MW00489240

THE SEARCH FOR MY MURDERED SISTER'S BODY

THE
MIRACULOUS
JOURNEY

A Day Made in Heaven

DLANA HALL BODMER

AVIVA
PUBLISHING
New York

Published by:
Aviva Publishing
Lake Placid, NY, USA
(515) 523-1320
www.AvivaPubs.com

Dlana Hall Bodmer
Email: Dlana@TheMiraculousJourney.com
Website: TheMiraculousJourney.com

ISBN (hardcover): 978-1-950241-04-0
ISBN (eBook): 978-1-950241-05-7
ISBN (Audiobook): 978-1-950241-06-4

Library of Congress Control Number: 2019905841

Editor: Tyler Tichelaar, Superior Book Productions
Cover Design and Interior Book Layout: Nicole Gabriel, Angel Dog Productions
Author Photo Credit: Buz Bodmer

Every attempt has been made to source properly all quotes.
Printed in the United States of America

For Gina

Now I lay me down to sleep,
I pray to God my soul to keep.
If I should die before I wake,
I pray to God my soul to take.

— Our Childhood Bedtime Prayer

GINA RENEE HALL
08/24/1961 - 06/29/1980

...WHEN I CRIED OUT, YOU ANSWERED ME, AND MADE
ME BOLD WITH STRENGTH IN MY SOUL...

—PSALMS 138:3

THE
MIRACULOUS
JOURNEY
A Day Made in Heaven

Music became a part of The Miraculous Journey

Reading the lyrics of the songs helped me better understand their relevance during the journey as I'll explain in the pages ahead. Here is a list of the songs I will reference throughout this book.

Sisters' Playlist

- "After All," Theme from the movie *Chances Are*, by Cher *(ch 1)*

- "Evergreen," from *A Star Is Born* soundtrack, by Barbra Streisand *(ch 2)*

- "The One I Love" by R.E.M. *(ch 3)*

- "I Love You More Than You'll Ever Know" by Gary Moore *(ch 5)*

- "Lady in Red" by Chris DeBurgh *(ch 6)*

- "Lebanese Blonde" by Thievery Corporation *(ch 7)*

- "Not Going Anywhere" by Keren Ann Zeidel *(ch 6, 7, 8)*

- "Circles" by Jana Kramer *(ch 8)*

- "Just For Now" by Pentatonix *(ch 8, 15)*

- "Angel of the Morning" by Juice Newton *(ch 9, 10)*

- "Something Better" by Lady Antebellum *(ch 10)*

- "For the First Time" by John Legend *(ch 12)*

- "Wagon Wheel" by Old Crow Medicine Show, cover sung by Darius Rucker *(ch 14, 15, 18)*

- "Dream On" by Aerosmith (Cover sung by Amanda Brown on, *The Voice*) *(ch 14, 15)*

- "Photograph" by Ed Sheeran *(ch 16)*

- "Lost Inside of You," from *A Star Is Born* soundtrack, by Barbra Streisand *(ch 18)*

- "Sympathy for the Devil" by The Rolling Stones *(ch 19)*
- "Hair of the Dog" *by Nazareth (ch 20)*
- "Broken Together" by Casting Crowns *(ch 21)*
- "I'll Follow You" by Shinedown *(ch 21)*
- "She Talks to Angels" by The Black Crowes *(ch 21, 22, 23)*
- "American Pie" by Don McLean *(ch 13, 20)*
- "Woodstock" by Crosby, Stills, Nash, and Young *(ch 20, 21)*
- "Somebody to Love" by Queen *(ch 22)*
- "Let It Go," song by Pentatonix, Lyrics by Walt Disney Music Company *(ch 22)*

Others' Songs
- "Satisfy My Soul" by Bob Marley *(ch 5)*
- "Highway Don't Care" by Tim McGraw *(ch 4, 6, 13)*
- "The Prayer" by Celine Dion *(ch 10)*
- "Gravedigger" by Dave Matthews *(ch 14)*
- "It's Been A Long Way Down To Here" by Bobby Thompson *(ch 18)*
- "Your Ways are Higher than Mine" by The Collingsworth Family *(ch 19)*

ACKNOWLEDGMENTS

My husband Buz

My sons, Dan and Will

My daughter-in-laws, Bea and Adrienne

My family, all still with me and all from times past

My amazing, caring team whose support is always appreciated:

> Margaret, Sarah, Jennifer, Dave, David, Trish, Heather, Wendy, and Donna

My friends: Barb, Ginger, Katie, Annie, Brian, and all who supported me throughout *the journey.*

My amazing team of professionals who helped guide me during my endeavor of bringing this miraculous true story to fruition: Patrick Snow, Tyler Tichelaar, Nicole Gabriel, Carolyn Flynn, and Dr. Alan Stanford.

Special Acknowledgment to Those Never Forgotten

My sincere appreciation to all throughout the years who have helped our family and Gina.

To all of the professionals whose diligent and passionate efforts made the difference in securing a successful conviction and not allowing Gina to be forgotten.

To the many caring volunteers who spent countless hours in 1980 during the long investigation, and the extensive search. And, to everyone who has since joined in the efforts to find Gina just because they too cared.

To all those concerned citizens throughout the years who have fought the fight to keep Gina's killer imprisoned.

With heartfelt gratitude, thank you to all who genuinely love Gina. Those who never let her life be extinguished.

And to my beautiful, loving sister whose light will shine on forever.

A Memoir of Two Interlocked Hearts...like
a Candle Flame Illuminating the dark.

INTRODUCTION

This is a journey where the ordinary becomes extraordinary. At first, it may seem to be the story of a heinous murder, only parts of which were completely solved. It is, but it is so much more. It is a story about my quest for truth. A journey that pushed all the boundaries of my normal, limited thinking. Yes, it is a story about the tragic murder of my sister, Gina, in 1980, but interwoven into that story is a tale of love and forgiveness—the story about how light shines through the dark. This is *The Miraculous Journey*.

In May 2016, a new lead pulled me back into the web of lies surrounding my sister's murder, causing me to live the horrifying experience again. Truth became my soul's objective. I returned to where it all began, searching for my sister's hidden body just as I had during the summer of 1980. But this time, nearly thirty-six years later, new leads were revealed in a most unconventional way and the reality of an undeniable spiritual realm began to unfold for me. As *the journey* progressed, it led me into more darkness than I could have ever imagined. My quest to investigate the unanswered questions about my sister's murder opened my eyes to two new truths: 1) There is a power, a lurking web of evil, that does not want truth to be known, and 2) There is a supreme power of infinite love and omnipotence shining light on the truth. I became entangled in a raging spiritual battle. I experienced just how our lives can be influenced by these very real powers—demonic and angelic.

In the end, the power of it all was revealed to me, layering on more mysteries. One such mystery emerged with clarity as a visible, divine message. The what, when, and where are all documented in these pages, proof of the existence of this divine spiritual realm. The why of *The Miraculous*

Journey—its true purpose—will be revealed in the end.

This story is about so much more than just discovering the truth of what really happened that horrific night in 1980. I learned to ask the questions that matter, contemplating everything I thought I knew about this world. Ultimately, I learned to listen to my heart. Finding truth is a personal journey. I see now that *the journey* led me to examine my own life. Truths long shadowed by the heaviness of my own unforgiving heart came to the surface. And in this process, I was brought from unconsciousness to consciousness, lovingly apprehended so I would know what I needed to know.

The most profound question I have pondered was: Why did this amazing spiritual army cross the veil into my life? I healed my heart through love and forgiveness—and freed my soul. But there is something more, I think. Sharing these intricate, often humbling moments *exactly* as I experienced them progressively evolves the mystery into an awakening of truth—the only truth that matters. The divine message is clear—a truth the heart of our soul always knew and never forgets. An inspiring message to be shared with everyone so that you, too, can see there is a divine plan in life.

The essence of my sister's pure innocence and goodness lives on in this story. I don't see it just as Dlana's memoir. Nor is it only Gina's memoir. I see it as a memoir of two sisters.

This is our story. This is God's message.

A Note on the Text

The Miraculous Journey is one of two books I have written about my sister's murder. The second book, titled *Web of Lies Unveiled: A Day Made in Hell*, is a companion book that goes into more detail about the unraveling of the chronological facts of my sister's murder. Had I not experienced *The Miraculous Journey*, these facts would never have been unveiled. Gina's story would still be overshadowed by the 1980 composed story. It is time for Gina's story. It is time to share what transpired that horrific night, and it took two books to share it all. *The Miraculous Journey* is an inexplainable spiritual experience that explores the mysteries of how I came to know these facts. And, it is so much more. I hope desire and curiosity ignite you from deep within, just as they did me.

FOR FURTHER READING

As you read, you may be interested in other resources it was not possible to include in this book.

TheMiraculousJourney.com
GinaReneeHall.com

Online resources include an interactive map of relevant locations, author's notes, the video, case timeline, 1980 archive of newspaper articles, discussion forum, anonymous tip form, etc. Subject to change. Any web addresses, links, contact information, etc. may have changed since publication.

Be sure also to note the color addendum in the very back of this book:

Miracles of a Day Made in Heaven — A collection of the most relevant photos.

God's Canvas is a kaleidoscope of photos from the author's personal collection included to warm your heart and make you smile.

Tapestry of Life with Special Acknowledgments is a photo section of never-ending gratitude to the people in the author's life who have walked and will continue to walk in the journey with her—her family.

The *About the Author* description at the end of this book gives insight into the person who made the commitment and promise to God by faith to share *the miraculous journey* with integrity and genuineness so that others will, in turn, do the same....

Contents

LOVE IS NEVER GLAD ABOUT INJUSTICE, BUT REJOICES
WHENEVER TRUTH WINS OUT.

CHAPTER 1

AFTER ALL

*We would be back one day to tell the truth.
It has always been about two hearts connected forever.*

I t has been thirty-eight years since I last saw the smiling face of my sister, Gina Renee Hall. Forged in my mind forever is the very last image of her dainty ankle crossing the threshold as she left, adorned with a bracelet—two gold interlocked hearts. Our sisterly bond was strong because we had shared a challenging childhood together, during which time we had each provided the other with what she seemed to need most. Gina's gentle, humble ways brought balance to my strength and strong will. Her heart ruled her head. My head ruled my heart. My sister's last words as she walked out the door, "Listen to your heart, not your head," have reverberated through me since the day she was murdered at age eighteen.

On June 28, 1980, Gina said those words to me as she left to go out for a summer evening. She would never come home again, and neither did her body. My family did not have Gina's bodily remains to lay to rest so we could peacefully mourn. Without knowing the whole truth surrounding her death, we had no closure. We went through the motions of having a funeral, remembering all that was good about my sister, but it was a funeral without a body, a headstone with an empty grave.

For a long time, I thought I was at peace with never having found her body. I told myself it was just a body somewhere in the cold ground—not her soul. Through the years, I have felt her with me during my milestones, but always with the sobering reality that she was not physically here with me. All this time, I had hated the man who had robbed her of her life. I could not forgive. My heart was heavy-laden, always trying not to remember, but never forgetting.

Despite the unforgiveness buried in my heart, I still lived a fulfilling life. I always knew that was exactly what Gina would want me to do. If her life could be summed up in a message to share with others, it would have been this: Simply embrace all of life's everyday wonders because we do not know which day will be our last. True, but there was more.

Because I told myself that nothing we could ever do would bring Gina back to life, I went on living my life, pacified by the peace of believing she was in heaven with God, like an angel. I even let myself believe that God had *made* her first day in heaven, convincing myself God just wanted her for himself so He let her die. I justified her death with the thought that God himself knew how hard her life was going to be, and loving her so much, He just took her on to heaven. God did not do this to Gina. Pure evil did. This was the wrong path of belief to hold, but I did not know it until decades later. It was a belief that arose from my own thoughts. I put a big Band-Aid over the pain. A pretend healing.

In 2016, this self-created peace changed. My heart had never truly been at peace with Gina's death. It would take an absolute spiritual army and both of our sister strengths to help me see this truth. Until then, I had no reason to relive the story everyone had composed about my sister's murder. That story, composed in 1980, cast her murderer, Stephen Epperly, as "a victim of sorts" when "Gina refused her killer's sexual advances," which sent him into a murderous fit of rage.

Within three days of Gina's disappearance, Epperly, who had twice before been tried on rape charges, was a person of interest. And within five days, the one and only prime suspect. For two more months, my family and friends joined investigators in the search around the lake house, all through the woods, throughout the college town of Radford, Virginia, looking for her body. Seventy-four days later, Epperly was arrested September 9, 1980 and charged with first-degree murder. Though we never found Gina's body, the case proceeded to trial in December. The prosecuting attorney for the Commonwealth of Virginia tried Epperly with only circumstantial evidence—no body, no confession, no witness. He met that burden of proof. Epperly was convicted of murder in the first degree of Gina Renee Hall in Pulaski County, Virginia, and sentenced to life in prison. He is currently incarcerated at the Buckingham Correctional Center in Dillwyn, Virginia. Epperly has never told anyone where he disposed of my sister's body. This "no body case" gained even more notoriety in the many years since the crime. Eager criminal justice and law students, ghost hunters, cold case detectives, paranormal shows, and many caring people had gotten involved in her death—it seemed everyone else wanted to bring Gina home, too. Many have tried for decades to solve the mystery and find her missing body. But no solution was possible because the foundational story everyone began with made it impossible. We did not have all of the pieces to this puzzle. But we had enough pieces to secure a conviction, and that was what mattered in 1980.

That summer night, June 28, 1980, was filled with unusual circumstances often described in the media as a night of many coincidences. The truth is I had always known there were no coincidences. The story of what happened to Gina that night was just that—a story. Her murderer and his friends created the story. The *composed story* that became everyone's perception and accepted reality. In some ways, even I settled on parts of the contrived story myself, always knowing in my heart it was not all true. In 1980, the web of lies did not seem to be what mattered most. Gina would not have wanted me to fight that battle. It would not bring Gina home, and that was the objective.

What I know is that my sister left home that night driving my Monte Carlo, which she had borrowed to go dancing at the popular Marriott Inn in Blacksburg, Virginia. I never knew what friends she planned to meet, but according to part of the testimony and statements, she walked straight inside and sat down with a table of people. That sounds like her friends to me. And I know she did not intend to stay too long. My sister had been excited all week that her former high school sweetheart and closest friend was coming to visit in the early morning before he would be deployed back to Italy. In just a few hours, her wait would be over and he would be dropping by Radford on his way to Washington, DC. This anticipated visit sparked the joyful smile I last saw Saturday at 9:50 p.m.

The composed story portrays my sister as willingly leaving this popular dance spot to be with Epperly. That is the story they tell. The story of a teenage girl who left with a man, a man she would have just met, a man ten years older than she was—Epperly—as if this was a normal, accepted Saturday night practice. I call this the Wolfpack Mindset of bonding together, working together, hunting together, like a pack taking down their prey. But the ultimate objective was the opposite of a single wolf's true nature—wolves mate for life. Wolfpack seems an appropriate name for the writers of the composed story.

Time for the truth about the last moments of my sister's life—Gina's story—her voice.

The composed story begins: Gina pulls into the Marriott Inn parking lot at 11 p.m., exactly at the same time as five men arrive. Epperly and his best friend Skipper are in one car and Epperly's other three buddies are in a different car. (Names not given to protect their privacy.) All three cars coincidentally pull into the Marriott parking lot at the same time. Epperly and Skipper park directly beside my sister. A coincidence? Skipper says in his statement, "I did not know the girl and I do not think Steve knew her either. We all went in." Although the deposition statements of the five conflict in some significant specific details, they generally all agree on some details. They walked inside simultaneously. All three buddies say they noticed Gina inside the Marriott, even describing what she wore as one girl among many people in a very busy place. One of the three said she walked by and said "Hi" to the group. Gina knew one of the five and he knew Gina. I will call him the trusted buddy. The trusted buddy "thinks" he may have seen Epperly dancing with someone who looked familiar. Skipper witnessed Epperly dancing with Gina four or five times. Another buddy says he saw Epperly dance with several girls. Other people at the Marriott that night describe seeing a different man, who wore glasses, as Gina's dancing partner. That is not Epperly. The most intriguing description was given by Epperly himself. He said Gina was with a man in his early thirties, tall and lanky, with dark curly bushy hair and dark eyes, and who Epperly thinks was wearing a mustache.

Gina was noted to have sat with others as soon as she walked in. Skipper even stated he saw Gina walk in and sit down with someone at a table. She must have sat with people she knew, yet somehow Gina meets Steve Epperly, dances four or five times straight, and makes the decision to go happily and willingly to an unknown place with this man she's just met. Not Gina. I know my sister. All of this activity in only half an hour before showing up at a table saying she was being bothered. I have always known that their composed story was not the truth. I believe Gina was targeted the moment she pulled into that parking lot. Maybe even before.

Not even one hour had passed since everyone's arrival when Epperly supposedly approached Skipper alone to ask him for the key to his mother and stepfather's lake house to take Gina there. This would have been just after the timeframe when Gina was reported to have been being bothered. No one else, none of the buddies, witnessed this conversation. One buddy saw Epperly walk up and whisper in Skipper's ear. Another saw Epperly and Skipper follow the girl out the door. Both Epperly and Skipper state the reason for going out into the parking lot to the car was to get the key for the lake house.

In Skipper's initial interview with Trooper Austin Hall (no relation to our family), he stated, "Me and Steve planned to go to the Marriott and pick up a couple of girls." While in the Marriott, he noticed "Steve had met a girl later identified as Gina Hall. She was wearing a white pant suit with a *purple body suit on under it.*" Skipper followed them out to the car, gave them the key, and went back into the Marriott.

In Skipper's later handwritten statement from early July 1980, he writes: "Steve introduced me to Gina and I walked out slightly ahead of them to the car. I opened the car door and gave the key to Steve. It seemed Gina was *confused* as to whether I was going and whether she was going in my car or not. Steve did not in any way put any visible pressure on Gina to leave and she seemed willing. I am not sure she knew where she was going. But she may have. She and Steve conversed and Steve answered saying they were taking her car. Steve said, 'that's alright isn't it?' and she said 'yes'. I went back into the Marriott."

In his December court testimony, Skipper states for the first time that he saw Gina dancing with Steve. And also adds this new information: "Epperly asked to borrow my car." In the defense cross-examination, he stated, "Steve and Gina conversed, she mumbled something to Steve but I did not pay any attention to it. I don't know what she said, but he said, "We'll take your car. That is OK, isn't it? And she said yeah." Also adding, "She seemed to be confused as to what car was going and exactly who was going. I think when she came out she thought maybe I—".

Not much changed in any of Skipper's statements regarding the conversation that he said occurred in the parking lot. After he gave Epperly the keys, he turned around and walked back in. He said he did not see them leave or who was driving.

When cross-examined, Skipper was asked, "...so they got in the car.... Did you watch them get in the car?" He replied, "I turned around—." The defense quizzed him, "Do you know who drove?" "I don't know. I turned around and walked off."

"You didn't have another key to the lake house did you?"

"No."

Of most interest to me was when Epperly's best friend Skipper was asked by the prosecuting attorney, Everett Shockley, "Who all went out to the car?" Skipper replied, "Myself and Mr. Epperly and Gina." "Anyone else?" Mr. Shockley quizzed him. He answered, "To the best of my knowledge, no."

These are the questions and opinions that stirred in my own mind:

> The police assumed in 1980 that Epperly asked Gina to give him a ride, and because it was known that she knew one of the five, they surmised she trusted them all. Not likely. My sister still would not have left alone with anyone. *Broken car door pull.* Some believe Epperly broke it after he murdered Gina in a state of rage, not believing my sister was strong enough to break it, though she was.

> Skipper described to Trooper Hall exactly what my sister was wearing, even though he tells of only a brief introduction at the door while exiting the Marriott into a dark parking lot. *A body suit.* A body suit is similar to a one-piece swimming suit or leotard. "A purple body suit" were his own descriptive words of what my sister was wearing, his words recorded by Trooper Hall in his police interview. I wondered, *How would Skipper have known Gina wore a purple body suit and not a shirt?* It would have appeared to be just a shirt under high-waisted white pants, concealed under a white jacket. Unless somehow it could be seen or known that she wore a purple body suit—in the dark parking lot—or later? I guess the note could have been written with the exact words already in the mind of the note taker, Trooper Hall, or still in the mind of Skipper, having heard the missing girl description on the radio, maybe knowing himself the difference between a shirt and a body suit. I do not remember what I told the radio station—purple shirt or purple body suit. There could be many reasons, but the ques-

tion remains: What is the truth? How was that known?

Another simple question: If Epperly and Gina had planned to go any-where together, prearranged with Gina before going out into the parking lot, and Epperly knowing that Gina pulled in and parked beside them earlier, her car parked right there, why would Epperly even need to ask to borrow Skipper's car? Premeditation of a "just in case plan" on Epperly's part, to have the means to follow her as she left just in case the parking lot is not dark or private enough to carry through on his premeditated plans?

But what about his best friend? That scenario may or may not impli-cate him. Was he in on the premeditated plan, or did he just witness it, or was he clueless? Skipper's own court testimony about the Marri-ott parking lot is quite telling. It is a fairly straightforward question—who all went out to the car? Who was at or around the car or cars during this Marriott parking lot encounter? Anyone else…? "To the best of my knowledge, no." A simple answer would have been—*No one else—just as I named.* Why not an *uh, hum* or *huh, uh* like all of his other answers during his extensive testimony? In my opinion, the phrase, *to the best of my knowledge,* would not be stated unless a layer of non-truth existed somewhere. It is like someone saying, "Honest. I'm telling you the truth." There is rarely a reason to say that unless you have something more not being told. I wonder who else was there? Was someone with Gina? Were Epperly and Skipper alone? My sister would not have been standing at his car right beside the Monte Carlo confused as to who was going with who, where, and in what car, as was told because she never would have agreed to leave with him in the first place. Why would she even be confused if she had mutually agreed inside to leave and go to the lake house with Epperly? Besides, she would have never left my car, our one and only car, in Blacksburg forty minutes away. What exactly would Gina have been confused about? Is it all just lies to cover the truth of what really happened in the Marriott parking lot?

We could consider that Epperly manipulated Skipper from the be-ginning with the *I need the key story suggesting that Gina had already agreed to go with him....*or maybe, he did not. The key is *the key.* The justification for going out to the parking lot was to get a key from the car for Epperly. Skipper said, "I carry a bunch of keys on a ball—a chain." That would be a legitimate reason to leave his keys in the car. There would need to be a reason for going to the parking lot if, after the fact, something had gone wrong. *That was not good. What if someone saw me? Hmmmm, it's CYA time.* The key is the crucial error in his story. It is highly suspicious. A few hours later, Skipper shows up at the lake house with a female guest, who later stated, "We arrived at the lake house at 4 a.m. Skipper fiddled with some keys to enter the house when we arrived. We entered the home at the rear door through the garage." Skipper testified he only had one key to the lake house. And he states he gave that key to Epperly—the entire reason for going out to the car. And, he also stated, "We always use the back door to go into the lake house." The same and only door he had the one and only key to, because he also answered when asked if there was a key to the front door (the lower level sliding glass doors), "No. If there's one, I don't know about it."

The most interesting piece of this *key puzzle* is something Epperly and Skipper could not have known. Earlier, Skipper picked Epperly up, and before driving to the Marriott, they went out to the lake house "to check it out." This visit was witnessed by a man sitting in a boat on the lake in front of the lake house fishing. "*It was as bright as good moonlight,*" he said. His report revealed he saw two men enter the lake house at 10 p.m. This is confirmed by both Epperly and Skipper's statements. What does not align is that the fisherman's account tells of a different entry point into the lake house than what was explained by Skipper in regards to the one and only key to the one and only common entry. The fisherman states that the two men walked down the side of the house and entered from the front of the home through the sliding glass doors. And as they got in their car to leave, the car stopped and the short one with hair like a girl (Epperly) got out and walked back down to the sliding glass door. So why all of this talk about the key? I do not believe it was the true reason for going out to the parking lot. It was a composed lie. I believe there was another reason for being in the parking lot, and the games being played did not include walking out *with* Gina.

There was one of the Wolfpack's depositions that told me what I already knew to be the truth. "The white female walked out *in front* of Steve and Skipper." Epperly was fired in April 1980 as a bouncer at a local bar. In a police interview, the reason given was bothering girls—following girls to their cars. Skipper even confirmed this in his own interviews. The most obvious, ignored fact: The broken inside driver's side door pull strap of my Monte Carlo. That broken door pull strap tells the story of a petite, but strong girl holding onto it with all of her might. This most likely happened in the Marriott parking lot, but the lake house was still a possibility. No matter where, my sister was in the driver's seat and she was trying to keep that door shut with all of her might.

What transpired in that parking lot that led to my sister's death? What is the unknown "something of relevance" that caused this blatant skirting around the truth of who was in the parking lot at the car and why? Skipper states that my sister was willing when she was at the car, yet he testified he never saw her leave the parking lot—*willing?* That one word alone tells so much. If she really had just gone *with Epperly*, why would the word *willing* even need to be used by Skipper. Preconceived Wolfpack perceptions or lies?

The composed happy-and-willing-to-go story had begun.

I always knew beyond a shadow of any doubt that Gina did not "meet a man in a bar" and leave to "be with him," as the Wolfpack composed the story. They took a girl who was untarnished, which became the first mistake in their composed story. Gina was like a lamb, pure innocence and goodness through and through. Gina did not have a promiscuous bone in her body. She was loved by many who also knew the composed story was a lie, and those who knew came together that summer of 1980 and put forth a remarkable effort. This was Gina's goodness exuding from others in their caring actions.

The composed story carried forward while many facts were ignored.

What I never knew is the rest of the story.

The most significant witness statement ignored from this night would be made by Kim Jett and Bonnie Cook (Craig). I saw the reports—taken at two different times. The reports state that Gina was being bothered, but the reports did not tell the same full, detailed story that Kim shared with me. But one report told enough, and it confirmed what I always knew to be true.

Within a week, these two roommates saw Gina's picture as a missing girl.

They began screaming in their room to each other, "My goodness. That is that sweet girl who came by our table last Saturday night." They went directly to report to the police what had happened while they were at the Marriott the Saturday night before. Kim told me she shared these details with the police: Around 11:30 p.m., Gina sat down at Kim and Bonnie's table. Gina asked them if she could stay a moment to get away from someone who was bothering her. Gina was alone when she sat down with them because she came directly off the dance floor to the nearest table. Kim shared they were helping her because Gina did not like what had happened. It was very clear to them that she was bothered by what had transpired. Five to ten minutes later, a man came up to the table and said to all three, "Come on. Let's dance." Kim Jett looked the man directly in the eye and said, "What part of *No* do you not understand?"

"It was Stephen Epperly," Kim emphatically told me.

Gina stayed with them about fifteen to twenty minutes. Kim said Gina told them as she left their table she would be fine when asked to walk out with them. Shortly after, Kim and Bonnie left. If the Wolfpack's timeline is true, Gina stayed about ten to fifteen minutes longer, leaving the Marriott one hour after her arrival. Did Gina not walk out with Kim and Bonnie immediately because she actually was with another somebody—another girl, another friend, another couple? The evidence supports that this is a theory to be contemplated. The multiple plastic cups, a tray full of cigarette butts, trash, etc. found in my car were all indicative of others present in my car at some point during the night. All of those items were not in my car before Gina left. I know because I was very particular about my car. I find most interesting the two empty fast-food cups, a fast-food bag and an orange plastic Tennessee cup. My family were Virginia Tech and Kentucky fans, so there would just not have been an orange Tennessee cup in our possession. Who else came or left with Gina in the Monte Carlo? If Epperly took Gina, which I believe he did—*the broken driver's side door pull strap*, it would not be as if a drive-through to get fast food would have happened. And I know my sister...she would never have gotten fast food... that is not her trash! That trash belongs to two other people. Who?

In their first visit to the police, Kim said the police showed them an older picture of Epperly, but they could not be 100 percent certain from that photo. Shortly thereafter, they saw a current picture of Epperly, went back to the station, and told the police he was the man who had been bothering

Gina. They also had noticed Gina dancing earlier that night with a man wearing glasses, a different man. They continued sharing their eyewitness accounts with other authorities, trying to make people listen and understand what had happened. They kept insisting there was no way Gina went with a man she was trying to get away from. The reply she said she received from the authorities was, "No. Gina went to a party with this man *willingly*. That is what happened."

When I spoke with Kim Jett, I learned she had carried the guilt of that night for decades. She shared with me that not a week went by that she did not think about Gina and what Gina might be doing if she had just made her walk out with them. Kim was still distraught over Gina's death and that no one would listen to them in 1980. This is a woman who tried to shout the truth from the mountaintops, but her voice was not heard. The police reports validated that they had come forward in 1980, but the whole story she shared with me was not there. This is a woman who years later wrote several pleading letters to the parole board not to let Epperly out. She never quit trying to make someone—anyone—listen that she knew Gina did not go with this man of her own accord. She even spoke with a parole member who assured her that Epperly stays in so much trouble in jail that he most likely will never get out. That gave Kim some peace. Her conviction and efforts validate that this is a woman who knew the truth about the Marriott. A woman still trying decades later to make sure people knew that my sister did not go willingly.

I did not know Kim Jett until she found me. In 2016, I had seen her reports from 1980 and used the facts from them, that someone had been bothering Gina, but I did not know the rest of her story until later. I did not know that this was the same Kim I was searching for during *the journey*. The same Kim who will be referenced in the day-by-day recap of the 2016 journey. Kim Jett saw my married name mentioned in another book that had just been released. She contacted me, wanting me to know her story— the details she had wanted to share for decades—and to assure me that she had continued from that day forward trying to make others understand that she knew there was no way my sister went with that man. Her story brought tears to my eyes since I understood the weight of the guilt she said she had carried. Someone told me she had posted on a site that she was excited to have finally spoken to Gina Hall's sister. A few weeks later, she was dead. She told others her story before she died. Thank heavens I had the wherewithal to record our conversation. Her voice was finally heard. It is no coincidence that she found me before her death. She needed peace. She needed her voice to be heard.

Kim had come forward in 1980. Kim's story did not align with the Wolf-pack's story. He said—she said. *So, really?* This was one of the last pieces of my puzzle that came from one of many no-coincidence connections to validate the truth I had always known. *Why would my sister have left with the man that was bothering her?* In my opinion, the story of Gina going with Epperly willingly is a bold-faced lie by men in a parking lot. And what is sad, most everyone believed it except those who knew Gina. And what is even sadder, who else besides Kim might have known a different beginning to this story? The devil is in the tiniest of details about what happened in that Marriott parking lot—*"to the best of everyone's knowledge."*

Conflicting details exist within the various friends' statements, but one thing is consistent: Everyone who tells the story picks up Skip-per's wording and describes my sister as having gone "willingly."

The composed story prevailed. The lake house became a cabin. The upscale disco dancing place became a bar—a nightclub. And Gina went *with* him *willingly.*

It is time to tell another story. Sisters' story of two interlocked hearts stron-ger together, forever.

It was always untrue that Gina chose to go somewhere unknown with this man, alone, that she had just met. This degrading of her honor has always been unacceptable to me. This turmoil brewed in me for almost four de-cades. And it was this lingering seed of anger that fueled my pursuit in May 2016 when a viable lead surfaced from a very dark place triggering what I called *the journey.* An elderly farmer who lived beside Meadow Creek off of Dry Valley Road near Radford, Virginia, had passed away. After his death, his grandson reported to the Radford Police Department that his family had kept a secret for years that could add new information to the murder case of Gina Hall.

Here is a summary of what the grandson told the police:

> On Sunday, June 29, 1980, the same morning Gina disappeared, the farmer and his nephew went for an early morning walk alongside Meadow Creek near their property. They came upon two men stand-ing in the creek. The farmer saw a lot of blood in the water. At first

glance, the farmer believed the two men were cutting up fish, even commenting to the two men in the creek, "Looks like you have had a good morning with the fish." Their hesitant response: "Yeah," in a faint voice. The farmer was caught off guard when no more conversation was amicably exchanged. The farmer came into Sunday breakfast and immediately shared the story with his family. We do not know if the farmer recognized one or both of the men right away, already knowing of them personally, or if he made the connection later when Epperly was named the prime suspect as he watched the story unfold on local news. What we do know is that he immediately forbade his family to ever discuss it.

From that moment forward, the farmer theorized that what he had seen was not fish being cut up. He believed he had witnessed two men cutting up a body. And these two men were driving a white van that he saw backed down to the creek off the main road.

As the TV reports played out about the story of the missing girl, and police tracked Epperly as the prime suspect, the family would witness him emphatically declare to the TV screen, "Those police are all searching in the wrong place. She's not there.... That girl is not there."

From that point, and for all of those years, the farmer assumed that what he had witnessed in the creek that Sunday morning was the dismembering of Gina. It was apparent to the family that the farmer had been concerned for his family, so he did not reveal the story or talk to police at the time. And it was always understood by the family that they were forbidden to talk about it.

I can only speculate why the farmer and his family never told authorities. Maybe fear of Epperly kept them silent. Or maybe they knew exactly who the second man was, and that brought fear of reprisal. Obviously, they felt a profound sense of fear. Radford was a small town where everyone knew everyone else.

In the grandson's story, there was no question in the farmer's mind that he believed he saw a female body being cut up. He believed it was Gina Hall. If he had recognized Epperly, why else would Epperly have been standing in a creek early that morning, immersed in blood? It was horrific enough to be told that my sister had been chopped into pieces, and then to consider there could be an unconvicted accomplice. I questioned who else could be so evil as to dismember a body? Another detail haunts and nags at me: In the farmer's story, a white *van* was backed down to the creek.

In May 2016, when police questioned the farmer's grandson, they asked him what "not there" meant. Did he believe his grandfather referred to "not there" as the official police search area in the lake, New River, and the surrounding woods? And if those places were "not there," then where was *there*?

Throughout the summer of 1980, the massive search for Gina's body had extended from Claytor Lake, up and down the New River, and into the surrounding woods. At first, the lake and the river had been top priority. The next plan was to set a six-mile radius as the invisible boundary of the search areas. That search perimeter included the vast area of wilderness between the lake house where my sister's blood was found and the area where my abandoned Monte Carlo had been found. Local TV would cover these searches, but the searches were nowhere near Meadow Creek and the farmer's property. The intersection of Meadow Creek and Dry Valley Road at the second bridge was approximately eleven miles from the search areas—at least a twenty-minute drive on back roads. But if one crossed the lake in a boat to the shoreline directly opposite the lake house, it would be in the vicinity of the Meadow Creek area and other areas of interest.

Lt. Andy Wilburn of the Radford Police Department told me the farmer's story. Andy had entered my life a few years earlier when he was half-jokingly charged by his chief to "Go find Gina Hall's body," having just worked on a cold case of another young woman who had been murdered. Andy then wondered, *Who is Gina Hall?* It was not long before he too was captivated by Gina and her case. Technically, Gina's case was not a cold case because we know her murderer, but Andy thought of it that way because authorities had never found her body. It was unfinished.

The day I sat listening to Andy tell the farmer's story, I had no strength, holding my breath until my lifeless body had no choice except to gasp for air.

"I believe it could be true," Andy said.

A longtime neighbor of the farmer vouched for the farmer's honesty, telling Andy, "If he said he saw it—then he saw it." That neighbor also informed Andy that Epperly had a relative who lived nearby, which could explain why Epperly was in that remote stream, familiar with it as a place where a van could easily be backed down to the edge of the water.

I hung my head at the new reality of this horrific news. The farmer was now dead. I left it to Andy to figure out if the farmer's story could be true.

That was his job, not mine. But in the coming weeks, that changed. Without a choice, it became my quest.

The farmer story incited my heart again. I felt more hate than I could have ever imagined possible. My heart hurt. Angry thoughts raced through my mind. "How dare Epperly rape and murder my sister, and also do this to her?"

And, two men? Who was this other man, and why had he never been brought to justice?

The farmer's story was just too gut-wrenching to fully absorb. My response to Andy that day was a potent silence, as long-suppressed emotions raged in my heart—vengefulness, hate, and intense anger.

That night, at home, I fell to my knees and prayed to God to help me know the truth. I cried uncontrollably for Gina; my sadness and grief were overwhelming. In the weeks that followed, the ache for my sister would not leave my soul. I could no longer bury my feelings. My mind filled with unwanted thoughts and images. Could the farmer's story be true? Is that why her body had never been found? Buried deep within my memory was the campfire rumor we had heard in 1980. Epperly's acquaintances reportedly told police that Epperly would sit around the campfire at the lake and boast, "The next girl I rape, I will cut her up and throw her off of the Claytor Lake Dam, letting the river carry the pieces away." Now, I wondered whether this could have been true.

In the days that followed, the farmer story would not leave me. What emerged was an unwavering desire to know the truth. I could not calm my eastern Kentucky heritage that raged from within, the quiescent warrior awakened, fiercely erupting after having been dormant for decades. I became determined to prove the farmer dismemberment lead wrong—or if right, find the second man and seek justice. Emotions raged with an intensity just as though no time had passed. It was the summer of 1980 all over again.

My sharpest, most heavily burdened memory of 1980 is the day I stood outside that lake house perched on a slight hill overlooking Claytor Lake. That was the day it sunk in: Gina was never coming home. We were told we were going to a *cabin* where the police suspected Gina had been murdered. I stood there wondering about the family who lived

PHOTO COURTESY OF THE NEWS JOURNAL, RADFORD, VA, PART OF THE NEW RIVER NEWSPAPERS

in this beautiful house. I questioned silently in my mind, *How could it be possible that Gina was murdered here?* It felt like a movie, not real life. She had called me about three hours or so after she left that Saturday night. She was calling from a lake house. In my statements to the police, I had told them I was awakened by the ringing of the phone at my bedside. My conversation with Gina was very short. I fell back asleep, maybe because in my head I never expected anything could actually ever be wrong, and I must have thought she would be on her way home because I had told her to get on home. When I awoke in the morning, I remembered the call—an apprehensive, nervousness in her voice, her tone out of character, and I realized the words she had spoken did not seem right, recalling exactly every word that was said. Days later, as I stood there by the lake's edge looking up at this home overlooking the lake, my sister's words still echoing in my mind, the intended message from the phone call became clearer.

Early Sunday morning, June 29, 1980, at approximately 1:00 to 1:30 a.m. the phone beside my bed had rung, waking me from a dead sleep.

"Dlana?" Not *hey, sis.*

"Gina?" It was her voice but not her.

"Yeah." Also not in character.

"Where are you?" My first dazed thought had been that she had wrecked the car. She was calling me and not already home, so something must have happened.

She answered quietly, "I'm at the lake."

I felt relieved that she had not been in a wreck.

"What are you doing out at the lake?"

"I am looking at it."

No emotion. The normal response might be something like this if the composed story were true: "I am here with a guy named Steve looking at the lake," or "I came out to be with Steve" or any of those responses, but even those would not have been in character for my sister. "I am with my friends" could have been a very, very slight maybe. It simply would never have been, "I am looking at it."

Standing at the lake house these few days later, only then did I understand she had been trying to tell me she could see a lake so that I would later know where she had been. She already knew she was in serious trouble.

"Well, who are you looking at it with?" I had asked that night.

Her response—one word.

"Steve."

"Please, you need to hurry on home. Remember, you have company coming early in the morning," I had said. But she did not respond with words. A soft somewhat mumbled, uttered sound, then click. That one word, "Steve," was the end of our conversation. Her voice. The last word ever.

Not Epperly's composed story that "she told her sister she would be home soon"—the story that carried forward.

If my bubbly, happy sister had been at this lake house *willingly*, her first words would have been something like: "Sis, you should see this place! It is beautiful and just like what you have always dreamed about, an A-frame house, full of windows with a beautiful view." She knew of my aspiration of living one day in the mountains of western North Carolina in a home just like this lake house home, a wall of windows with a view. Had things been normal, she would have continued by saying, "Don't be mad at me! I drove your car out to the lake and will be home shortly."

I will never have peace about that phone call. It will forever haunt me.

However my sister ended up at that lake house, whether of her own free will or not, she was immediately aware of her dire situation. And somehow she called me, her words unforgettable. I believe she was forced to call me. In 1980, the most logical explanation everyone assumed was that Gina may have been naive and easily manipulated by the smooth-talking Epperly. Many theorized she may have thought *everyone* was going to a party or to a different dance spot. Who is everyone? The police continue to build their theories from the foundation of the composed story: She arrives at the lake house, finding herself alone with this man, and that is when she calls me—before the violence begins. So, this scenario would mean a mutual agreement to go to the lake house together. Consider, if it happened in that manner, his violent intentions would not have been known to Gina when she called, so she would have had no reason to be out of character in her tone and conversation. And if she had had a reason to be afraid of him, there never would have been a call. His *modus operandi* (MO) is consistent in all of his rapes. His violent rage is swift, calculating, and premeditated. It would have been too late to call me. Something far worse scared her in her call, causing her out-of-character words and the nervous edge in her tone. She had already been taken from the Marriott parking lot, had been taken inside the lake house, and Epperly had made her call. He had no choice but to be more calculating. He needed time. He already knew what was going to happen. And calling me bought him time. Time he would have needed. He had already been seen in a public place where she was last known to be, and he had even been witnessed as the one bothering her on the dance floor. He would not know who might have seen him leave as she left. I believe he followed her out to the parking lot at the Marriott. And because he had already done the deed of taking her, realizing others would know, he needed a backup plan. Calling me was his safety blanket. Epperly also would not have known I was asleep. In his mind, if she called me, it would keep me from calling the police right away when she did not return home immediately from the Marriott if I thought she was *with* someone—not him in particular—just someone. And that would mean at least twenty-four hours. He did not plan on her knowing his name. A name she possibly heard used by someone else. Click.

And because her valiant last word spoken to me was "Steve"—a name she may have known or just overheard, I only now can imagine what punishment that one word brought my sister after the phone call clicked dead. But she was strong. She told us what we would need to know. Steve...and lake.

At 3 p.m. on Tuesday, sixty-two hours later, Steve Epperly became a person of interest.

PHOTO COURTESY OF KATIE MONROE

Simple story: *Girl meets boy. Girl refuses boy's sexual advances. Boy becomes enraged and kills girl.* Seems a logical storyline. What happened

PHOTO REPRESENTATION OF A 1975 CHEVROLET MONTE CARLO DOOR PULL

was just not that simple. And I emphatically repeat—Gina would have never gone with him alone by herself, anywhere. That was Epperly's mistake: Assuming she could just tell her sister she was at the lake with someone she chose to be with, and no one would ever know who or where. Epperly or Skipper would never have had to tell any of what transpired had Gina not given us that one word—Steve. Skipper must not have known until later that Gina had actually named Steve to me. He learned that Tuesday morning at the Barbell Club when the trusted buddy told everyone that I had called his mother looking for my sister, inquiring if anyone knew a man named Steve. And, we must never forget the broken driver's side door pull strap.

The day I stood there by the lake looking up at that lake house, the place where my sister may have drawn her last breath, guilt took hold of my heart like it was somehow my fault. I questioned whether if I had only just gone dancing with her or not fallen back asleep after her phone call, she might still be here. I never should have let her go without me. I was the big sister. I had always protected her. Gina was my friend, my deepest soul connection. That grim day standing there in front of the lake house, the reality of her death felt overwhelming. My boyfriend Buz must have seen in my face that I was on the verge of breaking down. He knew it was time to get me away from there.

The drive back to our townhouse in Radford from the lake house along Hazel Hollow Road took forever. As I sat in the passenger seat, I hung my head out the window, looking up at the sky. An uncontrollable, piercing cry poured out from my shaking body all the way to the townhouse. I had never felt so alone. Gina was gone. My screams were wrenchingly violent, and I could not stop them. I now wonder, *Did Gina somehow hear those screams…or feel my sadness?* I know God did.

Back in our townhouse, I lay in bed, still sobbing, trying just to breathe, remembering all I could about a few nights earlier when I had last seen my sister. I thought of her innocence, making me so angry that it had been taken from her so quickly.

Then I remembered her beauty, her hair always styled to perfection. She had teased me just days earlier when I lazily wrapped my dirty hair up in a bandana during exam week and let it go. That good memory brought a smile that broke through the sobbing anger, a small measure of her goodness shining light on a very dark moment.

I thought of the very last moment I saw her. A petite five-foot sweetheart of a smiling, happy girl and her last face-to-face words of wisdom...

"Sis, you have to stop letting your head get in your own way and start following your heart. Listen to your heart, not your head. Heart, not head."

LISTEN TO YOUR HEART, NOT YOUR HEAD...

CHAPTER 2

EVERGREEN

Our sisterly bond was forged by strength when we were just little girls.
Our love forever strong.

O ne memory from my childhood is like a crisp, clear scene from a movie. I am a little girl with a serious grown-up look on my face. I am looking down at the face of my cute, smiling toddling sister looking back up at me. As I hold her hand, we walk up the hill. The walk always seems to be so far away. The morning air is thick with fog. A little eerie, but I am not afraid. I know where we need to go. We are headed to Mr. Odell's house. We are hungry and I know he will be eating breakfast after a late shift in the coal mines. I also know he will welcome us with open arms. He is always a little bit scary to me as a child, his coal-blackened face and the whites of his eyes so pronounced. But he is a kind man, always offering to share his cereal right after he says his morning blessing.

Those trips up the hill to Mr. O'Dell's happened when I was six years old, after our life changed forever. One early morning before this, Gina still must have been hungry for some cereal. As toddlers can do, Gina woke before everyone else, went into the kitchen, lowered the oven door, and climbed up on the stove, snagging the knob with her pajamas. The switch came on and caught her pajamas and rubber diaper cover on fire. The rubber intensified the flames quickly adhering to her skin. The scorched linoleum floor, just to the left of the kitchen door, would be a constant reminder. Just a few seconds in Gina's life story irreversibly changed Gina's life forever.

For a long time, my baby sister was gone. She must have spent six months of her toddler years in the University of Virginia burn ward far away from home. This accident and all of the trips back and forth must have taken a severe emotional and financial toll on my parents. All I knew was that Gina was not home.

I always wondered exactly what happened to Gina. The vivid image of that black spot on the kitchen floor where her pajamas had been ripped off and flung to the floor are imprinted in my mind forever, but they were all I could remember of the incident. I had always believed Gina must have been hungry to have climbed up on that stovetop to get something from above. Maybe that perception is what drove me to make sure Gina was never hungry again, walking her up that hill to Mr. O'Dell's.

Gina's burns were extreme, leaving her severely scarred. Seventy-five percent of the right side of her body was burned, damaging not only her deepest layer of skin but also the sub-layers of muscle and tendons. When she came home from the hospital burn unit, a trapeze bar was installed in my bedroom. The terrible accident meant we had a circus in our house. For her, it was for physical therapy. For me, I got to hang upside down for hours at a time, swinging from the ceiling. That same year when I was five, Gina three, and John Jr. a baby, we lost our mother. We did not lose her to death. We lost her to an era, the 1960s, when women's health issues were not fully understood. She was taken away. She never lived with us again. I never knew if Gina's tragic accident precipitated our mother's illness or if our mother somehow caused Gina's accident.

I have no memories of my mother before I was nine. Twice someone brought her to visit with us, when I was nine and again at twelve. The first time, I felt reluctant to go to the car to see her, but once I saw her, I was not afraid. For years to come, I would hold that beautiful image of her from that day in my mind. The second visit was much different. I was older, further removed by time, but in her mind I was still just a little girl, just like when she had left.

What I do remember is that when I was rambunctious as a child, adults would say, "You're gonna get taken away like your mother if you don't behave." I was always being reminded of my mother's illness, but I really did not understand as a small child what had happened. I was always told that Gina's burn accident happened because my mother was lazy, always lounging around smoking cigarettes, reading magazines, and not watching us closely. My dad never spoke of my mother, but these words from others influenced my perception of my birth mother.

Years later, in the last months of our dad's life, I asked him what happened to our mother. He looked down, shook his head, and replied, "I had no choice. Your mother came after you three with a butcher knife. I did everything I could to try to help her."

After my dad's remark, referencing the three of us, I knew my mother's illness must have peaked after she gave birth to John Jr. I began to contemplate whether our mother had had postpartum depression. In a short span of time, our mother became pregnant for the third time in five years. During her third pregnancy, she experienced the emotional trauma of watching her little girl suffer extreme pain. About five to six months later she gave birth to John Jr. She could have had a mental breakdown because of the accident leading to a difficult pregnancy or a pregnancy-induced psychosis? It would be hard for a mother to bear seeing her little girl be hurt that badly. When did her illness culminate, the day of Gina's traumatic injuries or the day John Jr. was born?

I never knew the answers I needed to be at peace with this part of my life until recently when I met my dad's closest friend from those early years. He answered the questions I had always wanted answered. Our mother did not cause my sister's accident. My dad and my mother were sleeping and it was just that—an accident. And after that day, Elana was never the same. The emotional trauma of Gina's accident was the stimulus, the climax of her illness after John's birth. Seems a possibility of a culmination of all factors. It is still hard to say what completely broke my mother—the possibility of a misdiagnosis is certainly a factor to consider. Whether it was postpartum depression or postpartum psychosis, my mother was taken away to St. Albans, a mental hospital. There, she received the electroshock treatments that froze her mind in time—an event that would change her life forever. Diagnosis—schizophrenia. I was still five when my mother was taken away, so that tells me the butcher knife incident probably happened right after John Jr was born. This institutionalizing of our mother would have devastating effects on all of our lives. Many lives changed from that one moment in time.

I was the big sister. My job was to protect when Daddy was away. I was the tough, older one. At a very early age, I learned to be a child mommy. Those nights when my daddy would leave to go coach or referee, I remember sitting at the window, watching for him to return. Maybe I was afraid he would one day be gone just like our mother.

Three years or so after they took our mother away, my dad remarried. Mama Joan became our mother.

In those early years as a new family, we lived in the South Coeburn house. It was all pink when we first moved in. Our dad quickly painted that house green! A clump of bright yellow forsythia bloomed in the yard, forming a natural cave that Gina and I would play in all day long. We imagined we were Batman and Robin.

BIG SIS! LITTLE SIS

Gina often went away. Throughout her childhood, she had had multiple surgeries to mitigate her burn damage. Some areas, like her chin, lower thigh, and upper arm, received skin grafts to minimize the appearance, but most of her scars were deep, grotesque, and not reparable with plastic surgery. The last surgery at age eight was the most difficult. The day she arrived home, I hid myself in the Bat Cave, ready to jump out and surprise her. As she walked with Daddy from the direction of the carport, I saw the reality of her childhood. Thick bandages encircled her tummy. Without

MAMA JOAN AND DADDY DANCING

this surgery, she would have lived in immense pain. The surgery would allow her scarred skin to stretch and grow as children do. The two-to-four-inch wide cut left a deep rut in her torso that wrapped around her waist. She could have been sad that she had missed the summer fun, but my sister was always cheerful, and she did not seem to mind standing on the sidelines as she healed, watching our yard games of freeze tag and kick the can. So she had not missed the summer of '69. Our memories of that time were bountiful, spending hours catching the summer evening fireflies and searching the grass endlessly for four-leaf clovers.

Every summer, we would spend time with our dad's family. During those summer weeks in Kentucky, Gina and I would spend all day in the beauty salon our aunts owned watching Auntie Jel and Auntie Red toil at making everyone beautiful. At the end of the day, our turn came. They washed our hair with banana-scented shampoo. By the time they were done, we felt like princesses, swiveling in the chairs, looking at ourselves in the big mirrors. Gina dreamed of going to beauty school when she grew up.

I was the lively one, full of energy. A childhood friend recently shared with me how I used to win all the marbles while we were in grade school. I had forgotten this part of my life until he jarred my recollection of those intense marble games on the dirt patch. It was so much fun to knock out other people's marbles, winning their marbles for my collection. I was one of the few girls playing this stereotypical "only boys welcome" game.

As the oldest, I was Daddy's helper. Whenever something needed to be mowed, lifted, or moved, I was there at my dad's side. Always the tomboy of the family, I questioned many times why I had not just been born a boy. Maybe simply being John Hall's firstborn—John Hall the football player, the athlete, the coach—made me feel as though I was like a son to him. Independent, tough, and competitive, I also chose early in life to be resilient, persistent, determined, and a little stubborn.

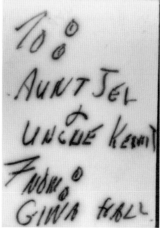

Gina was the quieter one, never in trouble, always pleasing everyone. She was the perfect Girl Scout. I believe Gina learned how to be extra-appreciative and kind when she was in the burn ward in Charlottesville. I often think of all the people there who touched her life, and she theirs—people who were there for her during this challenging part of her life. Even with all that had happened in her life, she embraced life for its good. She was an angel.

Gina loved her pets, Princess the white Pekingese, Hans the miniature Schnauzer, and Taffy the Siamese cat, whom she had trained to use the toilet. Don't ask me how! Gina was also closest to Mama Joan, always at her side, helping with whatever needed to be done. We would get a new baby brother, Garland, when I was ten. Gina spoiled both of her brothers rotten. She was a kind soul. She cared about others first, always. Her love for her family was never questioned. She poured her love into her baby brothers. When John Jr. played high school varsity basketball, he credited Gina for his success. As a sophomore, he was good, but not as good as he thought he was when a few of his fellow varsity players landed on the injured list and he moved up into one of the five starting positions. One day, John Jr. was strutting down the halls of their high school when Gina walked up to him and whispered in his ear, "Looks like you are strutting down the hall—big time!" She gave him a good talking to about humility. He took note of his gait and paid attention to his actions. This is one of his favorite last memories of his sister. This team would later go on to compete in the state championship on the same weekend I married my husband, Buz, in 1981. There were smiles from heaven.

Our family always had one primary focus—sports. Most of our memories revolve around some athletic endeavor. Gina was more girly girl than

I, but she was tough. We were on the high school tennis team together my senior year, a girls team I helped start a few years earlier. She was a great golfer and the only girl on the high school team. We both loved being part

of the Coeburn High School marching band. I played the trombone, but she carried the big drums. Petite, yet so strong! The cadences she would play still echo in my ears.

Our love of music came from our church life. We were raised Methodist, but some of my fondest memories came from the revivals where old-time music filled the air. I can still hear that mountain twang in the melodic words of "Amazing Grace" and "I'll Fly Away." I must have been grateful for the many caring people who surrounded us with love. Sometimes it takes a community to raise children. I cannot say that I learned every tiny detail of the Bible, but I learned what love was. The fellowship of my church family was an important part of my life. This foundation became very important in Gina's life. We would learn verses in the weeks of Vacation Bible School, but to say I was raised learning the Bible from one end to another would not be true. Going to church was just what we did. It was never something not done every Sunday until I moved from home. I married a Southern Baptist and we raised our boys Baptist, then Methodist, then Baptist again depending on where we lived. As they grew and participated in the many special travel sports teams, church went down the priority list, though I still sporadically attended for most of my adult life. Then about a decade ago, I left the traditional church. More about that later.

One Christmas, Mama Joan organized crafting the ornaments for the Christmas tree that would become a fixture in the Coeburn United Methodist Church for years to come. This was a dream day for two young girls, Styrofoam, shiny beads, glitter, decorations, and hot glue guns. I remember starting mine with a circular Styrofoam ring, a sort of 8-inch-wide doughnut. I decorated it with small strings of gold beads and shiny glitter. As I worked over it, we were reminded that it was circular, a beginning with no end, symbolizing eternity. Eternity had no relevant meaning to me as a young person.

In high school, my church became the home church for The Joy Express, a nondenominational singing group for teenagers that met Wednesday nights. This became my trusted tribe of teens, where my friends and I would openly discuss with each other all the teenage issues we were facing. On weekends, we would load up in our Joy Express greyhound bus and travel up and down the East Coast to sing in churches. We did not sing hymns. We sang contemporary songs, such as the Doobie Brothers'

"Jesus Is Just Alright"; Peter, Paul and Mary's "Blowing in the Wind"; *Mac Davis' "Stop and Smell the Roses"*; and Carole King's "You've Got a Friend," changing the words ever so slightly so we could share a message of love. Our lead guitarist played a mean chorus to Led Zeppelin's "Stairway to Heaven" and would go on to become a bank president. At the end of our performances, if so moved, some of us would share a story.

Once, as the fifty-passenger Joy Express Bus traveled to New Jersey, passing through the valleys of Virginia, I looked out the window to see one beautiful tree perched on a slight hill in the middle of a clearing—no other trees within sight. The tree was majestic, with perfectly shaped branches. At the Sunday performance, I walked up to the microphone, sharing my story of that tree coming to my teenage mind and concluding, "No one ever needs to feel alone, like that tree all by itself, because Jesus is always with us, especially when we feel alone. All anyone has to have is a tiny little seed of God, and it will grow into a big, strong tree, never being alone. God is all around us, and that majestic tree must make Him smile."

That same year, my dad went to the high school guidance counselor and coordinated a plan to *get Dlana out of town and on into college*. Somehow, I found myself being a high school junior and senior in the same year. I had the grades. And it certainly sounded like a good idea to get out into the world from the small town where I had lived. I always wondered what prompted my dad to do that. Was he worried I would marry my local boyfriend, or better stated, get pregnant and never live the life he believed was best for me? Was it my contentious relationship with my stepmother? Maybe the truth was I just wanted to be somewhere else...anywhere other than where I was, and my dad knew this.

So when I was seventeen, I left home. I graduated early and headed to Radford College in 1976, about 140 miles away from Coeburn. As my dad and I walked up the sidewalk to Bolling Hall, a freshman all-girl dorm, he kicked away empty beer cans from the sidewalk, the leftovers from the upperclassmen's early arrival. In the '70s, Radford College's partying atmosphere had a reputation all in a class of its own. I am positive my dad did not know this! I studied his contemplative look as he turned to leave. Seeing the excitement on my face, I think he felt he could trust his decision and he relished the thought that his firstborn was attending college.

Buz and I met right away, in my first fall quarter, at a recreational activities class playing games like Duck, Duck Goose. During a get-to-know-you activity, we were instructed to share something we loved. I heard this deep male voice in an unfamiliar northern Virginia accent say my favorite words, "I play tennis." I lived for tennis. He was cute, and he played tennis. What could be better! We connected on a first date for a shared sub from the Deli-Mart and a game of tennis. Of course, I knew I needed to let him win, and he did, despite my wearing the shortest of my cut-off jean shorts, which should have been a distraction. There is a reason they called them hot pants in the '70s. All through our college years, Buz and I were inseparable. We enjoyed long adventurous drives. We loved being outdoors, hiking to beautiful, untouched places. A fond memory that always brings smiles is the time Buz and I left the hiking trail at The Cascades, climbing up a steep mountain to perch on top for the view. After the strenuous trek, we sat down and he opened the backpack he had given me to carry. He had put a six pack in my backpack and, unknowingly, I had carried it up the mountain for him. We laughed for ten minutes—a warm Wiedemann beer, $1.69 a six pack, with a million-dollar view looking out over the beauty of the Virginia Blue Ridge Mountains. There is a reason behind the slogan "Virginia is for Lovers." Nature comes alive everywhere. And Buz and I created many wonderful memories discovering and exploring together.

The summer Gina graduated from Coeburn High School, she would beg me to come home from Radford for a quick weekend visit so I could take her to Norton to our favorite disco-dancing places. We would sneak out of our parents' house and drive to Norton ten miles away to dance the night away. Looking back, I'm sure Daddy knew we were sneaking out! Gina's favorite pastime was dancing. She helped Miss Vicki, the local dance instructor, choreograph dance shows and teach the younger children tap and jazz. Gina could tap like crazy, and she could turn somersaults and handsprings with ease. On the dance floor, Gina was a disco queen. A beautiful dancer. Although she was self-conscious about her scarring, I never saw her let her injuries keep her from finding joy. She always dressed nicely— that was important to her, tailoring her clothes herself so they would fit her petite frame perfectly, camouflaging her scars.

Gina would often travel to Radford to visit Buz and me. One very special weekend, she came up so we could see *A Star Is Born* with Barbra Streisand and Kris Kristofferson. The movie theater was so crowded that we had to sit in the balcony. I remember how we laughed because one of us had to sit on the aisle steps, but we did not care. We were both enthralled with the music and the love story, the idea that one love that is shared by two is ageless and evergreen.

I was always in a hurry. I had graduated from high school early, and I would graduate from college early, too. I was racing through life. That seemed to be the continuing underlying theme of my entire adult life—that is, until after the summer of 2017.

In November 1979, at age twenty, I quickly landed my first teaching job. I was excited to stay in Radford teaching one-on-one in a new Individualized Title program for underprivileged children at Belle Heath Elementary. Soon, my dad persuaded me to come back home to Coeburn for an opportunity I could not resist—my own classroom of first-graders at Coeburn Primary School. A lot of factors could have led my dad to seek out this opportunity for me—bringing me back home. Perhaps too because I had fallen in love with a northern Virginia boy who did not fit any preconceived idea of what my dad envisioned my life should be. Buz was not a golfer like my family's number-one focus, but he shared many similar interests with me. At the top of the list was our love of nature. I always loved being in the woods. The only time my family saw woods was if their golf ball sliced into some trees. Little Stoney, Bear Rock, and High Knob were some of my favorite places to be. I was athletic, always hitting a ball of some kind just like my family, but my heart was always in nature. Buz was just like me. By this point, we'd been dating more than three years.

And yes, our worlds were so very different. Something as simple as giving directions highlighted the different culture from one end of Virginia to the other. In Northern Virginia, road signs led the way. In Southwest Virginia (SWVA), we had our own way of giving directions. When I wanted directions to someone's home, the answer might be: "After you pass the second big curve, you will pass the old oak tree that has been there since I was a child. Right after you pass the corner where the old church burned down, you take a left turn, and follow the gravel until you cross the creek. Let's see...Hmm...after about three or four more curves, start looking to the right for the house on the hill!" They are all on hills! The crazy thing is I knew where they were talking about. We now have street signs, and numbered roads and we have caught up with the metro areas of Virginia, but when I was young, that is how we did it. Others drew their own conclusions about how we gave directions, but, of course, I never fully realized it until the day in court years later when the defense attorneys attempted to paint a picture that neither Gina nor I knew how to find our way around Radford. Just because we were from a rural area did not mean we did not know where we were going. We found our way around Radford quite easily, even if the defense did try to make it out to be a big metropolis! Radford was just another small town like so many others in America.

When Gina would come visit me during her senior high school year or her early college days at Emory and Henry, her favorite thing to do was to drive to Kroger's across the New River or to the Thrifty grocery store on the west end of Radford, located in what the locals referred to as the Thrifty Shopping Center. She would go to buy apples, always conscious of eating only healthy snacks, not finding them readily stocking my shelves in my home when she visited. I was the chocolate candy bar girl then, as I still am now. Gina was very disciplined with good reason.

After Gina turned eighteen in August 1979, a new concern about her health emerged. She told Mama Joan that when she gained just a few pounds, her skin would slightly stretch, bringing her intense pain. Gina had just discovered how delicious ice cream tasted and had put on just a few pounds. After that intense round of pain, it had become clear to her that she could never become pregnant and bear a child. Her skin would have never stretched to allow her to carry a child and go through labor. She was reluctant to talk about this new reality. "I don't even want to have children," she told Mama Joan, as if to justify the realized reality of her life.

While Gina was attending her first year of college at Emory & Henry in the fall of 1979, she would send me letters, sharing her hopes about her recent request to transfer to Radford being approved. She was enthusiastic about attending a larger university with a comprehensive nursing program.

Dear Dlana, Howdy!

Hope you and Buz and your job are coming along well. Aren't you proud of John—14 points! Hope the ballgame was fun at VPI. I never know whether recreation involving the whole family will turn out to be fun or fights. Boy, I'd love to call you but I can't afford it. I had a blast at CVC and hope to get accepted at Radford for spring even more now than before. I went to CVC Homecoming and loved every minute of it. Especially when Norma walked out (first freshman to be in the court in a long time). Even though she lost I was happy for her. Oh yeah, I didn't drink. I didn't find it necessary. Aren't you proud of me? Why don't you write me back a short letter telling me if you think

I'll get accepted for spring transfer. I am awfully worried.... Take care, and look happy (whether you are or you aren't). I am going to send you this little message and hope you read it every time you begin to frown or grouch about something. For instance, when it rains does it help to complain about it? Will it change? Do people want to hear your complaints?

Dlana, I'll love ya forever and thanks for everything that you've done for me and I haven't gotten to thank you properly for before. Your sis, with Love, Gina

Gina got accepted for a transfer to Radford to complete her freshman year. She would miss her friends at Emory & Henry, but she was so excited to be coming to Radford. She knew her path was college, even though her heart was in cosmetology. By the spring quarter of 1980, Buz and my sister were up in Radford while I was back home teaching. Gina was faithful with her letters.

Hey Sis, Love you!! (Written across the top)

Dear Dlana,

I am now in my music appreciation class being culturally exposed to the strings and I am about to fall asleep. Anyway I am writing you another letter because the other letter would just be old news now since I talked to you last night. Don't think I am awful because I am writing this letter while listening, at least I am listening; most everyone else in here is asleep. Now I am wide awake because I am thinking about what to put down here. Since I'll be seeing you soon, I guess this should be a short letter. So I'll just give you an outline of what's happening with me. I am enjoying Radford and hope and pray I keep liking it. Liz is really nice, and we are getting along just fine.

I know you're curious about Buz. We haven't talked that much but when we do run in to each other he fills me in on how you two miss each other. He misses you, as I guess you already know and I am sure he is as lonely as you are. But he'll be ok and so will you. Boy, will there ever be "Love in the air and everywhere else" when you two get together again. I think you'll end up closer cause you'll appreciate every second of being together. Anyway, I just thought you might want to hear how much he misses you and that you'll work out. I am trying not to sound nosy but you sounded worried last night about him so I thought I would tell you what I thought. So here goes,

"Everything works out for the best."

Yeah, Buz misses you, I miss you too. But I don't miss going home that much. Last weekend was fun. I miss Daddy, Joan, John, & Garland so tell them Hi & walk Hans once for me. I hope everything works out with you, your job, and everything else. I care a lot about you and I want you to be happy so don't worry too much...I think I'll run later on. I feel so good cause I lost 6 lbs and even though it's not that noticeable, it makes me feel better.

PS I didn't mention my "love life" cause it's definitely no big deal to me right now.

Looking back at Gina's letters, I see the subtle hints. She was running a lot on campus. She was not focused on a love life, and she was still not eating fast food. She must have been feeling the pain that would come from the stretching of her skin, so losing just those few pounds made her feel better.

And, in a second letter:

Dear Dlana,

I am in music appreciation again and I have listened to half of that and I think I have listened to a sufficient amount of it. Anyway this is going to be a short letter. I missed my first class and I'll explain why the next time I see ya. I hope I don't miss anymore. I am going to study today and go to Kroger's and that's about all I have planned. So my day will be pretty boring but it will be a busy one. I hope you have a nice week at home as well as at school.

"Miss Hall" that really sounds neat!!

The main reason I wanted to write to you is to tell you I appreciate you and Buz taking me out to eat and to Gail's and everything else. I really think a lot of you.

Even though I was not in Radford in the spring of 1980, I still had my Cedar Valley apartment until the lease was up in June. I visited most weekends, but Gina never told me why she missed class that morning, and I never asked. Maybe she just overslept like most college students missing those early 8 a.m. classes. She did share that she had had a discussion with my old roommate regarding my bedroom, as though she were not happy about something she saw. Now, I wonder. Perhaps she had stayed overnight at my apartment and did not make it back to campus in time because of this discussion. I got the impression from Gina that it was regarding using my bed as a drying rack, and she had to sleep in a damp bed. So I know she spent time overnight in my apartment, which was at least putting it to good use. My apartment was just a mile walk from the RU campus. I was aware that Gina would go up to my apartment on occasion just to have somewhere different to be. This is important to understand because my old roommate, Gail, who still was in my apartment, dated a local guy, Epperly's buddy, *the trusted buddy*, who at the time lived in the same complex, same building, one floor above us. Just a few months later, the trusted buddy would be associated with the details of the weekend Gina was murdered.

I planned to go back to Radford for the summer session to begin work on my master's degree in education leadership so I could become a principal. This desire was not so much about continuing my education. I just wanted to be back at Radford to be with Gina and closer to Buz. So as the summer of 1980 dawned, Gina and I became sister roommates. Buz had to return to northern Virginia to work as he did every summer so he could save money for his upcoming year's tuition, his final year. Gina and I decided to sublet his townhouse. Staying together would save our dad money. We were excited to get to spend the summer together in Radford.

I had not been there very long before I realized my sister had adjusted quite well to her new school. Gina started introducing me to her new friends, but we spent most of our time studying. That June, we were very busy with school.

Gina had had a serious boyfriend during her junior year of high school. A year older than Gina, when he graduated, he joined the military. Their relationship was in a temporary break status, mutually agreed to be on and off for the years while she was finishing school and he was deployed in Italy. They both agreed she needed to enjoy her senior high school prom and casual dates for company, which she did. She had been on a few dates, more like friends just getting together to eat pizza or go to the movies. Two weekends before she was killed, I had arranged a casual pizza date for her with a friend of mine. The weekend before she was killed, she drove home to welcome her fondest friend back home from service. I can only imagine the conversations they had because she was on cloud nine all week.

As she said, her love life was no big deal. She was happy with her life. When her best friend would be on leave to come home to Virginia, they would always see each other. On the last day of my sister's life—Saturday, June 28, 1980—Gina told me she was ecstatically happy, yet sad at the same time because he was scheduled to come the next morning—bright and early at 6 a.m. or so to spend time with her before he deployed back to Italy. Had her life not been cut short, Gina may have quit school that summer and joined him overseas before the summer was out. "He asked her to marry him," Gina's spring roommate had told me.

This letter that I found in Gina's papers confirmed her excitement about his upcoming visit.

> Hey Babe,
>
> I was glad to receive your letter and especially thrilled to know you are looking forward to seeing me. I know I can't wait to see you! My letters may not always show it but you are always in my heart. I will be home in June.... It has been exciting living here in Italy but I'm even more excited to see you....
>
> I have so many things I want to say but I'll tell you when I see you.

Sometimes when I read these letters from Gina's past, my heart raged with hate, focusing on Epperly and all that had transpired all over again. They reminded me of the life Gina never got a chance to live.

By Christmas of 1979, when she came home from college, Gina confided in me how scared she was of any future pregnancy. She may have been thinking about the possibilities of the proposal. I do not know what was on her mind, but I knew what we would do. "When that time comes," I told her, "I will carry your child." Even though I had not yet experienced carrying life within me, this was my sister, so I did not give it a second thought. This gave her peace.

Again, just a few weeks before she was murdered, Gina was still concerned about marriage, sex, and the possibility of what could happen to her if she were ever to become pregnant. We discussed that when the time came for her to marry, we would make our plans. I believe her growing feelings for this very special man in her life were weighing on her, hopeful that she could consider having a relationship with him in the future. I cannot know 100 percent for sure whether my sister had ever even experienced a sexual relationship, but I know this: She had experienced a loving relationship with this perfect gentleman in her life. And I know that my sister would never have put herself in a situation with a man that would just complicate her life even more. She was struggling with how life could be in her future. That tells me a lot. Sex was not a part of her life. But the dominating mindset of so many who did not know Gina was: How could any eighteen-year-old female not be sexually active? That mindset ruled the composed story. I even heard comments made from other women: "That is what you get when you go with a man you do not know." This was heartbreaking to me. How could others so easily judge when they did not even know Gina? Certainly, that too was the prevailing mindset of the Wolfpack.

The night of June 28, 1980, was a date Gina and I had been looking forward to for a while. We planned to celebrate the end of mid-term exam week by dancing the night away together, as we so often did. Gina was her happiest when she danced. Anyone who lived their young years in the 1970s disco era knew what this meant. In Radford, it meant: Disco Depot. Gina on the dance floor was a beautiful, graceful sight. I was always in awe of how she took on dancing like it was art.

But early that evening, Buz and I had a terrible fight—our first fight. After about a month back in the social environment of college life, I suddenly contemplated that after almost four years of dating the same boy, maybe I should consider dating others. I had been dating the same man since age seventeen. To a twenty-one-year-old, it was a logical thought process. Now, I know to contemplate the origin of such thoughts that came from out of the blue this day…*since he had gone home for the summer…I met him so young…what if he is not the one and only*….It was my fault. I had spoken the words he found unforgivable: "I think we should date other people." Furious, he stormed upstairs to my bedroom. I believed it was the absolute end. I had really messed up. I was listening to my head, convincing myself to take a logical, rational path. The only reason Buz didn't just leave right then was that he had agreed to drive a friend back up to northern Virginia early Sunday morning.

I was devastated, so I told Gina I wanted to stay home. Gina decided to go on without me, her heart set on dancing. I told her it was okay to take my brown Monte Carlo, and I must have known she would have others with her and that all of our friends would most likely be there. I had always thought of the Marriott Inn as an upscale, safe dancing spot.

"Will you help me clasp my necklace?" she asked, her hazel eyes dancing with excitement. Eager to be dancing within the hour, smiling delightfully at the prospects of seeing her friends, that was Gina. When Gina smiled, her high cheekbones would be so stunningly pronounced that I always wondered why I did not get some of those same genes. I jokingly accused her when we were little of sucking on too many jawbreakers. As I pulled her shoulder-length hair up so I could clasp her necklace, I noticed it fell perfectly back in place. Gina's shiny, healthy hair would bounce with every step she took. Today, the '80s are known for big hair. Gina did not have to tease and spray—her hair was naturally thick, and her hot curlers would set the feathered, wavy layers in perfect harmony so no wind could blow them out of place. Even when she hadn't styled it, her hair framed her face with little swirls.

In the townhouse was a small landing so that when you came in the front door, you could either go up the steps to the bedrooms or down a few steps into the living room. I walked her to the steps of the landing, noticing how put together she was, dressy white pants riding high up on her waist specifically chosen to camouflage her deep scars, hugging only her ankles where she had cut slits to tailor to her petite stature, and her purple body suit matching the straps on her shoes. This night she wore a white wrangler jacket that we shared, her sleeves neatly rolled up, highlighting her bronze tan she had worked on earlier in the day, sunbathing while napping in the privacy of our backyard after a hard few days of exams. And even though it was summer, she would never have taken the jacket off, always conscious of her scarring. As she left, I plunked down on the living room floor, glum about my angry boyfriend locked away in my bedroom upstairs.

Just as fast as Gina had gone out the door, she came running back in, bounding up the stairs. "I can't go out dancing without my ankle bracelet!"

That ankle bracelet would become a part of the murder scene, evidence used later in the trial. That ankle bracelet would be found in the shag carpet at the bottom of the spiral steps in the lake house, broken from her struggle to break free from her captor—or captors.

When Gina descended the stairs, she stopped on the landing, tapping her feet excitedly, spinning around to tell me goodbye again. As she looked down, she saw my tears. I had held the big ones back as long as I could. I looked up at her through watery eyes, and there she stood, beautiful as ever, the delicate gold chain on her dainty ankle. We both had the same designed bracelets—two hearts interlocked, symbolic of our sisterly bond.

Then she gave me those last words of sisterly advice:

"Listen to your heart, not your head…. Dlana you always think too much! Just follow your heart and you will know what you should do. Heart, not Head!"

And then Gina left, driving away in my Monte Carlo. I climbed the stairs to her bedroom, watched some TV, and cried myself to sleep, wallowing in self-pity.

One day in 2016, I reread Gina's letters. I found something she had written in January 1980 while still at Emory & Henry. It seemed so prophetic to me in light of all I was experiencing. She had attached a written excerpt of 1 Corinthians 13, as part of her letter.

> "Love…It is never glad about injustice, but rejoices when truth wins out…"

> "All the special gifts and powers from God will someday come to an end, but love goes on forever."

> "I love you and hope one day we both can live up to that paragraph above."

> Gina

Every time I dress for the day, I think of Gina. This framed letter now hangs on the wall beside my makeup vanity. It seems the right place—the world of beauty. Every time I get my hair done at a salon, I think of her. I appreciate how hard it is for a beauty stylist to stand on her feet and hold her arms up all day. It takes a lot of upper body strength. It's a hard day. Yet their days are filled with shared stories. Gina would have entered cosmetology joyously, carrying on the tradition from our Auntie Jel and Auntie Red. In my memory, I see Gina and I as little girls, swiveling in the chairs after the salon emptied out, playing dress up in front of the large mirrors together, making our little girl dreams come true.

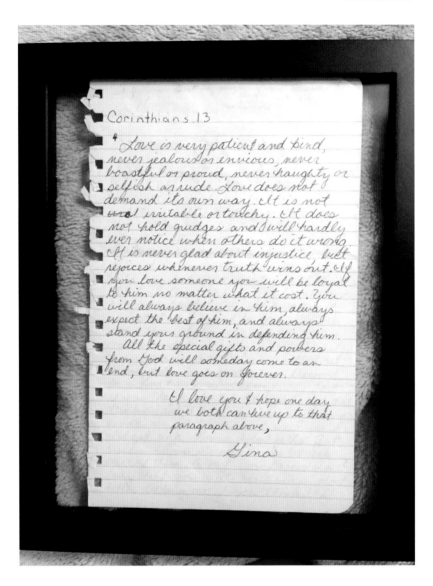

Corinthians.13

4 Love is very patient and kind, never jealous or envious, never boastful or proud, never haughty or selfish or rude. Love does not demand its own way. It is not irritable or touchy. It does not hold grudges and will hardly ever notice when others do it wrong. It is never glad about injustice but rejoices whenever truth wins out. If you love someone you will be loyal to him no matter what it cost. You will always believe in him, always expect the best of him, and always stand your ground in defending him.

All the special gifts and powers from God will someday come to an end, but love goes on forever.

I love you & hope one day we both can live up to that paragraph above,

Gina

ALL THE SPECIAL GIFTS AND POWERS FROM
GOD WILL SOMEDAY COME TO AN END,
BUT LOVE GOES ON FOREVER

THE
MIRACULOUS
JOURNEY
A Day Made in Heaven

CHAPTER 3

I LOVE YOU MORE THAN YOU'LL EVER KNOW

This chapter goes out to the ones I love, from the one left behind.

Our dad was rushed to the hospital in April 2007, his colon blocked by a softball-sized tumor hiding in a bend of his lower intestine. The tumor had already broken the colon wall into the body cavity, making it inoperable.

As my family and I faced his death, I pondered the significance of his life, reflecting on the memories, good and bad. Our lives had aligned in a way that shows how we are two connected souls. I began to understand how my strength was similar to his. We had both lost a parent earlier in life—my dad, his father; and me, my mother. We had both lost siblings early in life—my dad, his brother and a sister; and me, my sister. As he was dying, I realized he was my last connection to my ancestral line. Everyone had passed before him.

Sundays after church when we were kids, Daddy would drive us over into Eastern Kentucky across the mountains, heading to his childhood home where genuine Kentucky Fried Chicken awaited. Our fondest childhood memories were created on those Sunday afternoons. Our dad would play music on the eight-track: the Righteous Brothers singing "Unchained Melody" and "You've Lost That Loving Feeling." A favorite song was "King of the Road," which is what I imagined my dad to be, driving that living-room-on-wheels that was his '60s-era sedan, snaking through those curvy mountain roads. Then there was "Downtown" by Petula Clark, which ignited my curiosity. *Where is downtown? Where is the city traffic?* I wondered where that place was, the place "where all troubles would be forgotten." My dad's music transported me to other worlds, like Otis Redding's "Sittin' on the Dock of a Bay." Then there was my music, The Monkees telling me I could be a believer. Elvis telling me about idealized love, not just in his music, but also in his movies that would "babysit" us on Wednesday afternoons while Daddy worked. When I heard Nancy Sinatra sing, "These boots were made for walkin,'" I knew I was going somewhere, much farther than across the mountains to Kentucky.

Every time my dad arrived home, his mama and sisters would spoil him rotten. He was the baby of the family. Even though we were surrounded by family, three loved ones were always missing—their brother William Hiram Hall who died in October 1941 from a brain tumor at thirteen; a sister, Sara, who died in a tragic car accident, July 1966 and whom I knew as "Auntie Sara." And the patriarch of the family, William Milton Hall, who had been murdered in 1944 at the age of forty-three, long before I was born. The story, as it is told in our family, is that my grandfather was murdered for something he believed in. He was an advocate for coal miners, helping organize the unions in Harlan County, Kentucky. Our grandma, whom we called NaNa, traveled with him once to Washington, DC, which was quite the experience for her! She was very proud of her husband and the work he did, but it would come at a great cost.

In Appalachian lore, that period was called the Bloody Harlan years, when violence erupted in the 1940s that would continue well into my teen years in the 1970s. In my family, we knew what the phrase, "blood on the coal" meant. On that day, October 20, 1944, my grandfather had just dropped off my then-nine-year-old dad and his sister at school. Minutes later, a coal truck rampaged off the mountain, smashing into his vehicle. This questionable tragic accident was not investigated as a murder, but that is how my NaNa always saw it. As my grandfather lay dying, the coal truck driver who had run him off the road pointed a gun toward all of the surrounding witnesses, stating he would kill them too if they came close to my grandfather's vehicle to try to help him. Our grandmother told us she was alerted right away that her husband Milt had been in a terrible accident. Somehow, my NaNa made it to his smashed car before the rescue or the police arrived. She did not cower to this mad man's threats. She ran right past him into the arms of her dying husband. His death was suspect because of his association in forming the Unions of Eastern Kentucky to help protect the coal miners and their families. But in those times, no one would do anything. There was a war in Europe, and there was a war in Appalachia America. Families were divided between non-union and union. Fear ruled. My grandfather's killer was never arrested. My grandmother was left with four children to raise as a single mother in the 1940s. Her strength was unwavering.

When my grandfather was just a teenage boy, his father, my great-grandfather, had been the Sheriff of Letcher County, Kentucky. Being a jailer would have been a challenge anywhere at the turn of the century, but in Eastern Kentucky, it was daunting. My grandfather most likely learned strength from his father in those formative teen years—strength he would need since he was very young when he left for World War I. My NaNa once shared her love story of meeting him on the train platform dressed in his uniform. My grandfather was no stranger to the loss of a parent, having lost his own mother when only sixteen. My great-grandmother died at the age of thirty-nine, a month after the birth of her eighth child. My cousin would say she just had too many children! I would say you could never have too many.

Eastern Kentucky made American history with its feuds. My NaNa's ancestry can be traced to the renowned McCoys of the feuding Hatfield and McCoy families. I became quite interested in the stories of these distant relatives when I first noticed a family tombstone with an entire family buried within days and weeks of each other in the Hall family cemetery that sits on top of a mountain in Ermine, Kentucky. In my research, names in the Hall 1800 genealogies tell the story—Big Bad Hall, Gunsmith Billy Hall, " Hog" John Hall, Bad Bill Hall, Bad John Hall, Bad Lewis Hall, Thomas "Devil" Hall. I was glad to know that my great-grandfather was just called Big Will Hall. No Bad or Devil in his nickname. Names like this certainly rouse my curiosity about my family history preceding my great-grandfather and others who lived in the mountains of Eastern Kentucky.

I know my grandfather was an amazing man because my NaNa loved him! And it is easy to see why she loved him after reading the kind words shared in a local news article at his death.

WILLIAM MILTON HALL
JAN 1, 1901 - OCT 20,1944

WM Hall Meets Untimely Death.

The passing of Mr. Hall was not only a severe blow to his bereaved family but to hundreds of people throughout the country and southeastern Kentucky as well. Milt as he was familiarly known to his intimate friends will sadly be missed by his family, the U.M.W.A. of A, which organization he represented, his neighbors, his county, and his country. He was a valuable and tireless worker in the war effort and in many instances was responsible for the success of the Bond drives, Red Cross Drives, and War Fund Drives. He instilled the spirit of patriotism among his fellow workers and citizens.

A heartfelt letter addressed to my NaNa was sent to the local paper by John L. Lewis, a man both loved and hated by many for his leadership in the American organized labor movement. He served as the United Mine Workers of America's chief founder and president from 1920 to 1960.

Mrs. William Milton Hall

Whitesburg, Kentucky

I was shocked and grieved to learn of the tragic accident which befell your beloved husband in the course of his duties this morning.

The United Mine Workers of America has been the beneficiary of his loyal, efficient, tireless services for many years; and especially are the Mine Workers of Kentucky indebted to him for his courageous and bitter fight down through the years against the powerful forces arrayed against our Union in that state. He has contributed greatly to the building of our Organization into a strong and progressive unit, equipped to protect and advance the interests of our membership. All who were privileged to know your husband will mourn his untimely passing and will feel that our Union and its membership have suffered a profound loss.

Will you please accept for yourself and for the other members of your grieving family my heartfelt sympathy in this hour of your deep sorrow; and believe that I understand the magnitude of the personal loss which you have sustained.

Sincerely yours, John L Lewis

And Big Sandy Elkhorn Coal Operators Association, Ashland, Kentucky

Many consider Lewis the civil rights leader of the coal miners. His face is recognizably familiar to most by his thick, pronounced bushy eye brows.

It saddens me that my great-grandfather buried his son Milt, and his son Milt buried one of his sons William Hiram, and his other son John, my dad, never got to bury his daughter. I often ponder the strength of my soul family. And I imagine that tears flowed from heaven when the violence spilled into Gina's life.

JOHN L. LEWIS PHOTO FROM MY PERSONAL COLLECTION

Daddy never talked to us about his father. I know his father's character of caring about others and the tragic early loss of his father imprinted on my dad's life. Its impact was apparent in the paths my dad chose to take in his life. He learned early on the struggles families can endure. My dad would passionately tell me, "People do not ever make a lot of money selling life insurance, but they must. It is the right thing to do." The experience of being raised with no father impacted his life forever, but his father's legacy lived on in the countless families protected.

My dad had grown up poor in the Appalachian Mountains of eastern Kentucky, working for a dime a day as a young boy, guiding donkeys into the coal mines. His sister Sara would tell her daughter that as the youngest, she and my dad would be the ones to split the one egg that would be laid in the morning. My dad must have known hunger. But I am sure it changed for the better with NaNa and Auntie Jel and her husband, Uncle Kermit, leading the family. The entire family worked together to open a small business—a soda shop, serving fresh grilled burgers and, at times, graciously serving food free to people who could not afford to pay.

My dad was the first in the family to go to college. His mother and sisters were proud when he earned a scholarship to play football at Virginia

Polytechnic Institute, known today as Virginia Tech in Blacksburg, Virginia. The day he arrived to see the massive gray stone buildings at VPI, he thought the campus looked like a prison. Three times, he "escaped," hitchhiking all the way back to eastern Kentucky. NaNa would always know he was on his way because the recruiter would call and give her a heads up. The third time this happened, she met her son at the door, gave him a glass of water, and made him turn around, hitchhiking the 200 miles back to Blacksburg. I am sure she so wanted to hug her son and keep him home, but she made the right choice, knowing this was important for his life. She was the strength needed to set him on his path.

So Daddy played football and he was good at it. He went on to receive many honors. The recognition he was most known for was the Southern Conference Jacobs Blocking Trophy, which in today's world would be like getting conference lineman of the year. To this day, that 1954 team is the only undefeated team in the school's history. Deep lifetime friendships formed among his teammates, and those friendships would prove vital to us during the summer of 1980, as we searched that same area, up and down the mountains for my sister's body. The happy, cutting up memories of his college years were forever overshadowed by his daughter's murder.

After my dad graduated, he returned to eastern Kentucky to coach at his

former high school. He fell in love with my mother, married, and moved to Coeburn, Virginia, where their life together began. And we three came to be.

The day our mother was taken away, her parents explicitly told my dad, "If you think we are going to take those children, you have another think coming." Our dad responded, "If you think you are going to take my children, *you* have another think coming."

Daddy was on his own, a single man raising three children with a mountain of debt to climb from a double dose of life—Gina's accident and our mother's illness. He would always have a way to bring in extra income. That was how daddy became known all around the town of Coeburn and beyond as The Dessert Man. He would spend his summer break, from teaching and coaching and refereeing high school sports, baking pies that he would sell. He would ultimately leave teaching, but not youth athletics. His involvement with athletics and the youth of our community was always a part of his life. By my late high school years, his many years of hard work had paid off and his business ventures began to thrive. He never quit making pies, always sharing his sweets and bringing smiles to many faces.

Aunt Sara and NaNa would take turns staying with us in Virginia during those early years, quickly stepping up to help care for us. They became a stable fixture in the tumultuous life of three young children. We were ages six (me), four (Gina), and one (John Jr.) when we learned

about death. One day, Aunt Sara was coming over from Kentucky, driving my dad's light blue Mustang across the mountains when suddenly the tire blew out. She veered into a cliff and died.

I remember standing there waiting for her to arrive, and then hearing the news. Some neighborhood children taunted me that my aunt's head had been cut off. *Why were they saying this to me?*

Daddy carried the burden of this loss his entire life. Aunt Sara had had four children of her own. His love and support of Aunt Sara's first born, my cousin Lana Carol, was evident especially during her college years. My dad had a special relationship with two of his nieces and a nephew. They loved him dearly.

NaNa, Auntie Jel, and Uncle Kermit lived in my dad's childhood home, which his father had built for his family. My childhood memories of this wonderful place always warmed my heart. Recalling the lush flower gardens full of colorful butterflies that Gina and I would endlessly chase always brings my biggest smile. In her kitchen, Auntie Jel would always have crispy fried chicken, delicious tender pork roast, fresh green beans and corn from her garden, pecan-topped sweet potato casserole, her extra-special best-recipe-ever broccoli casserole, plus homemade rolls, hot cornbread, and sweet, lemony iced tea. She always offered an array of desserts, including usually a homemade pie—sometimes chocolate, sometimes coconut, or lemon meringue, butterscotch, strawberry cream, cherry, or pecan. The scent of whatever was in the oven would waft out of the house to greet us. Maybe it was the Crisco, maybe it was the dab of bacon grease bubbling around the chicken in the skillet that made the fried chicken so perfect. Every bite was crunchy, yet deliciously moist. Spending Sunday afternoons at Auntie Jel's house was serene. That was always her demeanor, but one family story stood out. When her sister Sara was going through a nasty divorce, her ex demanded a refrigerator and an old pop-up trashcan be given back, saying they were his. Auntie Jel said, "Come on over and get them," then calmly stepped out to the kitchen, separated from the main house at that time. She took a hammer to that silly metal trash can, marring it with hundreds of dents. It seems I resonated the most with my Auntie Jel's resolve.

Those Sunday visits with his family were special to my dad. After NaNa died, my dad took her seat at the head of the table for the Sunday family gatherings that Auntie Jel seemed effortlessly to make so memorable. While everyone else would pile up in their cars and head to church together, Auntie Jel would stay home preparing Sunday dinner. As a child, I never knew her spiritual beliefs. When she fell ill in later years, I would take a shift staying with her in Kentucky, relieving my cousins, and I got to witness her daily routine. She arose early each morning, following the same ritual. She would prepare her freeze-dried Sanka instant coffee, then feed the animals, the wildlife, and the birds, no matter the weather. This was how I came to understand what she believed in.

A favorite memory of my youth was my scruffy Uncle Ashland. NaNa had a baby brother whom I adored as a curious little girl…the dirty, bibbed, overall-wearing, unshaven man whom our aunts would make eat in the kitchen at the kids' table with us when he did not clean himself up. I loved this uncle! He would hug me and Gina, his scraggly beard scratching our faces. Gina would turn her face away, scrunching up her nose from the scratchiness of his face against hers. Uncle Ashland was a true mountain man, who spent his  time searching the forest for ginseng to sell. He would sit on his porch playing a harmonica, his dog singing along, howling in tune.

One time, NaNa and I went to clean Uncle Ashland's two-room house. She loved my floppy, green hat, a quintessential 1970s flower-child hat. I had adorned it with hippie slogan buttons and peace signs. She decided it was perfect for her. That was our NaNa. As we cleaned, we laughed and reminisced. Before our dad remarried, when my NaNa came to stay with us in Virginia to help my dad raise us, she taught me how to remember good over bad. Every time I came to visit her, she reminded me of those tender years when she had been our caregiver. Sometimes she laughed as she pulled out the Sears & Roebuck catalog and perused the shoe section, with its photos of "old lady shoes."

She would look down at her own shoes and laugh hysterically. "Look what I'm wearing now; those same old lady shoes we used to laugh at when you were a girl."

This laughter had been so important to me, remembering the good moments of our past. And I am sure laughter was always important to our grandmother, overcoming the bad with the good. When I think of NaNa and the quilt of her life, I realize she was no stranger to sorrow, losing her beloved husband so early. No mother should ever have to bury her own—a son and a daughter, and especially a grandchild in the manner we lost Gina. Her ancestry undoubtedly added strength. Still, no matter the endurance, these early losses of her life must have been heart-wrenching. Such moments can be the knots in our quilt, the parts of our life story that influence, direct, and change our paths—the parts that make us resilient.

My dad first faced cancer when I was fifteen. By that time, he had been married to Mama Joan for almost six years and had a fourth child. Daddy always had the same routine when he shaved. Someone once told me that when I was just a little girl, I told them, *"My daddy smells better than anyone in the whole world"*—it was his after-shave. That smell is my dad. A smell that meant stability in a little girl's life. One morning while shaving, he noticed a small bump on his neck and showed it to Mama Joan. She knew immediately he should go to the doctor. She had always told us she had heard her grandmother's voice in her head, telling her to pay attention—*It is so small, you will miss it*. Of course, I never really believed her, until now. It was cancer, Hodgkin's lymphoma. Radiation and chemotherapy were in order, and that saved his life for the moment, but most likely increased the risk for a second cancer.

After he survived cancer, he was a much calmer, more peaceful man. I see now that the bout with cancer provided him with an inner strength that would help him five years later, when his daughter would be brutally murdered.

Every now and then the pre-cancer, less-calm version of John Hall would come back out. I wonder what Gina would have said to Daddy had she been here for this next story. Our youngest brother, Garland, was playing in a high school basketball game, a nail-biter with seconds remaining. He was standing at the foul line with two shots; he took one, and then time out was called. The referees mistakenly recorded the jersey number of the player at the foul line, and after time out, called another player up to the line. Before anyone could even look up, my refereeing dad was out on the floor letting those refs know how to referee, with two policemen right behind him. It ended well, but everyone in the county heard about that moment. Daddy took his competitive sports very seriously. I believe that is why I ended up living back in southwest Virginia in his later years. It brought my dad much pleasure to watch his grandsons play sports. Moments like these created some of his happiest, easiest times of life.

My dad was a great man. His kindness always prevailed. He had *heart*. And he recognized *heart* when he saw it.

TROOPER AUSTIN HALL (PHOTO COURTESY OF *YOUR VIRGINIA STATE TROOPER* MAGAZINE)

Austin Hall was the initial lead investigator for the Virginia State Police on Gina's case. He once shared a story about my dad that happened earlier during those initial intense days. A story that still touches his heart when he thinks of John Hall. My dad approached Austin and said, "Austin, I thought the state was gonna send in some scuba divers and a search team?" Austin thought they would, but he had to share his disappointment with my dad. "Sorry, John. They are not coming and will not be coming. It was not in the plans." Austin said my dad did not get angry or upset. He simply asked Austin's permission to call a friend my dad knew, first graciously seeking Austin's approval before he made the call. Austin quickly answered, "John, if it were my daughter and I knew the President, I would not hesitate to call." So my dad made his call. The memory of what happened next still brings a smile to Austin's face. Within hours, the sergeant pulled into the parking lot on two wheels, jumped out of his car, and asked the men in an excited voice, "*What have you all done?* We just got an order from Governor Dalton's office. We are to give a daily report to the Bureau of Investigation on the Hall girl that is missing. The divers are on their way." But it would be this part of the story that touched Austin's heart. My dad was offered a state investigator from the Bureau to take the lead. He politely declined and asked that Austin Hall remain point man. My father knew his character. And he saw Austin's light shine like a beacon, helping us walk this very dark path. *This is a good man. He will care about Gina*, my father must have thought. And my dad was right. It would be this man's impeccable notes that helped guide me through the mountains of information in 2016.

The devil is in the tiniest of these details.

I often contemplate the many crossings of paths in our lives that become so relevant in the future. Many stories intricately woven together, changing the directions of people's lives.

Kneeling at my dad's bedside in 2011, I shared that I had carried the guilt of what had happened to Gina all of these years. As the oldest, I believed my job had always been to protect the others. I had always felt responsible for Gina.

In the last months of my dad's life, I had so many questions for my dad. I wanted to know about the day Gina got burned. What had happened? Who was there to help her? Who pulled off her burning pajamas? I do not remember seeing anyone with burned hands. All I could remember was the burn spot on the floor where her pajamas had landed. Exactly where it was—I still see it. A scorched, black floor. I believe my dad carried the heaviness of guilt of that split second trauma for Gina, his little girl's life changed forever.

That one trauma created a different path for many people: Elana, Joan, NaNa, Auntie Sarah, John Jr., etc. My life, too. I do not remember my dad ever being sad in those early years. I remember feeling happy in his presence. Daddy used to make us mayonnaise sandwiches. He could make them seem like a king's meal. He made us a lot more sandwiches of white bread and mayonnaise—just more fun to be had with those king's banquets! Mama Joan always said he was deep in debt when she came along. Now I understand the insurmountable financial burden of these two events. But it only made my dad stronger. Years later, his long hours of hard work paid off. So many other memories are clear, but why do I have no memories of our mother?

LAST GRANDCHILD

As my dad lay dying, I had so many questions I needed to ask him…but it was not possible. We always think we will have enough time to ask what we need to know, but then time runs out.

But that was okay! Our conversations throughout life were the right ones focusing on the happy moments. Most conversations with his children usually revolved around our children—his grandchildren. My sons' favorite memories of their granddaddy were his awesome love energy hugs. One time he let one of his granddaughters tie him up and comb his eyebrows. Now that is a good man.

When they rushed my dad to the hospital in early October 2010, he was facing his third emergency surgery, and we weren't sure he would make it through this one. He must not have thought so either because he looked at his children with a concerned look on his face as though he had something important he needed to say to my brother, half-brother, and me. His words of wisdom centered on his family, to always be loving parents and, of course, continue to work hard! Family was always what mattered most to him. But then they rolled him into surgery.

We waited eleven hours. But he made it through. He would spend the next sixty days recovering in the hospital. He made it home for Christmas. He checked himself right out of the hospital! He wanted to be home with

his family all together. In those last few weeks of his life, I would find inner strength—and many previously undiscovered skills, like administering morphine through an IV. In those last days, I thought a lot about Gina, remembering our life in those early years; looking out the window of my teenage home, I would see images of Gina turning flips and handstands across the backyard.

What I was going to miss the most was the way my dad and I shared our daily successes. For so many years, I would be crazy-busy and rush across the mountain to see him, driving so fast from Lebanon to Coeburn that I racked up several speeding

tickets. When I pulled up in his driveway, I would see his hidden smile as he pointed his finger at me and shook his head as if to say, "Too much trouble for you to have come over," knowing how busy my life was. My heart would smile, comforted by his way of showing he really was appreciative of my visits. Shaking his head or wagging his finger at me was just his endearing way of saying, "I'm glad you're here." His first words were always, "How was your day, Dlana?" He was genuinely interested in me, understanding himself what my life was like being self-employed.

After he became ill, he spent a lot of time on his porch. He must have sat there alone contemplating what was coming. His faith was strong, so he most likely didn't have to wait long for answers. He delighted in the hummingbirds and flowers all around the house. He never seemed to let on that he was afraid of dying. I knew he believed in his heart that he would see Gina again.

Something Daddy said in 1980 to the many newspaper reporters after Gina was gone has always stayed with me. "I just can't accept it. I sit on my porch at night and look at the stars and it just doesn't seem real. I expect her to walk up our driveway any moment." No parent should ever have to bury their child. My dad not only had to grieve the loss of a child, but he did not get to bury her. He never had closure because he never knew the truth of that night. I believe he somehow does now.

In those last days, I would watch Daddy, weak in his bed, grimacing from the pain even as I increased the doses of morphine, and I wondered if we could have the conversations I so wanted to have, what advice would he most want to give me before he died? Had I lived my life as he would have wanted for me? Success was a big part of our conversations. He always wanted me to strive to be the best I could be. For so many years, I had had a certain way of defining success. The origin was probably that day when I was a little girl, taking Gina by the hand, seeking something to eat. You learn to ask yourself, "How did this serve me?"

All these events had made us who we were, the stitching of the tapestry—a sister who wanted to protect her baby sister, but also a woman who was on a hamster wheel. My dad's dying got me off that track so I could begin to see what I needed to see.

When a body begins to die, its systems shut down. Pain escalates in the lower extremities and moves up the body. Even our dad's favorite burgundy pajamas, worn thin, were painful to his skin, causing extreme pain to his nerve endings. "White car," he mumbled. "Beautiful place." Someone he loved was with him, and the wind was blowing in his face. He was smiling. I was not ready to lose his strength. I still needed my daddy.

That night as he was dying, a sadness overtook me that I may not have lived up to his expectations. But, even then, I was stubborn. I did not want his expectations to be my expectations. In one area of my life, I knew he was not happy with me. I had quit going to a traditional church several years before and I knew it bothered him greatly. He knew I was still spiritual, but he worried I would not have the fellowship of a church family like he had experienced with all of his closest church friends, especially in times of need. I would tell him, "That is not why we should go to church, Daddy." Shaking his head, he would say, "I know, but it is a great advantage to have these friends in your life."

As I sat by my dad's bed, I remembered those early moments in my life when I first came to know the love that comes from within the heart of my soul. My NaNa would sit and read her Bible, and I would sit by her feet and watch her face as she read each word with devotion. I had been five or six when we first started walking over to a church not far from our home. Vacation Bible School had been in session, but what caught my attention were the yummy, mouth-watering banana popsicles. While I slurped, people told me about God, who loved me, and I sang songs about Jesus with the others: "Jesus loves me, this I know...."

Looking into Daddy's face as he was dying, I knew my strength to be there by his side came from a deep place of love. Quietly, I begged him, "When you get to heaven, please let me know what the real truth of it all is. Please show me what I need to know. I can't accept all I am told without understanding better what is the truth about life and this existence. I know I am to have faith, but something does not feel complete."

I told him I knew he would reunite with his family, his mother and father, his brother and sisters. "And most importantly, our precious Gina."

I said it, but I am not sure I really believed it in that moment. A big get-together, a welcoming party in heaven? I just was not sure. *What really happens to our souls when we die?*

So I laid my head on my dad's hand, while in prayer to God for his peaceful transition into the unknown, and I made a second direct plea to my daddy. "When you get there, wherever there is, please help me to know what I need to know. If any way possible, please help me know the purpose of all this."

These would be the last words said to him. I don't know if my dad heard my plea to understand God, my spirituality, my existence, my purpose. But I know God heard me. My dad was dead within an hour.

John R. Hall had led a life filled with trials and tribulations. His life was and will always be a life of significance. His strength came from a place of love, the heart of his soul. Surviving Stage IV cancer for almost four years is not only a testimony of his strength and love of his family, but also of his family's love for him. I know now that Gina was there, welcoming him home. I feel an amazing peace in knowing this. My soul family is a loving presence, always with me in spirit every time I remember their stories and how their lives connected to mine.

I wonder if our loved ones are watching us from heaven's grandstands. I do not pretend to know the truth of everything. As a Christian who believes in the Bible, I wondered exactly what this verse meant: Hebrews 12:1 tells me we are surrounded by a great, large cloud of witnesses. I hope whoever they are, they are cheering us on as we run the race of our life. I can only tell you what I feel, which is I am certain of their loving presence with me always. Every time I remember their life stories, I feel the connection of their lives to mine.

NaNa was a quilt maker, sitting in her rocking chair for hours, creating beautiful patterns, patterns that told the story of her life. In my office, I have hung the hand-stitched red-and-white quilt she made for me. I have come to see my life like those quilts, all of my life's moments becoming a part of a beautiful tapestry, connecting together the many pieces that make up my own story. All the pieces of my story connect to the stories of all of my loved ones, an interwoven tapestry, connected for an eternity.

ALL OF OUR MOMENTS BECOME
THE TAPESTRY OF OUR LIFE

CHAPTER 4

HIGHWAY DON'T CARE

Can we bring her home?

In 2013, Lt. Andy Wilburn of the Radford Virginia Police Department told me he believed Gina's body could be found and he hoped he could help bring her home.

My sister's case was considered a cold case by many, even though there had been a conviction. That her remains had never been found had drawn a lot of eyes to the case.

Throughout 2013-2015, I would visit with Andy on occasion, answering any questions he might have about Gina. He would keep me informed about Epperly and new leads, and I would share with him events I remembered from 1980. But starting in January 2015, the frequency of our conversations increased.

Andy started to win me over when I saw what he had written in honor of Gina's birthday in August 2014, a low point in my own life when I needed my sister's forgiving strength here with me. I was so busy in my own life, I really only paid attention to that last paragraph but that was enough.

> Life's journey takes us on a course that changes ever so slightly with our own goals and ambitions. That normally straight line will often dip above and below the path it should be on. Often, our lines are predetermined to intersect with someone else's line. The results of that contact, even if brief, can alter the course of each life after contact.

I'm on my path. I'm doing what God wants me to do at this period in time. I've been tasked with things to settle, investigate, and resolve because I am supposed to.

Approximately two years ago, my path crossed with a young lady named Gina Hall, whose life was taken in a brutal and senseless way. I believe it was not her time to go, but evil prevailed that night in June of 1980.

You see, Gina and I have a connection. Her spiritual unrest and my physical inability to rest have combined to bring a new resolve and passion to an unsolved mystery, the location of her mortal body. I work for her; I speak for her because she cannot. Many have concluded that her body will never be located. I do not agree. Hope is the keeper of the flame. It's what drives us all to do more, to do better, and to not let her or her family believe she is forgotten.

Sunday is Gina's birthday; it is also my daughter Katie's 18th birthday. My family will celebrate life, remember Gina, and hope that our connection will lead to her and our lives will touch again.

What won me over was I became convinced that Andy was genuinely passionate about my sister's case. Andy had known nothing about Gina's case when he first became involved. But as he gathered all of the relevant information, he became interested in putting the "soul-case" of her missing body to rest once and for all. As the years passed, he had several leads to follow—there have been many theories about the location of my sister's body. Many of these leads came from psychics, or what could be named as "gifted people—seers," and I know, too, that many came from those pretending to be psychic. And now I know the importance to contemplate what it really means to be a psychic, a medium, a soothsayer, a shaman, etc.

I still held Andy at arm's length, however, visiting him only so often. Oddly, though, when I would send him a text of a detail I remembered from 1980, he would respond with something like, "Funny u text me today, was talking about this in depth last night…. You available for a call?"

I first met Andy face to face in May 2013, when he sent me an email asking me to visit. I had not been back to Radford since 1980. Sitting in Andy's office for the first time, I scanned the room, seeing his wall proudly displaying his daughter's artwork. I also noticed he collected skulls. A photocopied picture of Gina, propped up on top of his filing cabinet, was visible to all who entered. Also, he had an old-fashioned flashlight propped on a shelf—the kind I remember from years ago, with big D batteries touching and connecting the battery power circuit through a long cylinder, which I thought odd and out of place. I would come to understand why in our later visits.

"You might find some of what I am going to share not the norm," he began, as he explained why he had contacted me.

A preacher who described himself as a "gifted person" had contacted Andy on March 3, 2013. This contact told Andy he could see dead people and the stories of their violent deaths, especially when he entered the scene of the crime, whether recent or long past. I will call this person The Preacher to keep his identity private.

"I see a lot of these," Andy told me. "I knew right away this one would be different."

The reason, he explained, was one small piece of information he'd uncovered in all of the files. Epperly had worn crepe-soled shoes that night—a fact not known to the public because never revealed at trial. When The Preacher described what he saw, he described the crepe-soled shoes. "That got my attention," Andy said.

The Preacher also shared with Andy that he saw a man tossing a golf club into the lake from the dock. The Preacher saw three people—two men and a woman—burying Gina. He could see car lights shining at the edge of the woods on them as they buried a female body. The field he described was adjacent to a row of four Victorian houses. Andy had tracked down those four houses. They once graced the land that would now be known as the Radford University Dedmon Center area near the soccer field. The legend at Radford University, fueled by ghost hunters' stories, was always that Gina's body had been put in the freshly poured concrete at the newly built Dedmon Center. In the Radford University archives, Andy found an aerial view map of the Dedmon Center as it was being constructed. He was relieved to see the site was not at the concrete pouring stages in this aerial photo from 1980.

"So I took that fellow for a ride," Andy said. The Preacher described one of the houses as colonial style, with a large lot cleared beside it. "'That is where Gina's body is buried,' he told me," Andy continued. "The lot was rimmed with tall trees." I contemplated who might have lived in that house in 1980.

At that point, Andy arranged a search of the Dedmon Center site, an area that is now near the RU soccer field. Twice, he arranged for cadaver dogs to search the area. The first search hinted that one of the dogs had found something of interest, but nothing definitive. During the second search, the dog led authorities to a bank behind a small shed above the soccer field. The dog handler told Andy that the dog would pick his best guess as to the location because the scent seemed to be scattered. These cadaver dogs are capable of detecting bodies that have been in the ground much longer than the thirty-three years that had passed in Gina's case.

To triple-check this lead, Andy met with a professor at Radford University who had a ground-penetrating radar machine. That search would ensue on May 9, 2013. After a few days of processing the data, Andy got a call letting him know the data had been evaluated. Andy and the professor met back at the site so the professor could show Andy the scan and the anomaly in that location. "It was the exact same spot," Andy said. "I knew it immediately."

The two men agreed that if they could get permission to dig from RU, they should.

"I was sure I'd found Gina," Andy said.

Together, Andy and the professor presented their findings to the president of Radford University. A limited scope excavation was approved for the small area where the anomaly had been detected. Authorities made it appear that it was the electric company doing a dig for a power issue because it was near a city pole. No one at the scene of the digging wore any identifying clothing to tip the public off that it was a police operation. On May 14, 2013, the city public works department started digging, excavating a hole 10 feet deep and 15 feet long by 3 feet wide. At the end, both Andy and the professor climbed down into the hole, absolutely dumbfounded that not only was Gina's body not there, but there was nothing to explain the anomaly the radar machine had clearly picked up.

"I was heartbroken," Andy said. "I really believed we would find Gina based on the psychic (*The Preacher*), the cadaver dogs, and the radar machine. How could all of them have been wrong?"

That night, his family was at the in-laws for dinner. Arriving home to an empty house, he sat at the kitchen table, head in his hands, in total disbelief of what had just happened.

DEDMON DIG

During the months preceding this event, his family had kept having issues with his wife's car doors locking on their own at random times. At first, they thought it was an electrical issue; then they started to notice that the days when Andy would work on Gina's case were the days the doors would lock. His wife would start to joke with him, saying, "My doors locked today. You must be working on Gina's case!"

After he worked through his emotions, Andy decided he'd better head over to his in-laws. He drove his wife's car over to her mother's and parked down at the bottom of the yard to be alone and think through his next move, still not ready to go in.

He walked around the yard just to think through the escalations of emotions throughout the day, the highs and the lows—the elation that he might find Gina, the crushing disappointment of standing down in that hole and finding nothing. As he walked back to his car, he noticed the car's headlights were on. He reached through the open window, turned the knob, and the lights went off. These were not automatic lights. His wife's car was a 2004 Hyundai, and the lights had to be manually turned on. As Andy turned the lights off, he stated out loud, "If that is you, Gina, just go ahead and turn those lights back on so I will know."

After that, he walked around the yard a few more minutes. When he returned to the car, the lights were on again. He turned them off. He got a lawn chair out of the trunk and sat beside the car. "I felt Gina so strongly that I could not control my emotions," he said. "I cried uncontrollably for several minutes."

"Gina, what do you want me to do now?" he bellowed.

Tell my sister.

"It was an immediate response," he told me. "It's as clear as anything I have ever felt. I did not need to hear the words. I knew what she wanted me to do."

He did not hesitate. He had been listening. "Tell my sister," he had heard. And he did.

"I will never forget the clear feeling that day of the Dedmon dig," he later told me. "I knew I was to meet you."

He had researched my family and saved my contact information, hoping that one day he would call the number to tell us he had found Gina. Instead, he called to introduce himself to me.

This was the day before my brother and I headed to a parole hearing. I agreed to stop by and meet with him.

I do not believe it was part of the plan for Gina to be found, yet.

Maybe there is a simple explanation why everything has been happening as it has—inexplainable happenings throughout the years.

Andy had copies of Gina's case file—multiple thick binders full of reports. Andy was curious if I could help him find Gina's body—his objective. He knew my eyes and ears were there the summer of 1980, and he wanted to know if anything in Gina's case would stand out to me. After all, I am her sister. "Go tell my sister" was always in the forefront of his mind. I saw and heard a lot that summer, but I did not know all of the intricate details I discovered simply by reading some of those old reports. I am confident no one has ever uncovered as much as I did just from reading Gina's case file. Even Andy, who was familiar with the case because of his interest in bringing closure to the Gina Hall cold case, did not glean from the reports the same as I, her sister, as I read them. I knew my sister. The mindset of a person and their objective when reading affects what facts are seen. No one would have ever absorbed all of the minutia of details as I could knowing and loving Gina. The investigators can learn a lot about the victims of their cold cases, every nuance, extensively from those who knew and loved them. And once truth can be known, as I desired, then other information begins to fall into place. It took a full two years before I would see how all of the old 1980 facts aligned to the new information that just kept coming. I now see why truth has been screamed to many for years from a realm I do not fully understand. Maybe it's simple: Light needs to shine in the dark. There is more to know.

Cold cases do not get warm unless a family member pushes for it and someone with authority makes it a priority. Our current resources are overworked, new cases pouring in every day so that no time is left to work old cases. NamUs (The National Missing and Unidentified Persons System) reports show 12,000 unidentified dead bodies unsolved to date. And the number grows each and every year.

Why do we actually have the name cold case? I understand answers seem impossible at times. The trail grows cold. But these old cases should never become "cold" because they sit on the dusty shelf. Thank heavens for that caring person who does not let it sit. This is a call to that someone from every little town to work that case assigned to them. Listen to your heart. Society needs to protect its citizens from those who have escaped and never been caught. Those living among us—their wrongdoings continuing to spread into the lives of innocent people, most interconnected like a web. The secrets of this web usually are exposed, one thread at a time—many around the forty-year mark. Why? A perplexing thought. Light and goodness shining in the dark, hearing the voices screaming for justice. I understand resources are limited, but where should our priorities be? This is not just about closure for families. The greater unseen advantage to society will be the many, many individuals living in the light, spreading joy and peace among their own circles, not living life in anger, hate, fear, guilt, unforgiveness, or unknowingness. We each affect the world we all live in together. We, each and every one, either spread light or dark into the world we live in...no in between! And the light trumps the dark every time, tenfold—thousandfold—a web of good illuminating our world.

What could be more important in a civilized society than to keep our citizens, especially our innocent children, safe from future criminal acts by those who have remained anonymous, some repeatedly? And, continued safety for victim's families from those who were prosecuted, but could one day be released, as my family is concerned will happen with Epperly as he ages and becomes a financial burden to the state? And, too, we must protect our jurors: Epperly sent a letter once asking for the name of *the little black juror*. That is just so wrong in so many ways. I have been unfortunately connected to this man and his story for almost four decades and I would not hesitate to emphasize—Epperly is unrepentantly, morally wrong.

I could not see the "all-American boy," as the media had trumpeted. What I saw was a man whose own mother tried to correct that narrative. Esther Epperly told the police and my family, "There is no doubt in my mind that my son had killed the Hall girl." This might be all I would need to share to introduce Epperly to you. Even his own mother knew his true nature.

Many stories surfaced from the statements written or shared in 1980 about Epperly's nature, before the trial—before the conviction—during that long summer as we searched for my sister's remains. Gina's file is full of them. Epperly's life was full of violence, yet not one of these stories ever resulted in a formal conviction until Gina's murder.

One time Epperly had attacked his younger, fourteen-year-old sister. Charges were filed, but never pressed. Epperly told police in a different county while being questioned in a later brush with the law that nothing had happened from his sibling scuffle because "The police were friends of the family and they did not arrest me." Why would the mannerly, clean cut, "small town football player on a pedestal" image reign over clear wrong-doings? This may very well be the beginning of Epperly's own creation in his mind as to how he could be perceived by others. He learned that the all-American boy image was to his advantage. Many believe his clean-cut appearance and smooth talking lured his victims. No—most never had a chance to *be lured*, as evident in many of his victims' accounts: "I heard a tapping on the window," or "As soon as I let him in to help him…" or "No warning at all," but everyone's perception was that the victims were deceived and manipulated by the all-American boy! No—what he did do was manipulate everyone else, and that became the exact perception he wanted others to see.

During the police investigation, various friends of Epperly were inter-viewed and shared their observations about him. Others' opinions seemed to matter to him. Epperly's showmanship was evident in the stories that came out: taking dares to swim across an icy lake; his football days not being about just playing to win, but playing to hurt; and other incidents of causing physical harm to others. Some never saw his violence. Many did. Words like "quick-tempered," "gets physical with women," and "violent tendencies" surfaced. But also "well-mannered," "perfect gentleman," and "fun-loving" came from those who only knew him as he wanted them to know him, such as his teachers and casual friends. Two words surfaced consistently: confident and arrogant. Many times, "See Something, Say Something" should have prevailed, but it did not. And those closer friends who witnessed his rage shared another, darker side of Epperly. One man shared that once when Epperly was stopped in traffic on Peppers Ferry Road, he got out of his car, walked up to the car ahead of them, and "pull-ing the unknown driver out of his car, Epperly beat him to a pulp."

Many external signs existed of Epperly's psychological issues. A common theme surfaced in these interviews. It was apparent to his acquaintances, even bystanders, that Epperly was becoming more confident in his ability to become very physical with others, something many people witnessed. Witnesses also told police that Epperly had a fascination with fire. He was known to soak kittens with lighter fluid and light them on fire. I had heard these disturbing stories in 1980. My mind could not help but focus in on my sister and her burns.

Skipper had an interesting story to share. He told the police that a few years earlier, he and his girlfriend had dropped by Epperly's trailer, where he lived down near The New River close to The Sportsman Grill. After Skipper returned from the restroom, he saw Epperly had his girlfriend by the hair and was jerking her around the room. Epperly's job as a bouncer at a local Radford nightspot most likely helped escalate these violent tendencies, which were justified in an environment where they could flourish. And this story had a disturbing twist—a woman shared her rape story, indicating that after Epperly had raped her, she was made to have sex, not just with Epperly, but also with a friend of his. Who was his partner in crime? These many tales simply dumbfounded me. I will never fully understand what I call the Wolfpack mindset.

After Gina was murdered in 1980, Epperly's friends who were interviewed by police seemed to know well Epperly's "problems with girls," yet they had remained his friends. And they all knew his nature. All of these stories, yet none of his friends spoke up. The ego-driven male of the '70s, the all-American boy, got a "Get out of jail free" card, to quote my *Monopoly*-playing dad. The blind eye was prevalent then and prevalent now—the nature of this game.

Throughout the years, more stories about Epperly piled up in my mind. When someone takes the life of another, their own life becomes public. The investigation delves into their character, their background, their actions—everything is revealed. My attorney tells me that a prison or jail cell is not private—that any document or item in a cell is subject to inspection at any time. Perhaps because of my deep roots in the community, and because my sister's murder still weighs on people's minds, it's not uncommon for guards who work at the various state penitentiaries where Epperly had been housed to share tidbits with me about his life there. I only need say my name and the stories are shared.

Most disturbing is what I saw once with my own eyes. A list of approximately 100 girls' names that Andy and I refer to as "Epperly's sex list." Andy confirmed it was an authentic document. I imagine very few people know of this list. It is certainly a list that warrants a closer look. Epperly names the girls. He tells what cities they are from. Sometimes he adds descriptions about them. And when he does not know their names, other marking descriptions become their given name: "Girl with Big Boobs in x town," or "Fat girl that 'x' introduced me to." I hope this list can one day be verified and analyzed for any connections to missing girls, or rape reports by an unknown male, and most importantly, unsolved murder cold cases.

Epperly's trail of women was extensive, at least until my sister's death stopped him. Will we ever know the extent of his violence? How does something like this, all of this, go unpunished—ignored—in a civilized society?

Thank heavens, eventually, it did not and he is in jail where he belongs. Hopefully, he will stay there forever until he meets his maker and faces true consequences.

The accompanying pictures show Epperly's arrogance in the beginning, his true nature as he left the courthouse one day during the trial, and his shock after his verdict—his prevalent thought: *There was no body found, so how could this have happened?*

EPPERLY—BEGINNING OF DECEMBER 1980 TRIAL—COURTESY OF *PULASKI SOUTHWEST TIMES*

Never doubt Epperly killed Gina. His own words tell us so. This same confident, arrogant attitude is what led to his conviction in 1980.

The Supreme Court agreed. The ruling decision letter in his appeal case clearly agreed that Epperly's own words were relevant to making the decision to uphold his conviction. Three of Epperly's inculpatory statements were: 1) His exclamation complimenting the talents of Preston's tracking dog, witnessed by several including policemen. 2) His response to Trooper Hall, who after accusing him of the crime, advised him to consider how his cooperation with the investigators would affect the jury. Epperly's response, "I'll think about it," and 3) His request of a friend made before the investigators had even concluded Gina was dead, to ask his brother, an attorney, if there was anything they could do to him if they didn't find the body. The last was the most damning.

The Supreme Court ruled correctly in his appeal. The prosecuting attorney stated it correctly, "That's what brought it all about—sex. This man's raw desire for Gina and her rebuff and he killed her." The defense argued, "I submit to you, a normal, red-blooded American boy does not kill somebody because they didn't get sex." I agree. But Epperly is not a normal, red-blooded American boy.

EPPERLY—MID-POINT OF TRIAL—COURTESY OF *ASSOCIATED PRESS*

Epperly has not changed.

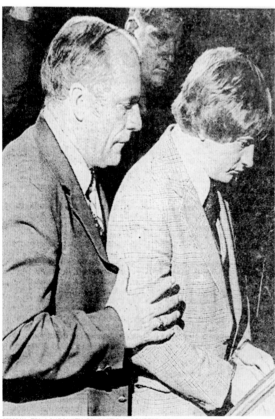

EPPERLY - TRIAL ENDS WITH CONVICTION—COURTESY OF *WASHINGTON EVENING STAR*

Over the years, Epperly shared stories with cellmates, but they have all been rabbit holes. It seems like he's been planting stories about cemeteries, caves, concrete foundations of buildings…many wild stories, as though he has enjoyed watching everyone chase their tails.

One such story came from a prison inmate, a local from his own neighborhood, who happened to run into Epperly in 1986 out in the prison yard. They caught up with each other talking about their cases. This man shared with authorities in 1990 that Epperly had told him he had buried Gina in a grave in the cemetery on the dead-end road near where the car was abandoned. Epperly claimed a boy from the Alley family had helped him. Police, of course, checked the Alley boys out. There were four brothers, two very young, one a teen and one twenty years old in 1980. I always wondered if the inmate was telling what he believed to be the truth. Why would Epperly accuse a boy by the last name of *Alley*? Could it have to do with a second story I would hear? That Gina was buried in the trenches that had just been dug and filled with gravel for the foundation of the new *Allen* building at Radford University being built very near the Dedmon Center construction project. There would have been a field between the two, spanning both sides of the railroad tracks. That made me think about the Preacher and his visions that led to the Dedmon Dig just over those tracks. Knowing now how manipulative Epperly is, it would not surprise me if Alley and Allen were just his way of messing with everyone.

One former cellmate came to the Radford police of his own accord after being released from prison in 2015, the thirty-fifth anniversary of the case. His statement was that Epperly had said in reference to Gina Hall, "Everyone is driving over that bitch every day." This statement comes across like a statement made in rage, not one of intentional misdirection. I think this cellmate's story warrants credence.

A big source of speculation over the years is why Epperly has a *better than others* situation in prison. He had all the amenities possible, even though being in jail might not be construed as posh—an adjective once used to describe his cell. The financial source is probably not his family since I learned once at a parole hearing that a member of his own family was slated to sit on the same side as my family at that day's parole hearing. Too many people have shared that they too wonder who kept Epperly up all of these years. My money is on a woman providing him with all of the amenities. Pen pal relationships form in prison. It is very common. And Epperly would be a maestro at orchestrating many relationships, simultaneously. But could there be more? Inside connections?

The majority of his prison years were spent at Bland Correctional Facility, known as an in-between place, where prisoners go from municipal jails to state facilities. Bland is a farming prison that supplies meat and vegetables to the other regional facilities. One guard told me they referred to it as a "hug-a-thug" prison.

Epperly was slated to be transferred to a higher security prison after I presented to the parole board our family's concerns for our safety, having heard of his troubles that landed him in solitary confinement at Bland so close to our home and knowing of the discovery of his meticulous records tracking the guards watch-post timings. The parole board listened and arranged for his transfer to Buckingham. This gave Andy an opportunity to barter with Epperly. He was allotted one hour to "visit." He hoped he could get him to tell where he had put Gina's body by allowing him to stay at Bland—the country club prison in comparison to Buckingham. Epperly gave Andy nothing.

I believe Epperly cannot tell. Telling will either lead to other victims, or it is not possible because Gina's body is not just hidden, but scattered or completely destroyed. Telling relinquishes what he holds on to in his own mind—power over others. Or maybe it is as simple as cowardly self-preservation.

We can never forget Epperly's arrogant confidence. I believe wherever Gina's body, or parts of it, is, there will be others. And I always remember it is not her; it is just a body. She left it the minute she drew her last breath. Where is Epperly's hidden graveyard? Even if it only hides Gina and no others, it is a burial place. It is a trophy graveyard—that's how he sees it because it is the only power and control he believes he holds. And he has to hold on to something. But it's not the only reason he can never tell.

We are all guilt-ridden at times in our lives. A convicted person, guilty or not, rehabilitated or not, at the least would eventually have words to share with the family of the victim. That never happened. My friend Annie shared with me these amazing, healing words to be repeated every day: I'm sorry. Please forgive me. Thank you. I love you. Words when spoken aloud resonate goodness. *Epperly*...say these words and free your heart —a heart where evil resides.

Epperly is not guilt-ridden. Epperly has no remorse.

CHAPTER 5

BRING ME TO LIFE

*Eyes are the window to one's soul. I felt as if he could see into my soul—
deep inside of me, a soul yearning to be awakened.*

My oldest son was getting married on May 14, 2016, and I was excited to be gaining a daughter. We were headed to her home on a beautiful Caribbean island for the wedding. One of my favorite places is the Bioluminescence Bay, a spectacular place for my family to celebrate together. A few days before we were to leave for the wedding, I sent a note to share my good news with a new friend I had met one year earlier. I remembered he was familiar with the Caribbean, and I knew he could give me some off-the-beaten path ideas for our trip and offer advice about my sons' interests in surfing and caving. Just a week later after contacting him, I would hear the farmer's story, and then this trusted friend would become a crucial part of my quest to know the truth about my sister's murder. I will call him Nola to protect his privacy and because I met him in New Orleans, Louisiana.

In June 2015, I attended an educational event in New Orleans. For this small town girl living a simple life defined by every standard measure of normalcy, this global gathering was a favorite! It's an honor to achieve one invitation, much less having achieved twelve to date, and I was excited. I always welcomed making new acquaintances and spending quality time with my long-time friends. I am glad that gender or age never became a stumbling block for my friendships. Two of my closest friends, both guys—one being my brother—were sitting somewhere in an airport, their flight delayed, so

I joined others for a welcome event and an evening of great music. Most of the people I meet within my familiar, trusted circles are wonderful, good people. I have always been lucky to have great friends, girls and guys! And it would be this night that I made a new, young friend. As I got to know this new person, I could not shake this feeling that I had known him from some place in my past. It was an unfamiliar, nudging feeling, but it was his eyes that seemed so familiar. No matter how much we age, the eyes never seem to change. Some say the eyes are the windows to the soul. His soul was apparent. I only saw goodness. Curious if our paths had crossed before, I launched right into a probing conversation. Preoccupied with our conversation, we looked up and everyone else was gone. Rather than try to catch up, I knew the morning would be an early one, so heading back seemed a better alternative. I was familiar with the area, knowing I was not too far away from my hotel down by the Mississippi River, but I still did not want to walk back alone. I asked this new friend if he minded walking me back to the casino area, and he kindly agreed. The casino was directly across the street from my hotel, which would get me close enough.

We walked up Bourbon Street slowly, talking and not even noticing the bustle. Although Spanish was this man's first language, he spoke English quite well. But it was his words of wisdom that enthralled me. He preceded to tell me things about myself that he could not have known about my life. "You have a big heart," he said. "Because you take care of so many other people in your daily life, you ignore yourself. Your heart needs healing—serious healing. You have dealt with some pretty bad stuff in your life, and it is affecting your heart. To be happy, you first need to believe you can be. First, quit taking care of everyone else, quit always looking to success to make you happy, and next, you need to learn to love yourself."

I looked down at his weathered work boots, hanging on every insightful word he said, noticing every slow step we took. This new friend seemed to know everything about me. Just moments earlier, I had not even known him. Or had I? As we turned the corner, intrigued by his wisdom, I decided it was my turn to find out more about this young prudent man. He shared the basics—husband, loving father of two little children, and so on. Then one statement stood out, as though he were sharing it with me to see how I would respond. "Have you ever seen a dead person?" he asked. "When I walk by a cemetery, I can see the ghosts. I have ever since I was a little child."

At first, I thought he was self-conscious about his gift, maybe even somewhat concerned, and that was why he had brought up the topic. I thought of moments in my many years of life that had given me a glimpse into this world of gifted abilities. I wanted to share some comforting stories. Once, a reflexologist knew I had broken my tailbone just from rubbing my feet. And I had—from a snowboarding accident earlier that year! A decade earlier, while on a spa tour on a cruise ship, an energy practitioner greeted me at her door by saying, "What is going on in your mouth? It's like metal or something causing you problems." I had just recently lost all sense of taste and smell. I always wondered, *How did she know?*

Then a story from 1980 came to mind. The authorities had brought in a nationally famous psychic to help with Gina's case. I shared nothing specific about Gina's case—just that I had once had a positive, unexplainable experience with a psychic named Dorothy Allison who had helped my family and helped many other people solve crime.

"Gifts are from God," I said. "God does not make anything imperfect. You have a gift that you did not ask for. You were born with it for a reason."

Nola confirmed that the experiences started early in his life. "I heard the voice of God clearly when I was just a little boy."

He told me stories of God and God's angels directing him on his path in life. My first thought: *Gina*. Not that I really believed Gina was a real angel, but that is what I would always think when I heard the word angel. Every Christmas when I sang carols about angels, I thought of Gina. I certainly believed in angels, but I had never really thought deeply about them until now. I always knew a guardian angel watched over me, but this young man was telling me with all sincerity that he actually saw his angels. I learned this verse licking those banana popsicles. Psalms 91:11—*He shall give His angels charge over you, To keep you in all your ways.* That gave me comfort as a little girl.

Of course, once we arrived at the casino, I had to stop and give that enticing penny slot machine just a few dollar bills. As Nola and I parted ways, we exchanged contact information.

The next morning, the first speaker was Shawn Anchor. He had a message about happiness that seemed to be just for me. It astonished me, moving me to tears. Everything the speaker advised was a repeat of the advice I had just received the night before from Nola. This coincidence was unnerving. For the first time, I was getting something seemingly meant just for me in a relevant, significant moment. This was not the usual fare that had always captured my attention in the past—how to be superwoman, super successful—this was different, and it was personal.

"We think happiness comes if we just do X, Y, or Z," I remembered Shawn Anchor saying, "and once we get X, Y, or Z, and we do, we will have happiness. Nope! We all, especially achievement-focused people, just keep moving the bar, and we never, ever reach satisfaction or happiness through success."

I was that personality. I kept redefining success as something bigger and better, so I never was satisfied when I attained my goals. The goalposts just kept getting moved—by me. My entire life had been about success—but when had it been about happiness? Happiness had not even been on my radar. My family brought me all the happiness I needed. But something did seem to be missing.

"Happiness comes first," the speaker said. Tears rolled down my cheeks.

Later that morning, I received a surprising text. My new friend Nola had asked me to meet him somewhere after the days presentations ended so we could continue our interesting conversations. He suggested the food court in the shopping area that connects to the convention center. I had walked through there earlier that morning from my hotel and noticed a favorite coffee cafe right there: Cafe Du Monde Riverwalk, famous in New Orleans for delicious sugar coated beignets and chicory coffee. That seemed a perfect end to a full day of learning for this food-loving girl.

The view of the Mississippi River was refreshing, and I felt rejuvenated by our intriguing conversations. We talked about everything—love, life, family, happiness, and God. We shared the stories of our life as if we were to give each other a small portion of advice we somehow knew each other needed to hear. It was as though he brought my heart back to my head—in balance—stronger together as it should be just like Gina and I always were together. Nola shared a dream he had had the night before and felt it was about my husband and me. Nola was not aware of our thirty-four years of marriage, yet he encouraged me always to look back and remember the first spark, that little something I saw in my husband Buz when I first met him so long ago. These conversations with Nola helped me find my self-worth, which had been buried deep inside.

It did not surprise me when he told me a year later that he knew his purpose in my life. It did surprise me when he shared that I had saved his life that night we met. I never knew exactly what he meant, but I tucked it away in my heart.

I left New Orleans having a new friend—a very gifted friend—and a re-ignited passion from my youth—photography. Nola encouraged me to purchase a camera, as though he knew my love of nature needed to come to the forefront of my life again—a rebirth of an inner desire to connect to God's canvas. We each told each other, "If ever you need anything, just let me know."

The summer of 2015, I spent extra time in nature, where I was always the happiest and closest to God, seeing the beauty everywhere I looked. I began redefining my happiness by not defining it with my successes. I began living in the present moment, working little by little on freeing myself from my past. I jumped off the fast-spinning hamster wheel of my life so quickly that I could have landed upside down in an unknown, unfamiliar place, but instead, I landed gently on gigantic fluffy white clouds. My new forever friend changed my life! There just are no coincidences.

My path had begun. I was reconnecting.

So almost one year later, I was excited to share the good news of my son's wedding with Nola. He responded with sightseeing tips about a few hidden areas of interest on the Caribbean island. He shared his favorite surfing spots for my sons. Recalling my stories of my arachno-phobia, he warned me which caves were full of humon-

MAROON BELLS COLORADO

gous spiders. He happily shared a quick update about how he was pursuing different interests to help people and serve them using his gift. Something about our conversation a year ago and his new interests made me ask a most unusual question just as I was heading out for the wedding trip. I had always thought about Gina as though she were an angel, and Nola and I had had conversations about angels; as we caught up, he mentioned a new term, "angelic realms" that sparked my curiosity. *Could he help my family with the thing that had been hanging over us for nearly forty years?*

I impulsively texted him the following request:

> I do not know if I ever shared with you that my sister, Gina, was murdered and her body was never found. Remember Dorothy Allison, the psychic in the '70s and '80s who solved hundreds of cases that I told you about? She gave us info, but we never found Gina. In the years to come, maybe think about Gina and see what happens now that our paths have crossed.

Nola answered immediately, asking me to give details—Gina's full name, a picture, and the last update I'd received on the case.

It was true that activity around Gina's case was heating up again. The TV shows about paranormal experiences would not let her case alone, even after all these years. Many more psychic leads were surfacing, to the point that it sparked a worry in me that people were not letting her rest in peace. I wondered if Nola could help me find the truth of where her remains might be and put an end to all of this; then, somehow, we would all have peace. For several reasons, Gina's murder had achieved national notoriety—especially because there had been a conviction without a body. John Russell, a Virginia State Police attorney who assisted the Pulaski County Prosecuting Attorney Everett Shockley, stated that Gina's case was one of only seven cases he knew of where a man was convicted with no body found, no confession, and no witness. Four of those cases were in the United States, including one of the infamous Charles Manson murders.

Gina's case was the first of its kind to be tried in Virginia. In addition, Gina's case had drawn nationally renowned psychics like Dorothy Allison, boosting the media's sensationalistic approach. *Newsweek* had described Allison in an April 17, 1979, article as a "playwright, referring to the television picture that flips on in her mind's eye and filled her vision with landscapes, buildings and faces—the faces of young accident or murder victims, and the landscapes that usually conceal their unfound bodies, and the visions turn out to be close approximations of grisly reality." Allison had described in multiple interviews that she was simply born with the gift. Growing up, people had thought her a witch because she had described a vision of her father's death; a few weeks later, he had died of pneumonia. Throughout her life, she told her family she would not see age seventy-five; she died of a heart attack at age seventy-four.

Allison was most famous for her work on the kidnapping of heiress Patty Hearst in 1974. She also worked on the 1976 Son of Sam murders. In October 1980, she was in Atlanta investigating an ongoing series of murdered children (the Wayne Williams case) while also scheduled upon her return for a second phone conference with authorities involving Gina's case.

On May 10, 2016, just as I was preparing to depart for the wedding, I touched base with Lt. Andy Wilburn in a text to get the latest update on the case. A parole hearing was coming up May 19 in Roanoke, the day after we were to return from the wedding, and Andy had already asked for my brother and I to stop by Radford to see him that day after we made our case at the parole hearing—something we would have to do quite often as Epperly came up for parole every one to three years depending on what the parole board ruled. They were starting to trend sooner, rather than the maximum three-year deferral.

The night before my husband and I left for the wedding, I was up all night packing and scurrying about the house. We had an early morning flight. But I felt it urgent to provide more detailed information to Nola. As my husband drove us to the airport, I texted details to Nola that I had not thought about for decades.

> My sister, Gina Renee Hall, was 18 when she died; I believe raped before she was murdered. Stephen Epperly, 28, was sentenced to life in prison for the crime.
>
> We never found her body so there is still a lot of activity around the case.
>
> I was the last one in my family to see her that night. I was supposed to go with her but did not because I had a fight with Buz.
>
> Sometimes I believed had that night not happened as it did, Buz would have never come back and I would have never had my amazing boys. Update: The oldest just finished medical school at Mt. Sinai and will begin medical residency at Harvard. The youngest is living his dream being out west with an awesome new career he loves. One that lets him be in the great outdoors.
>
> Gina called me around 1 a.m. sounding nervous—out of character. She said she could see a lake, but I don't think she knew where she was. I asked her who she was with and she answered with just Steve. Then click. She never came home. He killed her and disposed of her body.
>
> There was enough evidence to sentence him to life in prison even though we never found Gina's body.
>
> Since my daddy died in 2011, the case seems to have lots of activity.

Lots on the internet if you need more. There is a cold case investigator named Andy I met in May 2013 who has been in contact with me. He has some stories and leads—many from psychics, etc. He believes strongly that Gina is communicating with him.

Andy also suspects that Epperly had help burying Gina that night. This theory was not really given too much consideration in 1980. Police found blood on multiple levels of that lake house, and they believed Epperly acted alone.

On May 19, I go to the parole board to make the case that Epperly remain in prison. We do fear if he is ever released, he will harm someone in my family.

I will send you the last photo we have, her high school senior picture. She was sweet and kind and full of energy.

I know how busy you are—a perfectionist, a workaholic, and a phenomenal father—but if you have a little extra time to think on this, I appreciate your thoughts. Thank you.

Nola responded right away, saying he would ask for guidance on this. He told me he would not do any internet research because he wanted to make sure the information coming to him was coming to him pure, not because he'd read it somewhere else. He said when he put his phone with Gina's picture on his heart, he felt love. "That is good," he texted.

The wedding was beautiful and a daughter had been added to our family. My first experience with a song related to Gina's case came the night we arrived, meeting my future daughter-in-law's mom for the first time. The open air restaurant was noisy and energetic, yet it was as though I could only hear the music. This long song playing in the background kept drawing me back in. It was more than just that. I heard the words as though they were meant for me personally—a feeling from deep inside, a thought prodding me to listen. "I love you...." I dismissed the experience as emotional excitement for the wedding, but I still purchased this beautiful, soulful song "I Love You More Than You Will Ever Know" by Gary Moore right away. Little did I know then that it would become the first song in what I would call Gina's playlist.

Nola sent a note to say he was receiving information about Gina.

> It's not related to what happened to her. Just some things that maybe only you know or could interpret.
>
> Let me tell you first how angels communicate with us humans. They are always talking to us, and all we need to know is to learn how to listen to them. Angels talk in different ways to us, like through symbols, understanding, dreams, situations, direct messages, songs, feelings, and intuition.
>
> Once we learn how to hear them, we know how to differentiate between us or them talking. Some people get mad when we tell them something they don't expect to hear, but it is something that needs to be communicated. Even if it doesn't make sense for me or you now, it will in the near future.
>
> I have been receiving slowly messages about Gina through dreams, asking for them before I go to sleep. Not really about what happened to her, I think, or maybe yes in some things that you could interpret better than me as you are her sister.
>
> First, I received a message about a woman who was with her before, after, or present when that happened. That woman is not you. It is somebody else, but I couldn't see a face or a name. Then I received a message about one song Bob Marley sings called "Satisfy my Soul." Usually when that happens, there is a message in the title of the song or the lyrics. Try to read the lyrics of that song and see if you can interpret a message or something in that song.

"Tell me the name of the lake," he requested.

"Claytor," I replied with a heavy heart. I looked at the lyrics of the song Nola mentioned. All I could see was that I needed to satisfy her soul—like that was what she wanted me to do. I told Nola that I wanted so much to help her if that was what I was to do. And I wondered, who was the other woman—another victim who was with Gina?

On Sunday, Nola responded:

> This morning, I received a message in the form of a feeling in my body.

> I always feel a need to breathe deep and the question that always comes to my mind is "Why did you do that?" referring to the person who did this. The message this time was some things he did to her. It's not easy sometimes to hear those things—talking about you, I mean. You need to be strong to assimilate the things and information that is coming and is going to come.

Did Nola know I cried as I read this? I dried my tears, remembering he had told me to be strong. I am. I would be okay. I knew bad things had happened to my sister, but it seemed it was going to be worse than I ever could have imagined. I was troubled. Why would her soul need to be satisfied? Why now? If Gina was in heaven, why would there even be a need to worry about anything that happens here in this realm?

The next message sent from Nola was:

> Again today, the same feeling—needing to breathe and asking "Why did you do that?" I started to feel changes in my body about some things she experienced. I felt pain behind my neck at the level of my shoulders in the center of my spine, blood pressure around one of my eyes and nose. Information is coming slowly about things that happened and how it happened before information about the location. This is for one purpose we do not know yet, but there is a purpose behind it. Dlana, it is going to be hard, but at the end, calm and satisfaction will come to your life and the ones around you.

Nola was feeling Gina's pain, and that worried me. I did not want him to have to hold her pain. He assured me:

> The pain is in the past. She's happy. She is grateful. She is pure love now. Don't worry about me. The pains are not strong. They always come gentle but enough to tell what it is. It's perfectly normal.

Two days later, Nola told me he was getting something about a person whose name began with W. "I just remember Will...," he said.

"He was there that night right after Gina was killed," I replied to Nola.

The day we returned home, the day before the 2016 parole board hearing, Nola asked for a photo of Gina's murderer. I sent the first pictures I could find—two newspaper photos from the December 11, 1980 edition of *The Roanoke Times*. The photos were taken on the first day of the trial during a "field trip." Epperly was walking second in line behind his attorney Glenwood Lookabill as the judge, jury, attorneys, and court officials all followed the railroad tracks that crossed the New River to the trestle that spanned Hazel Hollow Road, Pulaski county, Virginia.

Nola responded back:

I can see in Epperly's face in the picture a lot of nervousness and lies. His face is not normal—maybe because they were very close. Where was this picture taken?

The photos had been taken the first day of the trial, December 11, 1980, as jury members were led on a tour, walking the same suspected path that Epperly took early that Sunday morning as he left my Monte Carlo abandoned underneath the trestle. Epperly and the attorneys are standing near the top of the train trestle that crosses the New River connecting Hazel Hollow Road in Pulaski County to the Radford side of the river.

EPPERLY HEADSHOT. PHOTO COURTESY OF *BRISTOL HERALD COURIER*

I found a picture in my old files of just Epperly and sent the headshot to Nola along with a picture of my Monte Carlo taken Monday afternoon, June 30, 1980, showing the scene the day my friends found my car.

Once my Monte Carlo was found around noon by our friends, Craig Runyon and Robert Lent, they alerted me and the local police. The abandoned Monte Carlo was parked almost directly underneath the train trestle, on the river side of Hazel Hollow Road, right in the bend of a curve. A Virginia State Police (VSP) investigator was dispatched. Trooper Austin Hall arrived and immediately launched an investigation. Police noted: Cups and trash were visible. Cigarette butts filled the ashtray, more than what any of our friends would have ever left behind, if any. An ignition key was found underneath the car on the ground at the rear of the vehicle, trunk lid up. Other notable details in the report: Short pine needles on the rear window, mud on the left two tires, spiderwebs on the headlights and window mirrors, and strangely, a screwdriver under the car beside the left front tire. And the most important detail—the inside car door handle, a long strap, was broken. One of the investigators at the scene that day in 1980 told me when I visited with him in 2016 that he would never forget the cattail seed pods stuck in the front of the car grill like those found at a marshy pond. This detail was never recorded. Details relevant to me now.

MONTE CARLO. PHOTO COURTESY OF THE NEWS JOURNAL, RADFORD VIRGINIA. PART OF *THE NEW RIVER NEWSPAPERS,* *JULY 1, 1980.*

Trooper Hall of the VSP discovered the blood stains in the trunk with visible strands of human hair stuck in the bloody trunk carpet. Thirty-three hours after having last seen my sister, I was certain Gina had been in that trunk—dead or unconscious. And later, the lab report would confirm she had been. Three strands of hair were compared to Gina's hair taken from her curlers. The blood was determined to be human blood and matched her blood type. A pubic hair was also found in the carpet in the trunk, plus, one light Caucasian hair, not enough to match, but light in color.

Police interviewed many passersby. A nurse first noticed my car at 5:20 a.m., Sunday, June 29, 1980, traveling the road she took each morning to work at St. Albans. Some saw the Monte Carlo with the trunk lid up, some with the trunk lid down. A few would state having seen "two white boys" standing behind the car near the trunk, Sunday at 10:10 p.m. The same nurse would also state she saw the car again Monday morning, parked in the same place, but this time she saw two white boys standing by the car as she passed. One of the most relevant statements came from David Sauls, a man who owned a bait shop 200 yards from where my car was parked under the trestle, and a man who served thirty years in the US Navy, fighting in Korea and Vietnam. Sauls told police that at approximately 6 a.m. Sunday, after he and his wife finished their morning paper route and were going out to get breakfast, they drove by and saw the same car parked under the trestle, the brown Monte Carlo that had run him off the road an hour earlier at 5 a.m. He reported the car sped around the curve, crossing over the center line. One tiny detail caught my eye—in Saul's interview with Trooper Austin Hall, he noted seeing a *van* parked near my Monte

Carlo at approximately 6 a.m. He had seen a van, just like the farmer had stated seeing in his story.

A police deputy also passed by early Sunday morning, but he first assumed my car belonged to someone fishing down at the river because the trunk lid was up. He made a mental note that two cars were parked beside it. One was a Cadillac. When he saw the Monte Carlo still parked there the next day while on his next shift, he got suspicious. He ran the tags and saw my name as the owner of the vehicle, but no record showed that it had been reported missing.

I had tried. As soon as I had woken on Sunday morning, I had called the police. I was told I had to wait twenty-four hours.

All day Sunday, the day Gina did not come home, I called everyone, searching for my sister. My friends came to help. Her friends, too. I shared all I knew at this point with everyone—"She was at a lake and I only have a name—Steve. I do not know anything else." I repeated to anyone and everyone I called Gina's exact last words to me from her out-of-character phone call. I even talked with the trusted buddy's mother who had lived above us in my old Cedar Valley Apartment from the spring. She now knew Gina was missing, so he knew. The fact that he knew I had called his mother about Gina missing was validated by his own deposition and also confirmed in others' statements. It would be the tiniest of details that tell so much.

While I was frantically calling everyone, Skipper was busy calling the Wolfpack to invite them to come out to the lake house for an impromptu horseshoe picnic gathering. Was Epperly in on it—an alibi picnic? So just a few hours after that late partying night, two of the three buddies were easily reachable—answering the phone, accepting Skipper's invite to the lake house, and when they arrived, Skipper and Epperly were there. All but one reconvening shortly after noon on Sunday at the same lake house where my sister just hours earlier had fought to her death. Spontaneous? I do not think so. Ridiculously obvious. Maybe it was the 10 a.m. drive on Hazel Hollow Road that same Sunday morning that stirred Skipper into action, passing by my Monte Carlo abandoned beside the road right in the bend of a slow-down-as-approached-kind of curve in the road. He drove by as he took his female guest home and then again as he returned to the lake house around noon. And the third time Sunday afternoon when he left the lake house.

While pitching horseshoes, one of the Wolfpack asked Epperly, "How did you do with the girl last night?" He said he had asked because Skipper told him that it looked like Steve was the only one who did any good. Epperly answered that he went swimming but she would not. And then the trusted buddy asked Epperly, "Was her last name Hall?" Epperly answered he did not know but she was from Coeburn. The trusted buddy knew right then that she was my sister. About forty-five minutes later, the short horseshoe gathering ended as quickly as it began. The two buddies left the lake house around 2 p.m., and as they drove by the trestle on Hazel Hollow Road, according to a police interview, the trusted buddy said to himself, "That looks like Dlana's car sitting there under the trestle." The next day, Monday morning, he heard on the radio that Gina was missing. That night, Epperly and Skipper visited him at work. At first, the trusted buddy was scared seeing only Epperly, but he felt relieved once he saw Skipper was with him. Epperly asked him if he knew anyone Gina ran around with. Skipper said this visit did not happen on Monday, but on Tuesday night. No matter, the visit was prompted by the trusted buddy's Sunday afternoon question alerting Epperly that he indeed did know *the girl*. The girl who was apprehended in a parking lot, now dead, that Epperly really knew nothing about until that visit.

The next morning, on Tuesday, Skipper, the three buddies, and a relative of one of the buddies who was a local police officer were all at the Barbell Club, and according to depositions, they were talking about Gina and Epperly. None of them ever immediately, or voluntarily without police request, came forward with any information they had, even after becoming aware that I had called the trusted buddy's mother searching for my sister. They specifically discussed my phone call. They were aware that Gina was missing by their own admission of having heard the radio ad. None of them went to the police even after Skipper came back by the club after going to RU to talk with Epperly and told them that Epperly said to tell all the buddies to play it all down. Even then, no one went to the police. Instead, playing it down is exactly what they did. The gossiping began, maybe even before the Barbell Club, but definitely Tuesday morning at the Barbell Club, as it was reported in their statements that this was the place and time my desperate phone conversation to the trusted buddy's mom became the hot topic. I believe it was these water cooler conversations that prompted Skipper to go see Epperly straightaway. Skipper now knew that Gina gave the name "Steve," and if we knew, then the police must know. When I called the trusted buddy's mother, and he shared the call details with the rest of the Wolfpack, the scrambling began. The composed story came to fruition because Epperly now had no choice but to go to the police. And he did by late afternoon. So in a way, my own actions led to the creation of the composed story I hated so much. The name "Steve" told to the trusted buddy's mother caused the dominoes to begin to fall.

We could surmise that if someone had any involvement, any connection to Gina and what transpired at the Marriott, especially in the parking lot, this reaction might be normal—*Uh, oh! We have to distance ourselves. We might be considered accessories somehow just for knowing anything about Gina and Steve.* These are not high school boys succumbing to teenage boy peer pressure. These are adult men. I can only surmise that Epperly brought fear to these men who could hold their own—real fear. How do we justify their actions? Here's the root of the problem with their composed story: I know Gina would not have gone alone to be with Epperly, so it seems something was still missing.

It could be something as simple as witnessing whatever happened on that dance floor that caused Gina to feel threatened that led to all of the secrecy. Something led to a change in the story from the original statement and the official deposition. The trusted buddy initially stated that only the three of them left the Marriott with three girls at 1:30 a.m. to go to their apartment. They stayed about an hour. He added, Skipper came by the Terrace apartments and picked up his female friend and left with her, but he was not sure what time. In his subsequent statement, Skipper is now with the three buddies when they leave the Marriott; all four went to eat pancakes, and then on to the three girls' apartment. This is not what was originally stated. I never knew all of the tiniest of details in 1980, like a trip to the pancake house that became a new detail weeks later as if it were just remembered that they had not left directly from the Marriott to the girl's apartment as originally stated—*the three left with three girls* now became four guys leaving together with a pancake stop before going to the three girls' apartment. *Was time being built into their story?* Was it all orchestrated to help someone have an alibi? If so, what leverage did this person have over Epperly for Epperly to have never expanded on the truth in all of these years? And, could there have been that much influence over the other three? Or, was it simply that the Wolfpack just expanded on their original statements, their memory corrected from three to four, from pancakes or not?

The trusted buddy's and others' delayed actions, before we even knew

Steve was Steve Epperly, confirmed the withholding of important information that could have helped my family and the police quickly identify Stephen Epperly. I trusted this buddy. He knew me.

I believe there is still more to consider than just what transpired in the Marriott parking lot. It seems something more than that needed to be covered up. Time will tell.

Gina was not logged as reported missing until 9 p.m. Sunday because the police would not take the report until a full twenty-four hours had passed. I called one hour early. By that time, I did not care about their twenty-four-hour rule anymore.

My friends went to several places Sunday night showing Gina's photo and asking about her and an unknown man named "Steve." I convinced the local radio station to announce she was missing. I still had not spoken to my parents. I tried all day to reach them, finally speaking to my dad late Sunday night when he returned home. Since I had been unsuccessful at getting the authorities to really listen to me, my dad made the difficult decision to wait a few more hours before leaving so he could stop in Wytheville at the VSP Headquarters in person to file an official missing person's report.

That night, Mama Joan said they both tossed and turned. As my dad prepared to leave that morning, Mama Joan noticed he had his gun. She asked him to please not do anything that he would regret and that would tear his family apart.

When my dad arrived in Radford early Monday afternoon, my car had just been found by my friends who were helping me to search for Gina. Daddy and I joined my friends and the police on Hazel Hollow Road. My dad immediately noticed the driver's seat was pushed all the way back, which was not how it would have been positioned had Gina been the last driver. My dad told the authorities, "Being so petite, Gina always pushed the seat up as far as it would go." Our friends also confirmed their experience of knees pressed into the dashboard when Gina drove.

When the police noted blood and hair in the trunk of my Monte Carlo, my car quickly became a crime scene. Within a day, the river and the woods near the abandoned car were being searched. Because blood had been found in the trunk, authorities dragged the river right there for her body. The news reports still focused on what police were treating as a drowning, but authorities already suspected foul play, even if they didn't say it publicly.

Meanwhile, in a different part of town, another story was unfolding. Before Wednesday night, before we even had proof Gina was dead, Epperly was visiting with a friend, William Cranwell, whose brother was an attorney and a member of the Virginia House of Delegates. Epperly commented repeatedly to Cranwell, "Would you ask your brother what can they do to me if they do not find the body?" *The* body.

Cranwell would testify to this during the trial. The initial report shows that Epperly would be heard by *three men*—Cranwell, Benny Martin, and a man named Tom Hardie—as saying, "What can they do to me if they do not find the body?", three times.

Those had been Epperly's words before authorities knew for sure even to look for a body—before we even really had proof that Gina was dead. Before we even knew about Epperly. Somehow, just days after the murder, Epperly was confident that a body would never be found.

So yes, I imagine Nola was correct—Epperly would have been nervous standing there on that trestle, the jurors following the trail Epperly had walked from the trestle to his porch. But did he have reason to be more nervous, walking by so many places of interest? He showed enough visible nervousness that from the picture taken, Nola would know which person was Epperly in the photo, his face not normal to Nola. Evil always seems to have a lingering trail. Was something right there that we all had missed? Before drifting off to sleep that night, I prayed silently in my mind for truth. Shortly after that exchange with Nola, I shared via text with him the last words Gina said to me. I told Nola, "My head always gets in my way. I can't change the past, but if she needs her soul satisfied, then I want to help her."

> I know is not easy as I'm telling you, but you are Dlana and I know that woman

> Her last words to me was to follow my heart not my head. Then we searched all summer and the trial ended in December and then I

He answered:

> People sometimes get scared when they know more about this world because they don't understand. We live in a world that is too much humanized—making us blind about the things that happen to us daily and

the things that are around us every day that we do not see. Everybody has intuition, but most can't see the difference between intuition and their own minds. They just do not pay attention to their intuitive side. We all have angels around us 24/7.

And about you, don't worry. Everything is going to be good—you will see. You have nothing to worry about in your future. Enough knowing how smart and strong you are.

This was new territory for me. I had an intuitive side—but things around me every day I couldn't see? I did recognize part of the message as something familiar and understood. I had believed that as a little girl, God had given me guardian angels.

The day of the parole hearing, May 19, 2016, after a wonderful wedding week laced with a few unsettling text conversations with Nola, Andy told me the farmer's story.

Nola had just told me on that Sunday before that I would need to be strong to assimilate the things and information that were coming. The farmer's story was beyond anything I could have imagined.

I had always had a sense that when I was on my knees, saying my prayers, God had answers for me. That is what I decided to do now. Pray. Cry. Beg God to hear me. Ask for help so I could know the truth. So that I could have the strength to do what I knew I would do in the days ahead.

I LOVE YOU MORE THAN YOU WILL EVER KNOW

CHAPTER 6

THE LADY IN RED

Listening to the whispers, hearing I love you.

"Want to experiment with something?" Nola was asking me in a text that came three days after Andy had told me the farmer's story. Nola instructed me to sleep with a notebook and a pen near my side. "If you wake up, take a note of whatever comes to your mind after you wake up or what you dreamed even if it doesn't make sense," he texted. "Do that for some days and tell me later."

He told me if I woke up repeating something or a song, make a note of that, too. "I'm going to teach you how to listen," he said.

I honestly did not know what to think about all this, but I trusted him. And I did what he said. I placed a pen and piece of random paper by my bed. I did not really think about it again.

The recent messages about Gina that Nola had shared troubled me. I kept thinking, *If someone wants me to know something, then please God tell me.*

I woke the morning of May 26, 2016 with a sore throat, fever, and chills. As I sat up, groggily swinging my feet to the side of my bed, I saw it, a note scribbled on that piece of paper I had put beside my bed days earlier, just as Nola had instructed. I was in shock. I did not remember writing this, but I must have…. *It is in my handwriting.* I sat for a moment and cried. What did it mean? How is this possible?

My head is underwater and I am breathing fine.

This note must have come from my subconscious, I told myself. *How could I write something down and not remember doing it?* It was all so confusing. My first thought was, *Could this be about my sister?* "My head is underwater." I wondered, *Is she trying to help us find the fragments of her bones hidden for thirty-six years?* I did not focus on the "I am breathing fine" part. I did not even question from where it came. I only saw *my head is underwater.* The farmer's story was still fresh in my mind.

Do our guardian angels intervene whenever needed or only when we sincerely plea to God for help? Does God then approve, saying, "Let's help her?" Would God allow my deceased loved one's souls to assist? Could it be Gina communicating with God's blessing? That is what it felt like—Gina. Did my spiritual army see the spiritual battle ahead, storming into the life of a still-faithful soul? Were they finally saying, "Enough is enough?" These are questions I asked much later. In the beginning, when it started, I was too confused to ask any questions except my own narrow focused question: *How is this message related to my sister?*

I had also written down a message that same night that seemed to illustrate a dream-like visual description that was not a dream because I did not remember dreaming it. The words were written in the night to be discovered when I woke in the morning. It was all so confusing. I will call these unexplainable experiences the only human words I know to use—a message, a vision, a note, a dream.

Here is that note:

> Three goldfish in very dirty water. One dead. Trying to get the other two into fresh water. I had no containers out of water for a while then got two of the goldfish into good water.

When I first read this, it seemed as though I could see the dead goldfish in my head, and it seemed I was sad that I could not save it. Yet I did not remember writing this down or seeing it in a dream. It was a message.

And, I also wrote these numbers:

9639

I was so overwhelmed I did not give this number much attention, eventually thinking it might be a route number, but I never found a road. In 2018, when I began writing this account of all that had happened, I simply entered the forgotten 9639 into a search engine. The first result: genetic code.

When these thoughts came with no control from myself, no knowing or remembrance, my reality and understanding of this world shifted. I did not stop to contemplate how or why. I only focused on a different why: Why this specific message, and what does it mean? There was really only one narrowly focused question important to me: What is this message telling me about my sister?

I was only seeing "*my head is underwater.*" I began believing the messages were from Gina because they were written as though she were speaking. And the recent experiences from Nola, Andy, and others made believing it was Gina seem reasonable. And much later, I noticed it seemed I wrote "*I'm underwater*" and crossed it out writing "*My head.*" Why? I was enough of a skeptic to further ask: Who is the real orchestrator of this? If it were my angels or God, why not tell me, "Gina's head is underwater"? Or better yet, "Gina is in heaven with us." And if not my angels or God or her, then who wanted me to believe it was her? And why did my mind only want to focus on part of the message: "My head is underwater." And even more confusing to me was actually seeing the goldfish dream-like message. I rarely ever had dreams!

Only one dream I had experienced repeatedly as a child vividly stands out. I am a girl who grew up in Appalachia America. I had never seen the ocean as a small child, not even on a TV. But in this recurring childhood dream, I saw a rushing wall of water come from around the corner of the tallest two-story building in Coeburn—the elementary school. I stood at the highest point, on a wobbly fire escape. Every time, in this repeating nightmare, the thrashing waves came from around the corner of the building and swept me away.

My first memory of the dream was when I was about four. The dream continued into my school-age years, attending school in that same building from my dream. Walking down those rickety metal stairs during fire escape drills would always bring about an intense fear. I never told anyone I was afraid. I just did it.

As I got older, about age eight, the dream subsided. By then, I had learned to bury my fears.

I let Nola know right away about the first messages. He asked me what

I asked for before I went to sleep and who I asked. I replied, "I asked for peace of mind. No one in particular. I thought about you telling me someone is protecting me."

Here is his reply:

> You are receiving some very important messages. They have always been talking to you, but you didn't know how to listen. Now you are paying attention and they are talking. Pay attention about little things that happen around you—they are not coincidence—and make a note. That's how you listen and learn to differentiate between your intuition and you. And let me know if you dream about any numbers.

I replied:

> I see numbers like 33 and 333 all of the time. I call it my lucky number— my age when I started my new successful venture, my son's football jersey number, and how old Jesus was when he died for me. I see the number all of the time.

He replied:

> You have a strong and clear connection. Always say thanks from your heart after you receive something.

Still, I didn't know who was communicating with me. Later, I would recognize that first scribbled note as a line from a song I had heard a dear friend play from her playlist. She spurred my creation of a personal library of music. Over the last few years, as I would hear her play her songs, I would download one at a time, growing my collection to only thirty to forty songs. I loved music, but to say that it had been a big part of my everyday life just would not be true. Instead of music, I would often listen to educational material! But this new interest had a subtle, new purpose behind it.

When I told Andy about the song lyrics, he said, "Oh, yeah! I think Gina communicates through song from what I can tell from my own experience."

He told me one particular country song always played when he worked on Gina's case—"Highway Don't Care" by Tim McGraw.

I understood why as soon as I read the lyrics. Andy had told me he cared if he brought Gina home. He had told me he was not surprised when he saw that Gina's birthday was the same day as his daughter's birthday. In recent years, he and his family had been lighting a candle for Gina when they celebrated the shared birthdays. Gina became a part of their family. He believed Gina was there with them for several years.

Andy shared that "Mrs. Robinson" by Simon and Garfunkel played numerous times, prompting his visit to go see Skipper's female guest when he discovered in Gina's file that she was a witness in the trial. "It was like she had been expecting me, waiting all of these years for us to show up," Andy said in regards to this visit. "Just plain weird." I would have a different experience when I met her. After I visited with her, I believed she was sincere in what she shared with me. She was believable.

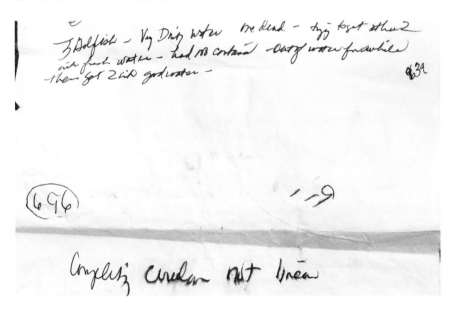

On May 28, 2016, I wrote these numbers on the same wornout piece of paper:

696

611 or 119

The 696 was circled, and 611/119 was upside down. So they were probably written at different times during the night.

On May 31, 2016, Nola sent me a note:

> Got another woman, probably with two names or two women, Andrea and Aurea. Probably another victim or somebody who knows him. It was sent as Aurea Andrea. I saw a 90-degree angle and Andrea on one side and Aurea on the other side. It could be a location between

two streets, an intersection or somewhere in Virginia. It could be Aurora also.

I am sure I missed this next message from him. Maybe I read it and just dismissed it because it simply did not register as I went on with my busy life. He shared:

I saw the woman again with Gina. A dark-haired woman.

And then the first real wow moment happened.

In June, I scheduled my annual physical in West Virginia. My son and his newlywed wife were visiting from New York City. Andy and I had decided to meet in Radford on my way to West Virginia.

Right as I pulled into the parking lot at the Radford police station, I got a note from Nola, a link to a song:

Lady in Red. That song was sent to me for you.

She whispered I love you.

I listened to it, and the song does whisper the same words at the end.

After visiting with Andy and his wife, I let my son take the wheel and sat in the backseat with my grand-dog Pablo. Nola had asked about my visit, so I shared with him Andy's latest thoughts about Gina. As the car started north up the interstate, headed to our destination in West Virginia, this is what I shared with Nola:

Andy says Gina does not know herself where she is, but he also agrees it is always a message about water. They now also agree she was most likely dismembered—the farmer and the creek story. Andy suspects who was helping him and he got away with it.

Andy and his family were also worried because the last time they had heard from Gina was New Year's. Andy and his family tell me she is with me now.

I believe she could be with us—maybe.... Maybe she heard my cries and pleas to be happy. That was all I have wanted for the last few years because of a personal sadness, and makes sense maybe why she was compelled to help me especially after the farmer's story.

But can Gina really help me? I am just not so sure about that. I believe God can.

How I had met Andy to begin with was that he shared he felt Gina's presence, and he had received a clear message, "Go tell my sister." Andy says that he now sees that Gina coming to him was not just about finding Gina's body, but that it may have been about connecting me to Gina. He told me he still needs to find her because he believes he is the one who will, and if he does, I believe he will find other victims.

As my son left the interstate, I noticed that the trees were gradually becoming thicker, the road curvier. I had always enjoyed the view on this stretch of road connecting Interstate 81 to Interstate 64.

Nola agreed with Andy that Gina was with me now:

Sun @ 2:35 PM

Tell me what you can find here

https://play.google.com/music/preview/Tld54pvcase4j2aa3ourploqjeq?lyrics=1&utm_source=google&utm_medium=search&utm_campaign=lyrics&pcampaignid=kp-lyrics

Gina loved to dance

I am at radford police right now getting ready to meet w Andy

Let me know why you ask?

Sun @ 3:23 PM

That song was sent to me for you

She said I love you at

> She doesn't worry about her body being found. Gina wants to see your heart healed. After that she will move forward after she looks at you with a grateful smile. She's going to move where she's going finally, but that doesn't mean she is leaving you; on the contrary, she will be always closer to you.

> She's advancing, but she is a little skeptical about what is going to happen to her when she reaches the end of the light. What is waiting for her there is something nobody could describe. She's going to let us know when she reaches the light, when she finally reaches her home.

I texted back:

> What do you think she meant by the song?

He replied:

> It means Gina misses you, but is happy where she is.

I replied:

> I am glad she is happy and where she needs to be.

Nola knew me. He knew I would have a hard time forgiving Epperly as he said I needed to, and a very hard time letting go of the possibility for justice to prevail if others were involved. The new thought that my sister might not be moving on ignited an inner resolve to finish this. There are so many different theories in so many different religions about what happens after we die—we lie in the ground, we don't lie in the ground...to heaven immediately, or to sleep waiting for the end of times—Rapture? Purgatory? Many conflicting answers. I have always believed Gina was in heaven. My beliefs were simple. And in my mind right then, in that moment, there was simply no human way to know absolutely for sure what happens after someone dies. No right, no wrong. I came to believe my sister needed me.

I looked out the car window up to the sky, wondering where the spiritual realm was, exactly. The beauty of what I saw told me God is right here, just as that lone majestic tree told me years ago as a teenager riding up through Virginia. God's canvas is always perfect. The sky seems more vivid when the mountains start to close in, the contrast of the green with the blue sky and white fluffy clouds seemingly bringing them closer to me.

Nola knew I needed to hear more. He somehow knew my heart's burden.

> Your hating him doesn't affect him; it just affects you. Your forgiving doesn't mean he's going to get away with it; that's not going to happen. He's paying and is going to pay for what he did, and he can't even imagine how much he's going to suffer. It's not in our hands. Your forgiving, even without his knowing, will make him talk. Your hate just helps him, and he gets stronger with it. Forgiving him will make him weak.

Nola was starting to break through my stubborn mind, but my concerns still were only about my sister. I replied:

> Please be there for her. Your strength and wisdom and love. Be there as my love, extended to hold her hand like I did when she was little and hungry.... I always wanted to take care of her and be her protector, and now, is she mine?

> I will forgive. I will pray about it tonight. I know what you say is true for sure.

Nola did not give up so easily on me. He replied:

> Remember when I told you once—I never understood how somebody could forgive somebody? That was impossible for me. Now I know how. Now I just feel compassion for somebody when they do some-

thing. I feel compassion because it is not in my hands to judge him or choose how he's going to pay for it; it's in somebody else's hands, and what is waiting for them is nothing near to good. Release all that hate to God. He is there, believe me. And his justice is perfect.

I told Nola that I asked for God's strength all of the time, and he said:

> He will give you strength but as I told you, you have to do your part.
>
> He can give you strength but you act to use that strength.
>
> Perfect worlds do exist but we are not one of them. We humans messed it up since the beginning and here we are.
>
> Just the ones that look to go back to that state by themselves will reach peace. You must need to work with yourself and don't put effort in changing somebody else. We need to evolve and change so they can then change themselves.

As I rubbed the ears of my grand-dog Pablo, I replied:

> It is like a domino effect on others. I change, and maybe it spreads?

Glancing out the window, I suddenly realized, *Where is that beautiful river? We should be passing it by now.* I always can look to the right of Route 220 and see the Jackson River that flows on through Clifton Forge. It connects to Cowpasture River, a name that certainly makes me laugh, and flows on to the infamous James River. My infatuation with rivers began when an enthusiastic grade school teacher visually brought the words to life from our Virginia colonial history book. Why am I not seeing it? I heard a ping, capturing my attention back to my phone.

Nola's wisdom texts continued:

> We are all connected, Dlana. My actions are affecting somebody else not necessarily close to me, but our souls are connected.

Please Be there for her. Your strength and wisdom and love   Be there as my love extended to hold her hand like I did when she was three years old and hungry and I would hold her hand and walk her up the street where I knew mr Odell would be coming home from the mines and eating cereal and I knew he would feed us   I always wanted to take care of her and be her protector and now is she mine?

Remember when I told you I never understood how somebody could forgive somebody. That was impossible for me. Now I know how. Now I just feel compassion for somebody when they do something, I feel compassion because is not in my hands to judge him or choose how he's gong to pay for it, it's in somebody else hands and I feel compassion and feel sorry for them because what is waiting for them is nothing near to good. Release all that hate to God. He is there believe me. And his justice is perfect.

I asked him about how my actions gave my sister's killer more strength. If I would just learn to forgive Epperly, would it, too, have an effect? Nola responded with a word I noticed he used a lot:

Exactly. He's going to feel it. It will soften that heart and mind.

Sitting in the backseat as we headed up to West Virginia, I was lost in thought while contemplating these stirring conversations with Nola. After a while, I came out of my reverie, looking around to see where we were and noticed that my son had taken a different route from the one I usually took. We were on back roads I'd never seen. When I checked my GPS on my phone, I saw it—Route 696. Right there on my screen, the road number 696 near a large body of water. I captured a screenshot and sent it to Nola.

My son, not knowing the area, had followed his GPS.

"Turn right. Keep driving to this water on the map picture on my phone," I told my son, "beside the road 696." All I could think about was "my head is underwater" and the number I had written down a week earlier.

We should have easily been guided to Interstate 64. Instead, we ended up at Pikes Pond, a huge pond surrounded with vast woods, not easily accessible. The front side of the pond borders the road. A house sat on the west end of the pond. A tall cliff wall bordered the back edge of the pond, making it seemingly, at first glance, inaccessible beyond the cliff wall to the woods behind it. *Why am I here? 696?* I wondered. This place is an hour and a half away from Radford. *What does it have to do with Gina?*

When we checked into the hotel, The Spring Dancers were performing a waltz, something they do every night at ten o'clock. All the dancers were wearing red dresses—ladies in red. Lady in Red. No, it couldn't be that simple.

I asked Nola if he thought I should just let him and Andy work directly with each other. But Nola told me I just needed to listen. Andy had told me I needed to be listening. Everyone seemed to be telling me that: to listen.

It's easier for you to listen as you are more than us. You are her sister.

Also, your heart needs to be healed, and you are the only one capable of doing that. Then you will hear and listen more.

You have a good heart for everybody, but you need to have a good heart for yourself, too.

When I questioned this, asking Nola, "How do I have a good heart for myself?" He replied:

Things from the past are there that need to be healed and replaced with love. It's not easy, but it is possible.

Nola forwarded an email from a friend who said her intuition was that Gina's body no longer exists. "Fractions of a bone are what are left." She, too, said the vital connection was me. She said Gina wanted us to know that it had all happened so quickly that she could not figure out what had happened, that there were things left unfinished, and that I was an important part of finishing it.

"There is water where she lies," the woman wrote. She further described Gina's resting place as being in a place with shallow water—something that looked like a mangrove.

Nola's friend asked him if he was okay with her contacting a medium she knew to ask about Gina and this pond. Curious, Nola agreed, but then he told me he received a clear message that Gina did not want that. So he advised his friend to hold off because Gina only wanted to communicate with us whenever she felt like it, not when someone else wanted to. Nola's friend understood. I would realize later I should have been paying closer attention to what Nola was saying.

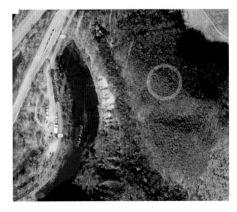

On June 7, I received an email in which Nola and his friend examined a Google map of the Pikes Pond area. He told me to go to the encircled area, coordinates 37.798734,—79.864321. Of course, I could not see a way to accomplish this by myself. He said he could see a symbol in the woods, and that is where he began focusing. I puzzled over his words: "Nature will reveal what it wants us to know."

Pikes Pond was deep with legends. People tell an old tale that years ago a train derailed there. The pond is so deep that no one ever retrieved the wrecked locomotive out of it. I visited the Allegheny County police, where officers shared the same story about the locomotive. I began to wonder if I needed to hire divers, and if it was even possible. In the aerial view of Pikes Pond, I could see what appeared to be a shallow place where soil might be visible under the water in the center of the pond—like an island. I never connected this pond's deep water similarities back to the Radford area until much later.

In a few weeks, I became so narrowly focused that I never could have simply given up searching for truth. I did not stop to contemplate the how or the why of the methods of communication. My only focus was my sister and why she needed me to find her.

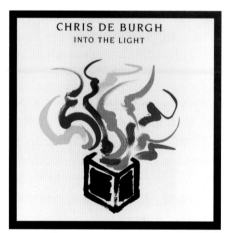

I pulled up the song I had downloaded after Nola first told me about the song by Chris de Burgh, "Lady in Red." As I was listening, my first thoughts were about how Gina loved to dance. Then, I saw it! Could Chris De Burgh be Christiansburg—a town that borders Radford?

Now the questions came a mile a minute. My mind raced. What is she telling me? Did she somehow die in Christiansburg? Was the farmer's story—Meadow Creek, in a Christiansburg zip code in 1980—the place where the second bridge crosses Meadow Creek on Dry Valley Road? That pointed to the farmer's story. Did she die at that creek? This thought enraged me. The troubling questions would not stop. Is there a connection to Christiansburg? Could she have been unconscious, still alive, when she was taken somewhere else in the trunk, in that white van—even maybe after the farmer saw whatever he saw? Maybe she was unconscious in the van and a second victim was being seen when the farmer interrupted them—if he had just been disposing of Gina's body, then why even need a van? Unless the person who helped Epperly just owned a white van. My mind was scattered. The image of a lady in red was haunting me. I could not escape the farmer's story, imagining her lifeless body covered in blood. How did my sister go into the light from Christiansburg, miles from the lake house? Or was the message to see simply: Into the Light?

Then I peered at the colorful box doodled on the album cover. The old box factory came to mind. Maybe that's the meaning. That building had been on the path that authorities took when they led a dog search in 1980 to track Epperly's scent from the trestle bridge to the front porch of his home. His steps passed right by the Old Colony Box Factory. *What is there that we missed?*

This was the battle raging in my mind.

No matter the message's intent, it would be a year later before I chose to believe that *Into the Light* was a good message. A colorful box covered with ribbons like a present was a good message. "I Love You" was a good message. Just as Nola said, "It means Gina misses you and is happy where she is."

It was time for one of my favorite annual educational events.

Arriving at my Vancouver hotel, the first thing I saw as I checked in was a mangrove. Yes, in the lobby, digital artwork showed a place that resembled the mangroves I had seen once when I night-kayaked a stream in Puerto Rico. Mangroves are lush with greenery and tree roots hanging out over the water. This picture looked like a mangrove, and in the shallow water

around it was a woman's body. It disturbed me all week. It actually was a form of digitized art and would move like a live photo, chest moving up and down like someone breathing.

Arriving back home in the peaceful mountains of southwest Virginia, I walked into my yard at dusk. While I had been gone, the yellow moon-flower had come up tall and was blooming—my dad's favorite flower. I used to sit on the porch with him around the Fourth of July, and we would watch the blooms pop open at night. Mid-June seems a little early for the popping yellow blooms. I had not seen it here at my home since about 2011, when he passed. I assumed I had killed it or pulled it up, thinking it was a weed. But this beautiful evening, the blooming moonflower greeted me home.

A good memory from our last summer together as daughter and dad flooded my heart. Those evenings spent on my dad's porch, his pointing to every weed that needed to be pulled, every job that needed to be done. And I graciously abiding his wishes.

"Dlana, go around and get the broom from the garage and go over there," he had said, pointing to the magnolia tree in the far corner of the front yard, "and knock those dead leaves on out. That way we can go ahead and pick them up before they fall!"

I had just thought to myself, *Surely you have got to be kidding me.* He was not! This was our dad.

Upon replaying this memory, the thought passed through my mind brief-ly: Could he have anything to do with all of this activity? It did begin after he died. *Or could it be that my dad's prayers for Gina were finally being answered?*

A full year had now passed since I had first met Nola—a strange, unex-plainable circumstance. I was starting to wonder about that no-coinci-dence meeting in New Orleans so I texted Nola: "Why did we meet?"

He replied, "I can't tell you now, but there is a reason we don't see yet, something else behind it we cannot understand yet."

"I do not think all of this is just about finding her body. I feel it is so much bigger," I texted back.

A simple reply: "Sweet dreams, hard head!"

Someone from the spiritual world knew of my questioning conversation with Nola because right after, standing in my bedroom, in my head as clear as if a radio were blasting the music, I heard the melody of an old song that was recognizable, yet not a part of my familiar, everyday life. A song I knew was just for me. I cried as I began to realize the power of what I was actually experiencing—a personal, caring relationship from the spiritual world that seemed to know exactly what I needed to know right at this moment.

Next, I wrote down:

Completing Circular not linear

As the weeks passed, I would think of it as *completely* circular not linear. Whenever I saw anything circular—manhole covers, culverts, circles of differently shaded grass—my narrow focus was on finding the circle that marked where Gina's body had been hidden.

The next weekend was my fortieth high school reunion. I reconnected with many friends especially delighted to see a close friend of my family I had not seen since the early '90s. On Saturday night, she pulled me aside and told me that after having seen me the night before, she'd had a dream she needed to tell me about. She used to spend time in the summers with my family, especially with my stepmother, who would talk about losing Gina so young, and to such a grisly murder. Mama Joan would share with her a specific theory of what she believed had happened to Gina's body. Mama Joan had long believed Gina's body was put on a train car full of coal, transported to the cargo ships, and had ended up in China. I never believed this wild tale about China, but many people at the time did including Mama Joan who always agreed with it. We all needed closure, each in our own way, so there were a lot of theories.

This person I had not seen in decades shared her vivid dream that Gina was in water. "The theory about the train is wrong," she said. "Your sister's body is in water." She shared she had not thought about us or Gina in thirty-plus years, so why now? She wondered aloud. "Water? The dream seemed so real. I never remember my dreams."

Back inside, for the silent auction, we had to place our tickets in one bucket or another. One had a photo of our old elementary school, the one in my recurring childhood dreams of the tsunami. I tossed all but two of my tickets in that bucket. I really wanted that old picture! Those extra two tickets I used for items that were brought by another old friend of Gina: a handmade replica of a log cabin with a red door and a small wooden chest with a deer on the front. My name was pulled as the winner of both items. At the time, though, I did not know to pay attention to the subtle hints: the one red door and maybe even the hunter's deer.

The next morning, on June 19, 2016, I woke up to this message scribbled on the bottom of the ragged, original paper I had placed by my bed almost a month earlier:

On the...hill...is where I'll find you

Underneath the word is stronger...

What hill? Hills are everywhere in Pulaski County. Could this have to do with the hill that I remember everyone saying Epperly went to after he was arrested and released on bond in November 1980? The police were watching him. They told us that Epperly headed to a high bluff, from which they said you could see everywhere—up the river, down the river, and even to the lake house.

I couldn't get it out of my mind that Epperly went up to that hill. Did he go up there to see if something was uncovered? What was he looking at from that vantage point?

Then a thought from out of the blue: *You have been there before.*

I had been a lot of places back in 1980.

On June 19, 2016, I woke to two unknown names written in the middle of the night on the back of an envelope left on my nightstand. To clarify, there was never any realization of having written most of these notes while I slept. I would wake in the morning to words that made no sense. Often, perplexing with no immediate interpretation. Still asking, *How did this happen?*

Denton Jones

Nancy Rae Lubick

How did I write names down in the middle of the night? Where did these names come from? Names that made no sense to me. I searched missing person sites, researched unsolved cold cases, and looked at Texas towns because of Denton and Lubick (Lubbock) and more. Nothing made sense.

Nola would say, "They are not towns. You have received full names, which is not the norm." How could my mind search towns when they were clearly names? And is Denton Jones one name or is it two—Denton—Jones.

Weeks later, a simple search landed on what I believed Denton—Jones and Nancy Rae Lubick meant. But my interpretation came with a perplexing, *Really*? A man named Denton Jones was

an actor on the TV sitcom *Two Guys and a Girl*, and a professor named Nancy Lubick was in the criminal justice department at Northern Arizona University. I did not know this. Justice + two guys and a girl.

Off my mind went. Justice for Gina, justice for other victims, if there were any. Maybe it is justice for Denton and Jones. Or does Denton Jones mean two guys and a girl? Did it mean—two perpetrators and a victim? Three perpetrators? Three victims? The farmer had seen two men. The preacher, one of Andy's leads, had seen two guys and a girl—light shining from car headlights on the edge of the woods, shovels in hand, burying Gina. A viable lead that led to the Dedmon Dig. The Two Guys and a Girl interpretation always seemed to surface as *the journey* progressed.

When I sent Nola a note wishing him a belated Happy Father's Day, I asked him why the friend with whom I reconnected at the high school reunion would have a message for me. He explained that Gina would use others to connect with me. I was too new to this experience to understand fully that he was telling me he believed he was really "connected" to Gina. I did not understand then exactly what "being connected" really meant. Looking back now, he even stated at one point, "Let me disconnect," but still I was missing it. I was not listening. I was not seeing. That narrow focus of only wanting to find Gina's truth was very strong.

Nola had an insight about this, which he shared in a text:

Gina is apparently losing a little bit of connection with other people as she's getting closer to you and you are getting more receptive to her.

I thought about that. I remembered that Andy had told me he and his family had had no contact from Gina since New Year's Eve, but I was not thinking in terms of "contact."

Nola said:

> She's getting closer to you.

I replied:

> But I need her to be close to you too. I am not sure I can do this without someone's guidance who understands this. You are the only reason I paid attention.

He said:

> Remember you were not listening before. Now you are. She has always been there; you just were not listening. Like I said, her priority for her is not to find her body. She doesn't need her body anymore. All she wants is to see you happy and resting about her, but if finding her body makes you and everybody happy, she will try to help you find her, not because it needs to be done, just because it will make you happy and finally give you peace of mind. Once she realizes you are happy and not worrying about it, she will continue where she needs to go, giving her confidence that it's okay to continue and nothing bad is going to happen.

I said:

> It makes me sad if she has been in limbo all of these years and not able to move on. Maybe there is not really time after we die.

Nola said:

> Nothing bothers her and she's not suffering; don't be sad for her. Be happy she is where she is; she doesn't want that.

But I had questions:

> So are the messages I am getting like 696 because she is helping us find her for us to be happy? Finding her would give others in my family closure. But I only want what she needs to help her.

Nola replied:

Finding her body is not going to help her; it is going to help you. And your family.

Your happiness is going to help her. If you decide to *desist,* it's okay. Nothing is going to change for her, but *desist* in a way that you feel happy about because once she sees you happy, she will continue her journey. Nothing is wrong if you *desist.*

I know you, Dlana. I know when you want something, you won't stop doing it until you're finished, but sometimes it is not what we want and we need to learn to accept things.

I wrote back:

I know. She is probably so tired of all the people trying. There have been so many stories and many seem-to-be as if messages from her. Like one psychic told Andy that Gina wanted him to tell someone named Kim that it was not his/her fault. Maybe Kim introduced them that night or introduced them at my apartment.

I have to know if someone helped him. There are just some details that point to him having help, and if so, that person should not go unpunished. But maybe not…. I just know I became very sad, more than the normal sad, the day I heard the farmer and creek story. All through the summer and the trial, Epperly was so confident we would never find her body. That makes me sad. Maybe there is closure in finding it and peace for me.

Once I set my mind to something, I do not let go easily. If she wants me to find her, I will not stop.

Nola needed to pause. He wanted to reflect. He came back with this text, speaking as Nola, my friend:

Now this is me. You are a hard-head girl.

Okay, now we can continue.

Nola was endlessly empathetic, and by now, he knew me well. He was patient with me, too, as I worked through the myriad of emotions coursing through me. He texted:

Okay, reasons why she's not moving are:

1. You are not happy about what happened to her.
2. You keep trying and that affects your emotions and energy (not just physically but spiritually too). Stopping you from being happy.

3. Finding her body won't affect Epperly's punishment.

4. You are trying to make yourself happy finding her body, but if you desist and are happy, it will be the same effect as if you found her.

If Gina wanted me to stop, then why the messages? I wanted to know that. Nola replied:

Because you want to find her.

She wants to see you happy. She doesn't care if you find her or not, but if it makes you happy, she will help. But not because she needs to be found.

With the clarity of hindsight, I see now that Nola was more "gifted" in many ways than I had ever previously realized. We had a very long, meaningful conversation that would become even more relevant as I walked ahead into this experience. Nola was becoming my anchor. My sister's life was helping me see what "into the light" means. And, I believe her life story was being used as a shining light in the dark. Andy had come into my life, and the farmer's story had come into my life and my mind's imagination. Now, everything felt unfinished, and it felt necessary to finish it. At the same time, for some reason, I was scared of something. I did not know what.

All along, Nola consistently assured me that all was well with Gina. She was at peace. The person she was most concerned about was me.

All is wonderful for her. You won't understand as human you are. She doesn't think like we think. Her mind is perfection now.

I bet she laughed when I called you a hard head!

There is so much good layered into Nola's words. And I know he is not perfect. No one is! Many would judge him just because he said he was "connected." There was a time in my life I would have too. Receiving is not seeking, but there is a very fine line. We might not have had the many parts of the Bible had some not been chosen as receivers. Again, a fine-line difference—a self-created path or a God-given path? Who am I to judge anyone else?

I find one word that Nola used as quite interesting. *Desist.* I had never really heard that word commonly used by anyone in an everyday conversation, at least not where I came from, and especially not by someone for whom English was a second language, as it was for Nola. While writing this account, I researched this word and found that although it is an uncommon word, it is used quite frequently in the Bible, especially in the book of Psalms.

Psalms 46:10: *"Desist, and learn that I am God, supreme over the nations, supreme over the earth."*

Psalms 37:8: One translation simply says, "Desist anger."

Another translation states:

"Calm your anger and abandon wrath. Don't be angry. It only leads to evil."

My thoughts right now as I write this—WOW! Anger had definitely been my deep-rooted problem for decades. I could have killed Epperly myself if given a chance. That is anger in the highest degree. That is hate. That is an evil that rots your very soul. God knows this! That is why it is written in the Bible and He led me to it.

I still cannot help but wonder to whom Nola was really connected. I did not seek it, and it seemed answers were coming to me from other places, especially through him. I did not always agree with everything Nola said about Gina and her soul, but I did agree with almost everything he said related to me. It seems someone, somewhere, wanted me to know the truth—not just about Gina, but about something else. I wondered for a moment whether Andy and Nola just thought it was Gina, and really it was our angels helping us. I believe God knew I needed to heal my heart, and the way to my heart was Gina.

On June 21, 2016, I woke to these words written on a random piece of paper left by my nightstand:

Song "Not Going Anywhere"

I did not hear this song. I had never heard it. I typed the title into a search engine, and…again, unbelievable! Nola would tell me that a song is just a way to deliver the message, like an envelope for a letter—you read the letter but you don't keep reading the address on the envelope. You just throw the envelope away—the same with the song.

Thoughts struggled to gain my attention. I questioned each line of the song as though it would tell me where I was to search: Pond. Vagabonds. Water. And one line which seemed to explain exactly how I had felt all of my life. My view of how I saw my sister was now starting to shift. I thought the song must be about how Gina must feel. I was beginning to believe that somehow a soul could hurt and be in pain. I wanted more and more to help her. Gina is somewhere never to be found—not going anywhere.

This song broke my heart.

Why does she whisper? I would wonder. *What is she afraid of? Who is she afraid of? Why else would she whisper? Is the answer to why she whispers somewhere in the song's lyrics?*

But later, the interpretation would be refined by my heart. Maybe our good angels—our spiritual army—were right here with me. Maybe it was a song to sing in our own voice—to each other. *I'm not going anywhere, sis. I have always been with you.*

CHAPTER 7

LEBANESE BLONDE

I always tried not to remember, but I just never could forget.

A ndy and I met with Everett Shockley, the prosecuting attorney for Gina's case in 1980. This visit verified most of the information I remembered from 1980 and refreshed my memory on other details. We were eager to listen to his opinions. He shared maps he had showing the exact locations of key places relevant to Gina's murder. Now, I could see where the bluff was: 5 marks the spot. I always wondered where exactly that bluff Epperly went to was located.

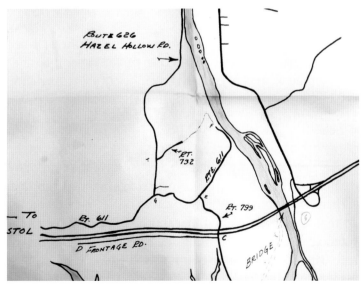

As we were about to finish, I asked Shockley if he still had notes from the Dorothy Allison interviews. He did. I took some pictures so I could delve into them later to see if his notes aligned with our notes and with my memory of the movie that had played in Dorothy's head in 1980.

Shockley surprised us with a revelation I'd never known: Dorothy Allison had told investigators in a second conference call to forget everything she had ever said about the case.

In 1980, Buz and I had followed verbal notes from Dorothy Allison's first conference, provided by my dad. She had advised us to walk a specific path, we believed from my abandoned car: "*Start there*," she said. "*Follow a direct path north to water...a cemetery. You will find a famous person's grave.*" We thought that the famous person might be military for some reason I cannot remember. So we started at the train trestle that crosses the New River from Hazel Hollow Road. Buz and I saw the nearest cemetery on our paper map, across the New River. We followed this path, which led right by Epperly's house. We did not expect that. We walked on up the hill to the cemetery and stopped. Dorothy had told us to walk north to water and Gina would be under rocks, but we stopped at the cemetery, stuck on finding the famous person's grave. A monument to Mary Draper Ingles, a well-known American pioneer and Indian captive, sits right at the entrance to this cemetery, but we did not connect it in 1980 to her being a famous person. We were still dumbfounded that we had gone right by Epperly's home and that it seemed to be a straight line from the car to his house and to the cemetery. And it was. It all lined up in a perfect straight line on the map as though I had laid a straight-edged ruler right down on the paper map and used it as a guide to draw a straight line. The memory of this experience would forever change my perceptions of what could be possible.

But this news that Allison reversed herself stuck in my head. It could be as simple as her frustration with what was happening that October 1980 in Atlanta, where she had gotten called in to solve the Wayne Williams Atlanta children's murders and a police detective branded her "that wacko broad." There were some VSP investigators down there who came back and said that she clearly named that murderer's name, but she was not being listened to. I now wondered if she had seen something too horrific to share with us—something that no good would come from sharing. Did she see something she knew was hopeless? I imagined the worst. The farmer's story. A body being cut to pieces in the creek. If Gina had been dismembered, as the farmer's story suggested, that might explain why

Dorothy Allison stopped her work on the case.

Though Allison had always drawn an array of skeptics, even among the detectives who were using her, she had solved hundreds of cases. In one article from that time, a skeptical detective had said, "Seeing is believing." Those exact same words had been written as another night note days earlier.

Allison had first started using her gift in police work in her hometown in Nutley, New Jersey, after she dreamed about a blonde, blue-eyed boy in a green snowsuit, his shoes on the wrong feet. He had drowned in the pond and gotten stuck in a drainpipe. She called all of her friends to make sure their children were okay. A month later, still seeing the little boy in her visions, she decided to tell police about her dream. They were stunned. No description or police report of the boy had ever been circulated. The little boy's body was found, shoes still on the wrong feet, still in the drainpipe. Allison had just provided closure for a heartbroken family.

Here were Allison's notes from the first 1980 conference call in late July. Allison was describing the vision she saw when asked about where Gina's body might be. These notes are telling, not only about where Gina's body might be hidden, but also about what might have happened at the lake house and who was involved. The answers may be here somewhere in her words:

flooding

water running constantly

historical

Mary Ingles (M circled)

to boat marina

restaurant - remodeled

1974 restaurant name changed

Name Plymouth

Smell leather

No body by 23

Name Marshall

Indian Burial

Grave Moore

Beside Indian Burial and Grave Moore

Roof 19 or 109. Switch numbers around upside down 61   601

date time or license

face North. Follow direct line North to find the body

rocks in area

Rock house marina

(The note taker may have written this from conclusions as written out to the side of the list: "Everything has an M" or maybe Allison had said it.)

Desire to be a policeman. Impersonate a policeman

Someone who is helping him

Go north

See 109 as going to place

Restaurant

Marina with boats

then cemetery "old, antique"

headstones laying down

Moore grave is third in then go to the water

Rocks - pile - she's under rocks

Courthouse to marina

Historical Cemetery - "real old"

from Moore headstone North to water.

rocks around body

white or silver car

go to library

frightened of factory not too far from courthouse

Call

When I scanned Allison's notes, my eyes landed on "factory." The old box factory? And, later, seeing "1974 restaurant name changed," I wondered whether someone connected to the case had owned a restaurant with a name change in 1974. And, "Plymouth/leather"—could this be a Plymouth dealership? And later seeing one of Epperly's cellmates' stories that Gina was buried in a fresh grave—a Moore grave? I searched for every Moore grave in Pulaski County through the findagrave.com website, then on foot to follow up on each and every one, considering all possibilities. "Historical Cemetery" captured my eye. And "Call." But most intriguing was seeing "*No body by 23.*" What did that mean?

Also listed were various magazine articles with this note: Get boy to read and get him to come out.

Family Circle 03/11/80; *Official Detective* 01/80; *Reader's Digest* 12/78; *Mc-Call's* 09/78; *Newsweek* 04/17/79.

I wondered, *Did she mean Epperly? Would he have read these notes and understood their relevance?* That would have been a smart thing to do in 1980, watching his reactions. That might have been more revealing than Epperly's reaction to Harass II, the tracking dog, when Epperly learned that Harass II had tracked him from the trestle to his porch. And especially when Harass II tracked right to the office where he was sitting in the Radford police station. Epperly's response, "That's a damn good dog." He repeated those words three times.

HARASS II AND JOHN PRESTON. PHOTO COURTESY OF *THE SOUTHWEST TIMES* FROM *YOUR VIRGINIA STATE TROOPER MAGAZINE*

What would Epperly have said if he had seen Allison's notes? Would he have understood what movie she was seeing, given that he knew the facts?

Reading back through my Allison file, one statement stood out to me in the *Newsweek* article "Visions of the Dead" from April 17, 1979: "Some policemen remain unpersuaded even at close range, and in fact all of her triumphs have been one degree removed from the dramatic absolute *pointing at the ground, saying, 'Dig here'* and watching as the body is exhumed." [Emphasis mine.]

Decades later, during *the journey*, three different gifted people would say a similar thing to me, using nearly the same words: "A dark-haired lady pointing to the ground."

How was it that three different people would come into my life at different times by different ways, with such similar visions and stories? All three described to me a woman they saw with Gina, a pretty, black-haired woman in a white nightgown that two of them described as tattered. Two of the three commented on the dark-haired woman's teeth. Two saw the woman standing on a grassy hill *pointing to the ground*. One saw a flat field at the top of the hill. Another saw the black-haired woman holding back the brush, and motioning him to come into a large brick house covered in brush, describing the home down to the detail of seeing purple and white flowers. They all would say, "The dark-haired woman is with Gina."

Who was this black-haired young woman they all described seeing with Gina?

The article would go on to quote a Nutley detective, "Professional investigators find it difficult to use an ordinary woman to find something they can't find. But when Dorothy gets involved in a case, all of a sudden things start to happen. I don't know how or why. That's okay. Dorothy doesn't know either."

The morning of June 22, 2016, produced a full slate of messages. In the middle of the night, I drew a picture that looked like a strange, *triangular mountain coming out of the water*. At first, I could not make out what I had drawn on the corner of an envelope left by my bedside. It was drawn with distinct, thick ink lines as though the lines were retraced over and over, repeatedly.

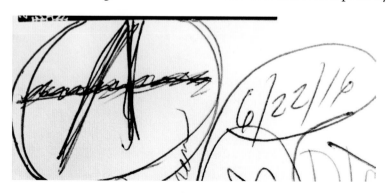

The same night I wrote:

8-1-35

Obviously, a date of birth. But I was learning that nothing is obvious.

And then this perplexing message:

Julio 9

I thought out loud, "Great, as if this is not hard enough already, I now have a Spanish-speaking angel!" I did not even know I could spell Julio. And still, I had no idea for sure what this message meant. The most obvious path seemed to be to pay attention to what had come up on July 9, 1980.

Curious what might be happening in the Radford area in the next few weeks, I looked at a list of upcoming events. A garden festival near the Ingles Farm stood out. My mind was constantly searching for answers to where Gina could be. The vast Ingles Farm had been a suspected search area for Gina's remains in 1980. Because of its history, this farm will be protected and undeveloped for many years to come. In 1755, Mary Draper Ingles and her two sons were captured by Shawnee Indians, Mary later escaping and finding her way back home five to six hundred miles, including crossing over the Appalachia Mountains and across many creeks and rivers. An obelisk-shaped Ingles monument made of chimney stones is in a cemetery north of Epperly's home—the same cemetery Buz and I had found following Allison's instructions. Recently, a second, newer monument had been erected as part of the area near the renovated Glencoe Museum, a historic Civil War home located very near where much of the circumstantial evidence was found, including Gina's bloodied clothes and a blue towel with critical implications for Epperly. Mary Draper Ingles certainly would fit the description of historic and famous, but at the time, we had narrowed in on looking for military headstones.

Three days later, I wrote this confusing message:

Bring Him to Va

same Rd

Airplane 12/1974

I had no time for new messages. I was still pondering Julio 9. That message just would not leave my mind. I thought to delve into the events of

July 9, 1980. In my files, I had noted items relevant to Gina's case discovered in the woods near his suspected path home. The day before, July 8, a short-handled shovel and a single shoe had been found. The Epperly home was missing two tools—a short-handled shovel and a mattock. But I had no notes about July 9. Still, this lingered in my mind: *What had happened on July 9?*

I had been asked to identify the single shoe—Gina's shoe. Gina had purchased that shoe when Mama Joan had taken us to a shoe store closing sale. We had liked bargain shopping together, and we had both liked this same brand, especially when it was on sale, so we had each bought a pair. The only difference in our shoes besides the size was the color of the band crossing over the toes. The band on her shoe was a perfect match to her outfit—purple, just like her body suit that Skipper knew she was wearing.

Thinking back to those days, I tried to remember what day the contents of mine and Gina's shared clutch wallet were found. Could that day have been July 9? No—July 7. I had been with the police search group that day off of Hazel Hollow Road about a mile toward the lake from the trestle on the river side of the road. The paper contents of our wallet had been neatly stacked, hidden under some dirt in a brush pile. My pocketbook had been stolen from my abandoned car and thrown over the riverbank a mile in the opposite direction of my car.

The most valuable piece of evidence was found on the day after July 9, 1980—the bloody blue towel.

Within two days of knowing that Gina was missing, three dear friends of my family—Jeff Kiser, Gary Welch, and Ronnie Arney, a young man who had played football for my dad during his coaching years—arrived in Radford, taking vacation days to help us search. Through those hot, early July days, while police divers searched the lake and the river, our friends kayaked the nooks and crannies of the New River banks. They also spent long days searching in the woods. Jeff spotted the blue towel on a scrubby bush in the woods behind the Thrifty Grocery, across the train tracks, over an embankment. The towel was identified by the lake house owners as being one of their missing towels. Finding this blue towel was a pivotal point in the investigation.

Police sent the blue towel to the laboratory. Human blood was identified, the same type as Gina's. With the discovery of the towel, we now had a trail—strands of Gina's hair from the refrigerator door at the lake house, hair stuck in blood in the trunk of my car, and now, hair on the blue towel. The police forensics lab took a strand of Gina's hair from her curlers and found it was similar to all three. Carpet fibers from the lake house rec-room were found on the utility room refrigerator door, in the trunk of my car, on Gina's underwear, and on the blue towel. The matches point to the blue towel being used to clean up the murder scene.

This towel, too, would become an important part of the December 1980 trial testimony, as would this day's events, Epperly's comments, and other statements made concerning the blue towel.

As I tried to puzzle out what the clue about Julio 9/July 9 might mean, I started to wonder what our three family friends would remember about their search. Could they remember exactly where they were on July 9, the day before Jeff found the towel? Following my hunch, I went to visit Jeff. I met him in Coeburn at the Pizza Hut. I had not been there in decades. It had been a favorite hangout when the first video games became popular—*Space Invaders* providing hours of fun in small town America.

"Dlana, please tell me you are not still searching for Gina after all this time," Jeff said.

I explained that no, I had not been continuously searching since 1980; I had just started a few months before. Not even the thought had crossed my mind in all of those years to go back and search for Gina's body—not until now.

The area where Jeff found the blue towel was extensively overgrown. I know because I spent many days searching that area in 1980 and again in 2016.

The towel was found up high, laying over the bush, perfectly, "as though it had been carefully placed there," Jeff now told me, "on top of a prickly, scrubby shrub, or if not placed, as though it was as lightweight as a hand-kerchief flung into the woods and gracefully landing on top, just as if it had been laid." This was how Jeff described it.

Why not just throw it off the trestle, letting the river carry it away? Arro-gance—no one will look long for a missing college student. Confidence—no one will ever find her body.

Jeff and our two friends had been working with a group of younger students who had come to help the search. That summer, Kitty Price and I spent many hours searching for Gina together. Even with the difficulty of the task at hand, digging through trash dumpsters together and finding bloody sheets and dead animals, new friendships emerged. One of those students would be in the group that found Gina's bloody clothes on July 19, 1980. So I asked Jeff, "Where were you searching the day before you found the towel? Could you have all been congregated in this same wooded area?"

"Yes," he said, "and I'll never forget what one of them said as we walked up."

One young woman in the small group said she had a message for them. Her grandmother, who had been worried about her being out searching in the woods, had instructed, "You need to tell those three boys a message." This had gotten the granddaughter's attention because she'd never told her grandmother she was searching with three boys. "Here is the message she has for you: 'Tell those three boys looking for the missing girl's body that they walked right by her. Her arm was uncovered, sticking out of the ground. Ask them, did they not see it?'"

"That story always bothered me," Jeff said.

Was that grandmother a seer? Even in 1980, there seemed to be a presence within the spiritual realm seeking to break through with truth—light shining in the darkness of this evil. Or was it the exact opposite—thoughts placed, intentionally misguiding us from the truth?

Could that have been on July 9? I wondered whether the grandmother's story was why I had been led to track Jeff down and talk to him—so that I would hear that message too?

Or what Jeff shared next?

"I cannot imagine how we did not find Gina's clothes the same day we found the blue towel," he said. "It was within twenty-five yards or so, and I just do not believe we could have missed seeing it."

Just as it haunted Jeff, it haunted me that somehow the search party had missed all of this evidence when it was so close in proximity. And they weren't the only ones searching. Many professionals and volunteers did not find them either. The tracking dog had already shown everyone that this was Epperly's path home from my abandoned car.

The News
JOURNAL

COPYRIGHT © 1980 NEW RIVER NEWSPAPERS INC

96TH YEAR— NO. 105   TWO SECTIONS   RADFO

Staff photo by Ray Downey-Laskowitz

In the search

Rescue squadsmen, search dogs and scuba divers were all part of one of the most intense searches ever conducted in the New River Valley, Saturday, in the search for Gina Renee Hall, a missing Radford University student. Police suspect foul play may have been involved and are searching New River and Claytor Lake.

On Saturday, July 12, 1980, an extensive search took place, organizing and coordinating many different authorities from across Virginia and parts of West Virginia. Claytor Lake and New River were their primary focus. About six State of Virginia divers and some volunteers worked the Claytor Lake area from the lake house to the dam, and the New River from the dam to the trestle. Even the search dogs were put on boats. One cadaver search dog can take the place of many people. This is a vast area to cover. *The News Journal* reported that it was the most intense search ever conducted in the New River Valley. Gina had been gone fourteen days.

A week later, on July 19, 1980, Gina's bloodied clothes, a mattock from the Epperly shed, and the blue-and-white-striped towel that Skipper's mother had listed as missing were found—nine days after the blue towel.

Jeff was right. Next to impossible. That made me wonder, *What if the clothes really were placed there after July 10?* If so, there were only two explanations: Epperly placed them, or someone else placed them, as if neatly bundled.

My mind contemplated the many possibilities.

The question to answer was: Why would Epperly just put her clothes, with blood all over them, bundled as if placed in a thick part of the woods within a half a mile of his own home? Maybe Epperly did it simply to mess with us or to draw us away from somewhere else. His confident demeanor, the cat and mouse game he likes to play with everyone, might just be the true source of how those clothes ended up there. Or someone else needed to make sure Epperly was the only one ever connected to that night, as he had been—someone with an unknown agenda. Either way, their ploy worked. Now everyone was focusing on the woods right off the path Epperly took, crossing the trestle following the railroad tracks home.

Sunday, July 20—the day after Gina's bloody clothes were found—approximately sixty to seventy uniformed officers, some carrying shovels, some poles, shoulder to shoulder searched this area. It was a sweltering hot day, three long weeks since Gina went missing. By then, the publicity around the case had heightened.

Still perplexed about the significance of Julio 9, I delved into the facts from 1980. A surprise surfaced. Epperly visited the blood center at The American Red Cross in Roanoke on July 9, 1980, right at 5 p.m., inquiring if his blood would be typed if he donated. This perplexed me—why? What was he thinking? Maybe her shoe being found—the first connector of him to Gina—likely dropped as he ran and turned to the right after crossing the trestle, started a domino effect, causing Epperly to react and scramble. I wonder how many times he retraced his steps looking for that shoe. I cannot get into his mind to understand why the first thing he did was want to get his blood typed.

I never once tried to think like Epperly until *the journey* of 2016.

The stories of the manipulation and scheming are really quite interesting. And it usually takes more than one to stay ahead of everyone else. Epperly always seemed to be a step ahead. This may be why he kept visiting the local police station. And he was not the only person who frequented the station during those initial weeks. Skipper was reported to have dropped by several times, telling the police that he was afraid—so afraid he was carrying his gun. Skipper was a man I do not believe would be that afraid of his good ole buddy Epperly, yet he was afraid of someone. And as noted in the police reports, another friend of Epperly's, Tom Hardie, kept coming by the station with Epperly. The police finally told Hardie, "If you are not his attorney," assuming he may have been by his attire, "then move on. You cannot be here." So it's an intriguing question—why did Tom Hardie accompany Epperly? And who did Epperly keep visiting at the local police station so frequently that reports were written about his cohorts? And that led to this thought: Perhaps Epperly had—*insider information*. It seems something prompted him to act on this day, Julio 9.

A lot seemed to happen around July 9, 1980, eleven days after Gina's murder. I continued to ponder so many questions, all stemming from one crazy message—Julio 9. This was the way I was thinking.

Jeff and I had reminisced about the local police officer who had come to my townhouse multiple times during those first weeks or so and repeatedly said to us, "There is just no way Stephen Epperly did this." So maybe the policeman Jeff and I reminisced about was the same one Epperly would visit. Maybe he was part of the tight-knit Wolfpack.

Jeff said, "It upset all of us. It all seemed as if to be trying to get us all to change our minds—trying to convince us that Gina had run away or that maybe we should look closer at Buz or Gina's old boyfriend as more logical possibilities." I always knew differently.

Was there a bigger picture I still wasn't seeing?

In 2018, I found my mother-in-law's notes she scribed from Buz's phone conversations with her during those first, frantic days when Gina was missing. Buz called his family daily with an update of what was happening in Radford. Real time notes from the very beginning, before we even knew Gina was dead.

My in-laws had lived a full and happy life. It was no coincidence that while writing this book at night, and helping my husband to clean out his parents' home by day, I was in the exact place where her notes and the Richmond, Virginia, and Washington DC area news clippings from 1980 had been tucked away. Buz told his mother that I described Gina as sounding drugged or sad in her phone call to me. This brings back that deep sadness forever in me, not registering until I woke back up the next morning, recalling her sullen voice.

Police & family convinced that Epperly was Clear—except for one—Diana. Diana does investigation on her own—finds out that Steve Epperly has been charged with rape + assault previously!

Tells police (Diana) found to be true.

July 1, 1980

Epperly submits to lie detector test. proven to be lying 7 times when asked if he killed Gina

As I read Buz's mom's real time-dated notes scribed by her as he shared exactly what had transpired after we learned who the mystery Steve was—Steve Epperly. I am reminded that everyone thought Epperly was innocent in those early days—except me. Mom's notes written during those first inceptive days confirm that was the dominant thought right after Epperly first shared with police his composed story that Gina had gone willingly with him to the lake house. I know my sister. And I still know her truth, now, just as I did in 1980.

Three heart-wrenching days after Gina did not come home, I knew Stephen Epperly had killed Gina. I am not positive exactly when Daddy came to terms with Gina's death. I believe he was still in denial for the first seven days after Gina's death. Maybe Daddy knew, like me, that day standing at the lake house that a search to find Gina had quickly changed to a search to find her body, but I believe it was the day he rode in the car with his daughter's murderer, as I'll explain shortly, that he finally gave up hope. Before that ride, I know my dad was still holding onto a tiny shred of hope that Gina was still alive. A glimmer of hope that she was somewhere out there holding onto her last breath. Everyone was still holding on to the hope that Gina was still alive. If they allowed themselves to believe he murdered her, that would mean there was no hope. I knew. I had heard her voice.

My dad's perception was continuing to be influenced by local positive opinions plentifully shared with us about Epperly, initially also believing Epperly's story himself—that Gina really did drop him off at his house at 4 a.m. And almost everyone else outside of my family were focused on her old boyfriend as a prime suspect in those initial days. Others staying in my townhouse recall, as Jeff and I did, the local policeman who kept coming by our townhouse for days, trying to convince everyone there was no way Epperly killed Gina. Even attempting to redirect attention to Buz. Almost everyone pointed to Gina's high school sweetheart. I clearly remember how Gina was so happy and excited about his planned visit, but I had forgotten that she had talked to him on the phone for hours before going dancing. This explained her smile and everyone else's prevailing mindset. *Boyfriend shows up. Girl stepped out on him. Boy kills girl.* My family was furious with this misdirection. Buz must have witnessed her hours on the phone, and just as I did not notice her talking with him, so too could she have easily called friends to discuss what plans everyone had for the night. She could have arranged to meet others she knew without me ever knowing about it, even a planned pick-up. Did Gina have someone else in the car with her?

Trooper Hall went ahead and gave Gina's friend a polygraph to clear him. He knew that would help others focus where focus was warranted. Epperly was given a polygraph test by Wednesday afternoon. Epperly failed. That test in itself is not conclusive. But seven times the test indicated failure when asked, *"Did you kill the Hall girl?"* and *"Do you know where Gina Hall's body is?"*

The first person my dad would call would be his old friend William "Bill" Cranwell, a connection from his Virginia Tech Football days. Bill was a necessary, local resource since he was a businessman who still lived in the area. Of course, everything kept happening so fast the moment my dad arrived Monday at noon that his call to his old friend kept getting delayed. What we did not know until later was that Cranwell was the same man Epperly turned to before the authorities even knew of Epperly. By Cranwell's early police interview statements and testimony later at the trial, we know that Epperly came to him before anyone knew Gina had been murdered—before the police saw the inside of that lake house and her blood. Epperly asked Cranwell three times, "What can they do to me if they do not find the body?" What Cranwell did not know when Epperly visited him was that his old football buddy John Hall's daughter was missing.

Many of the connections most likely started to fall into place for Cranwell when he met with my dad. Cranwell informed my dad he personally knew Epperly and could arrange a meeting so my dad could talk to him face to face. Even with all of this, I still wondered if Bill Cranwell somehow could not initially accept the idea of Epperly's guilt, having known him a very long time. This was a common feeling among many people. Epperly was still performing his Oscar act. Many had never experienced the true nature of Stephen Epperly. And many just ignored it. The truth of Epperly's nature was effectively being shadowed by everyone's own initial perceptions of him, some influenced by others' opinions. The initial reaction of almost everyone was that Epperly was innocent. Everyone except me, just as Buz's mom had written in her scrupulous notes. I knew Sunday morning that "Steve" was responsible for doing something very wrong to my sister, especially after learning by Tuesday night his full name, which led to quickly learning of his former violent history. I was the one who heard Gina's voice. No story I made up in my head could stop her haunting voice from echoing her last words spoken from that terrible night. For a long time, I had been trying not to remember, but never forgetting.

When Cranwell and my dad met, I do not know if Cranwell told my dad right away about Epperly's earlier visit and his conversations with him. I know Cranwell told the police because there was a report of the conversation. I believe Cranwell may have wrestled with what he needed to do. A later statement details a conversation Cranwell had with Epperly. He had offered to pay for Epperly to be given Sodium Pentothal, truth serum, and that if it proved he did not kill Gina, he said he would hire the best attorney for Epperly. Cranwell added, as he slammed his fists on the table, that he could accept anything except murder. The appointment was set, but Epperly backed out.

I could not understand, after all that had transpired in the last seven days, how my dad still could not fully believe Epperly had murdered Gina. I understand now, after becoming a mother. His hope never wavered because he was a father. Believing = No Hope. Sometimes, I wonder, too, if my dad's initial perception was also skewed because of the commonality between them all as Virginia Tech Alumni and former football players. My dad and Cranwell had played together. Epperly had been a walk-on football player at Virginia Tech in 1974, but he had quit by the fall of that year. A Virginia state policeman, as part of his investigation, spoke with two other investigators, one a Virginia Tech police officer, the other a Radford University police officer. Both gave accounts that several girls on both campuses reported rape incidents with Epperly, but would not put their statements in writing for fear of retaliation. The truth about Epperly was not well known. But my dad soon became aware of what he needed to see.

Sunday, July 6, 1980, undoubtedly became one of the hardest days of my dad's life—the day when he reconciled in his own mind what had happened to his little girl—the day he rode in the car with his daughter's murderer, carrying that revolver in his pocket. I find it interesting that others say my dad was checked for a gun. No, he was not. It took this ride for my dad to see what he needed to see. When the ride began, he did not know Epperly. By the end, I believe he did. That day my dad showed his strength as the man we always knew him to be. He remained strong beyond all comprehension. The pure will and strength it must have taken not to have used his gun that day is astounding to me.

Cranwell quickly arranged a meeting between my dad and the man who was the last person known to see Gina alive. My dad hoped if he met with Epperly face to face to discuss Gina's disappearance, Epperly might lend additional information to help us locate Gina. Epperly agreed willingly, confident in his demeanor, as consistently displayed throughout those initial weeks of July. The meeting would take place, as arranged, I guess with police knowledge since my dad was riding in the car with VSP Investigator Duffy when he recognized Cranwell's car pass them on Hazel Hollow Road. Another reason I am positive no one really knew what was in my dad's pocket, besides that he told us every detail of the ride, is the impromptu pulling over process of exchange, not the organized meeting place back near the landing at the trestle. They both pulled over, and my dad transferred into Cranwell's car, with Epperly already sitting in the front passenger seat. My dad sat in the backseat, taking note of Epperly's polite actions, clean-cut appearance, and neatly trimmed blonde hair, a refined, new cleaned-up look compared to the prior week. As Cranwell drove the backroads of the Claytor Lake area and Hazel Hollow Road, my dad intensely focused on Epperly, paying attention to every word spoken by him, not yet fully accepting him of actually killing his daughter because the hope was that she was only missing, not dead.

"I am sorry, Mr. Hall. I do not know where your daughter is," Epperly kept repeating.

They spent a long time together, stopping for a while at a spot that looked out over the lake. My dad would ask questions and Epperly, consistently polite, would say, "Yes, sir," or "No, sir." The more mannerly Epperly was, the more my dad began to waver, suspicious of Epperly's arrogance and confidence.

During the ride, my father's mood changed from hope to horror as the reality sunk in that his daughter's life had been taken, and this man was responsible. He finally reconciled in his own mind what had happened to Gina. His thoughts changed from hoping to find his missing daughter to realizing her murdered body was missing, hidden somewhere. From the backseat, as his good friend drove, my dad later shared with us that he watched Epperly's every tic and flicker and took mental note of every single turn of Epperly's head in hopes he would give a subtle clue as to what he may have done with Gina. I know in those moments, as it began to sink in with my dad, that he contemplated whether he should just kill Epperly right then. I am positive the anger he must have felt was insurmountable. But I believe he also must have realized that Epperly now held the secret of where Gina might be hidden, as they rode by the vast woods, lake, and winding waterways of this region. He knew if he killed his daughter's murderer, the secret would never be known, and he would never bring his little girl home. Because of this hope, he suppressed the rage. That hope came from his strong faith in God.

My dad would tell us later how his mindset evolved, spurred by Epperly's own guilty demeanor. After that ride, my dad knew his true nature. Sometimes evil has a way of just showing itself. My dad now believed, as I did, that Epperly had definitely brought lethal harm to his daughter. That day, when we both were standing outside the lake house for the first time, my suspicions too changed from hope that Epperly had only brought Gina physical harm to the reality that Epperly had indeed murdered my sister. Now, no hope remained. We all had lost hope that Gina was alive 188 hours after I had last heard her voice. The search now was for a hidden body, calculatingly disposed of by her murderer.

Conversations and corroborations stirred, carrying forward the formation of the coordinated, composed story. I am positive the local police and many local residents already knew of Epperly's reputation. It was a small town. Thank heavens for Trooper Hall. His focus was not misdirected by preconceived opinions about the local, smiling, football-playing, all-American boy—that was how most saw him in town. A friend of my family, Kitty McCoy, who lived in Radford, shared that when she would come home with a car full of groceries, Epperly would be the only boy to stop playing with the others and come and help her carry in her groceries. "Yes, ma'am. No, ma'am." A perfect gentleman. A Jekyll and Hyde. I am confident Gina quickly saw the bad side while on the dance floor at the Marriott. It would not have taken much for her to see through to his arrogance. Arrogance would never have been tolerated by Gina. Not for one second.

Seeing the old Washington newspaper clippings reminded me again of 1980. I would hear Daddy tell the reporters that he believed Gina either left with a man who knew me or knew a friend, and that she might have only agreed to go to a second place to continue dancing, not a party and not with a man by herself. Even Daddy was beginning to accept parts of the composed story. She never left to be with him. That was not Gina. Daddy would be quoted by many newspapers, but the nature of this statement would not appear in print, except in the Washington DC area newspaper, *The Washington Star*. Daddy was accurately quoted, "Gina's passion for dancing and her willingness to trust people apparently got her into trouble. Gina loved to dance. That was the only thing she really loved to do." I would later see that only the composed story created by a rapist, a murderer—a red-blooded, all-American *boy*—carried forward, especially locally, while my dad's words were not emphasized until the trial.

During our nights and days of searching, I had not been watching the news or reading the newspapers, but one day I was given a clipping of an article. The local newspaper had published a story that day that angered me to my core. My heart roiled when I read words like, "Hall last seen at a *cabin* on Claytor Lake where *she spent part of the night June 28 and 29*," and "*that she left a bar with a man she did not know*." One simple additional line would have changed the composed story. *The inside car door pull found ripped off as if she held it shut with all of her might.* But that was not the story told. Who had the influence in this town to spin it this way to reporters? To tell the media that Gina had told me she would be home shortly? That had not happened. Her last word was "Steve." Oh, yeah, Epperly's story prevailed. He was the one who said in his statement that Gina had told her sister she would be home shortly. And my statements sometimes were heard through the mindset that prevailed. And really, isn't the composed story almost always the prevailing mindset in these types of cases? She went *willingly*...a victim-blaming mindset. Then, and still now. Women, we all need to wake up. How many centuries must pass?

That was my sister and her honor. She didn't "spend the night" with men. Her honor was so easily dismissed. The composed story continued to be the story, and it had been so ever since 1980. Their story, not ours. Not my sister's story. Yet, it did not change the hearts of those who knew and loved Gina—the people who cared, who knew her and came to know her; law enforcement officers who spent their personal days off searching for Gina, a young girl they had never met; a young prosecuting attorney, Everett Shockley, who believed in the power of right to trump wrong; and a multitude of caring family friends who donated money so my dad could offer a $10,000 reward to locate Gina's body, thus bringing strangers to the woods to help us search. I believe my dad was a big part of the reason Gina's case did not fade away.

But what really made the difference was not just my dad. A community's caring efforts, the dedicated serving people, and everyone's love of Gina, knowing of her genuine innocence, kept the momentum progressing. And that was exactly how and why Epperly came to be arrested, tried, and successfully convicted. My family is forever grateful for all of the local people and authorities who worked tirelessly for Gina. Those who serve. Those who were not a part of the few, the interconnected web of influencers, elusively seeking to hide truth, compromising the principles of the caring, respectful majority of those good people living in this small town community. The amazing efforts of so many towering over the few. This was Gina and her light through the dark hours.

The essence of my sister's goodness still shining. This is the Light.

CHAPTER 8

NOT GOING ANYWHERE

Sis, I'm not going anywhere. I am right here with you always.

The anniversary week of Gina's death was a quiet reprieve from the messages, allowing me time to reflect on what I had unearthed from my memories of 1980. Now that I knew more about the day-by-day details of what we did not know in 1980, more was becoming clearer. The truth can set you free. And just like the summer of 1980 unraveled much of the truth, so too would *the journey* of 2016. Every encounter I had, every person I crossed paths with, added a piece to my one-thousand-plus-piece puzzle.

One such encounter that added an interesting piece was my visit with retired Special Agent W. B. Wilmore of the VSP. He shared this little, unknown fact: "Dlana, I will never forget a few years after Gina's death, I was called up to Radford to check out two bones found down by the river."

Two human bones had been found about 1985 by the riverbank, on the west Radford side of New River—a femur and a clavicle. Wilmore sent them to the University of Tennessee to be examined, and they had been determined to be male, age 35-40 years.

That these bones could be in any way associated with Gina never really crossed my mind until December when a second story surfaced and the dismemberment theories continued to emerge. Meadow Creek flows into Little River and then into the New River, a compelling thought. But they also could have been buried near there, washing free after flooding. In one of my notes, I wrote:

extreme flooding, torrential water all around me. I saw a man lose his leg. Very vivid dream.

Maybe the bones are not even related, but it certainly is questionable. Another mystery for the police. Two male bones—sitting on a shelf somewhere, unidentified.

Thousands of people go missing every day. Many longing parents tell themselves, "My child is just out there somewhere, a runaway, and one day will come home....one day." That could have been my family, still holding on to hope—grieving, fractured souls.

We were still grieving, and fractured, but in a different way—No body. No truth.

On June 30, 2016, I would wake to a simple, yet puzzling message:

Connect the Two

The following picture was drawn beneath those three words.

I spent the Fourth of July weekend with my best friend in her favorite childhood town, Kure Beach, North Carolina. That day, I had my first daytime thought that also seemed to be relevant. My friend was playing her songs, playing the same song repeatedly, which was unlike her. "I love this new song—'Circles' by Jana Kramer. I can't stop playing it." I was not hearing what she was hearing. I heard only part of me is broken / 6' down at the river is where you will begin to pick up the pieces.

On July 5, 2016, on my way home, while I was staying with another friend in Richmond, her mom came into the guest bedroom and handed me a book and an envelope that had a copy of a page from the book *Pearls of Great Price: 365 Daily Devotional Readings* by Joni Eareckson Tada published by Zondervan. The loose page was a copy of yesterday's daily devotional. She said, "I was just thinking of you and thought you might like to read it."

The July 4 passage was titled "Is It Coincidence…or God?"

Here is what it said:

God delights in arranging coincidences. Consider your Fourth of July Picnic. The sun is warm and the grill is working and everyone's bringing watermelon, but unknown to you, God wants it to rain. He wants your brother-in-law to help you hurry the grill inside the garage where you will stand waiting out the downpour. There you will get into a long conversation leading to spiritual ideas that will eventually lead your brother-in-law to Christ. How did God make this happen? Earlier today it was warm. But 5 miles away a colder jet stream from the Northwest was coming in. Yesterday it was 200 miles away above the Rockies, and on and on. God has been thinking about the brother in law for a long time. Whew! How does God manage it all? He does it. It's mind-bogglingly complicated. Divine Coincidences happen every day.

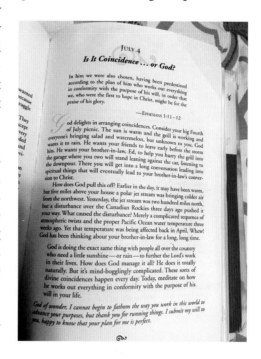

The verse quoted at the top of this devotional was:

> In him we were also chosen, having been predestined according to the plan of him who works out everything in conformity with the purpose of his Will in order that we, who were the first to hope in Christ, might be for the praise of his Glory. Ephesians 1:11-12

I needed that devotional in that very moment to remind me of the power of God. He has an army of angels helping assure that His Will, that purpose, is done. This was just the message that this confident, strong-willed, opinionated, hard-headed girl needed.

That whole week, I had really started to waver on my whole perception of what these messages were and where they were coming from. This verse helped.

The next day, July 6, 2016, the plan was to be in Radford, and the mysterious happenings kept coming. As I was leaving my friend's home in Richmond, I attempted to carry all of my luggage out in one fell swoop. Of course, at the bottom of the stairs, I dropped a piece and tripped over it. I laughingly said aloud, "I know, Daddy; five a day." I could just see Daddy wagging his finger at me. When I would do silly things, he would say, "I'm gonna increase your smart pills to five a day!"

In the car, my phone connected to the sound system, which just happened to be playing "Just for Now," a song from the Pentatonix album *That's Christmas to Me* that I had downloaded so I could play the song "Mary, Did You Know?" for my mother-in-law, who had Alzheimer's. I had never heard the song "Just For Now" before. The lyrics caught my attention: My dad always wagged his finger at me. I should have seen the humor in this instantly, but I did not. The lines would continue, but I would hear it differently: *I know **evil** had a boogie ride, but I am secretly on your side.* This was the first time I realized the breadth of what could happen. And it would not be the last.

On July 13, 2016, I wrote these words that would change everything:

> An island near where GII ends

And on the back of the paper, written the same night:

> James Young. Name on a map maybe

And, I had written:

> Maybe not the same message

Did I question somehow its source as I slept?

And, finally, I had written:

> a Dream
>
> I had a perfect rectangle, softened, round and like jello on my arm. I flicked it off and the rectangle just easily fell off and underneath was a plant growing out of my arm. I pulled it out with tweezers. It was growing on my skin like a purple-flowered weed.

At times, I would write *A dream*, yet it was not really like a dream but more like a dream-vision.

Then on July 17, I had another *dream vision:*

> I dreamed I went into the kitchen [my kitchen at home] and I was standing looking out a glass door. I saw six Civil War army men. They were dressed in dirty tunic shirts and holding rifles.

Stumped. I did the first thing I knew to do: Tell Andy. Andy said that it never stopped surprising him that when he needed to know something about Gina's case, it surfaced. He too shared that he had been interested in an island, so much so that he had brought in two cadaver dogs a year earlier to search two islands along the shores of the New River—a search he hadn't told me about until this day. It surprised him that I, too, was questioning an island.

"Why are you so interested in islands?" I asked him.

He replied that a paranormal TV show had filmed a segment on Gina's murder case at St. Albans in which they had used a "ghost machine" and the word "island" had come up. This just upset me. I dismissed it, but what did get my attention was the next part of his story.

When Andy and I had first met in 2013, I shared with him the 1980 Dorothy Allison story—the straight line when Buz and I had followed her instructions. After the word island came up, Andy was curious if that line would extend near those islands. It did. When he extended the line further, he said it continued across an island in the New River, and ended near the lake house, the scene of the crime. He was blown away just like we were in 1980.

Now, I was most curious about the islands, especially the one near the end of the 90 degree bend of Route 611.

I became obsessed with maps, stopping in at the Pulaski County Courthouse to view relief maps, hoping to see how densely that bluff was covered in 1980. Using satellite map imagery, I searched the area looking for roads that matched any of the numbers I had written down. As I was looking on

Google maps at the islands and the river edge of the properties that border Route 611, a distorted image in the current of the river caught my eye. I remembered Nola had said, "Nature will tell you what it wants you to know." The exact location of this strange image is where the shoals cross the New River. I captured the screenshot of the Google map image that shows the uncanny shape of a girl's body, to which Nola texted, "I look at this picture and always have the same reaction. Coincidences don't exist. Remember, no matter what anyone says to you, you need to go to that location."

The plan on this hot, sticky July day was to kayak down the New River from the boat landing away from the Claytor Lake Dam. I was hoping to get a closer look at the islands and the shoals where I saw the distorted image. Andy wanted drone footage so that he could survey the area from

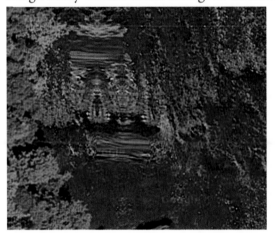

above. He surprised me when he told me he'd meet me downriver. Andy did not much like the idea of being on that river, which had a reputation for being dangerous. Buz and I had spent many days tubing at McCoys Falls during my college years. I had always heard the New River could be tricky.

"Someone's always drowning in it," said Andy, who is in the business of rescuing people. So before Andy left, he introduced me to a young man named Rob Stultz, a Radford K-9 police officer. Rob brought a trailer loaded with kayaks. I was familiar with kayaking in the mountain lakes, but kayaking a river is not the same, especially one so close to the dam where the water can be released with no warning. I took a deep breath as I pushed on into the water.

As we worked our way down river, Rob filmed with his drone. Rob and I stopped at the first island in the middle of the river. I got out of my kayak, walking all around the island and simply observed everything. I do not know what I was looking for. I was just looking. All I knew was that I wanted to go downriver to that area at the shoals where nature seemed to be telling me something.

As I kayaked down the river, I noticed to the left, before I got to the shoals, an orange stake in the ground in the riverbank. I passed a second one right before the shoals, so I paddled over and went ashore to look closer. It seemed odd for me to have noticed them. The stakes seemed to be marking off an area on the edge of the riverbank that normally would be underwater. Because the water was low, they were exposed. I had seen these orange and white stakes before when out west, taller ones used to mark the roads for the snow depths. These were only two feet high and stuck deeply, close to the bank of the river, marking this area.

I remembered the June 30 message—Connect the Two—not so much the words but the picture I had drawn. I believed I had been drawing these stakes twenty-two days earlier, but why?

A few weeks earlier, I had found Route 611—Old Rock Road—on the map. Some call it Wilderness Road because back in the day, it was the road that the covered wagons would follow to the famous pre-Revolutionary War bridge near the Ingles Farm.

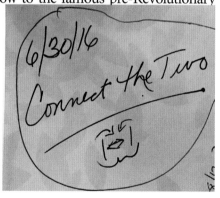

At the end of Route 611, only the large stone blocks remain of the covered bridge that once crossed from the west side to the east, having burned down during the Civil War Battle of Cloyd's Mountain. I had first wondered if the "Connect the Two" message could mean the old covered bridge because of the unusual picture I had drawn. I believed I was now seeing what the picture meant—the orange stakes, like straight lines drawn, not even fifty yards apart. But what did "Connect the Two" mean?

Standing on the shore, looking all around, I suddenly became aware that I was standing in a very remote, "no reason to be there" kind of place. This area of the riverbank was not frequented by people. The river was so low that the washed-out bank, hollowed out from past floodings, was way above my head in some parts, the roots of trees from above exposed in the dirt wall. And sometimes the river's edge was thick with brush and impassable. I was uncomfortable here. I walked back to my kayak and pushed it into the water, paddling toward the shoals.

My heart raced a little as I kayaked over the shoals. The shoals got shallower and swifter. You could probably walk from one side of the river to the other at this juncture, certainly when the river was low. The New River is the oldest on the North American continent and the second oldest only to the Nile. Some estimate it is over 500 million years old, an ancient river system that flows northward instead of south like most other rivers. Claytor Lake was created from this river. The Little River, which snakes between high cliff walls, enters the New River right below Claytor Dam, and Meadow Creek flows into the Little River.

Later, I would see fishermen walking the shoals. The legend told about this section of the river is that the shoals had been an Indian fishing place because of how the rocks come into a natural V where the Indians could easily build a fish dam. I imagined these rocks underneath caused the distorted shoal image I was seeing on Google maps.

In 1980, the authorities had stopped the flow from the dam. The objective was to lower the river so they could check the many rock ledges and crevices for Gina's body. The cadaver dogs had leaned over the boat's edge, doing what they do best—even over water.

Looking back over my shoulder and upriver, I saw a bluff in the distance, and suddenly, it was 1980. That must be the bluff where Epperly was known to be the day after he was released on bail after being charged with Gina's murder. Rob's drone snapped a picture that would have been the view looking back up the river from near the orange stakes. I was in the photo, standing in the river at the top of the island. Seeing how vast and wild this area appeared, I felt daunted. It should have made me stop and ask, "What am I doing here? This is impossible. A needle in a haystack would be easier to find. Just quit." I did not.

Downriver, Andy was waiting for us at an island close to the shore. From my kayak, I stepped into the water, directly into the thick plant life swaying in the river current. Anything might lurk underneath. I knew I would be shopping for muck boots that night. Together, the three of us walked the banks of this island and several other islands. My mind was searching for any image that could match the messages I had been getting since the end of May—fifty-six days since it had all begun. A large rectangular piece of Styrofoam had washed up on the shore. I took a picture of it because it reminded me of one of my dreams about a rectangle that was so light that I had easily flicked it off my arm. I kicked it over, looking for purple flow-

ers just like in my dream. Silly, I know. But I was looking at everything. Daylight was fading.

That night, exhausted after kayaking and searching, and having a follow-up eye appointment scheduled the next day in Richmond six hours away from my home, I decided to just drive on. I got a last-minute deal on a stay at the Hotel Roanoke, a beautiful historic hotel where I had spent my honeymoon in March 1981. I had not been back to this hotel in decades. As I settled into my room, I sifted through the tiny details I had gathered in the past month about Gina's case. I had more questions than ever.

On this night, my mind raced. A text from Nola broke my intense concentration. He said:

> They will be working with your intuition. Trust what you receive sleeping or during your day. Don't doubt and do what you are led to do. If you feel you cannot handle it, ask for a slow down to digest what you are feeling.... It is time to get more spiritual now to receive what is happening.

That night I dreamed. It was an unusual experience, as if I were seeing what I had drawn in the middle of the night in the shadows on the ceiling. When I awoke, I had drawn this picture, from images on the ceiling of lights and shadows making circles and rectangles in pieces. In the morning, when I looked at the drawing, it made sense. A large circle looked like a head, a line drawn through it. Another large circle looked like a torso,

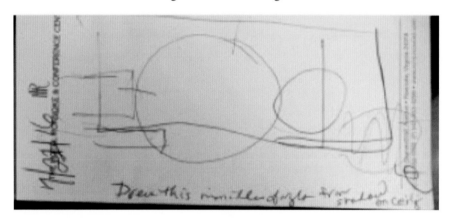

and two rectangles beneath that looked like legs. I had drawn what appeared to me to be a person. My first thought was recalling Nola telling me, "They will be working with you." They? *Who?* I wondered.

I did not contemplate long as the ping from my phone drew my attention away from my deep contemplations. Nola had sent a message:

> I don't know why I'm telling you this, but pay attention to butterflies.

I had noticed many butterflies on the river the day before. What did he mean, *pay attention to butterflies?* So I wondered, *Should I go back to the river today? Cancel my appointment in Richmond?*

I asked. He replied:

Keep your normal day. Don't change your plans. Let everything flow. Pay attention to butterflies when you go back, especially bluish. You will have a stronger intuition today. Pay attention and takes notes if necessary.

"Why butterflies?" I had to ask Nola.

> I had a dream yesterday where I saw black and white butterflies on a ceiling appearing out of nowhere; then one bluish purple butterfly came and landed on my hand and I gave it to a woman as a gift. I could not

see that woman's face. A butterfly represents guidance or a guide. That message was sent especially for you.

I rambled on and on to Nola about the details of the day before. I had noticed in particular the tiny periwinkle butterflies yesterday while walking the islands. They had sparked fond memories of Gina, when she and I were little, chasing butterflies in our grandmother's garden. He reminded me: one large butterfly. I also had paid attention to the hundreds of small purple flowers, like the one in my dream. I told Nola there were white feathers everywhere, especially on the islands, from all the ducks and geese. While walking around on the island, I even dug a hole under a small, dead fish I noticed, remembering my goldfish dream. I also told him about the hundreds of small mollusk shells stuck in the exposed banks of the islands and shoreline where the water was low. It seemed the river had been as much as fourteen feet higher in years past.

My thoughts were scattered. But no matter what I offered, Nola kept directing me to focus on the butterflies, sending one word in his reply... BUTTERFLIES.

They say patience is a virtue, and Nola had it. It was as if he were saying: *Really?!! Did I say anything about fish or feathers? I said BUTTERFLIES!!!*

I felt a sense of urgency. I promised Nola I would focus.

So on this day, Friday, July 22, I drove on to Richmond, Virginia's state capital, for that appointment, up and back, so I could meet Andy again Saturday for another day at the river. While driving, I could not stop noticing orange. I would see it everywhere. Of course, there is a lot of orange on an interstate, but I could not stop seeing orange—in the fields, on the buildings, absolutely everywhere. I surmised that when Andy and I returned to the river the next day, I was to take him to see those orange stakes. I knew it would be a long walk for him with his hurt ankle, but we just had to get back there. I was determined to make this happen.

Arriving at the river early Saturday morning, not knowing that the day that lay ahead would be the day my life changed forever, Andy and I began our walk up the riverbank, trekking right through the current most of the time. I wore both my new, thick muck boots and snake guards—double protection. Yet sometimes my stomach lurched to my throat. I loved to hike. But this was not hiking.

"We have to watch for a blue butterfly," I told Andy. "One large bluish-purplish butterfly."

Andy looked at me like I had lost my mind. But at this point, we both knew just to go with whatever came our way. The orange stakes were a good bit away. I felt we had walked far enough. About twenty yards ahead where a tree had fallen over into the water, I saw a large butterfly perched on the trunk. I looked at Andy and pointed. He had already noticed it, too.

As we approached, the butterfly remained, wings up, appearing brown. But when we neared the fallen tree and bent over to pass through, crossing over the trunk of the tree and under the limb into the water on the other side, the butterfly spread its wings, and they were as blue as blue could be. Blue, with dark purple flecks. The butterfly flew up to a higher tree branch, as though waiting for us both to cross through.

As soon as we stood up in the water on the other side of the fallen tree, the butterfly flew right back down, landing in the water right in front of us. It landed as if to be standing on the water; then it flopped over on its back, lying upside down in the river, its wings spread out softly, kissing the water. Astonished, we could not imagine what would cause a butterfly to do that. Andy took the piece of rebar he was using as a walking stick and lifted the butterfly up out of the water, gently placing it back on the tree trunk. It immediately flew right back down to the water, landing in the exact same spot again, flopping over on its back a second time. A beautiful, large butterfly floating upside down in the river as though it were playing dead. We would repeat the same experiment—scooping it up out of the water and lifting it back onto the branch, shaking our heads in awe to have just experienced what seemed like a miracle. As we walked away, the butterfly left also. We only went twenty more paces before I saw the orange stake. We were so captivated by the large butterfly that we walked right past the first stake as we approached the fallen tree. The fallen tree was in the center of the two stakes. The orange stakes definitely piqued Andy's interest, both of us logically assuming someone had marked this remote area of the river for a reason.

As we turned around, walking back toward the spot where the butterfly had entertained us, I took a picture of the tree in the water from the side where the butterfly had landed. Nola had said when you see the butterfly, start digging, and that is what I did. So we stopped, and I dug. I dug as long as I could. I broke Andy's shovel that day.

When I sent Nola a detailed note about the butterfly on the river, he simply responded, "I saw the markers." I wonder. He must have already known it would be a miraculous day.

Later in the evening when I got home, I looked at all the photos I had taken on our walk up the river. My eyes fell on the photo of the spot where the butterfly had landed. Then I saw it: One patch of sunlight glistened on the water. It looked just like a flash vision—a daydream I had had about a week earlier. I had written a note "*seeing glistening sunlight on water.*" The patch of sunlight was in the exact spot where the butterfly had flip-flopped for us. I zoomed in and immediately saw a face—Gina's face.

How had this happened? Only God controls the sunlight shining through the trees. (see next page)

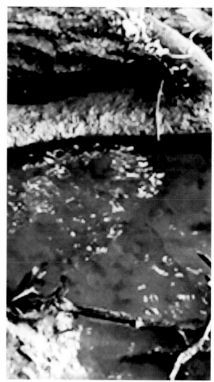

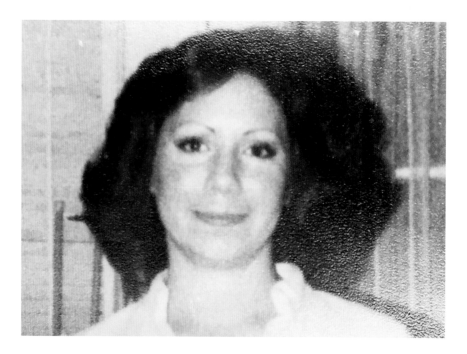

CHAPTER 9

ANGEL OF THE MORNING

All I ask of you, Sis, before you leave me, is to touch my cheek.

After the butterfly day, I would often look at the picture of the glistening water on the river, always seeing Gina's face—her eyes, her nose, her mouth, her hair. Every time, I would cry—tears of gratitude and tears of sadness. I was grateful for the miracle, but saddened because I kept going back to the river, digging with no success. I was undaunted. I so believed she needed me to do something right there in that spot.

Over the next few weeks, I convinced various people to go back to the New River butterfly spot. Some helped me dig; some just watched. My husband bore the brunt of it. Andy's son would even join me one day in digging at that spot. I could see my husband's patience was running out, so my brother came one day. They both no doubt wondered where this new, obsessive Dlana had come from. It all felt very urgent. I could not let it go. I knew that by disturbing the area, the water could move anything that I might uncover—if anything was there to uncover. I would even try to dig up under the tree, but it was nearly impossible. I just kept thinking about the earlier messages. "My head is underwater" *and* "6' down at the river that is where you will begin to pick up the pieces." No one could have convinced me to stop digging. I had seen my sister's face in glistening water on a tiny spot of a vast river.

Why this remote spot on the river? The butterfly could have landed anywhere on that river, but it landed there, near the distorted image of the shoals and in between the orange stakes that guided me back there. If Gina just wanted me to know she was with me, I would not have been guided back to this area. If God only wanted me to experience the miracle of the butterfly and see Gina's face in the water so I would trust and believe, then that could certainly have happened anywhere on the river. A place nearer where I parked my truck every day, not a mile or so upriver, would have been welcomed. I surmised at the time that because only God controls the butterflies and the sunlight that glistened on the water creating the outline of her beautiful face, God must want a truth to be known about this spot. *What?*

One day, while standing in the river in the exact spot of the river dig, I screen-shot my satellite location. A few days later, Sunday morning, I was looking back at my photos while waiting in the parking lot for Andy to join me. I noticed the red location marker was in the middle of what appeared to be the outline of a skull shaped by the trees around the water.

At times, I questioned my own sanity, but my love for my sister was stronger than all else.

I immediately sent Nola the picture on Sunday at 7:33 a.m. with this note:

> There is a skull shape near the shoals. The location where the butterfly landed—the red marker—is surrounded by a skull shape. See in the middle of it. That is where we have been digging, where we are going back to today. I do not know how we are going to dig that mud out, but I will find a way.

The whole time we were searching in Radford, I suffered excruciating headaches. They would start the moment I got off the exit to enter town. I first noticed the difference one day while riding in the car with Andy down Hazel Hollow Road. I actually commented to him, "My head always hurts on this road, and it seems to worsen in different places at different moments."

I asked Nola:

> My head hurts really bad when I get anywhere I know is involved, or am I just thinking about this too much? There is also a constant ringing in my ears. A white noise. Sometimes it comes, stays with me, and then just stops.

I was relieved when he answered that it was normal. He told me it happened to him in the beginning, when he had first "awakened" the fall before. I did not understand what he meant by this. I surmised at first that it must be something different from just opening up to these kind of messages because I knew he said he had always been connected with the spiritual realm since he was a little boy. I could only ascertain that what I was experiencing must have been what it feels like to have the angels touch your life. He advised me not to take pain medication, if I could resist it. I imagined it would do no good anyway because although he said it was normal, I did not feel normal. This was no regular headache. The energy reverberated at a high frequency inside my head. At the time, I stuck with the theory that the headaches were from a connection to the spiritual realm, and the sound energy was intense when I experienced it. Even with the headaches, I was feeling stronger than ever. Always, Nola reminded me, "Trust. Don't doubt. Follow your intuition." That was easier said than done.

Sitting in my truck in the police station parking lot waiting on Andy, I texted Nola:

> Is it only me who can see the face? Can you see it?

Nola assured me:

Yes I can see a face.

Responding in relief, I texted:

Good. I am not crazy. Makes me cry.

Nola replied:

No, you are not, just hard-headed. Don't cry. You need to be strong, as you are.

Sniffling, I replied:

I know. Andy is coming. I have to dry my tears.

Exhausted as I was each night, I would still wake to discover messages written during the night. On July 24, I wrote:

Shoals are not bad LL could be W. Very important the Wall.

The next night I wrote:

The river is low.

Yes, the river probably was low, but it sure did not seem to be low while digging underneath the water. I expected that the water would rise, but I did not expect it would be as high as it would be within a week. I wondered just how low it was, so I looked at the water table records for the New River. December 1980 was one of the lowest on record at 1.36 feet. Earlier in April 1980, it had reached a historic high at 12 feet. Were the islands under the water in June after the high mark in April, but when the river was at its lowest, the islands were exposed? Is that why Epperly went to the bluff when he got out on bail? From the bluff, he could see the butterfly spot. And surely, he would have noticed that the river was low. The banks would have been exposed like I am seeing now. What was he looking for?

The night of July 26, 2016, would be a busy night for messages.

I drew small connected circles, and wrote Raindrops on Water and glistening everywhere.

And these words written over top:

2nd picnic dream

And I wrote this perplexing message on an envelope I must have grabbed from my nightstand in the middle of the night:

Vision of Image in the water. Same place. Drew a picture.

That morning, after looking at the picture I had drawn, I wrote on the corner of the envelope my first thought: *Angel?* And a side note about hav-

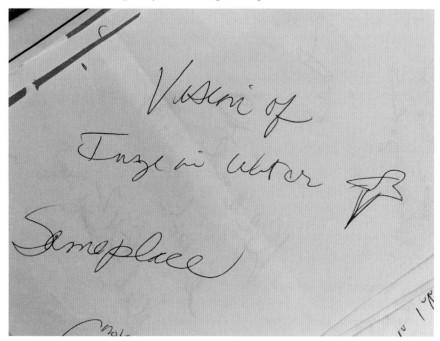

ing seen hundreds of birds the day before while at the river, flying above casting shadows down onto the water. I must have initially thought the symbol I drew that night was an angel or a bird. Later, I would think it looked like a symbol for a compass rose. I had so many initial thoughts about one of the most important messages I would receive.

There are many times when we can look back in our life and see clearly the moments of grace, those times when it seems God is in the details of an event, story, or conversation. This was one of those moments. The good is right there, but also in the background something else is trying to influence our perceptions, so we miss the good, taking a divergent path for a while. These subtle thoughts and urges influence our free will, our destinies, when we choose one path or another. We seldom recognize the power of it all—both the good and the bad. We just have to take the blinders off to notice the powerful influences within our everyday life.

At this point, the path could have gone either way—toward the darkness or toward the light. I was choosing my path—my destiny, my free will. No matter how much I meandered, eventually I would realize that the end result would still be God's plan. But all I knew then was to follow the clues I was getting. What I didn't understand was the spiritual battle I had entered.

As Andy and I walked up the river to dig, he revealed that one psychic had warned him Epperly was connected to the devil—that Epperly had the same ability to connect as gifted people can, but with evil, not God. It was like those movies where the fiddler sells his soul to the devil—the proverbial "deal with the devil"—but I had never fully believed in such ideas. It was one of those conversations that most people just do not have—too uncomfortable, so we just don't talk about it. This story started to worry me. Maybe Epperly—evil—was somehow influencing my thoughts. My mind worked away at this. Could that be? I had just experienced the miracle of my lifetime—seeing my sister's face in the water—yet somehow the darkness was creeping in, trying to make me not believe in what I had just seen. I wasn't going to let that thought get ahold of me.

Totally exhausted after a day at the river, I pulled the car over to rest, even though I only had thirty miles left to drive home. I took this debate to Nola:

> [Andy] says a psychic told him that Epperly has a gift but that it was evil-based. Not good like yours. This made me worry about the messages coming from another place. Yet, I saw her face in the water—the sunlight. Could evil be doing that to me?

> I am so confused. I know you told me some of the messages may not apply and to be careful. These signs in the water and the butterfly are amazing, unreal, and the message: My head is underwater. So very sad, really.

Downhearted, my frustration came through as I continued my text:

> I know that 36 years is a long time, but she is communicating with me now for a reason. I feel a sense of urgency. Now that we have dug there, one flooding could cause her to move, maybe move again. I dug 3-4 feet down where her face was in the water.

> I dug out large, rectangular, shale flat rocks that did not match river rocks. I guess they either slid from above when the tree fell or they were placed there. The flat rocks were all in one area, right where the butterfly landed, lying on top of each other.

The river is actually down in flow about 6 feet. We will not be able to look much longer when the water begins to rise. It was a bigger problem today than yesterday. Hard to dig under water. It is daunting. I really believed I would find her. My head did not hurt there. I dug for six hours straight.

Nola texted back:

Don't despair. Gina's body has been hidden for decades; you have just spent days looking for her. Don't lose your trust and faith. If you feel unprotected, ask for protection. If you feel you need to move to another place, move.

I had to ask Nola again:

Do you see Gina? I see not just a face, but Gina's face—her eyes, lips, hair.

I repeated:

Can you see her or just a face?

He replied:

Yes. I see her now. It is Gina. Nobody better than you to recognize her face.

We continued to debate about the possibilities as my mind searched. Had her body been disposed of here? Or could she have been at Meadow Creek, as the farmer said, the river carrying her here? Nola asked me why I doubted the farmer's story. He said he thought the farmer's story could be true. I thought I was losing my mind. I thought I would continue to debate and debate until I knew what was true. I worried that evil would capture me—that I would think like my sister's killer.

"You can't. Your mind is not like his," was Nola's simple, yet profound response. He kept assuring me that no evil was with me. Nola kept me grounded and focused on what we both believed was the right path. I put the story of evil connections out of my mind.

Nola kept saying to me not to worry about whether the messages were from God. If they were from God, I would know it. He wrote:

God is going to show you it is God.

These would prove to be prophetic words.

I went back up the river to the butterfly spot Saturday, Sunday, Tuesday, Friday, and Saturday again. Soon I was running out of people who would go with me. First, they would entertain the possibility, curious, but when they saw me digging up a river, their support would waver. The only thing that stopped me on Wednesday and Thursday was lightning. The rain came and the river rose. That must be why I wrote "*raindrops on the water.*" This was urgent for me.

After a day of digging in the river, no matter how tired, I headed straight to the shower, scrubbing the back of my legs vigorously, trying to remove what I imagined were microscopic river bugs. My day's experience would vividly fill my mind. Sometimes I surprised even myself at what I could do once I put my mind to it. I am not always a tomboy, still a girly girl at times, and thoughts of encountering bears, rattlers, and copperheads was not my idea of fun. And, the spiders, huge and seemingly everywhere—sighing, *UGH*, I closed my eyes, letting the water rinse away these images. My mind refocused on the beauty of the day—the birds, deer, and butterflies.

On July 30, I had two messages.

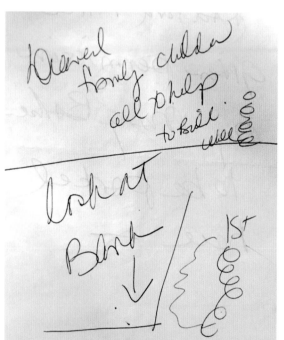

I would write this message, its meaning not understood until two years later. And even then, how can we really know its true meaning.

A dream–a family, children, all helping to build a wall

And, a single word:

EXACTLY

I had dug at the river the day before, so when I saw this word, I first wondered whether I was digging in exactly the right spot. Andy and I had walked on down the river to see the second orange stake and then came back and started digging where we thought the butterfly had landed, before I saw Gina's face in the water that glistens in the photo. Maybe I was not digging in the exact spot.

Why was Gina's face there in the water if I were not meant to dig? What exactly was I looking for—a skull? A body? A weapon? A chain used as weight to hold down a body, the huge, large flat rocks placed on top that I had discovered while digging. Something could be there, or I imagined something could have just moved there and become lodged under this fallen, yet still rooted, alive tree. None of this seemed normal for a riverbed. I know flooding. I have seen it. While living in the Shenandoah Valley, I had helped people whose homes washed off their foundations, walls still intact, floating down the Shenandoah River. Somehow, breaking through was the thought: *How could anything still be here?* Yet, I still dug. I had to try, even though I knew the chances of finding anything—if anything was even there to find—were nearly impossible. I just had to have faith and trust and believe that the butterfly had landed there for a reason.

The last day of July, out of the blue, I had a deep desire to find my study Bible with a sense of urgency. I had not seen it in many years. I looked everywhere. Then I stopped, took a breath, and calmed myself. I thought, *When did I see it last? Where have I put it?* Then, I just knew. I went straight to the bottom of my closet. On a shelf inside a plastic shoe box was my old study Bible. I opened it to the very page where I had placed the last photo I had ever taken of Gina. Both delighted and amazed, I snapped a photo as proof of another providence to show my husband. Gina was sitting on a couch in our new townhouse in Radford, just days— no more than a few weeks and maybe just hours—before she died. She had jeans and a pretty pink shirt on. No makeup, and looking groggy since we had probably just woken up. She still was so naturally beautiful to me. I could see the elegance in her long arms and graceful hands. I had not remembered this particular photo. I did not even know I had placed it in my Bible decades ago. I studied the picture. Behind her was the landing where I had last seen her tap her feet…that ankle bracelet still vivid in my mind. I noted the purple flowers on the table. I had dreamed of a purple flower. I asked myself, *What am I to see here?,* as though it were just another clue. And then my heart would pull me back. A photograph frozen in time. The only picture I actually have of just her. I saw Gina's beauty. I saw her gentleness. I remembered how smart and kind and generous she had been. I saw my sister in every way I could remember in that moment. All of the good and none of the bad, until my head started again. *What am I to see in this picture? I am sure there is a reason I felt the urge to find my Bible—what is it?*

In the photo I had taken of Gina's last picture, I would later see that I had captured the Bible verses exactly on the pages where I had placed it many, many years ago. I had not paid attention to the pages of the Bible where I had found it when I opened it and took this picture out. On the edge of the photo there were just enough words—one line—so that when I searched these words, I could find the exact verse in the Bible. The verse—"how the Lord had shown great mercy to her"—was easy to search. It was Luke 1:58. When I opened my Bible to read this verse, I saw another one right above the left hand corner of the picture:

"For with God, nothing will be impossible." — Luke 1:37

And the purpose powerfully rewarding. I had brought my study Bible out of the bottom of my closet and into my life again. Not right away, but later.

I was beginning to see better the connections between our physical world and the spiritual world. The messages would always come when I needed them most. I have since learned that I can ask for guidance, open my Bible to any spot, and find that it will be relevant to whatever is needed in that moment. The perfect answers. One night just as this book was 99 percent complete, I was upset about a conversation I had had about writing this book and sharing *the journey,* my memoirs. The advice shared with good intentions was that I would be risking everything I had spent my life building by publishing this book. My response was simply that I have faith and if that be the purpose, then that will be what it will be. I believe in my heart I am being obedient to God. But still, that night I prayed for guidance holding my Bible. I opened to a page I had never read. I saw the red words—

"Now the Lord spoke to Paul in the night by a Vision, 'Do not be afraid, but speak, and do not keep silent; for I am with you, and no one will attack you to hurt you....'"

— *Acts 18:9-10*

I also noticed Acts 17:23-33. I know my truth.

The next day, an acquaintance asked me, as he perplexingly shook his head, "Dlana have you been to Africa? I just saw an image of you in my head, peaceful in the grasslands of Africa." I knew I was receiving a clear message not to worry because God was answering my prayer, which will become apparent in the later chapters. And just a few days later, I was told by a lady, "For some reason, I feel I am to tell you to listen to a song by the Collingsworth Family called 'Your Ways are Higher than Mine.' You are going to need to listen to its words every day. I knew then that even after the book was published, I would still have mountains to climb. We truly live in an amazing world!

My daddy was always right. Fellowship is good. It is harder to break ten pencils bundled together than it is to break one. Strength is gained in togetherness of like minds, whether in a traditional church or a fireside group. But I was alone. I had cut off my nose to spite my face when I left my church, but I had also learned a valuable lesson. One verse simply has to be looked at in the context of the entire Bible.

One man's insistence on the interpretation and meaning of one verse from 1 Timothy had caused me more than a decade earlier to leave my regular church. He interpreted that verse as: "You have no voice. Your place is in the kitchen, not teaching." I had taught my fellow Christians' sons and daughters in Sunday school, but my opinion was not needed or respected in a mixed company adult class because I was a woman. I know not all church members behave that way, and I had to be responsible for my actions. But I am a hard-headed woman. My dad was so disappointed in me. My decision broke his heart. I still went back to his church, sitting with my dad on that same wooden pew from my youth, when I visited him. I had left the traditional church. But I had never left God.

I made a choice. I had veered from my path—my purpose. An influenced choice in so many ways. I now can just chalk this one up to one man's need to have power over another, but then, at that moment, that one "thought" won the battle. The truth was twisted. But my spiritual army never gave up on me. God's love was always with me.

So now, instead of one man's interpretation of one verse, telling me a woman has no place or voice, I searched to know of women in the Bible like Deborah, who was a judge and led an army. She showed compassion and became known for her wisdom and courage. Her faith in God provided light to the people she served. Or Ruth, the great-grandmother of King David who taught us to let go of the past through, bravery, faith, and obedience. Or Esther, an advocate who helped preserve the Jewish people, her courage and risk unmatched. And her actions ensured the bloodline of Jesus would be preserved just as God had said: Woman's seed—Jesus—will bruise the enemy's head. She showed incredible bravery to risk her own life to save the lives of other people. Hannah, the mother of Samuel, is an amazing story of faith. She left her son in a temple to serve God all the days of his life; he would become one of the greatest prophets (1 Samuel 1:11). Jesus' mother Mary exemplifies purpose by trusting and obeying God. There are many other women of the Bible who exemplify love and trust in God. Jesus treated women with respect and dignity. He valued women and their role in society. He did not follow the Jewish "rules" to not speak to a woman. Jesus spoke publicly to a Samaritan woman to the surprise of others. His conversation can be found in John 4. This woman went on to be a voice for Jesus in a world where it was a risk for her to speak. All of these women were given a voice. Jesus' example is still not followed in so many cultures today. This injustice brings tears to those in Heaven who see the disparity.

So again I was led on the right path. God is almighty. The devil, evil, the Enemy, the negative force—whatever anyone wants to call it—it's only mighty, not almighty. And at this point, I knew God was present on my journey. I knew then Gina was not alone. She had a spiritual army on her side.

I woke early Monday morning, August 1, to another busy night of messages. Buz and I had a hard day ahead of us in Radford so I glanced at them quickly.

I wrote:

> Could feel prickly sensations tonight a physical feeling noticeable to me like energy moving

And:

> Brochure Va.
> Pain in Heart

Ingles Ferry
Red Door shut and walked to it.

When I first saw these lines, I added this interesting notation at the bottom of the page: *It is evident in the difference in the handwriting of the first three and the last, the last line being different.*

I had written Ingles Ferry over the earlier message of red door…. Each one in the list was circled.

And this dream vision that I could see so clearly, evidently describing exactly what I was seeing:

I drew a chain fence with words "concrete or pole" written above, and chain below. Can see road gravel, maybe concrete (maybe orange tip?) Low to the ground 1-2 feet

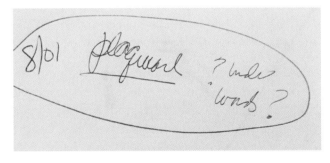

And in a different place, these curious words were written:

Plaquard
Under words?

In this seemingly simple note, I had written "plaquard," not "placard."

Why would this be misspelled? I wondered. I was waking to see words I did not remember writing, but if someone or something were guiding the writing, why would it not be spelled correctly? I am a stickler for correctly spelled words. It appears that I started to write "plac," but then seemed to change to a "qu." Who was in my head? I recalled how many people had told me, "She is whispering…. You are not listening." I guess a whisper could be spelled by me as p l a q u a r d instead of p l a c a r d while in a dream state. Still, this was not my own handwriting—the "p" was so different and "placard" was a word not commonly used by me. When I think of this word, I think of historical information markers along the road.

My initial thought about "Brochure, Va" was: A Virginia travel brochure like "Virginia is for Lovers." And that seems to go with a placard, where words would be like a historical marker. I looked for brochures at the travel rest areas I passed for anything that seemed to be a clue for Radford in a brochure. I focused on Civil War information that might be in print for that part of Virginia, thinking maybe I would see something there.

The red door note was different from the other lines. *He walked to a red door?*

And this dream-like description:

> On a big boat, looking for a lady who I need to talk to. She wanted to go to a different place so went down. I lost her. Followed? SURD?? (scared) down into the boat. Passed by people I knew **** [Here I named a person I had not seen or even thought of since High School], and Mama Joan. When got there no longer in a boat but in my office. Deep in the bottom of boat and these two women needed to see me. Rough women. Smoking. Asked to put out cigarette-she proceeded to put cigarette out on my thigh and burned me. Then they both started beating me up. Could not get to phone or Buz.

There was no logical reason why I would dream about these rough women or this person from my long ago high school days. Nothing had happened in my life, or in the passing of my day, to cause this kind of dream, or for me to see that vision of a single chain fence with concrete poles so clearly. No fences were down at the river. And now it seemed I was a character in the dream. And the image of those rough women would not leave me for days, seeing them, clearly in my mind.

My mind thought the worst, knowing of Gina's scarring on her thigh from her childhood burns. People can be cruel.

Looking back, this dream may have been the first clue about who else was at the lake house. In 1980, I never believed the "willingly" part of the composed story, but I never once questioned Gina not being alone with Epperly. I never really questioned what was found inside my car because I did not know in 1980 all of the details of what was there. Hence, I never even thought about anyone besides Epperly being in the car with my sister. I never thought about others being at the lake house before 4 a.m. when Skipper and his female guest stated they had arrived. I always imagined Epperly took Gina from the Marriott parking lot or did not let her leave *if* she dropped him off at the lake house. Knowing about the broken car door handle further validated my theory that my sister never went willingly. But a party at the lake house was nowhere on my radar in 1980.

I found and visited with Skipper's female guest, still genuinely grateful she had not arrived at the lake house any earlier than 4:00 a.m. She felt she could have been murdered also and considered herself blessed that she was still alive today, having survived that night. She did not learn until days later what had happened there at the lake house moments before she arrived. This witness was sequestered for the trial to testify to what she says is an image she will never forget. She added, "I only saw him [Epperly] once again after that night when I first saw him wiping himself with the blue towel—something I will never forget seeing." She described that moment as being frozen into her mind forever. She had to walk by him as she entered the courtroom, and her voice still quivered as she shared with me, "Epperly looked right at me, and I read his exaggerated lips, 'You Are Dead.'"

Another timeline question arose when I learned about the bass fishermen story: Two bass fishermen reported in 1980 that they heard a boat start up, go out to the center of the lake near the top of the dam, and then stop. The boat then started up again, and returned to the lake house. Other witnesses stated the same. But the bass fishermen held the rest of their story secret for decades. Andy believed the bass fishermen's story when one of the two recently came forward and shared the rest of what he had witnessed that night. My Monte Carlo pulled out in front of them from the side lake house road onto Claytor Dam Road no later than 3:00 a.m. On their motorcycle, with a big bass strapped to the back, they followed the slow driver who never turned until Hazel Hollow Road.

The facts I was discovering from the police reports and interviews, the miraculous no-coincidence experiences, and 20/20 hindsight gave clarity, revealing a viable theory. The lake house party was starting to come to light for me, but I was yet to fully see what I was to see.

For decades, I had never tried to reconcile anything. My role was to keep Epperly in prison, working every parole hearing with the same diligent effort for my family's protection. And for decades, I had never forgotten about Dorothy Allison. I never could mentally grasp how Dorothy Allison could give us visions, or how when Buz and I had followed a straight line on the map from my car to the Ingles Monument, it had crossed over Epperly's house, and now Andy had extended the line and it had landed at the lake house. I was curious. What else would that line cross? So now, thirty-six years later, I was piecing together a map with all I knew. When

I traced that perfectly straight line on the map, I realized the line crossed the New River exactly at the same spot where the butterfly had landed. Exactly where I had seen Gina's face. Nothing is impossible for God and his spiritual army.

DOROTHY ALLISON — 1980 LINE EXTENDS TO CROSS THE RIVER AT THE BUTTERFLY SPOT

The car - under the Trestle; Epperly's house second ave and Wirt street (man symbol) ; the monument- cemetery; the star - the place on the river where the butterfly landed. The house - lake house. Draw an imaginary line from my car, over Epperly's house, through the cemetery, across the islands and to the dig spot near the shoals on the river. A straight line.

CHAPTER 10

SOMETHING BETTER

No wall is too tall to look for you. We will find you.

W e spent all day Monday, August 1, probing holes with metal rebars in as many places as possible. We poked thousands of holes in the riverbanks, all of the banks around the islands, up on the islands, and the entire walk by the river's edge to the area where we had seen the butterfly and I had seen Gina's face in the picture. I thought digging a big hole in a river was hard. It was nothing compared to how tired I was after this grueling day. Andy and I enlisted others to help. I brought along several people I knew could handle the terrain. Fortunately, there were still good people who were willing to help. Andy's psychic friend from the Dedmon Center dig—the one I call The Preacher—joined us. As we poked holes, I got to know him. I listened as he recapped detail by detail the images he'd had of my sister. He was conscientious about my feelings, knowing some of what he shared was hard for me to hear.

While at the butterfly spot, I climbed up the fallen tree to the flat area above, up off of the bank, to probe holes. Remnants of an old trash dump were clearly visible. I looked up to the sky, to the top of the cliff wall, imagining the dumping site. Could this steep, rock cliff face I was now seeing up close be the "wall" from an earlier message? This day my husband would be the hero. I just did not know it yet.

That night, too tired to drive home, I stayed in the area. Buz caught a ride home with my brother, neither of them planning to return for the big job slated for the next day—the cadaver dogs—the reason we were making all of these holes. After probing all day with a metal rebar, my hands were bruised and blistered. Exhausted, but starving, I went to dinner, plopping down at the table, lazily placing my good purse up on the top instead of in the chair beside me. A few minutes later, the handle flopped over on a lit candle and caught fire. The waiter hopped to quench the fire, but I had already smothered it out with my cloth napkin. I could not even hold my fork that night to eat, so I just used my hands. I bet the staff really questioned who had walked into their restaurant! A little laughter is good for the soul. I am starting to wonder who else laughs with me.

Andy had arranged for a full search day. The plan was to have three teams of dogs to cover the vast area, but an emergency search for a lost autistic child in another part of Virginia became top priority, as it should. Two of the teams went there to help, one planning to rejoin us by late afternoon if all went well. I can only hope that the child was found alive since the afternoon team did join us. Rascal and his two handlers arrived early that morning. I had high hopes for the butterfly area of the New River. The islands were important to Andy. I concluded by now that the island just got me to the river, and the river got me to the orange stakes, and they led me to the butterfly spot, like breadcrumbs leading the way.

This was my first experience watching the work of cadaver dogs. As the day progressed, we really had no significant actions by the dogs to note. The dogs were working hard, and I was, too. My hands were definitely not accustomed to pushing a three-foot metal rebar into a hard summer ground as deep as it would go. By late afternoon, I started sitting on my T-shaped rebar, letting my body weight do the work. The dogs were getting tired, too, but we still had not made it to the butterfly area up river. I pleaded with Andy to see if he could make it happen. Because we had already prepared that area, poking holes the day before, Andy arranged for a boat to meet us at the landing to bring one of the dogs, Rascal, down river to the butterfly spot, avoiding the long, difficult walk up river.

At the butterfly spot, the dog sniffed all around the tall mound of dirt piled from my river digging. Right before we were to leave the area to go back upriver, I asked if the handler would take Rascal one more place—up on the hill above the fallen tree to the dump site. Up there, the dog laid down in a spot two times—in an area directly above the tree that had fallen over.

The handler then took the dog back down to the river spot, circled, and took him back up to see what he would do. He laid down again and even scratched. This was approximately six feet from the riverbank's edge where the tree had fallen into the river. The handlers were not sure by the way Rascal had laid down that it was significant enough to warrant digging. They surmised Rascal may have just been tired from the long, hot day and was acting out, wanting to please his handler. So they called and had a second handler and the fresher dog that had just arrived to be ready at the boat landing. The boat was on its way back to get them.

While we waited for the second dog, I probed more holes, moving a lot of the small rotten trees out of the way. The second dog also did not pick up anything down by the river where I had dug. But up top, the dog did pick up where I had moved a small, *light rectangular rotten log* while probing more fresh holes as we waited. He showed interest there. It was about twelve feet from the other dog's spot. We did not dig because they said it was only a slight interest by the dogs, not an enthusiastic interest. I thought to myself, *But what if it is just a small body part—not a whole body? Or could this be where her body landed, dumped off of the high cliff above? And later, he crossed the shoals, with his tools to bury her at the old dump site.*

As we loaded the second dog back into the boat to leave, I felt quite saddened that we were leaving. The boat was pulled ashore up river about sixty feet from the fallen tree, near where the second orange stake was. As I sat there in the boat, looking back down river at that fallen tree in the water, I saw the biggest spider I have ever seen in my life. Seeing a spider as big as a baseball, on the same tree I had just straddled so many times in the prior weeks, was quite disturbing. We pulled away, heading up river toward the opposite shore, the river higher than it had been, but still low for a motorized boat. All I knew as we left is that I would be back very soon to dig where that dog had laid down up above at the old dump site... just in case.

Andy still wanted to make sure we made it over to Meadow Creek before the dogs left. The first time Andy had taken me there, I had felt overwhelmed with sadness—a normal emotional reaction from having just heard the farmer's story. But today, as we arrived, I became physically ill. I sat on the concrete edge of the new bridge, looking at the old abutments and wondering what it had looked like in 1980. I imagined how one could easily back a van down to the creek edge. The dogs covered a lot of Meadow Creek, but to no avail. The handlers could see the disappointment in my face. They reassured Andy and me that they could always come back and try again. "The area is vast," they said. "There is a lot of ground for the dogs to cover."

Bones can be recovered decades later and analyzed. What I had not told the dog team was that we suspected the search could be for even smaller fragments—if the farmer's story were true.

On my drive home from that long day, I decided it was time to call Mama Joan and confide what had been happening.

"Dlana, you are not giving anyone money, are you?" she asked.

I was sure she was wondering about Nola.

"Of course not," I said. "The only money I've spent has been on gas, hotel rooms, and…oh, yeah, a metal detector I used at the river spot. I plan to buy a GPS tracker. But that's it."

Nola wasn't like that. He had previously told me he never wanted to use his gift for financial gain, saying:

> About making money with my gift, if you find her, I don't want to be recognized for that, not even my name. I will live with my happiness to be helpful with the gift God gave me; that is enough for me. Peace makes me happier than anything. Money is just paper compared with that satisfaction.
>
> God will compensate me his way if He wants to.
>
> My gift will improve and bring more gifts to me to develop to keep helping people and be in peace with myself. Gina connected to me for a good reason. Because she knows my intentions.

Did I have peace like Nola? Not yet. And, in a moment of clarity, I was starting to see a purpose: to save my spiritual life. That was all my dad wanted for me. I had asked Daddy when he was dying, once he got to wherever, to somehow please let me know what I needed to know so I could better understand everything I had started to question. I wonder if he heard me. I am sure God heard me. Maybe my dad is still praying to God for my soul and God hears my dad.

I shared with Nola my excitement in realizing the power of it all:

God is all knowing and all powerful. He can make the butterfly land
in the water and He can make the image of Gina's face appear in the
sunlit glistening water.

Nola's humble response:

That's Him.

There was such peace in knowing this.

On August 4, 2016, a melody woke me from a dead sleep. I recognized it
as Bonnie Tyler's "Holding Out for a Hero." I was singing the chorus when
I opened my eyes.

The lyrics really caught my attention, although I was not really sure what
the song's meaning to me would be until a few days later.

And the next night, August 5, would be another busy night.

One line written: 3-4 snakes under bush beside the water.

A song waking me from my sleep, a melody I recognized—the lyrics from
"Boys 'Round Here" by Blake Shelton. A note written: The song in my
head after the snake dream.

Another would say: Nature - following sounds like a recording.

And then on a separate small sticky note, one word: BOG.

And another note, Orange (cone) (overwater) written exactly like that.

And in the morning hours, another melody woke me, except this time
I did not know the distinct melody in my head. A message was written
sometime before awaking to that unknown melody:

Angel in the Morning

I did not connect these words to the melody of the song playing in my
head.

The melody echoed in my mind. My best friend Barb was visiting me for
her birthday so I kept humming the melody until we could figure it out.
My friend has a repertoire of music in her head, so she recognized it immediately, even coming from a tone deaf hummer like me. As she played
the song, it was the same as I had heard, and its title almost matching the

words written earlier, before I woke. Did I hear a whisper incorrectly? I must have heard "of," but written "in" because after reading the lyrics of "Angel of the Morning," I knew that song was a clear message. My emotions swelled.

The lyrics of the melody I had heard in my head broke my heart. With tears in my eyes, I belligerently spoke to the sky. "No, we are not quitting. I am not stopping. We have started this, and we are going to finish it." That was my attitude, right or wrong. I felt I had no choice. I see now—I am hard headed.

My best friend and I decided after I had a good cry that we both deserved a delicious cheeseburger and an old-fashioned milkshake in honor of her birthday. And a big dessert that we would share!

Saturday, August 6, would be my last day down by the river. Of course, I wanted to go right back to dig the spot at the dump site where the cadaver

dog had laid down and scratched earlier in the week. I pulled out all the stops to get Buz to go back to the river to help me. And it would be a day I was so glad he was with me.

I did not know this would be my last walk to the butterfly spot. Many signs could have stopped me from returning—the enormous spider, the snake dream, the rising river. Walking through the woods, up the riverbanks, through the river—it was a place that had become quite familiar. But this time, the familiar path had changed. The river was rising, so the butterfly spot was much more difficult to access on foot. While forging through a different area of brush, I stepped on a particularly fierce nest of yellow jackets. I received several stings, but they were not harmful enough to make me stop. While digging at the dump site up on the hill above the fallen tree, Buz and I were not getting anywhere. We dug a hole 2-3 feet deep—wide enough for me to stand in right at the spot the dog had scratched. I removed every tiny rock, carefully inspecting everything that came out of that hole. I would take a break and look up, wondering what was up on top of the rock cliff *wall* that bordered this area. It appeared that many years ago, people had dumped trash from up there to here below, so I wondered, *Is there a road?*

Dead trees were everywhere. I kept moving dead trees, digging underneath them like in my rectangle dream—light, soft rectangles with purple weed flowers. Buz kept talking about erosion, saying that after this many years, the landscape near the riverbank would have changed dramatically. I recalled having read that the highest crest was thirty-six feet in 1940. That flooding would certainly change the landscape.

In 2015, the second day I had met Nola at the food court, he had shared with me a dream he'd had about my husband and me the night after he'd first met me. The dream had three parts: Water, dead trees, and erosion. Now, I was experiencing all three of those with Buz at this digging site. In Nola's dream, I was standing on a balcony, looking out across a large body of roaring water like a creek or a river to the forest on the other side. I was sad and worried because all of the trees were dying and I could not understand why. Nola said my husband could not see the trees in the forest across the creek dying because he was focusing only on the water eroding the banks and could not see past it to the other side.

I had wondered when Nola first shared this dream with me what it could possibly signify. Dreams can be interpreted in so many ways from so many different points of view. I never would have imagined then that one year later I would be back to Pulaski County digging and searching again. Did Nola know? Or was he just the messenger? What did he see or know the night he met me? And that dream he had was about this day a year later. *How can that be—it's like a plan?* There seemed to be a predestined plan for my life that others were playing a role in.

So maybe Gina was buried up above the butterfly spot, but because of the erosion, part of her had washed down into the water, or maybe there were several smaller spots and only her skull had moved or slid into the water when the tree fell. Or maybe this dump site could be a graveyard marked by two orange stakes placed deep in the river's edge. I wondered, *Can the orange stakes be seen from the bluff? Yes, I am sure this area could be easily seen maybe with a naked eye, definitely with binoculars. I wondered what anomalies that radar-detecting machine might find here.*

On the walk back out, downriver after digging at the trash dump site where the dog had laid down, I again tangled with another vicious insect—a hornet's nest. They dive-bombed me from every side. Some got stuck inside my clothes as I ran. I was stung all over—at least ten stings. Someone wanted me out of the woods!

After getting stung twice by insects, Buz reminded me of the time he and our youngest son were bushwhacking a new hiking trail on the Clinch Mountain. All Buz knew was that his linebacker of a son was barreling toward him, sending Buz airborne. Our son had stepped on a gigantic hornet's nest. We laughed about that. Buz was sure I, too, could have elicited linebacker skills had he been walking in front of me this day. I kept calling my attackers "bees." Buz said they were insects. I called them all "bees" even though I knew they were not the same. We laughed. He jokingly said, "You don't have a word bone in your entire body," meaning I do tend to be a lazy talker when it comes to my use of words. I grew up calling them all "bees." Then Buz mentioned something I wanted to know more about— the cliff wall. "On the day when we probed holes," he said, "I climbed up the cliff wall. I was curious where it went."

That would have been a hard climb freehanded, so I fussed because he could have fallen.

"Yeah, if something had happened to me up there, no one would have found me because no one really knew that I had climbed up there."

In my head, I heard, "If I had been stung by a bee up there, no one would have ever found me." Bee. Buzzz. Buz. *Buz was the hero. What is up that cliff wall?* It would not be until a few days later that I figured out the significance of those insects as other "bee" stories would arise.

On Sunday, I invited the family back for a second summer picnic. We were not down in the yard for very long before thousands of sweat bees swarmed the yard. Yes—thousands. I am not exaggerating. They were even on the doors of my home. The croquet game in the backyard was the most entertaining. Mama Joan is serious when it comes to her croquet skills, and she was intent on beating her granddaughters, but those little bees were getting in the way of our game. Finally, we all just had to quit. I had never seen a single sweat bee around my house. I rarely had seen one since I had been a little girl. This was becoming a "bee" weekend for sure.

Monday afternoon, August 8, I went back to Pulaski County Courthouse to look at old maps on my way to Richmond, planning a stop at RPD (Radford Police Department) for a day of case file reading. I needed to slow down, back up and punt and start trying to figure out what all was happening. What I had discovered in my research was a bit overwhelming. Gathering the facts takes effort. Truth reveals itself effortlessly. After the long day at RPD, I made myself take a mental break. A night at my honeymoon hotel again seemed a perfect plan. On my drive to the Hotel Roanoke, good memories of my honeymoon filled my mind.

Buz and I had eloped. Spontaneously. That morning, March 14, 1981, as we left northern Virginia, we had not even an idea where we would get married. In January 1981, I had bought a wedding gown, and we were preparing invitations for a June 1981 wedding. In early March 1981, I learned that I had been pregnant for at least a month. My dad had already offered us money to skip the June wedding entirely; he knew it would be difficult to connect families from two opposite sides of Virginia. I should have taken it. Instead, I have a wedding dress hanging in my basement with the price tag still attached!

Buz was finishing his last month of college, when all of a sudden, I was waking in the mornings, sick to my stomach. I could not stand the smells from breakfast being cooked. In the mornings, I would crawl from my bed to my bathtub and continue to sleep while the tub would fill with water. I was exhausted, and I did not know why. My stepmom did. A sure sign to her was when I walked into the kitchen and turned green at the smell of bacon. She quickly made a doctor's appointment for me, but the blood test said I was not pregnant. Relief!

However, I had a second appointment in Kingsport, Tennessee. The person who did my ultrasound told me, "There's nothing wrong with you. You are just pregnant."

To hear this news at age twenty-one was a little tougher than I expected. Just nine months earlier, my sister had been murdered. Only a few months had passed since Epperly had been convicted. An appeal had already been filed before we even left the courthouse. As I drove the mountain roads back home from the doctor, I trembled to think how I was going to tell my dad. For a brief moment, driving off the mountain seemed to be a better choice than facing him. In that very moment, I made my choice—a choice to become the best mom I could be.

When I got home, I told my dad. He smiled ever so slightly. He nodded his head in the endearing way only my dad could do. He was going to have a grandchild. Next, I called Buz, whose only response was, "Just make me a boy!" And I did.

Next, I headed to northern Virginia so Buz and I could break the news to his parents. Buz's parents graciously received their new daughter-in-law to be. I never once felt like an outsider to my new family. They welcomed me with open arms. His mother had actually been born in SWVA. Ironically, her dad moved her and her two sisters when they were teens away from SWVA in hopes they would not marry coal miners. And now her son had married an SWVA girl from coal country. Life is always interesting! Before we left, Buz's mom took what would become our wedding day photos with her small 110 camera. We waved our goodbyes as we left, eloping to who knows where with no plans.

So we drove down Interstate 81 looking for a small church in which to be married. I spotted it off in the distance from the highway near Staunton, a quaint country church with a bell chapel. When we drove up to ask if someone could marry us, the pastor was someone Buz had known from his youth. What were the chances of that?

After the ceremony, we decided to stay at Hotel Roanoke for a one-night honeymoon. For our honeymoon dinner, we went to the mall and bought two baby books, one on infant care, the other on baby names.

Entering the lobby of Hotel Roanoke again, the memories fresh in my mind, I had to laugh remembering a honeymoon spent reading about how to change a diaper. For just a few moments, those abundant memories erased my exhaustion and my preoccupation with my hunt for Gina's body and my quest for truth.

After the chance meeting with Nola, I had retrieved those old photos Mom had taken and placed them in my office so I could see them every day. The day in New Orleans when we tried to decipher his dream's meaning, Nola had reminded me always to remember the first spark that brought Buz and me together in the first place, contemplating if the erosion dream could signify our long marriage.

That night, my mind kept wandering, thinking about those thousands of bees and getting stung twice by the yellow jackets and the hornets. I decided it was time to ask for guidance as Nola would do. I prayed that I might understand what was up with all of the bees.

The next day, my mind wandering off. I remembered a story that warmed my heart. When I was in college, I would call Buz "Buzzy Bee." I would draw flowers with a bee flying above. This was my signature line in every letter I would send to him. Gina knew this. I had not thought of this for years. I doodled as I did when I was just seventeen. I smiled, my heart listening.

But that did not last. My mind was back on the search. The hero song lyrics from an earlier song message came back into my mind: Buz was up where the mountains meet the heavens on top of the high cliff. Buz was up there…he was the hero, the superman climbing that wall. The cliff wall bordering the old dump site where the dog had laid down up above the tree where a butterfly had landed, showing us the spot where my sister's face glistened in the water, a place where nature—the shoals—had showed us the way. Was I being directed up there? What was up above that cliff area?

But later, my mind would take off in a new direction, remembering that Andy had told me that Skipper had just come back to the area, living part-time in Radford to help take care of his mother. I thought of the line in the song "Holding Out for a Hero": I wondered, should his approach stir the fire in my blood. Is that how Gina felt? Daddy? Or, just my mind misinterpreting the song lyrics. I like my first thoughts—Buzzy Bee.

While in Richmond, I was having dinner outside at a rooftop restaurant with some friends. As I was telling them about my crazy bee weekend, a huge long black bee landed on my right arm. It was over an inch long. My friends just looked at me. How could I just sit there with a bee on my arm? They had no idea what I had been doing. That little bee was nothing!

The next night, Wednesday, August 10, while still in Richmond, staying in a historic hotel, I experienced something I had never experienced. A dream in a dream:

A Bad Nightmare

While asleep, I dreamed that I closed my eyes, and as I was falling asleep, I saw glistening water everywhere, so I smiled and knew all was what I thought. Then I saw all kinds of scenes flashing by quickly—a fountain with fish swimming in it, a large house—a stone brick mansion. Birds, ducks, snakes, bees, spiders.

I want to write down all of these I see… It was crazy—a lot was coming at me; then my shoes were coming out and I put them on the table, and it was storming-wind, black skies, thunder, lightning. Bad storm in my room, scary all around me. I was shaking, so I called my friend to help me-to see if she was here and if I could get her to come and see. Leaves and sticks and a mess were everywhere in my room. Then my shoes were lined up on the table. Then two men in wheelchairs (construction workers I had seen at the hotel but handicapped men in my dream) came into my room. They went into the closet and got their sweatshirts out and left. Now my shoes were lying on the side of the table, not under it. Others came in and out, but no one saw the mess. The pieces of nature were all in my room.

I was so scared! I knew Gina was trying to tell me something. I could see her. She was there. Daddy was sitting off to the side in gray clothes and wearing black glasses. He was skinnier. He looked up and asked, "What are you doing?" I told him I was looking for Gina. Daddy said, "Why now?" He sounded like he did not think I should be doing it right now. He said, "I never did." He just looked down and shook his head.

The flying animals were flying at me. The snakes were chasing me. The spiders were everywhere I turned. The ducks, birds-everything-seemed crazy except for the fish in the shallow water fountain. It was as though God was telling me all was going to be okay. I sat and cried and went back to sleep. But I was asleep.

All in a dream within a dream. I dreamed that I was in a nightmare dream.

In my dream, my dad was dressed in older era clothes. A gray Members Only 1980-style jacket from long past. Big glasses, not wire rims like he wore in the 1980s. I saw black thick plastic glasses, like when I was a little girl. This was the first time Gina was in one of my dreams. I could see her. I had never had a dream in a dream before. I did not even understand how you could dream that you were dreaming in your dream.

The next day, after my dream, I received this shocking note from Nola:

> Got message. Dad feels sorry about you because you still want to find her, and he shakes his head once more telling you hard-head. Don't take it wrong, please. It is what is sent to me.

Unbelievable. His timing undeniable. How did Nola see the same thing I had seen the night before in my dream? And yes, my dad had loved to jokingly call me a hard head. And, it seems, so did Nola. But how could he have known what I had dreamed? Or did he see my dad as I saw my dad—in my dream? Was my dad shaking his head because he was clearly upset with my current narrow focus of searching relentlessly, or was he shaking his head because he could see the battle I could not see yet? Were *they* watching us from the grandstands of heaven? Was my dad there for my safety, disapproving but still being a dad? And most confusing, how did Nola know? Was Nola connected to the same conscious field I was connected to, at the same time? Shaking his head would certainly be what my dad would do if he were disappointed in me, yet sometimes, he would shake his head in endearment of whatever I was doing. It was his way of showing he loved me. Nola could not have known this about my dad. How could Nola see the same as I did? It was as if we were all connected with each other within a realm of consciousness.

I wondered, *Can my deceased loved ones watch and see what goes on in our lives?* I had never really thought so. *Why would they need to if they are in heaven?* Where was the information *really* coming from? Did it always come from the same place—a good place?

After this, I began contemplating what I was experiencing. Could this have come from a dark force? Why would my dad show guilt in heaven? Was it guilt or only how I interpreted his actions? "I never did" was clear. I knew my dad and did not believe he would have ever said that to me. It was a lie. He had looked. We all had. Could it be interference? Could it come from both places, good and bad simultaneously? Could there be influence on our lives from the spiritual realm through a conscious realm within us? Was there a part of us through which influence can occur? Are our minds constantly influenced by powers ever present, unknown to us in our daily lives?

We are not just physical bodies with brains. And our spirit and our soul are not the same. They all should be guarded. Proverbs 4:23 says, "*Above all else, guard your heart, for everything you do flows from it.*"

Is this where we connect with God? Is *your heart* being referenced to guard the spirit within us—the heart of our soul? Could consciousness be our soul? Could this be the part of us that can live forever? Guard your heart—your soul.

Listen to your heart, not your head!

I was starting to learn we cannot believe everything we think because we do not have control of all our thoughts. Only now I was realizing that many of our thoughts are not only influenced by others, but also there is a spiritual influence.

I believe the heart of my soul is where I connect to God. And it is through this relationship, just as a father loves a child, that my spirit seems to awaken my soul to remember the truth it already knew.

> *"You shall love the Lord your God with all of your heart*
> *and with all of your soul and with all of your might."*
>
> — Deuteronomy 6:5

As I was walking out of my hotel room, I noticed the art hanging on the wall. The picture showed a scene that looked exactly like the river where I had been digging. *Really?* This picture so eerily reminded me of the daunting tasks of the last few weeks of my life. It even had the tree limbs in the water like the river spot covered by rising water. I thought, *Yes, the river is high now.* And then I would see someone standing in the river in the picture, and I would think of the shoals and how they could have easily been walked by Epperly in the early morning hours from his home when he so calculatingly disposed of my sister's body. I would be saddened for just a moment with the thoughts that maybe I had been missing the messages all along. I would calmly remember: *One step at a time; you are doing all that you can do.*

I had received a text from my good friend Barb: *A song, The Prayer by Celine Dion. Somehow, I just know you are to listen to this song.*

I needed to put on my happy face and go to the final presentation before finally heading back home.

I simply had to know more. That nightmare was too real. But I trembled at the thought. I asked Nola to pray for me. What he said would take hold in me and change me irrevocably.

> Get used to praying for yourself. Of course I am going to pray, but God always listens to everybody, no matter who that person is.
>
> I know you do it unintentionally, but asking somebody to pray for

you, deep inside, it means a lack of faith. You do not *really believe*
that just one prayer by yourself…is enough to make God help you.

I did believe that when I talked to God, he listened. In my belief system, I
knew we did not need a priest or someone else to intercede. But Nola was
showing me more.

Talk to Him like you are talking to me. Make a conversation. You
will hear him, too.

I know now that this August nightmare had been an attempt to bring fear
into my life—to make me be afraid so I would stop. And had I quit, we
would not have what happened next. It was a battle—plain and simple. A
battle I never even realized existed before *the journey*.

Nola reassured me I could ask for God's protection.

Nola told me God would send his angels to protect me.

After hearing that, I knew I could go forward.

And I remembered Nola's words of wisdom: ***He is going to show you it's Him.***

ABSOLUTELY NOTHING IS IMPOSSIBLE—
SEEING IS BELIEVING!

CHAPTER 11

IF

I am in a good place. I see no reason to bring me home.

A meeting was arranged with the current owners of the historic Ingles Farm on Route 611. We had searched that property extensively in 1980. The old farm runs on both sides of the river—covering a lot of acreage. The current owners had graciously given me permission to park at the historic ferry site on the Pulaski County side when I came to the river to dig. Andy and I had a list of specific questions we wanted to ask. I was most interested in locating a graveyard on the property, triggered by the 1980 Dorothy Allison notes. I had already researched several old maps looking for the forgotten "antique" cemeteries, sure one must be somewhere on this historic property.

As we entered the property, passing the old tavern, I realized I had been there once before, in 1980. A memory flooded over me, crawling on my hands and knees through the brush, knocking spiderwebs out of the way, searching for my sister's hidden resting place. We had come to the same place, the end of Wilderness Road on the old Ingles Farm, where my friends had discovered disturbed ground—perhaps a freshly dug grave—the first thoughts in 1980. Entering the old barn on the property, I had screamed, receiving the shock of my life—a six-foot-long snake hanging from the rafters. One more of my haunting memories of the summer of 1980.

Today, the owner confirmed that in the area near the far property border between the New River and Hazel Hollow Road was an old graveyard—a slave graveyard from long past with no markers. My thoughts from with-in sadden me. The owner drew us a map and said we would know when we had found it because *there would be a placard* marking it. That was a last-minute thought he added at the end of his instructions. I just looked at Andy. Placard had been one of my earlier messages. I decided right then I would be back tomorrow to find that graveyard.

Our questions about the graveyard prompted the owners to recall that three Virginia state policemen had come down from an eastern Virginia headquarters about nine years ago to check out a lead that an Ohio psy-chic had called in. The area they were interested in, where the owner had taken them, was in this same area. That they had driven all the way to Radford was a sign that they had given this psychic some credence. Andy was surprised. He shared that he had not seen this information in Gina's file. At this point, I was starting to realize that every day, every encounter, could tell us something we needed to know. I was always to be listening.

The Ohio psychic claimed Gina was buried in a dry creek bed that some-times has water and sometimes not, right where the "S" curves are located on Hazel Hollow Road. *Sometimes water, sometimes not,* just as Nola and his friend had said. The three policemen came and looked, but that was all—no cadaver dogs, just looking.

Why are there so many stories over all these years? Why so many random places? I started to wonder if the clues were adding up to a scenario in which there were other murder victims. I was starting to believe I was to find more truth—justice for other fractured souls—maybe connected to Epperly, maybe not.

When I asked these questions of Andy, he would point out, "The clues may not be about where we end up, but about leading us to where we are to end up next."

On and on it went. I just kept seeing that beautiful butterfly, Gina's face in the water, and the thousand bees.

After meeting with the couple at Ingles Farm, the next morning, Friday, August 12, Andy and I planned to go to the "S" curves and find that slave graveyard. Andy brought along Kevin, a volunteer who often helps him. I brought my brother. From where we had parked, the four of us walked to the top of this wooded area, following the owner's hand-drawn map, searching for the slave graveyard. On the way up, to the right, was a dry creek bed in a deep gully that caught the strong current of rainwater from the top of the mountain. I was curious what was at the bottom of this ravine. Reaching the top were flat fields of tall grass, which meant snakes. My anxiety calmed when Kevin said to me, "I feel such an amazing good presence." I felt his genuineness, and it gave me comfort, even though I found myself in the woods, again, searching for my sister's grave. I know now that this man really did feel the presence of angels. And he believed he felt Gina's presence.

Entering the slave graveyard was like entering the centuries of our past. It appeared that it was common in those days to bury the dead and cover the mound with rocks. If no one had walked there in 1980, a grave would have certainly just covered over in a very short time and blended right in. I remembered Dorothy Allison had said we would find Gina's body "covered with rocks," but how would anyone ever know who was buried where at this point? There were only remnants of graves. Rocks once placed on top of the mounds were now scattered about. No markers or headstones remained to tell us of the dead's past. Bodies need to be left to rest in peace, but Andy told me they cannot rest if they die traumatically like Gina had. *Can they rest if they die a violent death?* I wondered, but then I remembered that Nola had said, "Gina is in a good place. She is pure love."

It was easy to see how these lands connected together along the river. Epperly had been a record-setting track athlete, someone who could have easily run through these woods undetected. One witness had seen him at 5 a.m. Sunday in the Thrifty Center parking lot. His mother had seen him in the front yard as she went to church at 9:30 a.m., and at noon for a quick lunch, and again that afternoon at 4:30 p.m. A hunter friend had told the police that Epperly knew the woods "like the back of his hand." Epperly had been an avid hunter; it was known in 1980 that he hunted on the Dalton farm right across Hazel Hollow Road.

This place—the one I would come to call the muck place—was close to the location where in 1980 we had found the contents of a clutch wallet my sister and I had shared. All the contents of the wallet, including her checkbook and identifications, photos of my spring class of first graders, Gina's blood donor card that showed O positive, and other miscellaneous pieces had been neatly stacked and *placed* together, partially covered with some dirt, and set under a pile of brush and trash. This muck place area was about two miles from my abandoned car and a mile from where we had found our important papers from the wallet. Gina's bloody clothes were also found stacked, *placed* together at another location across the river, not even a mile from the abandoned car. All were miles away from the lake house crime scene. It had never made sense then, and it still made no sense now. These items had not been disposed of in a state of chaos. It had all seemed intentional.

This felt like following breadcrumbs—like I was retracing the steps Epperly took.

The four of us walked back down out of the woods to the flat area where we were parked on an old tractor road that I am sure had wound through the woods for many years, even before tractors. All of our faces were red and sweaty because it had been an exhaustingly hot, humid August day. The shade at the bottom felt good as we stood around my Ford F-150 and shared notes of what we had seen up on the hill in the woods. I saw vastness—a million places a body could be well hidden. And as we conversed by my truck, I noticed a large blue butterfly. I just smiled and paid attention to my next thought, my eyes drifting to the area below us.

The deep, rocky, dry creek ravine intrigued me. Shaped like a V, it would fill with water when it rained, roaring down the mountain. At the end of the ravine was a pooling small pond, trickling on into a rocky creek bed that separates Hazel Hollow Road from a sixteen-plus-foot cliff wall. I was paying better attention to those subtle urges that led me closer. I stood for a moment just looking at this alluring place, captivated by the unique landscape.

I had not noticed Andy walking down there. The place had already caught his eye, too. He turned and yelled, "Come on down here!" He pointed to the rocks hanging over the water and added, "It looks just like the Vancou-

ver picture you showed me." Plants jutted out from the rock cliff edge over the water. I drew closer and saw a triangular rock sitting straight up in the murky black pool of water, just like the picture I had drawn on my nightstand writing pad on June 22. I just knew I was somewhere I was supposed to be. The whole place was picturesque—and familiar.

My mind quickly diverted to only seeing the triangular rock as a clue—to dig exactly at this spot. I took photos of the area, knowing I would be back.

Later that night, while resting from the extensive day of searching, I was reflecting on the many places my day had led me. Looking back through the photos, I discovered an absolutely flawless miracle. In my photo, I saw the image in the water beyond any doubt, recognizing that it mirrored the symbol I had sketched on a piece of paper while sleeping, weeks earlier, on July 26—having no clue then as to its true meaning.

The photo captured the perfect light-shadowed images, casting a shape just like the symbol I had drawn. I captured not just one, but two images on top of the water. My very first in-

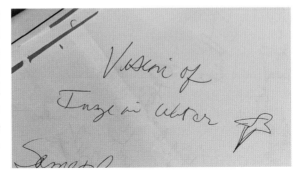

terpretation was that it was a sign—like angels or souls guiding me to this exact place. I reconciled for a brief moment that only God could control nature, so it must be a message directly from God. It must be God's angels.

Then my narrow focus kicked in. One of the images was clearly smaller than the other and shaped as though it could be a child—a little girl in a dress. The most prevalent thought came as I recalled Andy's questioning me about a six-year-old child being with Gina.

As I sifted through my mind, I remembered conversations from Andy about what I call the "flashlight stories." Andy had asked me out of the blue one day if my dad had known a six-year-old who had died. So I asked everyone in my family. My cousin, it turned out, had a story no one in my immediate family had known. When my dad was just a little boy, he and his boy cousins were playing inside a car. They knocked the car out of gear, and it rolled back over my dad's younger girl cousin. She was around five years old when she died, not six. Daddy never shared this heartbreaking story with us.

After I learned this, I asked Andy how he had thought to inquire about a six-year-old girl who had died. He replied that this little girl was "with" my dad and Gina. It came to him when he was asking yes-and-no questions directly to Gina, using the on-and-off flickering of the flashlight as the answers.

So quickly my mind then interpreted this beautiful image as a message trying to tell me there were two victims, not just one. And one was a little girl. The place matched the Vancouver picture and other messages. That bolstered my certainty. This was a place to search—to dig. I would dig, hoping I would find just one small bone fragment. I was digging for proof that would reveal truth. The muck place seemed to be a logical place to dig.

Looking back, I realize now that I had become a spiritual battleground of light and dark. I was not fully seeing the true miraculous message of this image. At first sight, I thought God's sunlight had made the image of two angels so I could see another miracle, trust, and believe. Then my mind steered quickly away with that single thought—a six-year-old little girl. These shared thoughts by others were taking precedence in my mind, influencing my decisions. I landed on this one thought: two victims. It was as though I did not have control of my own thoughts, and as though others' thoughts were influencing my thoughts.

Day after day, I would drive back to the muck place in Radford, in silent thought, asking myself for the full two hours there and the full two hours back, *What if I do find Gina's body? What if I don't? What is the real purpose of all of this? Am I to walk the same paths as I did in 1980? For what reason?*

I didn't know. I just dug.

The muck place had earned its name because of the thick black sludge of rotting leaves infusing the creek. The rotting smell of the black muck nauseated me in the August heat. The dark waters would not reveal what lurked beneath the rippling surface. None of that mattered to me as I kept reaching in carefully, lifting the rocks out and digging in the muck.

No one could have persuaded me not to dig at the muck place right in the spot of the light images on the water. If someone had drawn a cartoon of me, I would have had an angel on one shoulder and a devil on the other. That's how powerful the spiritual battle raged inside of me.

The more I turned over these thoughts in my mind, the more the darkness crept deeper into the crevices of my heart. The image of a small child returned to the forefront of my mind. Two angels—there must be two victims—Gina's soul with a little child. This one thought came to dominate all my other thoughts, influencing my perception of what I saw.

Some mornings I woke up, having written "my left arm itched" or "my right arm itched." I would see blood drawn where I had scratched my arm so intensely while I slept. I grabbed on to the only logical theory I could come up with. The itching must correlate with a specific direction from the muck place. As I lay there in bed contemplating, I began to think of myself as a compass because I had written:

> The sun setting at my head and rising at my feet, so my right arm must be south. My left arm pointed north.

Should I walk in a specific direction from the muck place? The battle was real. I began interpreting the miraculous image as a literal compass with its only purpose being to point me where my sister's remains could be found. And my itching arms pointed the way. Much later, I would come to understand that my intuitive thoughts of the image representing a compass was in an indirect way a correct interpretation. A thought that should have led me to see what the light miracle really was an image of, but it did not. The narrow focus was too strong. I would not see the full truth of the image until almost a year later.

I had witnessed many miracles up to this point in my journey, so why did my journey need to continue? I had just experienced the miracle of light. But with that miracle came a real force within my life—a spiritual enemy. This was an enemy who would not want me to awaken to the real truth—the true message of the image in the water: Love. I was experiencing the battles we all experience every day, often not even aware when in the midst of it. My battleground was an intense desire to prove that farmer's story, right or wrong. My path was still influenced by pride and ego. All I could focus on was Gina's guiding us to her body. I was missing the true message. I still needed to win the spiritual battles in my own heart. I still needed to make sure my mind was not being influenced. How do I know this? Later, I would write a message that told me:

> The mind is the enemy's playground.

So I will call this powerful, influencing force the Enemy because that is what I was starting to understand. Battles have sides, and anyone on the opposite of my side would be an enemy: The Enemy. Spiritual battles are a part of this world. But battles don't have to rule! Life can be amazing, peaceful, joyful, and full of bliss.

PINNACLE NATURE RESERVE, RUSSELL COUNTY, VIRGINIA

One day, my husband stood back and watched me dig in the muck. He crossed his arms over his chest. Clearly, he was starting to worry about me. "Enough is enough," he said.

Buz insisted I take a break. This was an emotional roller coaster. I was exhibiting a balance of strength and resilience that came from somewhere within just like it had my entire life. I agreed with him that it was time for a day of fun. Instead of hiking in the woods searching, we hiked to our favorite waterfall. Instead of digging in the water, I played in the meandering creek with my Rooby Doo—Ruben, my special rescue, a mix of lab, pit, and boxer. Our dog learned to swim that day, and our laughter was abundant.

We strive for the perfect balance of emotions—sadness and joy—but sometimes our hearts get filled with muck just like the endless black sludge of that murky place where I dug. Nature has two sides to everything. Some emotions seem not to be from nature, but self-created by man, designed by the Enemy. And when so, they do not have an opposite, balancing side. This is part of the muck that influences our minds to our own detriment.

When I finally hit the bottom rock layer at the muck place, I realized it would be almost impossible to break through. The rock in the creek bed was just as hard as the ravine above. All that washed from the rocky crevice above ended up down here, apparent by the many animal bones I would dig out. If Gina had been placed in the ravine, the dry creek bed covered with rocks, sometimes wet, sometimes not, at the S curves, then it was certainly possible that eventually she would wash down here. What I was curious about is what happens to bone over time. Andy arranged for me to meet with an anthropologist for a quick lesson on human and animal bones.

Already I had been contemplating another way to tackle this muck. I had asked a friend who owned a well-digging business if her company's equipment could penetrate the muck. Yes, it would work, she told me.

For thirty-six years, the creek had washed layers of rock and debris over this spot. What had it looked like in 1980? Had it been like now—a hardened creek bed bottom—or had it been a bigger pond of water, covering a larger area? And every time I looked up I wondered, *What is up on top of the muck place cliff wall?* How could she be both at the river and here? How could she be in so many different places? Nola had said to be patient and the messages would make sense later.

All that summer of 2016, I was reliving 1980. It felt so unnecessary to walk this path again, yet it was necessary.

I found solace in remembering what Nola had said, *"He is going to show you it is Him."* How did Nola know this? When he had said it, I never dreamed it would be like this. I had thought of God showing me in some way that was not visible, through my feelings or thoughts. I had never imagined anything as concrete as a butterfly landing and then seeing Gina's face in the river's glistening water—and the muck place photo unknowingly capturing an amazing miracle of light.

I did revel in the undeniable proof in the photo. I felt it was of God, transforming Light into this perfect shadow-lit image. At first, I thought it was the sunlight, not the angels, making the images until I looked closer and saw that each image had a clearly defined ball of concentrated light energy from which the light spreads across the water, mirroring the symbol drawn, authenticating a "*Vision of Image in the Water*" foretold by my spiritual army. This was a Day Made in Heaven. The light shining out from the image like what I can only imagine an angel must look like floating on water. God's angels lying in the water.

Not until almost a year later would I see clearly the message I was to see. What the image was undeniably an image of. I was simply unawakened to the real truth. What I sensed then was that it was some kind of proof:

- proof of communication from one realm to another
- proof of a spiritual existence in the form of light energy
- proof of the real power of our creator

But I didn't understand the full message yet.

CHAPTER 12

FOR THE FIRST TIME

Live. Love. Breathe. Awaken.

An Absolute Miracle—that is what I had just experienced. First I had seen my sister's beautiful face glistening in the water where the butterfly performed its rhythmic dance, kissing the water with its wings. We can believe in miracles. But we were to see more—a divine message shared by God's angels.

When autumn is coming to the mountains, it brings foggy mornings with crisp cool air and afternoons warmed with sunshine. The last flowers burst into bloom in my garden, a prelude to the necklaces of yellow, orange, and red that would adorn the mountains in just a few weeks. At the end of summer, I found myself at the Russell County Fair, a thrilling and delicious scene with big prizes and stomach-dropping rides, cotton candy, and candied apples. Every year, my employees and I set up a big red tent featuring a colorful spinning wheel where children could win prizes. It was an unchanging day, predictably similar year after year.

But this year my week was different. The physical changes in me were odd and dramatic. Perhaps the search for Gina's body and the emotional turmoil in my life were taking their toll. I found it hard to concentrate at times because of a white noise in my head. Excruciating "headaches" would descend on me, at times accompanied with vertigo, especially when I was in Radford. The changes were noticeably going into overdrive. After being a meat-and-potatoes girl all my life, I suddenly, overnight, could not stand the taste of meat. I could not get enough vegetables. My fingernails, which had never been strong, all of a sudden were not brittle, and easily grew long. At night, the skin on my arms would itch so much that I would scratch frantically, drawing blood. My tummy was swollen like a little Buddha statue.

And the most surprising of all of the changes: I could not even kill a spider. I was carrying spiders out of my house—all fear had disappeared. One day, I sat perfectly still as I watched a large, wide-bodied spider scurry across the floor. For fifty-plus years, I had been terrified of all things spiders. Not even a week earlier, I would have been yelling "Help!" while swiftly jumping up on my couch. Now: No screams, no fear. Where did this newfound love of everything come from? How did my intense fear of spiders just disappear overnight? Killing any living being just seemed so wrong—even a spider. It was as though I felt this spider had a right to live, even if he was in my space. Of course, I still prefer spiders to live outside, so that is where I take them. I cannot explain how this happened. I can only imagine that it has to do with this amazing spiritual world that connected into my life, bringing with it abundant goodness.

That summer of 1980, while searching for Gina's body, I had crawled through places I would have never gone under normal circumstances. I still see the huge spiders in their webs right in front of my face, but that summer, I was numb to the fear. Even though the fear was still real.

An early memory of my arachnophobia comes to mind—a memory of my scruffy Uncle Ashland. He lived in a two-room house down by the North Fork of the Kentucky River. Before I went to Uncle Ashland's house, I always made sure I went to the bathroom, because otherwise, I would have to go to his outhouse, and that meant spiderwebs. My fear of spiders was very real, and in the outhouse, their webs multilayered like a highrise apartment building. Going to the outhouse was not happening! Those trips down to Uncle Ashland's were colorful, to say the least.

One night at the county fair, I noticed I lost my balance easily, and had to take Buz's arm as we walked up the hill to the grandstand for the live music. I did not want to miss our son's best friends, slated to entertain that evening. The feeling was weightlessness. People were noticing. I greeted the grandfather of some of my son's friends, and as I was climbing into the bleachers to speak to him, he said, "What in the world, Dlana? You've been hitting the bottle early!"

I could handle this balance issue short term, but I was questioning if this was going to last forever, *How am I supposed to work and function?* However, I did—2016 becoming my best year ever. That reminds me of that one tiny verse in the Bible that my dad shared with me decades ago—1 Chronicles 4:10. Many refer to it as the prayer of Jabez. My dad gave me a little book written by Bruce Wilkinson called *The Prayer of Jabez: Breaking through to the Blessed Life*. I have always known that if I just did what I believed was right and treated others as I would want to be treated, all would be good. This little book added an extra prayer to my life. I learned I was simply to ask as Jabez had.

I was growing concerned, concerned enough to think about seeing a doctor, concerned enough to ask Nola about my weightlessness and balance issues. He responded, "I experienced similar symptoms in the fall of 2015." That was after I had met him in June. He called that experience his awakening.

"Go out and walk in the grass barefoot. You will ground yourself," he advised. I did, and it worked.

He texted:

> Awakening never stops as long as you keep looking for it.

And I replied:

> I feel God's love. Everything is alive. I am awakened more than ever to the beauty that surrounds me. You said Gina just wants to see me happy, smiling from within. I believe my loved ones are in the grandstands of Heaven cheering in excitement for me. My sister is dancing.

I was changing, too. I had always thought of myself as nice, but this was different. I felt nicer. I felt more goodness and kindness through all of my connections with people. I was noticing the great feeling that came over me when I shared my smile with others. I was creating a whole environment of positive feelings around me. I loved to help people, and now, I was helping people in so many unexpected, wonderfully rewarding ways. At the fair booth, smiles were abundant. Smiles were free! This year, I was more aware of the differences in the children's eyes at the spinning wheel. I have always had a deep love for all children, which is why I had chosen to be a teacher in my earlier years. I shared with Nola that it was as though I could see light in their eyes, especially the youngest. And I believe they saw the same in mine by the way they looked directly into my eyes. I felt their trusting, loving innocent nature as I had never felt it before. I felt it in my heart.

My text conversation with Nola ended with a comment that caught his attention. I could feel his smile in his reply:

> Look what you said, "Amazing to just follow my heart and do what I am supposed to do." Now you are growing. You just found *it* yourself.

In the last days of the county fair, while taking a break to sit in the shade, I visited with my son's best friend from high school. I knew he was an avid outdoorsman and would be quite familiar with the Radford area as a former RU student, so I quizzed him about the nooks and crannies he was familiar with, since I was especially curious about a bog-like area. Just then, as I visited with him, I got a text from Andy:

> WHAT have you been doing?

As I puzzled over this, Andy continued. He had gotten a call from Kevin:

> Tell her she is not ready.

I asked Andy:

> For what?

Andy didn't know. He just said, *You are not ready*. He said Kevin was adamant because Gina had visited him twice the night before, wanting him to tell me that message. I had only met Kevin at this point once before, that day on August 12 when I had taken the miracle picture of the images on the water at the muck place—the day the angels had lain on the water.

My first thoughts were, *What am I not ready for?*

I continued my quizzing of my son's friend asking about a BOG area and old roads. I knew he used to fish the shoal area frequently. He told me I could use a computer app to see old roads, going back in time. With this one tip, I would later verify that there was a visible road in 1980 that easily led off Claytor Dam Road, up the hill, right to the cliffs, high up above the dump site—the flat area that sits six feet up from the butterfly river spot. I wanted to see a 1980 map rendition to know if Epperly could have driven up there and dumped my sister's body off that high cliff. There was a 30-40 minute period missing in the timeline between the lake house and running Mr. Sauls off the road. I wanted to know where Epperly went. A local, long-time resident shared that the aligning cliff area was a well-known meeting place for partying. In 1980, there must have been easy access to it. And, at this juncture in September 2016, I did not know about the 3 a.m. bass fisherman story that really hurled more doubt into the composed story's timeline when trying to follow Epperly's early Sunday morning path.

One day, at the Pulaski County Courthouse while researching another clue, I asked the clerk to search the database for any home owned by *James Young* because of the message I had received suggesting this *name on a map maybe.* On her computer, I noticed the parcels were marked with hyphenated numbers. My thoughts: *8-1-35?* Later, using the Pulaski County GIS site, scanning every lot number all around the radius of the lake house parcel by parcel for 8-1-35, finding the closest, 058-01-34 on a parcel of land between the Ingles farm and Young Road. I found all of the similar numbers except that one—and I found one lot with no numbers marking it. Surrounding that unnumbered lot were other similar numbered parcels. That particular lot had a tiny blue circular outline indicating water, but I did not connect this right away. Later, in November, I would see the eerie, murky pond hidden down over the bank bordering Claytor Dam Road on this unmarked lot. Epperly had traveled this route in my car early that morning after he killed my sister. It was the only direction from the dead end lake house road. I wondered, *Was this parcel with the hidden pond ever numbered 8-1-35? And, it did not surprise me that there is another parcel labeled 068-1-35 across the lake.*

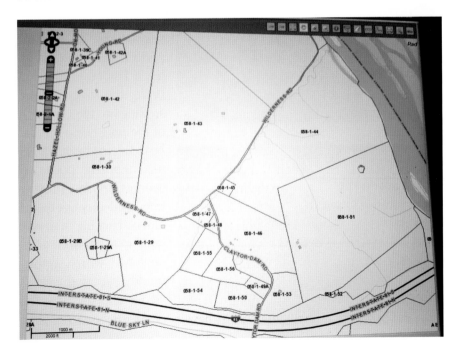

The battles in my mind would continue. The farmer's story kept rattling around in my head.

That first week of September, I continued to have confusing dream messages, like this one:

> All of a sudden, I had an entire half of a house I had never seen. It needed to be updated and remodeled, but it was large. A construction man and woman were there. She tried to buy all of the old toys for $11,000. I said no. We would go through it ourselves. The right side of the house was a row of windows looking out over a large creek with large pine trees blocking the view of the creek. I kept running into the contractor and his wife no matter where I went.

When I woke from the dream, I drew a picture of where the kitchen was and the wall of windows and a large table.

Could my dream have been of Epperly's house? I drove to his home one

day and sat in my truck, just looking at the house. A row of pine trees edged the property, separating it from an easily accessible alley with at least twelve, very tall pine trees all in a perfect row along the alley. If I stood in his yard, under the large window, looking in the direction of the pine trees, I would be facing the river. I imagined Epperly pulls my Monte Carlo into the pine tree-lined alley just before dawn, backing into the yard up to the shed door, only two wheels getting muddy, raising the trunk lid up into the branches of the pine tree, the same

rotting pine tree trunk remnants still visible where the tree had once stood right beside the shed door. Epperly opens the trunk lid into the pine tree limbs, sprinkling the pine needles on the rear windshield, getting the tools so as not to be seen crossing the street with them, driving back to Hazel Hollow and leaving my car under the trestle. Epperly then goes somewhere, somewhere he has already used to hide his crimes in the past, and buries my sister, crossing the trestle before or after, then walking on home and leaving the tools behind. This shed  roused my curiosity. *What was in the shed at the end of the row of pine trees? Is something still hidden there? Does it have a dirt floor? What was it used for?*

The shed on the home property haunted me after the pine tree dream. Taking my sister to that shed would have been quite an arrogant move. I am not sure even Epperly was that confident. My mind began working the possibilities. Did he really do the worst atrocity imaginable—dismemberment? My mind took off on a wild tangent, rethinking the farmer's story, or should I say the *concept* of the farmer's story.  Epperly had bragged that he would dismember his next victim, but no one in 1980 had really believed he could do that. What if the farmer had been a seer, the vision of dismemberment seen in his head, the same visions so many others saw? Perhaps he saw the terrifying flashes of a scene while walking the creek, a movie in his head playing out as it happened in another part of town. He then shared it with his family in a way they could understand, as though he had actually seen it. My thoughts took off, contemplating whether the actual place was somewhere else, not Meadow Creek. Could it be the butterfly spot at the river below the dumpsite from the high cliffs? The muck place or another out of the way pond? It could even be the shed. Everything Epperly needed was already there. His graveyard for his victims a forgotten dumpsite. His plans set in motion long before he murdered Gina. A plan involving somewhere familiar for when a decision needed to be made quickly. He was calculating, and his decisions of what he would do the next time were already known to him. This was not an impulsive, chaotic, *I accidentally killed this girl—what do I do now?*, kind of decision. I do believe my Monte Carlo made it to the shed as described. At the least, to get tools, but I am not so sure about Gina's body. But if so, dismemberment certainly could still be a possibility. If this had been his thought process, it was so wrong. So disturbing.

I contemplated: He had from 5:15 to 9:30 a.m. when his mother saw him out in the yard as she left for church. In the yard? Is that where a man would be hanging out after having been out until 4 a.m.? No. He would be in bed like every other all-American boy after partying—Boy? Twenty-eight years old. He did something during those four hours. What? In Skipper's handwritten statement, added as though a last minute thought, he wrote: "Please add to page 9: Mr. Cubid Epperly (Steve's Father), was outside crying and I asked him what was wrong." He said: "... I just lost the best friend I ever had. He explained that Spanky, their small dog, had been hit and killed by a car. I said I was sorry." The reason Skipper had gone by the Epperly house late Tuesday night was because Trooper Hall had instructed Epperly after his initial 5 p.m. visit at VSP headquarters to go tell his friend that he wanted to talk with him ASAP. Skipper did not want to call Trooper Hall from his grandmother's home where he was living, so he went to the Epperly home to make the phone call. That does not sound like he *willingly and voluntarily* went to the police on his own. He was told to call.

And this could explain the dead dog: a little dog yapping at the shed, so Epperly killed it. He could have dismembered her right there. And he could have buried her right there, somewhere near. He could have done a lot between 5 and 9:30 a.m. and covered a lot of ground between 9:30 and noon. Scattered? By noon, was he finished? He was always so arrogant and confident.

And this was the evil monster I needed to forgive.

This is crazy thinking. Maybe the pine tree dream is about something else, I told myself.

While I was puzzling through all of this, Andy was discovering a new lead. All along, he'd been having what he called "secret squirrel meetings," his term for police tips where someone wanted to meet him "in a remote location." At first he expected it to be a tip about a drug connection because the tipster had told him that Gina had been dismembered and scattered from an airplane. There could not be very many people who owned airplanes in this area. Who had airplanes then? People in the drug trade.

Airplane = Drugs.

I had told Andy about the 1980 "scattered" rumor and the reference to Ohio. At the time, we had believed it to be a far-fetched theory. And since 1980, I had not even given it a minute of thought, until my 1974 airplane message in June 2016, prompting a recall of the 1980 scattered theory. Had we known in 1980 what we know now, it may not have been such an implausible theory to think Gina's remains had been scattered somewhere. And maybe we could have better understood why Ohio was part of their message. It's the tiniest of details we have to pay attention to. Andy concluded this "secret squirrel meeting" had nothing to do with drugs. It still, however, pointed me to a new line of inquiry: the drug connection.

Andy's "secret squirrel meeting" proved to be full of surprises. He learned of a national team of gifted people who in 1980 had been asked to help solve Gina's case as a favor to a local resident. This man was associated with that government-based team and verified that this was where the 1980 "scattered" theory had originated. I questioned why a federal government team would be interested in Gina. Unless there was some connecting factor of something or someone they were already interested in.

The source talked about a concept he referred to as Mind Reach—a new interest Andy had started to practice.

We discovered one Saturday that Andy had picked up remote-viewing techniques quickly. As soon as we arrived to our meeting place, Andy handed me his phone, "Read this." The time-stamped text he had sent himself earlier described exactly what Buz and I were wearing. It could have just been a lucky guess, but not in this much detail. The end of his text read "...and you could not decide on the hat." That morning, hours earlier while still at my home 115 miles away, I really could not decide what hat to wear. I had pulled my hat box off the top shelf and tried on several different hats. When Andy told me that, I just looked at my husband in utter surprise.

I was starting to believe in what was possible. I was venturing into areas that might be perplexing and a little mysterious—I was venturing into the power of our own minds.

"The way I see is not like a clear picture," Andy said when he described his Mind Reach experimentation. "I might describe a green and white item as a tent, but in reality, it might be an awning." I still questioned the right and wrong of it, but all I wanted was the truth, and Andy really believed it could be done and he could use it to find my sister.

One day, a relative of Andy's who lives in North Carolina was giving him a hard time about his opinion about ghosts and the spiritual realm, so he told her everything he saw around her, from where he was—Radford. His descriptions were startlingly accurate. She admitted he was right, but she was still not open to the possibilities. The limited boundaries of our own minds and beliefs influence our perceptions and can be unbudging even when we experience verification of the extraordinary. This is what we do. I would have been skeptical, too. We just cannot see what is possible—to see what surrounds us. The power of our minds is the answer. But it can also be the downfall. We can never fully know who is behind the scenes, possibly influencing the outcomes. Changing our beliefs almost seems impossible, but it can be done. Change your experience, change your mind; change your perceptions, change your reality. Sounds easy. It is not.

I remember doing the same as Andy's relative during the 1980 investigation, when authorities received a call from the parents of a seven-year-old girl who claimed to have visions about the case. My dad also got a call from a woman speaking on behalf of the little girl, sharing the same story as told to police. Then my dad received a map of the area that had been described. I recalled thinking out loud, "Really, Daddy—she's just a little girl. How could she know?" I questioned it all.

The searchers were looking in the wrong area, she would say. The girl psychic pointed authorities to the Virginia Tech campus, saying Gina was buried at the edge of the woods under a tree. The woods were located on the east side of Route 460. If a person stood in front of Hillcrest Hall, an athletic dorm on campus, and looked across the football practice field, that person would see two trailers, one white, one green. The girl psychic had told the police that Gina was buried between those two trailers.

What I didn't know until 2016 was that the girl psychic had also told police that the spot could be identified because they would find a pair of broken eyeglasses. Gina wore brown tortoise-shell eyeglasses with round lenses when she drove. Gina was seen dancing with someone at the Marriott who wore glasses.

This tiny little fact, buried in Gina's file, matched one of my messages:

> Glasses broken and muddy looked like leaves on them

I now wonder whether a different victim from the past connected to the same murderer or connected murderers was being seen in the eyes of this child. I then wondered, *Did any Virginia Tech students go missing while Epperly was there?*—the same time frame when there were two trailers near the football practice field?

I still struggled with the very idea of using psychic gifts for good because according to the Bible, we are not to seek answers from the dead. But in my case, I was not seeking it. I had asked God for help. And the messages just came. And this child had reached out to us. Most of the people I crossed paths with on *the journey* were not seeking psychic communication. The messages just came to people, sometimes just from being introduced to me as Gina's sister. Some, unknowingly, just shared thoughts that came into their minds. Some dreamed, sharing vivid memories of relevant, related dreams. Some, like Nola, asked God for guidance and for God to send his angels to help. And some, like Dorothy Allison, were very aware of their own connection to a spiritual realm—acting as receivers of transmitted messages to be shared to help fight the presence of evil. Yet I also suspect that some of these very real experiences have behind them hidden agendas unknown to their receivers. The agenda is to deceive—masters of deception. Even messages that can appear to be good can be from a deceptive, familiar spirit—a place of darkness. But I had to ask myself, *Why would the Dark show Nola, Kevin, and The Preacher the actual acts of a crime?* I saw Kevin's face the day he stood with me, visions of Gina coming into his mind like a movie, describing what she was wearing, seeing her standing by a car as though a scuffle had occurred. Yes, it was to some degree information he could have surmised from what was publicly known, but in actuality, everyone told the story that Gina went in the car willingly, so the scuffle he saw by the car conflicted with what was assumed by everyone else. The expression on his face, the vision he saw, was more. He could see the violence. He was seeing what someone somewhere wanted him to see—what really happened to my sister beside the car, maybe in the Marriott parking lot. And all Kevin did was stand beside me and the visions came.

Would an Enemy not want to keep his evil web a secret? The visions, the movies that played out in these people's heads, were very real. The little child psychic emphatically declared we were looking in the wrong place. The farmer emphatically said we were all looking in the wrong place. The visions were very real. I simply asked myself, *Who put these thoughts in their minds? And how can we discern the difference between those that are true and those that are intended to deceive?* There are hundreds of stories about good angels helping people. There are no coincidences.

My struggle was that if all of it really originated from a place of evil, then that would be a timeless orchestration of deceit and unbelievable connections, a power controlling not only us but also nature and sunlight. A power that not only controlled the present, but also the past and the future. If this is true, then this Enemy frightens me to the core. I believe in my heart that only God can do *all* of this. The Enemy is mighty, but only God is almighty. And the Enemy succumbs to God. If there is something to be known, light will shine in the darkness. We just have to pay attention.

As a woman of faith, I asked myself whether my messages were coming from the side of the light or from a dark realm—fallen angels, demons. If they were from the dark, what was their objective? I cannot help but think about the power of a single thought later changing the interpretation of a divinely inspired message. Seems the deception begins in our own thoughts just as a message I received so clearly stated: *The mind is the enemy's playground.* Then again, if the dark side can communicate, influencing our thoughts, the Light can, too. The Bible talks about the good and bad spirits. The Bible talks about angels—good and fallen. I used to think it was all just a movie plot—not an actual war between good and evil. Now I know our good angels are extremely busy. How many angels we must need—an infinite number.

Many times, people tell stories about the moments after losing a loved one, when they receive a comforting message. And there are stories of miracles, when people hear angel voices. I believe in angels. Andy shared with me that he thinks lost souls need closure, so they come to us. And when someone dies traumatically, like Gina did, they cannot move on. And that maybe these souls need peace. He wants to help them. He wondered if some just never knew God.

Gina did—she loved Jesus with all of her heart.

I do not know the answer, but when you experience the unexplainable as I have, an answer certainly is desired. There is really no way to understand within our human world the depths of the spiritual world's powers right here in our midst. I know now, by experience, the absolute power of it all. I am starting to understand what being controlled by a power unrevealed means.

As I was contemplating Andy's stories, my dreams, and our differences in beliefs, I ran across a true story—a biography of Protestant preacher Johann Blumhardt, titled *The Awakening* and written in the mid-1800s. It was no coincidence that this story appeared as my first-line item during my internet search for a particular topic. In it I caught glimpses of both Andy's and my theories. The demons are real just like the Bible tells us. Jesus calls them the wicked. The last demon to be exorcised by Blumhardt from a possessed woman screamed out, "Jesus is the victor!" Many witnessed the exorcism. By the end of Blumhardt's life, an immense awakening had spread from village to village in Germany because of the miracles that had been seen and heard. The demonically possessed lady in this story did not seek. She just ended up living in a home where a murderer had lived before her. I never thought much about demons, but I certainly do now. This evil presence had lingered there like a seed. Demons do live among us. This story made me wonder, especially when I thought about Epperly.

I did not know for certain who was communicating with me. Whether it was, as I began to believe in the beginning Gina's soul, or whether it was God's angels, I cannot say. I only know this: I sought God's guidance when I fell to my knees in prayer that night after I heard the farmer's story. And I met Nola before all of this seemed to begin. And my daddy died before all of this. And Andy and the preacher, and many others, all before.... And, and, and...unfolding as if time is not relevant. The puzzle pieces were beginning to be laid out on the table.

At first, as *the journey* reopened the events of June 1980, I listened to everyone else. Then, as it evolved, months later, I learned to think with my heart, not grabbing onto every idea that blew in the wind. This was hard for me. I tried to take each day as it came, seeing what I was to see. What is really hard to fully understand is how all of the storylines from *the journey* seem to be connected—like a master plan. What I mean is that just as my journey was stirring to life, so were other people being stirred to enter my life—different people experiencing the same storyline at different times, from different places. Even people before *the journey* began. Mostly, I felt it all was from a divine place filled with love. Sometimes, though, I also felt it came from a power I prefer never to experience again.

But sometimes you aren't given a choice.

Andy planned a second visit with the tipster so I could meet this intriguing and complex man with many interesting stories to tell. We ended by asking him to request that this gifted government team please take Gina's dental records and help. For some reason, I do not believe dental records will help them see where she is because dental records were how a body was mostly identified in 1980, and Epperly would have known that. It would be one touching, personal story that the tipster shared that would help me understand something I needed to know—the very reason I was there that day. He talked about many different times when the last words a loved one shared,

especially before a tragic accident, became relevant advice in the life of the loved one left behind. The person, seemingly gone forever, is not really gone at all. The tipster said if we look back, and really think about the last words shared, we can see the messages clearly, sometimes even prophetic, becoming relevant in our lives. This one moment gave me such clarity. *Sis, listen to your heart, not your head.* I was getting it!

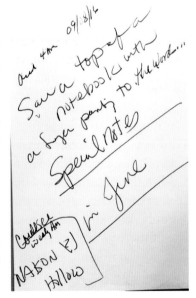

That night I truly saw an angel. That morning when I opened my eyes, I had written:

Saw a top of a notebook with a beautiful finger pointing to the Word-Special notes in June.

When I woke and saw this, it was not like before, always being surprised in the morning by what was written. I immediately remembered what I had seen in my sleep, so much more than just this description. It seemed as if an angel had visited me. So real—as though it had really happened. I could feel the goodness still present. I could see that finger as beautiful and graceful as truly no words could ever begin to describe. The finger had pointed and glided across the top of the page in my dream vision. I could see the long, elegant illuminated finger pointing to the top of a notebook page, pointing right to my writing, with a beautiful golden light shining all around the words… "special notes in June." And the words "the Word" seemingly added in a different handwriting or maybe written at a different time in the night.

My angel visit last night was different than the other earlier messages I would not even remember writing, seemingly random words at times. Last night was different. It was as if I were awake and actually seeing an angel telling me to go back to the beginning—the June notes.

I went back and read all of my notes from the month of June. I was still holding on to the possibility that all messages, even in the beginning, were relevant to Gina's case. I still was not seeing what I was to see. This was the stronghold I was fighting. I was starting to believe that Gina needed me to find her, not just for her, but now, also for others.

Many of my messages were starting to make sense now. Whether this voice was Gina's or some other being's from the spiritual realm, I stopped worrying about it. It just did not seem to matter because it was not something I could control. I let life happen. Someone, somewhere wanted something known.

The search for my sister's body was about the only thing that could have pulled me out of my day-to-day hamster wheel life and caused me to re-examine my own life journey. This felt urgent to me, and simultaneously, like something that had been set in motion years ago. The day I was born? The day Gina was born? I should have been driven to the point of physical exhaustion and mental confusion, but I was not. I kept going. I was noticing, more and more, a clearer connection to God. As the spirit realm continued to send these messages, my heart opened up more. God was more visible than ever in everything I saw.

My senses woke up to the world as I had never really seen it before. Peace—no fear.

I had always loved and appreciated nature. This was different. Nature's beauty was vivid, connected to me in the purest form. The sunlight brought dimension to the clouds, outlining the leaves on the trees.

I smelled the rain. Waking early to hear the birds, I smiled and went through the day, smiling at the beauty that surrounded me everywhere I went. The sunrises, the sunsets, the glorious colors of God's canvas in every moment—I noticed them all. I would need this solace, these quiet moments of good, as the next few months in my search intensified—the true battles becoming more apparent.

I believe those who have known me would describe me as having always been a kind, generous, loving mother, and a person of genuine integrity—pretty much an all-around okay person. Far from perfect, though. None of us are. What I experienced was a deeper change—a much more meaningful awareness of the world's beauty, and our connection to it, which increased as *the journey* progressed. If this were an awakening, then I was happy with whatever happened, whoever caused this—that someone decided to wake me up so that I could open my eyes every day, greet the morning in gratitude, and end my day in appreciation for the bright moments of my day and the even brighter paths to come. The Light was shining through. I still see God in everything every day! I would quietly think to myself every single moment, *Please God, don't let this go away! Oh, yeah! Nola said it will never go away as long as you look for it.*

The problem was I was also still looking for something else...the truth from a very dark, elusive place. This very elusive web of evil that I was beginning to uncover was beginning to cover its tracks, just as it had in 1980. The evolving storyline illustrates why I believed I was starting to feel the dark creeping in, and why my spiritual army was becoming more prevalent—I was getting closer to the truth, piece by piece. I needed more strength. Maybe that is why the angel had visited.

CHAPTER 13

AMERICAN PIE

*I have faith in God. And my faith took me to where
"them good ole boys" became known.*

A round this same time, I found out about another cold case
murder that had occurred in Pulaski County. The murder victim had been a Gary Romano, from Bluefield, West Virginia. He'd been murdered around midnight to 1 a.m. Monday
morning, June 30, 1980, within twenty-four hours of Gina's murder. I was
surprised. I am not sure if my dad had been told about this. We were fighting our own battles. How could two murders be committed so close together in this quiet little stretch of Virginia and not seriously be considered
as possibly connected? Preconceived perceptions. He was a drug dealer.

The June 30 note I had written *"Connect the Two"* quickly surfaced in my
mind. I received the message on the same day—June 30? It must mean to
connect the two murders. My first thought was, *Could this person Gary
Romano have been in the wrong place at the wrong time, perhaps seeing
Gina being buried or being killed—becoming a second victim?* The connection intrigued me enough to ask Andy to send me the only information he
had—a brief newspaper clipping of the case, one paragraph.

Monday morning I just happened to be standing in my office by the seldom used, antiquated fax machine when a fax came across. It was an invitation to a continuing education class in Princeton, West Virginia, over
an hour away. It would not be like me to even consider going, but in that

moment, it seemed like a good idea. Being the time stacker I am, I decided to take one of my employees with me so I could use those few hours in the car wisely, teaching and training every opportunity I got. Sarah, another team member, reminded me later that we would drive right past Bluefield, knowing of my curiosity about Gary Romano. Sarah handed me an address she found online.

Early Wednesday morning, as we drove to Princeton, I asked Kynan if he was okay with making a quick stop in Bluefield on our way home. I shared why and figured it was worth a shot to try to visit Gary's parents, not knowing yet that they had both already died.

Arriving at the training, I scanned the roster. My eyes landed on a name: Peter Romano, Bluefield. Kynan and I just looked at each other in awe. *Could he be related?* I was at a class I normally would never attend, and now I would meet the brother of Gary Romano on a day when I had already planned to visit his parents. Happenstance? At this point, I was starting to see there were no coincidences in my life.

Peter told me everything he remembered about his brother's murder. Information that later would be confirmed by VSP. Peter had only been eighteen when his brother was murdered. He sorrowfully shared that he had spent an entire year trying to find out the details of why his brother was murdered. I understood. When we lose a sibling, it takes away a piece of us. That piece is magnified when the loss is traumatic and mysterious. Answers are needed to peacefully mourn. Peter shared that his mother had never healed from Gary's murder. Her sadness was always there, taken with her to her grave.

Peter said he had quickly learned he was investigating something an eighteen-year-old should not be involved in. Gary, twenty-four at the time, had been connected to drugs and "bad people," something the police had discovered, but the family had not really known. Gary was found in his blue truck, shot in the head execution style. Peter mentioned that Gary's guitar and a 12-gauge shotgun were missing from his pickup. The truck was discovered in a grassy spot on the side of Interstate 81 a few miles south of the Claytor Lake exit at a construction site.

On that day, Peter was home waiting for Gary to pick him up and take him to the beach so they could celebrate his high school graduation. Gary planned a stopover at Claytor Lake to visit with his parents, who were there camping for the weekend. A lifeguard at Claytor Lake Park in his earlier years, he had once resided in the Claytor Lake area in an apartment beside The Hitching Post. The police believed he was associated with one of the 1%er motorcycle clubs that frequented The Hitching Post. These clubs were also referenced in Gina's file by an investigator who referred to them as "hippies" gathering at the lake. They were certainly more than that. They were known as an above-the-law, 1%er motorcycle club who held a stronghold in the New River Valley.

This is his timeline: Gary was with friends from Bluefield hanging out and playing music Sunday night. He left and returned with a friend whom none of them knew. His musician friends describe this unknown man as keeping his head hung down, not really making eye contact with anyone while they all enjoyed picking music around the campfire. A composite drawing of this mystery man seems a familiar hairstyle—a familiar chin. Gary left the campground around midnight. His last sighting was when he stopped off at The Claytor Lake Motel to shower at a friend's room.

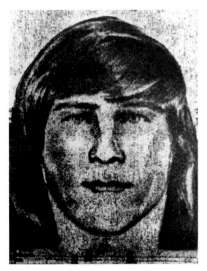

In the 1980s, Pulaski County was considered a midpoint of the drug distribution route between the South and the Northeast and according to the Commonwealth Attorney at the time, Everett Shockley, it was a hotbed for drug trafficking. At the time, Gary Romano's murder was written off as related to his drug-dealing connections. It is still a cold case today.

The most interesting fact I would learn would be the reports of a Ford LTD, possibly green, that pulled in behind Gary's blue pickup, as confirmed by two eyewitnesses. Police have a partial fingerprint from the truck handle. Skipper owned a Ford LTD—a brown one as noted in the reports, not a green one.

When the police found Gary Romano, he was wearing women's underwear. I began contemplating how this might connect him to early Sunday morning at the lake house. These could not have been Gina's panties because I had identified hers as part of the bundled pile of clothes placed in the woods. Those panties revealed evidence of her struggle—the fibers embedded, matching the carpet fibers from the recreation room in the lake house. Whose underwear could this be? The police just assumed it was his, saying, "He was a funny, you know, that kind of guy who wears girl's underwear." Perceptions. Not facts. If the evidence were still in a police file box, what would it reveal—maybe even the same carpet fibers? I recalled "Connect the Two."

Ketamine (an anesthetic) was a word that came up during 2016. If someone had wanted Gary Romano dead, they could have drugged him (or not), dressed him in an incriminating pair of women's underwear, driven south a few miles to a construction site they already knew was there, pulled off into the grass, positioned him in the driver's seat, and shot him in the head. What happened at that lake house that could have led to this course of action and Gary Romano's fate?

It seems most likely the underwear was the answer. Romano's own fetish choice as the police surmised? Or, could it be a very clear, strong warning sent—*Drive to a specific mile marker to see with your own eyes what could happen to you if....* Or the other, more obvious choice, Epperly taking care of loose ends leaving behind the panties as incriminating evidence. But why? Maybe we could connect the two if that someone who knows the underwear is hers comes forward to tell VSP and then they too will know her truth. Her voice. Romano was targeted. It was not a random act. The message I had received on June 30—"Connect the Two"—became apparent. Now, I see that a message might have two parts, multi-purposed. The picture, a different meaning—the orange stakes at the river butterfly spot—and the words, connect the two murders. And still another simultaneous meaning: Gary Romano had been murdered on June 30, 1980; I had written the words "Connect the Two" on June 30, 2016.

I just couldn't believe that two murders happening in a quiet remote corner of Virginia within twenty-four hours of each other would not be connected. How could they be a mere coincidence?

And it was no coincidence that my professional life would produce a training that would bring me to West Virginia, a place I should not have been under normal circumstances, to meet Gary Romano's brother. I had met him right when I was supposed to meet him.

Of course, now the obvious question was not whether the murders were connected, but *how?* Romano's girlfriend told the police that he had kept his drug ledger in his guitar case, and both the guitar and its case were missing from his truck. The missing ledger might have connected the dots as to whom he would have been with the night before. Romano's 12-gauge shotgun was also missing from his truck.

Next, I would write down this crazy note that would bewilder me for weeks:

Naison Hollow

Naturally, my thought when I first saw it was, *That's a place.* Hollows are commonplace in SWVA. A hollow—pronounced *holler* by many—is a term used for a road that winds up into the mountains and usually dead-ends. The mountains are so tall along the road's sides that the sun does not shine through very long during the day. For weeks after the message, I had been looking for such a place—but then one day, I entered just these two words into a search engine and the first line that came up was Maison Hollow, the body style of a hand-crafted guitar. I remembered Gary's missing guitar, not handcrafted, but maybe relevant. *Whispers—M or N?*

And then I discovered a most surprising fact. On June 29, 1980, early Sunday morning, approximately one hour after my sister called me, there were multiple reports of gunshots. *Gunshots.* Neighbors reported hearing several cars drive down to the lake house around 12:30 a.m. Several bordering neighbors reported hearing two distinct gunshots shortly after 2:00 a.m. from the direction of the lake house. "It sounded to me like a 22 rifle with a crack in it," one neighbor told police. About one or two minutes later, he heard a loud blast like a shotgun. "A 12-gauge," he surmised. "The sounds came from the direction of the lake house."

The same lake house where Gina was killed.

The police did log checking out the gunshots. They learned of a small cannon that would be fired by a local resident every July 4. The details indicate that little cannon was not fired, yet it seemed to be this thought process that derailed the continued investigation of the gunshots witnessed by several neighbors. It is apparent from how many interviews were conducted that this cannon theory preoccupied the investigators' minds. Was it a misdirected focus, steering the investigation further away from the truth? Maybe preconceived perceptions? Remember Kim Jett and her report of Gina being bothered inside of the Marriott. Another preconceived perception?

At this point, I was still only asking—Was Romano a victim or a villain? Somehow, had he known Epperly or Skipper from when he was a lifeguard living in the Claytor Lake area? Two Guys and a Girl was in the forefront of my mind. At this point, I was still thinking passersby, unexpected guests, believing those gunshots were from a few people—two, not many. It would be late fall before I seriously entertained the idea of a lake house party or a party at the dock beside the lake house. The messages would come and paint a different story.

The day before Gina's birthday—August 23—was the last time I dug in the muck at the muck place.

But the muck place was not to be forgotten. It is relevant.

On Gina's birthday, August 24, I met with VSP Special Investigator Santolla, who was assigned to Gary Romano's murder cold case. We went to Interstate 81 where Romano was believed to have been murdered. The investigator stepped off the 345 steps on a secondary road that ran parallel beside the interstate, marking the spot that aligned with Romano's truck. Standing there, looking down into that ravine, I felt a whisk of air gently kiss my face—the same feeling I'd had when I first stood at the Dedmon Center after Andy filled me in on the Dedmon dig. Of course at that time, I had just discounted it as the chilly wind. Now I was noticing the differences and I did wonder.

I could hardly restrain myself from climbing down into the ravine even in the high heels I'd worn to work earlier that day. Santolla did climb down in there, and I was glad he did. He saw nothing of relevance. I trusted his wisdom gleaned from his many years of experience.

My mind circled back to my original thought: *Did Romano see something? What if the lake house is not the connector? Perhaps it is the construction site there on I-81—wrong place, wrong time—that connects his murder spot to Gina.* One of Andy's clues had been the song, "Highway Don't Care."

Of course what did I do? I kicked off those high heels and spent the next Saturday searching the culverts and the ravine off of Interstate 81. I found an old mid-'70s Ford LTD hubcap stuck in the ground on top of a rotten tree. Of course I knew this hubcap was not *the* hubcap from the car that had pulled in behind Gary's pickup, but I was to see it so that I would connect the two, recalling the details of Romano's murder and the Ford LTD. The subtle clues were just reminders to pay attention to something else. And somehow, that chill told me this murder was connected to Gina's murder. My mind may have been working overtime, but this was my new reality.

That same day of Gina's birthday, this line awaited me on the notepad by my bed:

Don't forget DS think through this

DS—David Sauls? In 1980, David Sauls was the man who had spotted the van near my Monte Carlo after he had been run off the road at 5 a.m. on Sunday—by the same Monte Carlo. In 2016, I found the police report of this incident. I had remembered hearing about it in 1980. When I asked Shockley about it, he said he had never heard the name David Sauls or the car story. *Curious.* Austin Hall did not recall anything about it either. This was an important piece of evidence in the night's timeline. Sauls' first interview was a short line item on Hall's many interviews taken during a police roadblock, interviewing everyone who passed by the trestle. It was in this brief note Sauls mentioned seeing a van that morning. Sauls' second interview with police authorities was more detailed, as was his wife's.

This one little important message reminded me of something I had seen before. Now having learned that David Sauls was not even part of the trial proceedings, and knowing now that Shockley or Trooper Hall had not heard that name, I was perplexed about a document I saw with my own eyes. Purported to have come directly from Epperly's cell —a document Epperly had in his possession that had the name David Sauls written on it with a list of other people's names and to dos—names seemingly related to Gina's case, numbered as though Epperly wanted to deal with it in some manner like a priority list of sorts.

Throughout the years, many people have sent me information about Gina's case in random ways, and often I would even see information, not realizing its origins, or it would have no relevant meaning like this list. Now I was curious.

Why would Epperly be fixated on David Sauls? Something just does not reconcile as to why this man's name made it on Epperly's list. Could Epperly have somehow known about Saul's statement given to the police regarding the 5 a.m. reckless driving behavior when Shockley was never even told about it? Maybe Epperly recognized Sauls as the bait shop owner when he ran him off of the road. Could Epperly somehow have knowledge that Sauls had spotted the van, relevant to the farmer's story having seen a white van backed down to the creek? This would certainly warrant extra attention from Epperly if the farmer's story were true. Who had white vans in 1980? Mostly construction workers, painters, a mental hospital, drug dealers, and hippies.

The next day, I had this message:

DREW IT BEFORE. LOOK BACK

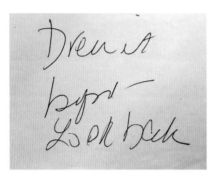
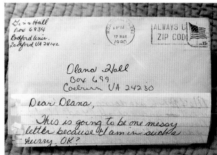

Drew what? This one didn't even look like my own handwriting. Curious, I looked at Gina's letters just to see if any of the writing was similar. Of course, that could not prove anything one way or the other, conclusive beyond a shadow of doubt, but it certainly was interesting. I could see similarities in her numbers and the numbers I wrote down in the beginning: 6s and 9s. The "a's" and "b's" written in the messages were different from my handwriting, the "b's" similar to Gina's handwriting, yet still, it bothers me that I would have even gone down this rabbit hole.

I saved my dad's letters, too. A relished Happy Valentine's Day note scribbled quickly on a memo pad sheet! Or my most appreciated notes that always came with just two words—Love, Dad, and a hundred dollar bill enclosed, often with an extra note—*for medicine* knowing that one of his grandsons was sick. He always just knew.

I looked back at all of my messages to see what I had drawn—the orange stakes, the triangular rock, the light rectangle with a purple flower, the dismembered body, the rocks, the wall, Civil War soldiers, and most importantly, the symbol of the image in the water.

What was I to see?

The night messages continued coming closer together. Sometimes I call them dreams, but they are more like flashes of different scenes: First the driving scene with huge rocks. Then I am with girls being chased. Then I am with Buz again. These visions are not really dreams. They are a description of the scenes, like watching a movie flashing by in my sleep state, and sometimes I would wake like this night and write the details down on paper of what I had seen, not really understanding what I was writing. But the majority of the time, the messages were just written in the night with no memory of even writing the message. As I later pieced together all of the pieces—the story I believe we are to know, the answers to my questions were layered in the vision messages.

September 8, 2016

I had a dream I was driving to meet Buz. It was getting dark. There was a huge landslide with rocks and dirt everywhere. The rocks were huge, and I did not know if I could make it through the small space, but I couldn't go back so I went on through. They were flat-faced huge rocks. Then I made it to meet Buz.

We were eating, and I knew we were being followed.

The girls tried to get me in the bathroom. We fought. She escaped by running out the door. We hurried to leave, packing everything fast because the man and the woman were coming to get us. The man was fair-skinned, tall, with a small-build and blondish. We made it to the bus. They did, too.

I had to go to the bathroom before getting on the bus. Buz and I also had a lady who was going with us.

I was surprised we were taking the bus to Norfolk.

September 13, 2016

I asked did others help or did he kill them too.

And a dream vision: Lots of chains. Chains hanging from ceiling. Wood platform in background. Empty. Abandoned.

And a message: I was helping my friend, but then my friend decided to stay, and since I witnessed, I had to chain her up and not let her go.

September 16, 2016

> Dreamed about a woman with a large scar on her right cheek (purple). She had black hair, was pretty, and wanted to move from here. She was from Nassau originally. She had a baby and was moving to Roanoke. The scar could have been a bruise because it was purple. She was going into hiding. In her hands was lots of food to take. She was taking the baby and food until (illegible-maybe "husband") would move her to Roanoke.

My messages were getting more complicated, with more layers of meaning. Who was this black-haired girl? She kept surfacing in so many different places. Nassau, the country? Or somewhere else? A victim maybe with a bruise?

About a year after this message, Andy told me about another cold case murder in a town in Virginia during the time Epperly had lived near there.

On the paper, I would write:

KNIFE DREAM STAB

Nola got a message about a knife, too. A knife and a staircase. This had made no sense, until now, weeks later.

I would never have thought a knife had come into play. I do not believe that is what killed Gina, but I did wonder about its relevance after I ran into an old family friend—another unexplainable experience. I had not visited with Susie in years. That night, after seeing me, she had a dream. The dream still frightens her to this day. She shared, "I've never been a dreamer, and this was so real." She somehow knew she needed to tell me. "For some reason, Gina is on my mind. I feel this dream has something to do with her."

A beautiful, black-haired girl had been in Susie's dream. The girl's hair was perfect as though sitting over her

shoulders, her skin shining in the sunlight. But a man was taking liberties with her. Susie described this man as having a small build and curly hair. A rough-looking man. She said it was a chaotic dream centered on a woman, who just sat there, in the light. All of a sudden, Susie was in the dream and this same man was in her face with a knife at her throat. She said, "It was not a big knife; it was like a small knife we would have in the kitchen." The image of the knife in her face, at her throat, would not leave her thoughts. She said she was in a large room with lots of windows. She also recalled at this same party two people, a girl and a boy, who were going swimming. The swimming girl's hair was sandy brown and pulled up on her head. A year later, Susie called me to share that the details had stayed with her. The nightmare images would not leave her. She continues to say the black-haired girl is the most beautiful girl she has ever seen.

Nola had advised me to pay attention to the people closest to me. Susie was a dear friend of Gina and our family, but she would not have known about Skipper and his female guest at the dock swimming that early Sunday morning. Skipper reported in his statement that he decided not to swim, but he said of his female guest, "she peeled off her clothes, her swimming suit underneath." *Peeled off—really?*...words tell so much.

The same details as in Susie's dream would surface much later in the dream of a close friend. She and I shared a hotel room during an overnight event. She awoke and immediately began telling me about a very vivid dream she had had. I just kept listening. The similarities were frightening. Her childhood home, a man with a knife, the commotion outside, everything except the black-haired girl. The only new detail was that in her dream, the man with the knife was blocked by a wall that all of sudden was there in between them.

So why a knife?

A steak knife was on the lake house owners' list of known missing items. The bloodstains on Gina's jacket were more concentrated on the back shoulder area. Why would that be? Epperly was a strong man, so why would he need a knife? Could there have been others, multiple men? That missing kitchen knife surfaced in the utility room weeks later. Skipper's mother just put it back where it belonged, never calling the police to notify them that she had found it. They learned of this months later.

And then on September 22, 2016, I had this very strong image, a weird un-

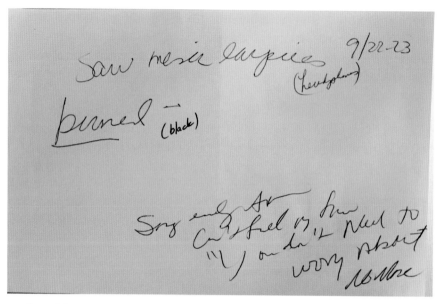

explainable vision that would later validate to me that there is no human explanation of *the how* behind my experiences. This message is significant in realizing just how much I cannot begin to explain or fully understand.

I wrote:

> Saw music earpieces (headphone) <u>burned</u> (Black)

I could see these black headphones as though they were just suspended in the air. In that moment, I assumed it had to do with the music because the same night I also had written this down in the corner:

> Heard song in my sleep. Can't feel my face-you don't need to worry about

> No more

The "No more" is in a different handwriting and does not in any way resemble my handwriting.

Seeing those black headphones scared me, but I was learning; time would tell.

I realize that many of my messages are confusing. They were to me, too. I really could not keep up. New messages kept coming, and my mind would go on to the next steps without a chance even to absorb those from the day before. Some days it was like when I was just a little girl on a hot summer day trying to drink from a water hose with the pressure turned all the way up. The new messages were coming at me full blast. I didn't know it, but some of the messages were becoming darker and more revealing. It was not as if there were a 1-800 number I could call to inquire about what was happening to me. I just took each day as it came.

I would never return to the river spot, and I did not return to the muck place again until October. All of this information over these three months had fueled my mind to be searching to get into the killer's mind. No one should have to do that.

OUR BELIEFS OFTEN COME FROM OUR EXPERIENCES WHICH
BECOME OUR PERCEPTIONS. THOUGHTS AND DECISIONS
ARE INFLUENCED BY PRECONCEIVED PERCEPTIONS.

CHAPTER 14

WAGON WHEEL

Where do we draw the line? A thin line that
should never be crossed intentionally.

Andy had a big day planned for us. He wanted to look at caves. Dana Harris from the local crime lab was a cave enthusiast who had often, over the many years past, thought of Gina and where she might be. He knew Andy wanted to find Gina, and he graciously wanted to help. We would meet up on September 17.

Our early drive to Radford began with one of those perplexing *no-coincidence* music experiences. If the truck radio was on and my phone is near, my playlists played. One of the first songs I ever downloaded was from the TV show *The Voice*: Aerosmith's "Dream On," sung by Amanda Brown. This day, my iTunes playlist decided to give me multiple duplicate repeats of the song.

After it had repeated several times, Buz said, "Please change your playlist. I don't want to hear that song again."

I did wonder too, *Why does that song keep playing?* I looked and that song had been duplicated six times on my playlist. Maybe I had somehow done that accidentally.

"Well, I can turn on Pandora," I said.

And when I did, the very first song playing was "Dream On" by Aerosmith. I laughed for ten minutes! They—whoever they are—do have a sense of humor. It was in this moment that even Buz scratched his head.

I do not know how melodies came into my head, waking me from a dead sleep. I cannot explain how songs seemed to play right when I was to hear them. I cannot explain how the lyrics seemed to fit the circumstance right when I was to understand something. I could not even begin to come up with all of this orchestrated, intricately designed plan. I learned just to let it happen. And happen it did. One of the first songs I ever downloaded was from a 2011 collaborative album by Yo-Yo Ma, Stuart Duncan, Edgar Meyer, and Chris Thile called *The Goat Rodeo Sessions*. I found the title intriguing! One day, I realized, as I would near the Radford exit, the same song from my collection would shuffle on: "Here and Heaven." I snapped a lot of pictures of my dash displaying song titles.

So when Andy organized this day of exploring caves with Dana, my husband and I joined them with curious intent. Little did I know that this day would be when the confusion from the chaotic messages would spiral into an understanding, but rather than bring clarity, it brought a deep, perplexing concern.

This Saturday's focus was to locate the many caves in close proximity to where my car had been abandoned in 1980, assessing the possibilities of whether any caves align with the secrets of the night that Epperly had kept for decades. We met the two men early that morning at the Radford police station. That was the same Saturday that Andy showed me the time-stamped text telling us what we were wearing. And I really could not decide what hat to wear for both in and out of the sun caving! The Radford Police Department building had been the old box factory in 1980. It was suspected that Epperly had walked right past this building on his way home after crossing the trestle. Sitting on the back deck of RPD, I looked out over the lawn, noticing for the first time several large boulders. In 1980, these boulders would have been hidden, surrounded by the woods. Nine days earlier, I had had a dream about big rocks, huge flat-faced rocks, just like these.

I had the Boulder Rocks dream on September 8; I saw these boulders on September 17.

Andy's friend Dana captured our attention with old maps and lots of knowledge of where the caves were, specifically caves that would have been more visible in 1980, their locations possibly known to Epperly, a lifelong resident.

In a quick while, we were standing at the opening of one particular cave ten feet up on the bank near the trestle. Several of the caves were right on the presumed path Epperly walked that early morning as he crossed the New River on the trestle. Buz and Dana went inside the caves, looking  for any crevice or small hole that might have been blocked or covered years ago. These type of small cave openings are all over this area. I agreed with Andy—what could it hurt to look?—but I would leave that to them. I wanted to walk across the trestle while I had permission.

Again, I found myself in a place I had been before, a place from the summer of 1980. Standing on the trestle looking out at the vastness of the woods and the New River, I thought, *Why would Epperly go all the way to Meadow Creek with so many places right here to hide a body?* Unless maybe he was on the

PHOTO COURTESY OF KATIE MONROE

other side of the lake for a reason--the boat? And the more I thought about it, the more I was starting to believe others had to have been involved. I glanced down to the area where my car would have been abandoned. I thought of the many statements of the activity witnessed around my car. Cadillac, van, two white boys at the trunk—twice, trunk lid up, trunk lid down. But for almost four decades, the story was always Gina alone willingly with Epperly.

To my left was, Bissett Picnic Park, which now extended closer to the trestle. In 1980, the area was thick with woods, old Indian lore describing the park area as being riddled with hidden caverns. Andy once shared a story of cadaver dogs finding Native American bones in caves near the New River in this park area. I knew of underground, disappearing rivers, dropping into the subterranean cave systems. I wondered, *Could it even be possible that cave passageways could exist underneath this river? If the topography was just right, they might connect one side of the riverbank to the other, maybe even opening right on the St. Albans land directly across the river.* St. Albans' caves were on the agenda for later in the day.

Climbing down into the ravine, I stood in front of the remnants of the large stone block foundation for the old trestle. A bumblebee disappeared into the earth at the foot of it. I thought, remembering the bees of August, *Pay attention to your thoughts.* I was looking at the vastness of the area, the melody in my head from the song "Gravedigger". It was probably just my own head recalling the lyrics of a Dave Matthews song, but how could I really know for sure? I was certainly close to many areas of significance, but I just did not believe Epperly had buried her whole body in a shallow grave nearby. It was searched so intensely in 1980, but if he had, I know my sister would have been grateful for the rain. Epperly was already so confident by Monday morning that she would never be found, but then again, she could be there somewhere closer than I thought. Where?

Realizing I had been gone for a while, and that my husband and Dana might be finished checking the caves, I climbed up and headed back. Arriving back at the truck, I saw that the Virginia Tech game Andy had been listening to had brought a smile to his face. The team must have won. I shared with him a thought I had while standing on the trestle looking up-river toward the I-81 bridge. A report I had read in Gina's case file from a Harrisonburg man who called into RPD to report that he thought he had seen a torso floating in the water as he drove over that bridge. He was not a local. He must have thought he saw what he saw to have made that call.

"Quit getting caught up in the minutia!" Andy exclaimed. He would tell me this when he would see my mind work like this, remembering every little detail I had read or heard.

Andy viewed everything from a larger perspective, and his police experience taught him to see these witnesses' and their "wild stories" as just that. I agreed. Some were far-fetched, like a torso floating down the river, seen from a bridge as one drives by. But not all of them were to be discarded or ignored. We can't forget the mountains of minutiae. We can't forget two human male bones found on the Radford side riverbank in that same general area. In 1980, hundreds, if not thousands of calls and statements were made to the police, in an era when everything was recorded on paper, easily lost in piles of paper. Andy approached Gina's case from a fresh perspective by interviewing many people, following new leads, and organizing others to search areas of interest just like today. I felt that with the passing of the years, perceptions could change and stories could evolve. I had sought truth from the initial words and leads from the very beginning, from 1980's initial weeks, before perceptions and composed stories could change. I believed everyone or anyone involved with that night thought it would all just go away and never result in anything happening with the case. They could never have anticipated John Hall. I found their words of utmost interest. I wanted to see all of the early minutia hidden in Gina's case files—boxes and boxes of single page reports. The tireless hours of the police and their recorded "first hand, in-the-moment interviews," from the beginning, not weeks later. The stacks of information—the minutia that no one else would have taken the opportunity to delve into as deeply as I would being Gina's sister. And I did not get to see but a small part of it. But I saw enough. The discrepancies in the many initial statements versus later statements was very telling. So much minutia a second book came to fruition to organize the chronological timeline. I learned quickly to search for the minutia—the hidden gems. And it would be the tiniest of details—the connecting pieces of a night of many secrets—that would become relevant, matching my messages in my quest for truth.

We loaded back up in my Ford F-150 and headed off to the next location— St. Albans Sanatorium, a mental asylum around which many paranormal ghost stories have sprung up over the years. The asylum had never been on my family's radar in 1980, and I do not recall it being on anyone else's. Dana had ascertained from his old caving maps that there were several caves near there, and it seemed one of the largest caves was now located under a parking lot on the St. Albans grounds built for the new asylum building. I do not know if that cave was searched before it was filled in and covered up in 1980. All my mind heard were Epperly's own words—"Everyone drives over...every day."

This was my first visit ever to St. Albans. As we drove past the back of St. Albans and pressed further into the property, I got a creepy, unsettling feeling. I reminded myself the focus today was caves. Dana knew from his old caving maps that there were many underground passageways in this area. We did find a sinkhole-like place covered in yellow flowering goldenrod and ragweed. Buz and Dana cleared out brush to see if they could find a cave entrance.

"A woman who works with me had worked at RPD in 1980," Andy told us. "She saw a vision right after Gina's death. She believes Gina came to her in a white, flowing gown. She was waving her hand, motioning to come in right to the entrance to a cave." Now I understood why Andy was so fixated on the caves.

An interesting tidbit—Romano was part of a cave rescue team when he lived in Bluefield, Virginia. I could not help but consider that if Romano helped Epperly dispose of Gina's body, a cave certainly would be familiar to him. Epperly could have known where most of the nearby remote caves were located. And then, if so, Romano would have been considered a loose end in Epperly's eyes. But even if not, I still believe Romano was connected to that night at the lake house.

My attention was captured by the tall pines in a row up on the hill overlooking the New River. I left Andy, Dana, and my husband in the fields and headed up the hill.

When I saw for the first time the new St. Albans building, construction completed in 1980, I knew then I would have to research the exact stages of its completion, right

down to the final parts— the sidewalks and that parking lot. Almost an impossible task.

As I walked around the new building, I came directly out in front of the old building. It looked nothing like what I had expected. My dream messages came alive. A row of windows faced the river, familiar from an earlier message and the old building—the brick mansion in my nightmare from August when it was dark and stormy around the mansion. The black skies symbolized the darkness I felt around this building, a place no longer a mental health facility, but now known for its ghost tours—a magnet for paranormal enthusiasts.

I turned around and walked toward the riverbank, wondering if I could see across the river. A steep, wooded hill dropped off right on Hazel Hollow Road. And then the experience became surreal. Looking down, I saw the chain

fencing I had drawn earlier, described as both concrete and metal poles. My exact words written had been "concrete or pole." I saw both, alternating. It was here. The similarities were uncanny. At this point, I was silently overwhelmed with emotion. I remembered that *orange* was in that same dream and that as we had driven onto the property earlier, I had no-

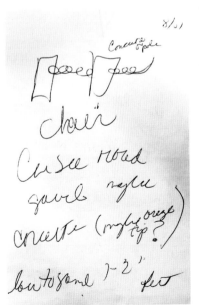

ticed an orange chain stretched across another entry point. I walked over to it and found myself in front of the side of the old building. And there in front of it was a raised area. It looked as though it could have been a fountain just like I had also written—a fountain in front of a mansion. A raised area encircled in old stones that had been filled in with grass and small shrubs. Clearly it had been something else in the past, a spring-fed fountain or old wells. When? I had to find out if there had ever been a fountain at St. Albans. I wanted to find out where the dining quarters were when the building had been operational.

As I kept circling the old mansion, I walked by a very large, rectangular piece of Styrofoam too big to move. As I turned the building's corner, I saw people painting T-shirts, preparing for the coming month of October's Halloween tours, with lots of shoes set on the ground next to their tables, details that matched my nightmare message. This was becoming quite disturbing.

I felt a strong pull to walk over to an old outside garden area near the back of the building. I walked right to this bench. There was my sister's name, Gina Renee Hall, engraved in the bench. It said it had been placed there in her memory by the Cool Kids Paranormal. I was both shocked and moved by the act of someone who still cared enough to honor my sister. *But why here, and who are the Cool Kids Paranormal?*

I just sat there on that bench contemplating my confusion. My August nightmare had taken place on the grounds of St. Albans. The one when my dad shook his head. The only time in my life I had ever experienced a dream inside of a dream. I remembered that in that dream, I had cried and fallen back asleep, and it had been as though God were telling me all was going to be okay. My mind dialed back to the very first dream I had had about the three goldfish. One of my first messages, three goldfish, one died, and I couldn't save it.

I wondered about the image from that August nightmare—the peaceful part with the fish. All of it had seemed crazy except for the fish in the shallow water fountain.

Today was becoming an emotional roller coaster. It was more than I could process.

That night, I texted Nola:

> How could I have seen all of this? It seems like I am seeing places before I am going to them. There seems to be a pattern.

Both curious and distraught, I started firing off my worries to Nola in long, erratic texts, contemplating for the most part, *How in this world could this be happening to me?* I told him I needed to understand this. It scared me to see these things I was seeing.

Later I received Nola's answer:

> Keep doing what you are doing. You are on the right path, but you must know where to stop if you don't feel comfortable. What makes the difference is intention. People, as society, block intentions since we were just little kids. They don't have the intention. The people in the Mind Reach experiments just make the intention and it happens. Intention = Paying Attention. Everything related to clairvoyance is intention. Without intention it won't happen.
>
> Take time to know what you are feeling. Enjoy and feel and know where things come from. Learn how they communicate and how they won't. Know the difference. That's the way you can determine if it is genuine or where it comes from. There are more things you don't see yet waiting for you to confuse you. You are doing good, but pay more attention.
>
> You need to learn to protect yourself from that negative energy now. Don't try to fly too high. Let everything happen by itself. Like in my case, all these things are interesting, but I do not want to look for something. Whatever comes comes as a gift. Everything comes by itself and when it's needed. What is not needed won't come.
>
> I just want to be 100% guided to do what God wants me to do. When you choose by yourself what you want to do, it is confusing and you could end up doing something that is not good or not allowed. Always ask for guidance.
>
> There is a thin line between these things and you need to learn what's what.

I had to ask:

> What do you mean intention? I did not want this. I did not have intent to dream about a chain fence with concrete poles or metal poles, and then actually see the fencing with alternating concrete and metal poles. What do you mean fly high? Thin line between what things? Them and us, being guided by wrong somewhere where I should not be? I only have you to trust when it comes to all that is happening. I know you, and I know you want only good for me, so I need to understand what I need to protect myself from.

Nola replied:

> Take your time. Grow like a baby and let it come and happen by itself. Gina is happy because you are finding happiness, remember? That's what she wants. You want to find her and that's what you are looking for, but that's not her priority. Her priority is to see you happy. To see you like you are now.

> Remember your daddy shaking his head?

Nola kept encouraging me to have ease with all of this, to let it come. To not fly too high—just to let things take their own course.

But Nola would also tell me later:

> St. Albans is not a place for you.

St. Albans is purported to be the most active paranormal location on the East Coast. That is a whole *lot of not good.*

Nola was warning me that the evil comes disguised.

I thought for a brief moment, *That's interesting that he said "daddy." The same as I say—not dad or father, but daddy.*

I thought about the many times I have had a subtle urge just to do something, like turn around in a room, or not go somewhere. That certainly would be paying attention, listening to the voice inside. But these happenings were not just feelings. These were visual premonitions of my future. He wanted me to tune in to these messages so I would know what was genuine, and what was evil. "Know the difference. There are more things you don't see yet, waiting to confuse you." He wanted me to be prepared. "Always ask for guidance. There is a thin line between these things. You need to learn what's what."

This is the first time I became frightened of what I was experiencing. I asked myself, *Could I really be dreaming where I would be going before I get there?* That is certainly what seemed to be the reality.

Upset, I closed my eyes and meditated in prayer, but I fell asleep:

> Daddy was with me, and we had to cross the road. It felt like someone was after us. Daddy stayed with me, but I was going to be late (for what, I don't know). We walked down a road. He

went on. I had to climb a hill. I could see stairs in the distance. [On my paper, I had drawn a flight of stairs up, flat across, descending down the other side and written on the hill.] I was worried about taking the baby (toddler) cause he would have to go down the other side but I knew I had to because I needed to hurry and someone was following us. I made it to class but had to change clothes, hippie clothes. It was chemistry class I was heading to. My daddy was shaking his head.

Why had my dad been in this message? *Was this a message...from him?*

The picture was a distinct drawing, like a trapezoid with a flat top and parallel slanted sides. Back in the '70s, when I was attending Radford University, I loved chemistry, and sometimes I dressed like a hippie. So maybe this was just a real dream about me, who I had been then. Then it made me wonder, *What if one of Gina's friends was a student, a chemistry major? Could there be a friend who would remember something?* Then, one day I saw it! The minutia. Could this report—the postal worker's report I had found in Gina's file—be about one of Gina's friends? Since the middle of September, the Wagon Wheel song had not stopped in my head or my dreams. The part of the lyrics I kept hearing was about A trucker from Philly heading to Johnson City, Tennessee. One little piece of paper—a police report taken about the naked and beaten girl picked up on the interstate by a trucker and believed to have been taken to Johnson City, Tennessee. *How did they connect?*

After I had received the message on September 7 about an old shredded blanket, I dug into research, reading everything. I was driven to know the truth. What drove me was an unrelenting purpose to know the truth of my sister's last moments as if she needed us to know. Love is a powerful, driving force.

As I absorbed every word I read, my mind weighed the possibilities. Andy had always believed Gina was still wrapped in that missing quilt. I wasn't sure. How had her hair been found, stuck in the blood on the carpet of my car trunk? It had been a thick, handmade quilt. Was Andy right? Was Gina's body still wrapped in that blanket? My mind worked to imagine it: Gina so petite, the blood would have had to soak through the quilt, her hair short, not long, would have had to fall out from inside a large, rolled quilt. And there was that one pubic hair found on the trunk's carpet. Maybe the blood and hair could have come from her bloodied clothes when placed in the trunk, but it seems most likely she was not rolled up in that quilt before she was placed in the trunk. It seems more likely she was just picked up and carried directly to the trunk. And I am even doubtful Epperly had her clothes in his possession after he carried Gina to the trunk. It is highly possible someone else had her clothes.

Then something caught my attention. Skipper's stepfather had given Trooper Hall a list of missing items: a blue towel, a striped towel, a small steak knife, a can of Dow bathroom cleaner, a Holiday Inn bath mat, a *gray blanket*, etc. I remember my stepmother bristled as she listened to trial testimony, upset that some seemed more concerned that the prized quilt was still missing than they were with the fact that Gina had lost her life. Skipper's mother had described the backing on the missing quilt as slate blue; His stepfather described it as gray. If I polled a random group of men, they would see little distinction between slate blue and gray.

As I researched, I discovered the story about the girl, naked and beaten, clutching a gray blanket around her, running out onto the interstate highway, picked up, maybe very near the I-81 overpass that crosses Claytor Dam Road, the truckers telling the story.

A rural postal worker had reported to Radford police Monday morning June 30, 1980, that while he drove his early Monday morning delivery route, he had overheard a conversation on the CB scanner between two truckers. The truckers were talking about a young girl who had been picked up. A girl, naked and beaten, wrapped in a *gray* blanket. The postal worker heard the truckers say she was so badly beaten that the trucker wanted to go straight to the emergency room at the nearest hospital, off the first exit possible, but she would not let him. The postal worker was not sure, but he thought the conversation implied that the girl rode with the trucker all the way to the end of his route—Johnson City, Tennessee.

The lyrics were now making sense from one of my earlier messages:

The Wagon Wheel Song

This is one of the most disturbing parts of this story. Who was that girl? Was she connected to the lake house? Was she so scared that she never came forward? Did she witness something she should not have seen? Did she even exist? But if she did, why did she never come forward with the truth—for Gina? Fear. I understand.

I believe the story about the naked girl wrapped in the gray blanket. I think it reveals much.

In 1980, I had had a CB in my Monte Carlo and an official handle "Buzzy-Bee." I would listen as the drivers of all of the eighteen-wheelers would chatter about the events of their day. Could this be what the bees were about—to simply remember my "handle" and connect the trucker's story to Gina's case? Gina knew this story:

Once, the winter before Gina was killed, I had made a stupid decision to get in my car when school let out and head to Northern Virginia during a snow emergency. Of course, I ended up doing a 360, to use my sons' snowboarding term—a doughnut in my Monte Carlo on Interstate 81, spinning into a snowbank, still in my dress attire from school—high heels! Those worked out well in the snow! A good-hearted trucker, holding back his laughter, gave me a good lecture and pulled my car out of the snowbank, instructing me to get off at the next exit. I did not. Buz was the destination! And I am positive I was the topic of some fun conversation for that trucker on his CB for hours. People love to tell their stories, over and over. I told Gina this story, over and over, so she would never do the same thing. This is why road warriors had CBs then, to help each other when people got stranded, or abandoned, or in trouble as this girl had been. The talk would have continued for hours, maybe days, spreading, always being discussed on their CB radios right as they passed the exact location of the event as originally shared with others by the trucker who picked her up. There is no way to know the exact time she was picked up. It could have been Sunday morning and the postal worker heard the truckers still talking on Monday morning in the proximity of where it happened. The story would just continue to be talked about at every passing of the mile marker by the many truckers until a new story came about. A lot like the 24-7 news of today, repeating over and over the same story.

Two dead bodies—Gina and Gary Romano—and now, a naked, beaten girl wrapped in a gray blanket, all within twenty-four hours of each other, all along a quiet stretch of the peaceful Virginia mountains.

So if the trucker story is true, which I believe it is, that girl could have wrapped herself in the missing gray quilt from the display rack in the master bedroom upstairs at that lake house. She might be the one my September 8 dream told me escaped:

> The girls tried to get me in the bathroom. We fought. She escaped by running out the door. We hurried to leave, packing everything fast because the man and the woman were coming to get us. The man was fair-skinned, tall, with a small-build and blondish.

My message was not about Epperly so who is the fair-skinned, tall blonde man with a small build? But the dream also would indicate there had been at least a second girl—a victim—there in the lake house. This also could explain the common O+ blood type found on two levels—upstairs and downstairs. Blood was found in both the upper and lower level bathrooms. It was assumed in 1980 that Epperly may have climbed the stairs after having killed Gina downstairs, grabbed the quilt, left Gina's blood on the upstairs bathroom light switch, smeared from his hand. But he was a man, and he would have had to first notice the quilt on the quilt stand in the master bedroom. Why would he take something he would know Skipper's mother would notice missing? I do not believe he would have. A sheet from a closet would have sufficed. I do not believe Gina was wrapped in anything, her hair stuck in the blood of the trunk carpet. Could some of that blood in the lake house be another girl's blood—a naked, beaten girl who grabbed the gray quilt, and escaped. Was she wrapped in that gray blanket that was missing from the lake house? Time would tell.

After learning about Epperly's mode of operation in his victim's rape reports, I began questioning how Gina ever even ended up downstairs if they came in the upstairs as Epperly stated. His mode of operation from multiple rape victims was consistent—swift. He would have taken her straight to a bedroom just as he stated in his own statement. But that was not the case when the downstairs carpet fibers were found on her clothes. I believe they entered the lake house downstairs through the sliding glass doors, left unlocked during that earlier visit to the lake house that the fisherman witnessed, before the Marriott. And the only reason to leave it unlocked was if guests were expected. It always goes back to the Marriott parking lot and the reason given for being there—to get Epperly the key to the lake house so he could take Gina there. Wow...*so he could actually take her there* reads as truth and twisted truth.

So many questions raced through my mind. By now, I was starting to understand why I had never accepted the story as it had been composed in 1980. This fueled my desire to know the truth even more. Who was wrapped in the missing gray quilt?

A story circulated in 1980 about the Sunday afternoon when Epperly returned at 4:30 p.m. from the lake house horseshoe picnic that Skipper had arranged. Epperly's mom confirmed this in her own report. According to the story, Epperly had told his mother that a man driving a Corvette nearly ran down a child in the street. Epperly's mom said he and his brother had "hopped in the Jeep and went off looking for the crazy driver."

Did Epperly have an underlying motive? He does not seem the type to care about a child. What was he really looking for? Maybe the girl who had escaped in the gray blanket? This mysterious girl would have been a loose end, just like Gary Romano.

And the interstate overpass on Claytor Dam Road is a trapezoid shape. Something to climb up.

As you drive to the lake house, you must pass under the I-81 overpass on the only road that leads to the lake house. The interstate is clearly visible above. The lake house was not that far away—maybe a mile. I believe the area where the escaped girl was picked up was this I-81 overpass that crosses Claytor Dam Road, which is why the postal worker overheard the truckers

when he was in proximity. Ironically, I was told that—*We miss you Gina*—showed up spray-painted on this same trapezoid-shaped overpass after 1980. Too many trapezoid shapes to figure out, as I would soon learn.

For now, I landed on the arched brick entrance at St. Albans. The concrete steps in a trapezoid shape matched the drawing and other dreams.

St. Albans continued capturing my attention. It was still bothering me greatly that so many of my dreams became real as I walked the St. Albans property. I looked back through my many photos from that eerie day. It was disturbing how many details about St. Albans were showing up.

Nola would tell me later he could see chains across a door. He described arched windows. I would discover later that half of the St. Albans building was closed down in 1980 and not used for decades. My research turned up a very old photo of the asylum, an aerial view. One detail caught my eye. To the left of the asylum appeared a curved white line, what could be the edge of a fountain. Now I wanted a historian to tell me exactly when this raised area had been completely filled in with dirt because of the details of my nightmare—the calm fountain with the fish, and my dream of not being able to save the goldfish.

The real surprise was when I saw the picture of the graffiti on the bowling alley's walls inside St. Albans. It had to be what I had seen in an earlier dream vision—the black, burned headphones. I knew then I needed to get inside to see it with my own eyes.

St. Albans had ties to Skipper's family. In fact, the family's involvement there spanned the entire history of the St. Albans Mental Hospital facility. It was the family business. Being a major employer in a small town usually lends to a position of power and influence. The original St. Albans complex was built in the late 1800s as a competitive boys school on land known for the Draper Meadows Massacre in 1770s, when a group of Shawnees attacked the white settlers. Stories abound from the days when the school was open. By 1916, the St. Albans Lutheran Boys School became the St. Albans Sanatorium for the mentally ill. The mental asylum was started by Skipper's family. This well-known mental hospital served hundreds of miles of territory for decades. By the mid-1940s, 6,500 patients had been through the asylum's doors. By 1960, it had become a recognized hospital for the region. My own mother had been taken there in the mid-1960s. The family oversaw it all, from being its founders to being doctors on the staff. Skipper's grandfather could have been my mother's doctor. This made my mind really churn at the connections of life's stories.

I had a vision the night of September 25 that would haunt me. I cannot begin to imagine how I saw this so clearly.

> I pulled back the carpet, and Gina's hand was there. The bones had been cut, severed cleanly. He had put her hand in my office, right underneath me.

I had never seen a picture of a crosscut of a wrist to even know what it should look like, but the detail was so vivid that I could have counted the tiny bones and whatever else is round in a crosscut anatomy of a wrist, seeing each cleanly severed bone as clearly as if I had looked right at a freshly cut wrist. Haunting.

Nola messaged that same day, telling me he saw a hand coming through brick. He also said he received "wood stairs" and "stabbed in the back—again."

When we compared notes, we had both seen the hand in the same way. I had seen it from the brick floor. He had seen it reaching through brick.

I was shocked at what I saw next in a dream vision:

> body cut off above the hips and was moving and sliding across the floor

Two nightmarishly vivid dream visions in a row, the severed hand and now this, beginning after I first stepped onto the grounds of St. Albans.

They were like clear pictures that woke me from a dead sleep. No story. No words. Just a glimpse of a vivid picture that I saw as clearly as if I were awake and looking right at it.

The same night, I wrote this note:

> Dreamed that I was swimming in a large place outside. Then it closed so I went over to the underground rooms. Swimming in there. Long Tunnels to rooms. Lots of different ones with doors to them. Then someone started chasing us.

Why did I keep seeing long tunnels with water flowing through them?

"Take a break," Nola said.

Struggling again with my experiences, I rattled off a response:

> I will slow down, but do you think I should not keep trying to find the truth about Gina? I feel I am supposed to. And the dream that Daddy was in came true last weekend at St. Albans, which is why I am dreaming where I will be in the process of searching for Gina. I want to find her and give justice to whoever if they cut her up. I am not sure I can have peace without finishing this, but I am trying. I will be away next week. I will try to take a break and listen to myself, and then, I promise I will slow down and see. Do you think it is about Daddy wanting justice? It seems illogical that anyone would ever get to that angelic place and want anything back here unless it is for the good of those still here. Maybe that is why I have such a sense of urgency, like something is going to change.

That week I had a trip out west, grateful to have it to occupy my mind. But someone somewhere would not care that I wanted a break. The messages did not stop coming, as though no time or schedules could be imposed in that spiritual dimension. And I now wonder, *How many dimensions are there?* How can we know? The Bible references a third heaven as though there are different realms. Nola had said Gina was in the third heaven. So why was I fixating on St. Albans? I have always known Gina was in Heaven.

As soon as I arrived at my hotel, I noticed a wooden, covered bridge walkway, up the stairs, across the road, down the stairs, reminding me again of the trapezoid drawing. And a Pier 111. Really? I redirected my focus on the beauty surrounding me—God's canvas. But that did not last long; the messages started coming full force.

PAY ATTENTION TO YOUR THOUGHTS...

CHAPTER 15

DREAM ON

I could not sing and laugh with her
because I was not listening with the heart of my soul.

A woman named Sherry, who had retired from the Ohio Department of Corrections, contacted me on October 1. Her email was too specific for her to be just another gifted person wanting to find Gina. My first cousin had connected us, and I paid attention for that reason, plus another—her reference to a large rock with a vertical hole. A trend was becoming obvious. People coming into contact with me, or others associated in the past with my family, seem to have sudden dreams, visions, or urges that were not the norm for them. Think of the multitude of people connected to *the journey* so far: Nola, Andy, Kevin, The Preacher, The Farmer, and on and on. The details of Sherry's vision were so precise to the area near the lake house, which is uncanny when you take into account she had never set foot in Virginia. In her email, she wrote:

[Do you know] of a road that headed west and had an approximate 30 degree curve to the left and at the curve on the right there was foliage, a house, or something that used to stand there years ago, many years ago. This area on the right where something once stood would not be easily noticed, but if someone was an old timer, they would know it was what was left of a lane or driveway or whatever property was there years ago. From that spot, if you look back across the road on the other side, you will see a hill or incline,

257

and only in the winter, you can see this big rock or more like a boulder. The rock is approximately 6 feet wide and approximately 5 feet high. Huge thing with a rather flat top, enough you could possibly lie down on it. Behind this rock there were burrows/dens from an animal. Epperly knew of these burrows/dens. I think because they were so large and they seemed to go almost straight down. He used this for an already-dug grave to save time in hiding his crime. I believed she was bundled in the quilt and placed in this area, and the rock, which will never change location over many years, was his marker to revisit his crime. This huge rock sits approximately 30 to 50 yards off this road and up an incline area, wooded/foliage. Its top is a little higher on the right side than the left. You would not be able to see it in the summer months very well from the road, if at all. I believe she has been placed in a vertical grave within his arms' length. This is very hard for me to share because I just don't know if any of this will help, and like I said I am not claiming to be a psychic and I have never been to Radford. I pray she will be found this year.

A few weeks earlier, September 22, the Google page was a cartoon depiction of a family of rocks. Remembering the earlier dream I had had about boulders, large boulders everywhere, I screenshot it. It reminded me of the Radford Police Station.

Time for a trip to Radford. Now I wanted to look for a big flat rock near an old lane and explore a long list of places of interest. What I hoped for was that if I drilled down through the whole list and kept on it, I would find exactly what

I needed to know. I wanted to be comprehensive. I didn't want to overlook a single thing. This was for my sister, and it seemed long overdue.

Buz and I went back to the muck place so I could go up on top of the hanging, plant-adorned, rock-ledge cliff that bordered the muck place. I saw a flat, untouched field of reeds; it was familiar, having seen it already in a dream vision. Another premonition. Walking through the flat-reeded area, I wanted to move every rock I saw, especially those stacked one on another. We found a shrine-like place with rotting remnants of what had been a very large tree that had fallen decades ago, and a large standing tree near it bore plaques of the Virgin Mary, a cross, and a religious figure. Were these out-of-place religious ornaments nailed into the bark as a memorial? Marking a grave, maybe? Whose grave? I cannot help but wonder about the black-haired girl. Who is she? Could she have been at the lake house? A witness who also became a victim of the night, a memorial justified because she was known and loved by another associated to the night. Or could the memorial have been placed there for Gina, in guilt, knowing where Epperly had buried her? The tree was within yards up above the muck place, high above Hazel Hollow Road. I even wondered if the flat-topped cliff rock could be what Sherry was actually seeing in her visions. It would look different in the winter. This area is part of the Ingles Historic Farm, protected for many more years to come from any potential development. Epperly would have known this in 1980.

A few graveyards were on my list to visit. It was time to rule out Epperly's stories that were wild goose chases, and nothing more. There had been that rumor in 1980 that Epperly had buried Gina in another person's fresh grave. I walked these old graveyards looking at the names and dates of death on the tombstones. I silently wondered if I stood

where she was, would I feel that gentle wisp of air? My next stops: The clearing area above the dump site and cliffs at the butterfly spot. The road on the old 1980 map must have grown up over time. It was getting late, and I knew I was pushing my luck with Buz. It was time to travel back home, but I had a sudden desire to go to the Dedmon Center at Radford University, on the opposite end of town. We had not been back there together to the university since our college years. I had only been to the

Dedmon Center the day Andy told me about the Dedmon Dig—the first time I had ever experienced a wisp of air gently kiss my face, but I quickly dismissed it as my own emotions.

When Buz pulled around the road encircling the Dedmon Center, I saw the exact picture I had drawn again—a new place, the steps up to the soccer stadium seats and down the other side. And in that same dream, I could have been the student dressed in hippie clothes going to chemistry class. I used to sit right across the road on a grassy knoll near the science buildings and study, before these buildings were all here. Now I had a new trapezoid place, two with steps: The concrete stoop at St. Albans and the Dedmon Center soccer field stadium seats.

This trip to Dedmon Center also got me back on my circular kick, *Completing Circular not linear*, looking for a circle under which we would find Gina's body. Even the grass was shaded in a circular pattern around a manhole that matched one of my longitude/latitude clues. This particular spot was very near the Dedmon dig. Andy had told me recently that he had recalculated the math and believed they should have been digging farther up, near the soccer scoreboard. But, of course, they could not get permission to dig again. I cannot help but wonder who in 1980 lived in the Victorian house that had once stood near this spot.

As we drove around the Dedmon Center, a large rock cliff across the river caught my eye. I had an urge to walk to the river's edge. I walked right up to a deep, vertical hole with petrified sides. The holes had obviously been there for a very long time. Why would RU not have filled them in? I now know that six-foot-deep, vertical holes exist, possibly remnants of boat dock pole supports from long, long ago, or trees that had simply fallen into the river, leaving behind their rotting stumps to petrify. Where else might we find the same? Someone familiar with these woods might know, realizing the convenience of using a vertical grave. Could there have been one just like this above the large cliff rock at the muck place, where the shrine was found?

Andy had always told me he could see Gina placed in a vertical grave, wrapped in the quilt, her arm and hand up by her face so someone could almost reach in and touch her hand by reaching down inside. Just like Sherry. Just like the  grandmother who had said, "Those boys searching for that girl walked right by her arm sticking out of the ground." And now another layer—that Gina was bundled in a quilt, placed in a vertical hole near a big flat-faced rock. All that took me back into the woods.

One day, Kevin and I were standing by the big rocks at RPD. He told me he had a very bad feeling. He could see an indentation in the rock. It looked to him like a place where a person, if they were to lie back on the rock, would fit. "Something bad happened here," he said. When I laid back against it, I understood what he meant. I remembered an online discussion I had stumbled onto when I was researching St. Albans a few weeks earlier. I discovered that the case of my sister's murder was still so alive and the name Steve Epperly had prompted two women to share their long ago encounters, easily shared now in the internet age. Both women shared similar stories about Epperly coming on to them by asking them to help him move. *Going to the box factory to get boxes must have been a common lure he would use.* Ironically, this old box factory building now houses the RPD. The large, flat-faced rocks adorn the surrounding grounds. This area was not only a place of interest to Kevin, but it certainly became a place of interest to me. All of these clues about boulders and holes, the Dedmon Center, St. Albans, the shrine, the graveyards—they made it feel like I was chasing clues but getting no answers, just more questions.

All of this just kept stirring my curiosity, and I began to wonder, *Could there be multiple places with multiple victims? Could that explain the deluge of clues—why there were so many directions to explore and all of them seem to be flooding me all at once?* If you looked at this list, Gina could be in a million places—in all of the places—if her dismembered body had been hidden like in a scavenger hunt. Or it could be that there were many victims—perhaps even another from that night at the lake house, but also perhaps victims from long before my sister encountered this man at the Marriott. Epperly's history of being a sexual predator showed up numerous times in Gina's case file, in addition to the two 1976 rape charges. There was much history of violence against women. Victim reports. This is not the case of an all-American boy, as if it only happened this one time, who in a fit of induced rage murdered my sister, as if it were her fault because she would not have sex with him. This was a serial rapist. And, as was yet to be seen—perhaps a serial murderer, too.

All of this weighed heavily on my heart. I wanted to walk away. Just quit. But truth was important to me. I have always been a seeker of truth. It was no longer just about justice in investigating the second man the farmer saw in Meadow Creek and what he had seen. It now seemed to be about something bigger.

I sent Nola the St. Albans pictures. His thoughts:

> I have a strong feeling she's there—the strongest feeling I have felt since we started.

In 1980, three major projects in the Radford area and several smaller ones on the RU campus had been undergoing construction. The prevailing rumor was that Gina's body had been placed in a concrete foundation being poured at that time. The new St. Albans building had just been completed and Dedmon at RU had already begun. Other RU construction plentiful. A distributing plant in Pulaski County was thrown out as another one of Epperly's red herring games shared with Andy by a prison-time girlfriend. Epperly was working in construction. And he knew concrete. That was his job in June 1980. So many theories centered on Radford University, many believing Gina could be in the concrete under the Dedmon Center spurring the legend of Gina's ghostly presence on campus.

I did find it interesting that on Monday morning, June 30, Epperly was pouring concrete on the Radford University campus. Details shared with the police by Housel, his June 1980 construction boss and longtime friend, provided the details of Epperly's job site for the day. A concrete stoop was being built at what Housel called the "brown building." Interesting that this boss was one of Epperly's chosen character witnesses.

My husband laughs when he recalls how in 1980 I marched my sassy self right into RU's President Dedmon's office and demanded the places where Epperly had worked be thoroughly checked. I never knew about this next place mentioned in this person's story.

Even though Housel reported the job site on that Monday morning was "the brown building," whatever that meant, a man who worked on the job with Epperly named Jay shared this story with his family: Jay always was the first to arrive to work, but that Monday morning when he got to the job site before the sun came up, Epperly was already there. Epperly was always late, but that day he was right there. Trenches for the job had already been dug and filled with gravel. Jay believed Epperly put Gina in those trenches. The trenches/forms setting the foundation for the *Allen building*. Shortly after Jay arrived, Epperly's friend, the psychiatrist's son, showed up flailing his hands as though excited or upset with Epperly. The two of them skedaddled out of there. "Flew out of there" were Jay's exact words. It was still dark when this happened, according to Jay's sister re-telling Jay's account of what he had witnessed. That account is somewhat similar to Skipper's account; Skipper said he did go to RU, but not until Tuesday morning after class, and after the Barbell visit, so not before the sun was up as told in Jay's account. And there is no mention by either of them of leaving quickly together as Jay had witnessed. Maybe Skipper visited both times: Monday morning, a visit to RU to find Epperly, maybe before dawn, and returned again to Epperly's job site Tuesday morning after the Barbell gossip when he first learned that everyone else knew too, including us, the name "Steve."

It would be interesting to run that radar machine over every spot like this stoop that was being constructed at RU Sunday and Monday, June 29 and June 30. Seems simple enough. *But how could we ever check all of those foundations?*

I prefer always to remember that it is just a physical body—a vessel for her soul, and her soul is not there. If he chose to bury her in concrete, then it would not be necessary for me to be on this journey because that could mean she was buried, alone, in one place. I was searching for the truth of what had happened that night. I was searching for her body because I believed there were other bodies. Other victim's bones lying with hers. A trophy graveyard. There were others who would finally have peace if her bones could be brought home—home to her empty grave.

I'm glad I had a lot of loose paper by my bed on October 1 because it would be a busy night of messages. And from the handwriting, I believe an "influenced" night from all directions.

The first crazy message that came October 1, 2016 was:

> drew 4 black dots in a row with the word Important written under the 4 black dots.

I had no idea where to begin on this message. A few days earlier, curious about some of the backroads near Claytor Lake, I asked our new caving friend Dana if he had any old maps that would help me. Three days later, he sent a map that included Route 611, Wilderness Road, looking very much then just like it does now. I had driven this road many times, parking at the end, walking up the river to dig at the butterfly spot where I saw Gina's face in the sunlit, glistening water. What I later saw on this old map were four distinct, round, black dots lining Route 611, the black dots representing where the houses had been in 1980. That was what I believed this crazy, off-the-wall message from October 1 was about. Or maybe the four dots are The Preacher's four Victorian houses that once stood in the Dedmon dig area? Is the interpretation a place with four houses? No matter—time to head back again to Wilderness Road. The "Wagon Wheel" song written the same night again, maybe for a new and different reason like simply wagon wheels, validated this choice right or wrong.

A second:

> One Door Wagon Wheel Song. Smaller crowd. her same

And a third:

> Wall-1/2 glass small sections. not all of it just part of it.

> It's under your nose

Right under your nose! Is someone losing patience with me? And what is "It"? This was definitely not my handwriting. Look at that "s." I am not even sure I could reproduce that "s."

I knew I was to listen. I knew I was to pay attention. I knew I was to *dream on.*

The Radford Police Station with the large rocks in its backyard was the first thing that came to my mind. But one evening, as I turned off Main Street onto the street that leads to the RPD, I glanced out my window to the right and saw it—*one door.* The Glencoe Museum displayed several actual doors in their frames as artwork in the yard. No walls. No ceilings. No windows. Just single doors—one door, free-standing intermittently in different places up on the grassy knoll.

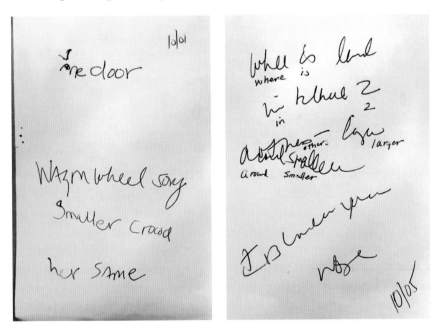

I walked up the museum hill, a property bordering the Radford Police Station, for a closer look. Buz and I had been there a month earlier. We had sat on the grassy hillside that drops off to the back of the museum, maybe 20-30 yards up from the train tracks and the trestle. We were having a picnic lunch on this grassy knoll, taking a break from searching an area of focus down over

the tracks in the ravine and the woods where Gina's clothes had been found. I had never paid any attention to the museum. I did not even remember it being there in 1980.

One red door. Standing alone, displayed as art.

Right under your nose. Red Door. Walked to it.

Other messages matching this place: Civil War, Va Brochure, wagon wheel days, up on the hill, placard. Under the words—*Under the placard?*

Now I was off in a different direction, putting the St. Albans no-coincidences on the back shelf for a while. Now I was focused on *one doors*. The museum, the old box factory now RPD, the asylum all seemingly logical "right under your nose" places. But even the RU Allen building would be an "under-your-nose-kind-of-place" because it houses the RU campus police. Of course, the most logical being Epperly's own home. It felt like Epperly himself was messing with me.

On October 11, I awoke in the middle of the night to a song melody in my head. It was a line from the lyrics of the song "Just For Now." I was now believing I was supposed to get my sister out of somewhere.

Some nights are just busier. I also wrote:

Same dream. The Chains. He would talk so he was a witness.

> 2 guys and a girl witnessed? 2 shots? My dream was about witnessing so had to help. Tied up.

And that same night:

> Red door walked to it? And, I drew a T with a capital A on each side A A.

And I wrote:

> Maybe just dreamed about an old, white-haired man.

> Triangular rock important in 2 dreams tonight. Passed it and went back.

And I had the following message:

> As we left there, before I was walking in dark halls-when I was showing my artwork -the things I had drawn, we were in a car driving together. I was in the front looking back.

I understood the triangular rock. The muck place. The dark halls and artwork kept coming up. But the most interesting this night was that *I was in the front looking back*...looking back at what? Other people in the backseat of a car? Looking for another car following behind?

And just two days later, I would wake and see what seemed to be a crazy dream from where I just do not know. Secrets of a female patriarch of a family who had had an accident—maybe a truck accident in 1996? *Could this be the party line that Nola had referenced?* Others breaking through. I called these type of messages *a dream*, but I later contemplated that even if I woke in the night, remembered a dream, wrote it down, then fell back asleep, not remembering in the morning having written a dream down—if that is what was happening with these dream-like messages, then I must question—how could I dream *1996*? So details like this, many in those scribbled night notes, tell me now looking back that these are more than just dreams. But at the time I only wondered whether there was a family with this history in the Radford area connected to Gina's case or to St. Albans?

And in this dream, I clearly saw the half-moon-shaped hole in the foundation top. This vision stayed with me longer than the others. From that day forward, I just knew I was to look for the half-moon hole everywhere I went, scanning the foundations where they met the walls and asking myself, "Why?"

This was that October 13, 2016 dream-like message:

> Big house? Secrets. Me and three friends visiting. They had
> killed five people, but I was not sure how. I wanted to see the
> basement foundation as home was built. But they were watch-
> ing us. One was crazy, so she slipped and told us five. So we
> got her to leave us so we could look.
>
> Strange family-everyone was protecting the mother. Lots of
> dark halls and passages down into a dark basement, but I
> needed to get down there. Something happened to the lady
> in 1996 with a truck. They laughed about it, but that is when
> she changed and became scared and little crazy. Got them to
> leave us behind so we could try to look for the five people
> that were dead.
>
> Thought there was a circular hole that could be partly seen
> under the walls where they attached to the foundation—I could
> see airspace like a hole in a foundation top and see part of a
> hole from the side of the wall.
>
> The lady was the boss and she headed the family. She killed
> the five people and they all kept her secret.

On October 14, I went to Radford specifically to go into The Glencoe Museum. The curator showed me a photo of this place during the Civil War
days. And, also, a telling photo taken around 1980. To my surprise, this old
beautiful Civil War home was completely engulfed in trees and brush. In
the upper right corner of the old Polaroid photos, the second-story roof
peaks up through the overgrowth. No wonder I did not remember it.

The curator shared, "This forgotten, ignored historic home was known as
a place for vagabonds in the '70s. The basement became known as a party
place to the locals."

His words brought an earlier message to mind, the song lyrics from "Not
Going Anywhere" by Keren Ann Zeidel.

This area borders the woods where so many people spent countless hours
searching for Gina. The train tracks and trestle are within 100 yards. This
location was just a few blocks from Epperly's home, an alluring place, hidden in the overgrowth right beside the old box factory in 1980. The discovered clothes, tool, and towel led everyone to search up and down the

Kallimorgen Island Parking Lot (before 1980)

tracks and in the ravine across the tracks. The house was barely visible to a passerby, and had been abandoned for decades. The unique shape of the windows of the basement door, just like I had described earlier from a vision, caught my eye. I was curious whether it had ever had a dirt floor or a bricked floor, remembering what Nola had said about the severed hand reaching through the brick.

Now restored, the beautiful Civil War home was perched up on a grassy hill. Could this place have been relevant to Epperly's life before he murdered Gina? What other secrets might this old house from his past hold?

Why was I led to this place—a place "completely out of sight in 1980," hidden by nature and years of neglect? It was bordered by the woods where a lot of evidence was found. It was so close to the big, flat rocks at RPD—the old box factory. Maybe Epperly had buried Gina right where the red one door artwork stands and the Civil War placard marked the spot—exactly. Right under our nose. The curator told me that in 1980, a landfill dump site had surrounded this barely visible Civil War brick house and the old Radford police station had backed right up to this landfill. This seemed too obvious, and why then would Epperly have been so confident we would never find her? Everyone in 1980 was looking for a body, not body parts. *Red Door, walked to it.*

I wondered, *Was this old landfill Epperly's graveyard? Now it's a parking lot that people drive over every day.*

It became apparent to me that this forgotten, ignored two-story brick house, completely covered in thick brush, might have been overlooked

in 1980. And the landfill had been an insurmountable task. And all of the evidence, placed, had led everyone away from the most obvious. This old Civil War home was now definitely another place of interest to me.

I remained haunted by an image I had always seemed to have had for many years as I would travel Interstate 81 on my many trips home from northern to southwestern Virginia. Heading south, crossing the long highway bridge that spans the New River near Radford, I would always unconsciously turn my head and glance up that river, quickly feeling sick to my stomach when the disturbing vision of a black trash bag would come into my mind, as though my sister were still in it. I believed this vision was just my imagination, but for many years, passing through this part of Virginia, with my boys asleep in their car seats, my eyes would scan the side of the road, all the way from the Radford bridge to the Claytor Lake exit, for a black trash bag. That was a memory I tried not to remember but never could forget.

Whether Epperly had dismembered Gina, and maybe even others, or not, his own shed could be a place to consider. Carrying a black trash bag across the street to the landfill would not seem out of place. Dismemberment never made logical sense to me. It would require more places to bury the body parts, and more places meant more chances to discover his crime. Or, in actuality, easier to hide his crime if a landfill were his graveyard.

On October 17, I saw the vision again of the hole in the foundation:

Doing good. Correct path. Foundation half-moon hole in top.

Can see it could be partly seen under the walls where they attach to the foundation.

Could see airspace like a hole in the foundation top and see part of the hole from the side.

Before I went to sleep on October 21, I despairingly thought, *Please, Gina, if you are in that museum, give me an idea of where I need to look. This is a museum, so I cannot dig up the entire basement.*

That night I had a dream:

> All of my credit cards were stolen. I was in a restaurant with friends. I opened my wallet and all were gone. (I had a clear picture in my mind of my beige wallet that is full of credit cards being all empty.) I went back to the hotel and sat at a desk trying to get the computer to boot up so I could call the credit card company.

I really thought this one must just be a normal dream. Then I remembered that when I had visited the museum, there had been a gift shop in its basement with a receptionist desk just like in my dream. I could see in my dream walking down the steps just like in the museum.

And then this detailed message:

> We were all together somewhere, maybe a picnic-like place, and I shared my food (1/2 a chicken), and I showed my artwork to my friends, but then I left. I was walking in a hall underground with dark and dirty floors. I was walking to a door. I passed two boys, and one was stealing my stuff from my bag on my shoulder. It looked like he had taken a white, small item. Right when I was walking up a few stairs and concrete stoop leading out of the dark halls, I yelled at him for taking my stuff. Earlier while at the table with others, the two women had been with the two guys. And the girl could have been with the "rock" looking one or the puny one.

I am showing my artwork again, having just written about walking into a dark hall underground and showing my artwork a few weeks earlier. Many questions arose from this one message: *Could the artwork be the one doors at the museum? And who were those two boys—the puny one and the rock (strong?) looking one? And what about the two women who had been with the two guys? Was this something seen at the Marriott earlier? Another layer of people? And a girl—not one of the two women. Who? And who is the puny one?* Probably not Epperly or certainly not Skipper who was much bigger than Epperly. Or, in a way, Epperly would be puny if only compared to Skipper. *And who is at the table—two women with the two guys—the*

Marriott? What had Gina owned that was small and white? She had worn a gold necklace that night. Andy would tell me he had always sensed that Epperly kept an item from each of his victims. And part of the St. Albans building, the King Center, has a trapezoid-shaped, concrete stoop leading out of those dark halls.

On the same night, I illegibly wrote and to this day, no idea:

> Nixier (or niyler?) Branch

And,

> I had to decide who got to stay with us. There were three or four of us. I decided to (cheat?) the others and ran, trying to lose them. And I had to hide my backpack with the info in it. Lots of rooms and tunnels with water in it. Just get across the street from the first place. It was my family's place, but after, it did not seem like it. I hid the backpack with me with all of my important info buried in it. But then got into the car and put the important stuff in the car because someone would find it.

I had no idea what that message meant. Did Gina have a backpack in the car? Was it Epperly's backpack with important papers? My first thought was that the museum is across from St. Albans, but then I concluded that since I was at the museum/landfill area during this time frame, across the street could be the Epperly home. I envisioned that someday someone would tear through Epperly's childhood home, piece by piece, and find these items, his collection, and there we would find something of Gina's. Maybe something white. *Maybe her teeth?* Such a disturbing thought.

The Epperly house surprisingly went up for sale in October 2016, having been in the Epperly family since the 1800s. I considered buying it under an alias, but as *the journey* progressed, I realized that would not be what Gina would want. It was just a body. She was elsewhere. And if her body, or bodies, were there somewhere, eventually it would be known.

A sense of urgency was building in me. The messages came in succession, one after another with layers of complexity, yet simple messages that could be seen interlaced within the storyline.

I was starting to become frustrated. If all of this could be told to me, then why could someone just not tell me where she is? Andy always believed she did not know herself. I was asking, *What is the real purpose of all of this?* I felt like I was on the brink of another change.

When I wrote down two full names—Denton Jones and Nancy Rae Lubick—or three names—Denton, Jones, Nancy Rae Lubick—I landed on two guys and a girl believing that was a correct interpretation. Is there any way to ever know for sure if our own thoughts that lead to interpretations are truly our own thoughts? Maybe I had just interpreted it wrong. If so, then how can "two guys and a girl" be the same as another's vision from three years earlier—two guys and a girl standing at a car with headlights on burying Gina. Maybe I was given this concept in a name clue, and not just given "two guys and a girl" because I could have easily surmised it just came from my own subconscious having known the story shared by Andy's Dedmon dig psychic, The Preacher, years earlier. Seems to me two guys and a girl is relevant.

I did stop and ponder at times, *Why not just tell me where Epperly hid my sister's body?* Later, I asked, *Why would it be some crazy puzzle-like game? Here are some names.... Now, Dlana, figure out what they mean.* Is there any way to really know the messages' true origin? It is more than I can comprehend at times. Is there some rule in that realm that says we can't tell you the exact truth because of free will, but we can guide you...and only when you genuinely ask for help can we intervene? I do not know the answer. I only can share what actually happened to me, writing down two off-the-wall names, with no prior knowledge of those names in my life and no cognizance of writing them. I still do not understand fully the origin of my experience and probably never will. But I do believe those who love me would not mess with me. And those who do not love me would revel in the game of deception. Why would Gina, or my daddy, or my spiritual army, give me these messages? Unless that is just how it works. I think of parts of the Bible where prophets receive messages that seem to be like riddles. Look at Revelation! I believe no matter the origin, it is still always God in control—God's timeline and we will know what we are to know when the time is right. Then it will no longer be a riddle! I do not believe God and His spiritual army would give me a perplexing clue or allow other heavenly beings to do so unless I just had to figure it out because there was a *process* that I had to come through. A larger message that I was to see and experience so I would understand, like learning to simply pause and question the true source of one message.

But then again, how can we ever really know?

I looked for pity from Nola. I told him:

> You said once you knew your purpose in my life and that I had to find it
> for myself. I wonder now what it will be. People need closure from bad
> things, and I want to help them. I don't like people to be hurt or sad.
>
> I just can't seem to accept that he cut her up and put her in all those
> places.

Nola was patient with me. He texted back:

> Let everything take place by itself. Try not to force it, and be patient.
> Everything will come by itself in the right time, not when we want….
> [There is a] lesson we need to learn first before it happens: Everything
> is in order for a reason.
>
> Just follow the guidance. It will make sense later.

Nola was right. I paid attention to my thoughts that seemed to come from
nowhere or would pop back up from an earlier message just like that June
22 airplane note I had written down. It was so specific and perplexing, yet
simple. A moment of understanding came when I plugged in "Airplane
1974" in a search engine. In December 1974, a TWA 727 jet coming from
Ohio had crashed into the western peak of Mount Weather, killing nine-
ty-two people. The Mount Weather Emergency Operations Center is located on top of the 1,700 elevation mountain that sits between Bluemont,
Virginia, and Paris, Virginia, 227 miles from Radford, three hours and
thirty-three minutes (333) away. *333—really?* A flood of questions filled
my thoughts until I landed on something.

Once, when Buz and I were first married and living in northern Virginia,
he had driven me up through that area and told me the story. "Bodies
were strewn all over that mountain," he had said. "Scattered everywhere."
At the time, Mount Weather was a top-secret government facility. One of
the most far-fetched theories from 1980, shared with my family as coming from an unknown source, was about an airplane going to a remote
place in Ohio and scattering Gina from the airplane. "Ohio," "scattered,"
"remote"—all in one rumor. It made no sense then. Now I know where
the rumor came from. That Mind Reach team. And Ohio did connect to
Epperly later. Ohio was connected to the TWA plane crash. "Scattered"
connected to the farmer's story, and to this plane crash. What did a plane

have to do with Gina's case? I would find the plane connection later, but in this moment, it wasn't about the plane. To me, it was about identifying bones. It was the DNA!

From this line of thinking, it also occurred to me that it would be good to get family DNA on file. Should we ever find unidentified bones, authorities would need DNA to match. No one had yet gotten DNA into the system to match to if my sister were ever found. Our dad had died in January 2011. The minimum we needed was DNA from my brother and me, but it would be best to have at least one parent. To find the way to Gina, I would first need to find my way to my birth mother. And that had just happened one year earlier.

FIGURE IT OUT!
"IT" WILL NEVER GO AWAY AS LONG AS YOU LOOK FOR "IT"!
"IT" WILL BE WHAT YOU WANT "IT" TO BE."

CHAPTER 16

PHOTOGRAPH

The Spirit of Life is like a tiny candle flame, glowing in the dark.
Tiny, yet powerful. The goodness of our actions spreads the light
out into the darkness.

For the better part of fifty years, I had not known where my birth mother, Elana Kay Holstein Hall, was. From time to time, I would think about trying to locate her. Several years ago, Buz and I had traveled to Whitesburg, Kentucky, for the Fall Heritage Festival, an event my first cousin, Auntie Red's daughter Lee Anna, helps organize. While walking up the streets, looking at the storefront windows, I reminisced about childhood summers spent on those streets with my aunts—their beauty shop, the drugstore with the forbidden *True Love* magazines lining the racks, and the mouthwatering milkshakes served in ice cold, tin mixing cups. Grandparents I had barely known had owned the Holstein Hardware store for many years, living in a big brick home on the hill behind it. Flashes of scenes from my childhood stirred. A glimpse of a blanket laying on the tarred flat roof of the hardware store where it seemed I had played once. I vaguely recalled going through a secret passageway, from the back right corner of the store that was like entering a dark closet, that led to the large home. By age five, I would not see the inside of this store or my grandfather, my mother's father, ever again. I only saw my grandmother, Rose Holstein, afterwards when she brought my mother to visit us when I was nine and twelve. And, once, after I was married. Buz and I drove there one day and I just walked up and knocked on the door of the large brick house. I wanted to find Elana. The door opened and I could see inside, dark and smoky. We were not invited in. As Rose stepped out, I saw the grand stairs behind her. I had climbed those stairs as a child. I knew at the top, to the right, would be a bathroom that was used by my older boy cousins. My mother had two brothers and two sisters. The visit was unfruitful. It was clear I would not find Elana through this distant grandmother. I was not disappointed. Having already had children of my own at this point in my life, I simply could not fathom how any mother or grandmother could be like that—it was beyond comprehension to me.

While at the festival, I met one of the aunts I'd never previously met. My first question to her was whether she knew where my mother was now. But she would not tell me. "It would not be good for you to know," she said. "And I am not really sure, anyhow."

The aunt insisted my mother would not even recognize me. "It would just be all around not good for you to show up," she said, and this insistence continued for a good ten minutes as she listed for my husband and me every reason I should not continue to search for my mother.

But then in 2015, a first cousin from Indiana whom I did not know, one of Elana's sister's daughters, called me out of the blue. She had just lost her mother, Elana's older sister.

"Would you be interested in some old photos of your mother when she was a little girl?" the cousin asked. She had all of my mother's special mementos like her senior portrait and a prom photo. Once, at my NaNa's funeral in January 1986, a stranger had told me I looked just like my mother. He had been good friends with Elana in high school. He had shared a story that made him smile—his memory of prom night. On that night, he pretended to be Elana's date, but really he was just helping her sneak out so she could see my dad. That prom photo with just her in it told me she may have only made a quick appearance at her prom. He shared that my mother joined my dad, and he went to the movies alone. The story I had been told decades earlier must have been true. My dad had just finished college and was teaching and coaching at Whitesburg High. I am sure this relationship was unacceptable. I was recently told by my dad's best friend that it was more than just unacceptable. Elana was the daughter of an affluent family who never accepted my dad as good enough for her. They did not recognize my dad's amazing accomplishments of having completed a college education while playing football in the days when that was a very hard feat to accomplish. Her parents' perception of my dad as being from the other side of the tracks caused strife between Elana and her parents. Elana chose my dad, and this one decision in her life may have influenced her parents' selfish decision not to help when their daughter needed it most. Her family abandoned her. And after her mental illness, they disowned her. She became a ward of the state of Kentucky. I often ask myself what kind of blood courses through my veins. And then I remind myself—John Hall's!

My mother posed for a prom photo, but her heart was elsewhere. I am proof of that: I was born ten months later.

I was elated to get these photos. I had no pictures of her. No memories. These told a story of the mother I'd never known. My mother was a high school majorette, smiling and happy, petite like Gina. Beautiful!

My cousin told me she had visited Elana a few times in upstate Kentucky when she was much younger. Her mom would go to visit Elana occasionally, so that was how she knew of her. "I have never understood why the family distanced themselves from your mother," she said. This cousin worked for the FBI, and she would eventually help me find my mother. "I wished I had found her earlier," she would tell me then. "She must have been so lonely."

All those years, I had been searching for Elana Kay Holstein, for some reason never once imagining that she was using the Hall name. When we found her, she was listed as patient Elana Kay Hall at a nursing rehabilitation facility in northern Kentucky in a small town bordering the Ohio River, population barely over 1,000. I was there within a few days.

The day my brother and I arrived and walked into her room, my mother looked right at me and said, sharp as a bell, "I have three children." She held up three fingers. *Where is the other one? One is missing*, she seemed to be saying.

Amazed, I asked, "Elana, do you know who I am?"

"Dlana," she said. "My little girl, Dlana."

My mother had been very young, eighteen or nineteen when I was born, and five years later she was taken off to St. Albans. There she would receive electroshock treatments that would change the course of her life forever. Her mind was frozen in time in a child-like state, yet she still knew certain things. The conditions of her room saddened us. She was sharing a room with two other people. We knew she had been institutionalized for more than fifty years, presumably in many different places. My mother had lived as a ward of the state of Kentucky. I looked around the room at her possessions. One shoe box sat at the foot of her bed. It was filled with small items—a Bible, tiny toys, a necklace, a little antique old doll and one aged, white baby shoe worn gray as though it had been rubbed thousands of times. *Were these ours?* Just a few objects. They must have meant so much to her. I noticed a few clothes hanging in her closet, and those on the floor, all dirty. Everyone seemed to like her and do the best to care for her, yet aside from the caretakers at the facility, she was all alone, abandoned by her family. It broke my heart to find her in this place.

When we visited, she lit up the room, giggling like a child. She told everyone she passed in the hall that I was her little girl. This was in the fall of

2015, after I had met Nola. When I look back now, I see that our reunion may very well have been one of the first steps in God's plan, so I would not leave this part of my life unfinished.

During our visits, we would go down to the cafeteria where she would watch television while she ate. She could identify animals that she would see on TV. She especially laughed when she would see dogs or cats on a commercial. And if she saw something scary like a snake or a crocodile, she would react as a little girl would react, holding her hands over her eyes and gasping. Her eyes would light up again when the screen would clear and something happy would come on. Her physical condition had been affected either by decades of psychosis drugs or she had had some form of a stroke. Her lips drooped, preventing her from speaking clearly. And she shuffled when she walked, her balance steadied by holding her walker tightly from fear of falling. She loved black coffee. And she ate every bite of her dinner. If anything was left over, any morsel of food, package of salt, she kept it. She would place it in a napkin, then fold the napkin ever so carefully, adding it to her walker's "hidden" compartment under the seat. That was her special things place. Every visit, I slowly introduced new things into her life. First, I wanted to see her have enough clothes, a TV, and a chest of drawers—the necessities. But that also meant jewelry! It was a joy to watch her play with the costume jewelry, taking everything out of the jewelry box I had given her, and then organizing it back in its perfect place.

Next, I wanted her to have copies of her photographs and my family's pictures, including the grandsons she had never met, framed to decorate her walls. We discovered how much she loved having baby dolls. When I would show up to visit, she would be lying in her bed, sleeping with a baby doll cradled in her arms. Not like a child playing with dolls, but like a mother yearning for her babies. And always, the three fingers would come up.

After tracking my mother down, I had a lot of trouble in the beginning just getting the state's guardian to return my calls. Shortly after my visit, my mother just happened to be assigned a new guardian after years with the same one. Soon thereafter, a third guardian was assigned who would be the one to help me. I wanted to move my mother to Eastern Kentucky, where we could visit her more frequently and make her last years more comfortable in a place where she would only have one roommate, could go outside on her own, and have good care. After a year of red tape, I did finally get her moved to a newer facility in Eastern Kentucky, in the same town where she had spent the good years of her life.

The only tricky part was that I had to transport her. To help me with the long, six-hour, "no idea what to expect" drive, I enlisted my brother. We loaded her up and moved her to Whitesburg, arriving with a paper bag of chicken nuggets and French fries, popular foods she tasted for the first time. When we drove past the outskirts of Whitesburg, my mother recognized it. She knew she was finally home.

Once I figured out the airplane 1974 connection, LeeAnna, my local first cousin, helped arrange to have a law enforcement colleague to help me administer the DNA kit. I really wanted my mother's DNA, but I did not expect her reaction to that uniform to be full of apprehension. I saw a true fear, an anger that rose from deep within her, when he entered the room. She watched his every move intensely with a frown on her tense face. I calmed her. It was all we could do to persuade her to let him swab her. She was visibly afraid. I am sure there was a deep history of restraint and other issues that certainly might explain her reaction.

What exactly had happened at St. Albans, when she was taken there? Time was forever frozen. And why do so many people believe Gina's spirit is at St. Albans? Is there a connection? Sometimes I wonder if Gina is comforting our mother. I do not know. All I do know is my mother is a joy to visit. Her simple child-like outlook offers a moment of grace. Her loving smile when we walk in to visit is soothing to my soul. I am grateful to have found her. There are no coincidences. I took a photo of Elana a few months after I showed up in her life. We now had flowers and colorful decorations. Comfy, plush, fun pillows. And clothes! Of course, I did not notice then the words on her shirt, maybe from the box of clothes Mama Joan gave me to share. Nothing is impossible, just like her sweatshirt said!

One day, Elana and I were sitting outside in the garden at her new facility. She enjoyed looking up at the birds and the clouds, smiling as though they gave her peace. It was spring, and a mama duck and her ducklings entertained us. As she looked up to the sky, I told her that was where Gina was. She just looked at me blankly but with a slight grimace, suggesting to me that maybe she understood. I asked her if she understood. She  looked back up to the sky. I told her again that up there was where Gina was—in heaven—and that was why Gina had not come to visit her, but one day she would see her again. Now, she seemed to understand, even though she still held three fingers up. I talked to her about Jesus being with Gina. I asked her if she knew the song "Jesus Loves Me." She smiled as I sang to her. I do not know if she fully understood, but I believe Gina is in her heart. I know God is. Being so alone for all of those years, in the simple quietness of her life, I believe she could feel and really take notice of the hugs from heaven.

In early 2017, unresolved pieces of my past surfaced in a no-coincidence fashion. A story told to me led me to a woman who had been my mother's best friend during my youngest years. Her joyful memory of my mother was that she had been a loving mom, and she reminisced with many heart-warming stories. They had let their children play together. The photos my cousin gave me align with her stories. This was how this woman saw my mother.

Sometimes I ask myself, "What part of my past defines who I am? What stepping stones of life have made me who I am today?" Being a loving mother is what pleases me most, yet I have no memory of my own mother before

age nine when they brought her to visit us. That day, her jet-black hair framed her face, her lips outlined in thick red lipstick. Immense joy filled her eyes, this moment of seeing her children for the first time in four years. How can it be that I had no other memory of her before that day? Was I really that good at burying bad memories? If they even were bad. Certainly, that would be a coping mechanism that could serve me well in the years to come. How could I have been so good at burying the disappointments of life before I even knew what disappointment was? The photos that my newly met cousin gave me did not look like disappointment. I have lived a life of many experiences that could cause me to dwell in my own self-pity, but no matter how bad they were, I seemed to see the good.

What I do remember from early childhood is how my friends and I played in the nooks and crannies of my neighborhood. Sometimes we'd climb down into the drainage holes to play, sinking into mud up to our knees. They were building a road by our house, and I'd ride my bike on the just-paved, not-yet-opened road, pedaling as fast as I could all the way from the top of the hill to the bottom. Once, I spun too fast and flew off my bike, landing in a pile of gravel. For the longest time, I had a tiny black piece of gravel lodged in my skin right under my right nostril. You can imagine the embarrassment I felt at school. It did not fully disappear until college! Another early memory was being cared for by the nuns at St. Mary's Hospital. I was in a metal baby crib. I had eaten a whole bottle of baby aspirin. Those memories are clear, so why did I have none of our mother? My dad and I never discussed her, except that one time when I had bravely asked about her in the months before he died. Why did I never ask more? I guess I thought there would always be a time for us, someday.

After 1980, we also never discussed the details of Gina's death. We never discussed evil. We discussed Epperly. We lived the nightmare of evil in 1980 so it was always understood, just never discussed. The concept of evil was wiped from our minds like a taboo subject. I find it interesting that the subject matter of pure evil was really never discussed anywhere, including in church. Why? Do we think if we ignore it, it will not disrupt our fairy-tale life? I wonder, if one has never really experienced evil, is it possible to fully grasp its influence in everyday life. Do we even realize a very real spiritual battle is taking place around us every moment of every day? I did not before *the journey*.

My husband once shared a concept with me from *The Black Swan* by Nassim Nicholas Taleb, one of his favorite authors. The world only knew of white swans, believing that was all that existed, until one day a black swan showed up. Gasp! There are black swans? Everyone's knowledge of swans changed. That is how I see everything in our world. We can never really expect what will come into our life, our world, and change our beliefs, whether we let it or not. I simply could not ignore what I experienced and turn it back into a white swan. And had I not kept a digital account and recorded everything and then looked back at it, I may never have realized the true extent of the darkness in the very real spiritual battle. There were only glimpses while living it, but I can see so clearly afterwards the external presence of its influence.

I ask myself now, What is evil? How would I define it? We don't think about the neighbor next door, or the all-American boy when we think of evil. We think of Hitler.

How can we reconcile evil in this world? That is a hard question to answer, but there is some solace in knowing that light, The Spirit of Life, can shine in the darkness.

I have some amazing nieces, especially talented in the acting and drama categories. I always enjoy the one-act plays performed by this group of very talented young people. They have consistently won Virginia High School League Class A State One Act Play competitions. They are always champions in my eyes! Their drama teacher often writes the content, always humbly giving his champion students all of the credit. The topic of one of their recent plays was the Holocaust. A big subject. They compiled true stories, touching the hearts of all who watched. The play was named *Spirit of Life*. These amazing young cast members performed the roles of victims of the Holocaust whose stories exemplified a lasting faith in humanity no matter how bad their situation. At the end of the performance, we would hear, "There is a miracle, the biggest miracle of this horrific event; it is the *spirit of life*, the connection they had one to another, to want to live, to help one another, to simply still have faith in God." Cast members proclaimed,

"Survive Spirit of Life." My niece joyfully repeated, "Unite in the Spirit of Life" at the end. It was an incredible experience to watch these young people tackle such a difficult topic—pure evil.

In their school play, their stories emphasized the miracles in a story where 9 million people would die, 6 million being of Jewish descent. The lines spoken at the end of the play would reference Power…Power to control others. Power over others. What a lesson for these young people to realize. Power is certainly at the root of many evil acts. Power can often spawn from a love of money, which is the root of all kinds of evil. I believe lies are at the root of pure evil—the Enemy's lies in the playground of our minds.

I, too, contemplate the times in history when our very souls are challenged in understanding the whys of life. When our faith in God is challenged. There was a center to this web of evil in the one act play, and its web spread, the smaller tendrils spreading this evil mindset even to the strangers lining the streets, who heckled as the Holocaust victims were rounded up to be brought to the concentration camps—heckled as if these victims were not even fellow humans. The web of this evil power infiltrated these bystanders' minds so that they would point fingers and shout, "Where is your God now?" as the cold, humiliated, beaten, separated families were marched onto the train cars. And with the point of a finger, the family member standing beside you would be gone. What power could cause these bystanders in a crowd to suddenly join in on the evil? The bystanders were becoming followers, not leaders. Is it fear of not being accepted by your peers that causes this type of participation? I would later write this very important message:

Fear is the Enemy's sharpest tool.

I now understand. Fear spreads through the tiniest webs to those standing next to each other, causing a stranger to join in and taunt the passing Holocaust victims from fear of not being accepted themselves if they did not participate. Once experienced, it becomes a part of their redefined life as a now acceptable action. We become numb to fear's effect. And not just numb to fear but also to acceptance of irreverence of God. God's name used in vain, maybe in a movie, repeatedly heard, numbs you, piece by little piece, until it becomes the accepted norm within your own mind. A new, tolerated reality.

Those actions—those statements that were made—are not of God. The Enemy was in the background of those thoughts. And once the dark power gets a foothold, evil prevails. When bad things happen, our faith wavers. Sometimes we even blame God. Why do people want to accuse God as though God caused this? God's spark is deep inside of us, there making sure the spirit of life survives. I believe the Holy Spirit is what moves the goodness of people, touching their hearts from within, igniting this amazing strength. The smallest of miracles can then shine through that intense darkness.

There will always be spiritual battles within our world. And there is no simple way to reconcile this travesty. What good can really come of any of this? What good came from Gina's death? What good comes when a woman is raped or a child is beaten or molested or mistreated? What good came from the electroshock treatments that left my mother's mind frozen in time for fifty years? I believe God's heart breaks, too, when he sees what humans are capable of doing to one another. Joseph said in Genesis 50:20, *"You meant evil against me, but God used it for good."* What good? The Good that triumphs over the bad when we do not let it rob us of our Spirit of Life, the goodness within ourselves, and the ability to heal when we feel God's presence and know of His love. The Spirit of Life united those victims whose stories these young actors shared, carrying them through their darkest moments, continuing to believe in the spark's existence no matter how dark it became.

Light will triumph. How?

One way is by simply knowing of the promise—life is eternal. When we leave this earthly, physical life, on the other side of the veil, evil does not exist. The Enemy is not there. He is here every day, every moment trying to influence us away from remembering this promise—influencing our Spirit of Life. Our inner soul, the heart of our soul, knows this truth. The veil can come down here on earth if we just keep that spark ignited. We can trust and believe in the peace of knowing this. We are all living life in a world that needs our sparks of kindness, our love, our spreading of the light.

I see this Spirit of Life every time I visit Elana. She brightens my life with her grateful giggle. As soon as I walk into the nursing home, the excitement bursts from her eyes. I see her Spark. It ignites my spark! Gratitude spreads. Smiles spread. Kindness, generosity, and truthfulness flourish when the Spirit of Life is present. I choose to look past the dark parts of her life, alone for fifty years. She could be bitter, angry, sad, harboring hate, blaming, or full of shame, but even in her state of mind, the light shines. And it blossoms into a beautiful soul full of love.

When I think of Epperly, I think of evil. I think of a web of darkness spreading its connected threads out into our beautiful world. The web grows and feeds off of itself to the point that it infiltrates where we cannot even begin to see and imagine. When evil is at play, the darkness seems to be visible in only one place. In reality, however, it is inevitably connected even if by the tiniest of threads to the larger web of darkness. I could say that the man who murdered my sister is the center of this web, but I believe he is merely one of the tiniest of the threads extending out from a very large, elusive web of connected evil. *The journey* revealed this web of darkness.

When I think of Gina, I think of good. I see my sister's life as this immense ray of light, shining a bright beacon from every corner of this dark web. *The Miraculous Journey* rouses questions we may not have even known to ask. Or questions we have always wanted to ask…but not sure how—questions about the truth of everything! Maybe we only need to answer one question—What is the Spirit of Life? The foundation of the Spirit of Life is Love. Just reading the Gospel of John gives so many answers to so many questions. The voice of truth, Jesus' words, in red print—a lot of the wisdom in that book comes straight from the Giver of the Spirit of Life.

I see Elana frozen in time, just like the story the photographs paint. And to know her now, her childlike behavior in still seeing me as her five-year-old little girl, is to understand what pure love really means. To know her is to understand—The Spirit of Life.

CHAPTER 17

JUST FOR NOW

Sis, I am gonna get ya outta there, if there is where you really are.

Walking into St. Albans for the first time was like walking into my own nightmare. Graffiti artwork had been painted on the bowling alley wall. Most of the building was dark. Halls were wide with dirty wooden floors. The wooden stairs seemed just to disappear into the ceiling leading to nowhere. Everything exuded a haunted feeling. Why, I did not know, yet.

Earlier in the day, I had met up with Kevin. I'd really pushed my luck with my husband, so I asked Kevin to help me work through a list of ten places I wanted to find. He and I began at the muck place, trying to zero in on a longitude and latitude that seemed to point us to a spot closer to the edge of the road, up from the muck place and creek. Standing there, I felt a burst of energy, almost as though I were standing in an electric field, which is why I gave Kevin the nickname "The

Antenna." Standing side by side at the edge of Hazel Hollow Road, up a small incline from the muck place looking down at the small body of water, I wondered: *Could it have been a larger pond in 1980? A pond with cattails?* A constant replenishing of fresh water ran off from the ravine above. Epperly's very first cellmate's story captured my interest. When he was first arrested, before he was tried, Epperly would have still been more confident and arrogant, maybe even bragging with a truth—"I buried her under a cow feeder." So I wondered, was the muck place a watering hole for cattle in 1980? The reeds grew plentifully in the flat area above the cliff, but I am not sure this place would have fit the description of a bog, a marsh-like area, back then.

"Let's meet up with Andy," Kevin suggested when we had trouble pinpointing the exact spot we were looking for with my new handheld GPS. If we really were searching for scattered bone fragments, they would be more deeply covered in time. A better way was necessary. I needed precision, a six-inch by six-inch spot, not a six-foot by six-foot spot, so I could locate the exact longitudes and latitudes.

I agreed to Kevin's suggestion. Plus, Andy wanted to see some of Gina's letters.

As we dropped in on Andy at the police department, he announced he was glad to see us. A writer from a local magazine was coming to do a story about St. Albans and Gina. This planned visit caught me off guard. Of course, he asked us to please stay.

I felt uneasy about the magazine interview, but then Kevin said, "Look at all the roadblocks we had today. Nothing working out as planned. There is a reason for this. This is where you are supposed to be today."

I know now there are no coincidences in my life, so I let the day continue to unfold.

Sitting in the police department conference room across from a reporter, it finally hit me why there had been such intense interest in St. Albans. Now I'd seen the brick mansion in person. The questions revolved around Gina and her murder, but the article emphasized the St. Albans paranormal mysteries and the ghost of Gina. My mind was a million miles away, asking how I could be participating in a paranormal twist on my sister's life. Andy told them about the letters from Gina that I had brought for him to see, and the photographer took a picture of one. It was decided that we would get a picture of Andy and I sitting on Gina's bench up at St. Albans.

I hesitated, but then I caught Kevin's eye and remembered to let what is to happen, happen. Andy had always explained to me—to justify the stories, interviews, and ghost shows—that when he gets interviewed, more information is shared, and, "It makes it more likely that someone will remember something and come forward." But publicity still stirred me up so badly. I wanted my sister and her memories left alone, but I knew this was never going to happen after seeing the haunting exterior of St. Albans.

Sitting on Gina's bench, Andy and I pretended to read Gina's letter together as the photographer took images. This really seemed to bother me. In that moment, I heard my dad's words echoing in my mind. In 1980, when I became upset about the media's presence, my dad had told me that all of the attention, right or wrong, kept interest on Gina and the case. Then one photo was snapped with just me. That is when a very nice, yet curious man walked up. He introduced himself as Ken, the leader of the Cool Kids Paranormal group that had built and installed Gina's bench. He explained they were wrapping up the last week of the Halloween tours. He said he was happy to meet me, Gina's sister, with a caring tone in his voice, as if he had known her personally.

"Would you like to go inside?" he asked.

Walking in, I first noticed the gift shop, which was selling St. Albans Sanatorium sweatshirts to help keep this paranormal playground afoot. Andy and I followed Ken down a long, dark hall to a grand wooden staircase. *Nola. His vision of the staircase.* The place was festively decorated for Halloween, when the St. Albans group held haunted house tours to raise money. Eerie, decorative chains hung from the ceiling. Wood floors and wooden panels surrounded us, and just like in my vision from September 13: "Chains hanging from ceiling, wood platforms, empty, abandoned." I also recalled my October 17 message: "Correct path. Foundation half-moon hole in top." I trained my eyes on the baseboard looking for a half-moon opening.

I was consumed by an intense feeling of bad. I should not be here. There were long dark halls like the tunnels from my messages and a leaking roof. I had an overwhelming feeling of worry for my sister.

Ken told me that he worked with another ghost hunter named Natasha. "We always hope to speak to Gina," Ken told me. "She is one of the most popular ghosts but our interest in her is personal."

I was still skeptical that anyone could be pulled from heaven to have conversations with anyone, yet that is what seemed to be happening in my life—a one-way conversation from somewhere. I could tell Ken was undaunted in his beliefs in the spiritual world of ghosts.

"Natasha is one of our most gifted members, the strongest connection. Gina approached her," Ken assured me. "Her love for Gina is strong."

Ken emphasized that Natasha was passionate about finding Gina. "Natasha was drawn to this building the first time she saw it," he elaborated. "She did not really want to ghost hunt. She backed out the first three times and finally gave in because of Gina. She was in awe of this place. She prayed to God to protect her before she went in. She felt it all was for Gina. She was drawn to the Grand Staircase."

Ken continued reminiscing, "On Natasha's second visit to St. Albans, she was drawn to the green tub room, where she was sure she felt Gina. She was overcome with sadness."

Natasha keeps an 8x10 photo of Gina in her room, Ken added. "Gina is the underlying purpose behind the formation of the Cool Kids Paranormal. That is the reason we have the bench. That is the reason you are here. To Natasha, this is all about Gina. And it brought us to you. Together as it is to be. I can't wait for you to meet her."

There are no coincidences. I knew standing there that I was supposed to meet Ken, and I felt as though I already knew Natasha. I wanted to meet her in person, and that is what I did a few weeks later.

It had been a summer of no coincidences, and now it was a fall of no coincidences. I did not question how this day was unfolding. I believed it was part of what I was supposed to be doing. "Would you show me the bowling alley, the kitchen, and the green tub room?" I asked Ken.

Before entering the bowling alley, I already had discovered that the black headphones would be painted on the wall, but seeing them in real time was surreal. The graffiti was exactly as I had seen in my vision. Immediately, I scanned the raised bowling lane floor for the half-moon shape I had also seen in my dream visions. That seemed like a logical place. We moved on to the kitchen and to a wall with a row of windows.

Both proved to be unsettling, but what happened next unraveled me—we visited the boiler room.

No doubt noticing the concerned look on my face, Ken said, "We also pick up the strongest connections in the boiler room."

The boiler room was downright eerie, with a room to the side that was covered in green tiles and had a bathtub in its center.

"When Gina first contacted Natasha," Ken said, "she was near this room."

The experience was so real, he continued, that Natasha was overwhelmed with grief, a deep sadness so intense that she promised she would never stop searching for Gina. "After that, we had to know. We needed to know why Gina seemed to be here." Ken and Natasha worked alone on trying to understand Gina's connection to St. Albans.

Ken shared that every time they held a spirit gathering, they would ask questions in the boiler room and around this room with that bathtub. One strange thing that would happen was that a reference to "the birdcage" would come up. The birdcage was a balcony with wiring woven above it like a giant birdcage. It was on the back of the building where asylum patients could be outside—fresh air with a view—but completely enclosed so they could not fall or escape. I cannot help but wonder about my mother

and her experience in this place. Somehow, Natasha and Ken knew that Gina's mother had been there. Someone somewhere wanted them to know this for a reason we cannot yet understand.

Ken shared other details that seemed unusual for him to know—Gina's favorite colors and other small details, like the name of our dog we only had about six weeks when we were little girls: Princess.

"Every time we connect with Gina, she seems to be afraid of someone else, like she is whispering," Ken said. "We think it is the Doctor (Skipper's grandfather)."

My heart sank.

The face of the red-headed girl flashed in my mind. I had met her while visiting a friend in Fayetteville during the Fourth of July weekend. As soon as she saw me, an image of a girl holding her neck as though she were being choked and could not breathe came into her mind. She somehow knew the image was Gina, and she knew Gina was my sister. She knew details of us when we were just little girls that she could not have known. She also told me she could see spirits all around me and two of them, who had once known me in life, were arguing about me. She added that one was wanting to save my soul and one was wanting justice and closure. I saw that she was visibly overcome with emotion. When I had asked her why, she answered with a concerned look, "Gina whispers." I wondered because of the way she answered me if that was not normal in what I surmised was her world of mediumship. I did not know that day exactly what a medium does, short of having watched the TV show *Medium* a decade earlier. I was a Patricia Arquette fan. In that moment, the only frame of reference I had to try to understand how she knew these things was a few weeks of experiencing the unexplainable myself.

I know now that there is just simply no way to know from where these experiences are coming. They do happen. I have seen the proof in their documentation. I see now that was Ken's role in Gina's story. And even when visions, dreams, and answers come without seeking, we must still understand it is impossible to discern the true origins. Our human interpretation that it is Gina's spirit is a natural one. I do not know the answer. No human can. Natasha would tell me later that she always understood there was no way to discern the source—angelic, demonic, a good spirit or a bad, manipulative spirit—that wanted secrets kept as she believed was happening with Gina. All theories swirling around in our world today cannot be validated because validation occurs within the limits of our own human interpretations, perceptions, and beliefs. Yet, new theories can emerge from our experiences. I now know there is a power in our world that is not to be underestimated. But this day in St. Albans, I did not know this. I was starting to believe that my sister was in a very bad place. A place where she was scared and alone, like she was being held there by someone or something and that was why she was whispering. I began believing she was unable to get to Heaven for some reason. This day gave rise to a *new thought*: I needed to get Gina out of there; I was worried about why she was whispering.

Seeing the shocked, concerned look on my face, Ken added, "The boiler room at St. Albans is the place where the ghost hunters have had the most contact with Gina. It is Gina's spirit that answers. We are very protective of her. She only comes when she wants. We do not let others bother her." He explained that the ghost hunters ask questions using a handmade board, adding, "I have proof, on video."

I watched as the proof perplexed me. Natasha asked "Gina's spirit," "What is the name of your cat?" A pendulum swung to each letter, spelling out T-A-F-F-Y. Now that was impossible for them to have known.

Their objective was always Gina and finding Gina and her truth. They were both led to St. Albans with many no-coincidence stories of their own that set them on that destined path.

Other questions asked were about what might have happened that night. Questions I had wanted to have answered.

"Who was with you?" Natasha asked. B-E-T-H.

I couldn't imagine who Beth was at first, but this name brought a memory forth from the trial. I vaguely recalled a friend named Beth from Gina's spring semester being called as a character witness in the trial. So now two first names had surfaced, as though someone wanted us to know something. The name shared with Andy—"Kim"—by The Preacher who said that Gina wanted Kim to know it was not her fault and now the name Beth delivered to Ken and Natasha. Could it just be intentional misdirection? But if so, it was truth used to misdirect. I wondered then, *Were they with Gina that night? Did they know who may have been*?

I kept watching with curious intent. Natasha asking, "How did you call your sister that night?"

I had never been able to reconcile this piece of the puzzle.

It spelled out, "After I was blocked, then I called."

My jaw dropped. This was just like one of my messages: *I was driving, and a car blocked me. Pulled in, and the car pulled in behind me. Blocked me in. I asked him (them) to let me out.* This heightened my curiosity. I was now shaking my head like my dad, in disconcerting confusion.

As we walked through St. Albans, my sense of darkness felt palpable.

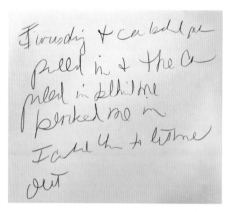

Now I needed discernment more than ever. This place felt wrong, and I couldn't say why. The thought of my sister's spirit being there was disturbing. *Was she really here? How could that be? Why would she be here?*

The more I researched St. Albans, the more I learned that many people connected Gina to this terrible place. I had been half-aware of those ghost hunter shows, but I had filed them under "sensationalistic TV." I did not believe in ghosts. One online article featured a comment from a woman saying, "Why would Gina's spirit be at St. Albans?" Exactly my question. The woman wrote, "Why would she not just be at Epperly's cell, haunting him every day? Makes no sense for her to be at St. Albans." I was quite distraught to see my sister's name associated with this disturbing place.

The most apparent connecting piece was Skipper's family. It interested me that the ghost hunters usually didn't read the trial transcripts so they didn't know much about the grandson. They most likely only knew the basic composed story that everyone knew. *Girl meets man at bar and goes with him to a cabin where she calls her sister saying she is with Steve and will be home soon.* All attention was on Epperly in the many stories thereafter. *Girl refuses his sexual advances. Enraged, he kills her.* Yet the ghost hunters came to the belief that Skipper's grandfather's ghost was causing Gina to whisper. As though the answers are related to that name. As though one ghost has control over another in some in-between realm, keeping Gina from moving on. How? This thought opposed everything that had ever given me peace about my sister's death—that she was in heaven. I now know to ask, *Could this all be twisted truths from actual truths, used to guide our thoughts purposefully in a desired direction.* Some truths were used, their purpose twisted, like the name of our childhood dog being given from a spiritual realm seemingly validating the communication between spirits and man. A truth: Princess was the name of our little dog. How can we ever discern the real origin? This story has two composers, from powers we cannot even begin to imagine continuing to plot out the story.

On this day, my ruling thought became: *This constant association of my sister with St. Albans paranormal activities might just be keeping Gina from somehow having peace.* Something inside me questioned exactly how the spiritual realm worked, and whether all these people could be pulling my sister back into this realm with their attempts to contact her all of the time. Or maybe it was somehow a disturbance of her peace. Not Ken and Natasha, because they told me Gina comes to them and they too believed they were to protect her and keep others from involving her during the spirit gatherings conducted in this place. I did not feel good about all of this. I wanted to get Gina out of there, if that was where she was, as I was starting to believe. I became resolute.

So then the question was: Who wanted me to come here? I was starting to see this experience differently. I had started out believing the purpose was guided by only God, because of the miracles I'd witnessed. I had thought I was to learn to have an open mind, to trust and believe anything and everything is possible. I believed God was in control of nature, and I still do.

And I believed I needed to find Gina's body, not as much for her, as Andy desired; not even for me to heal, as Nola believed; but for truth. Truth as if there was always a deeper, imperceptible reason behind it all.

If there were other perpetrators, we needed justice. If there were other victims, other people needed closure, too. I believed wholeheartedly that God was helping orchestrate this because an evil secret needed to be revealed. I had faith.

But please God, why St. Albans? Why were so many messages tied to this place? Could Gina really be stuck here? Was I supposed to free her? If my sister wanted me to get her "outta there," then that was what this hard-headed girl was going to do. Why was it that she always whispered? That thought seemed to come from a place of no peace. Was I beginning to create a different story, a divergent path? This felt urgent, like it was all going to change.

Andy was right. That article that was written would bring a story from the past right to me, just as he had always said. Publicity, any publicity, brings new information.

Out of the blue, an eighty-three-year-old woman called my office seeking to reach me. She had recently seen the magazine article about Gina and St. Albans. Andy and Kevin were right, even though I did not agree with the premise of its content. The article brought attention. The caller recounted that she had someone drive her "all the way down to Radford" from Vinton one day in 1980 to the Radford police station. When she told them she had an important clue in my sister's case, she said the "cops" drove her to the trestle where the car was last seen, as she asked. So many details from 1980 were resurfacing, all in a new light. A police report confirmed this visit.

Here is what she shared with me:

> As she stood there, she knew a young man (Epperly) crossed the tracks, and she could sense a car—a small white car, a Ford. She saw this young man at the trunk of another vehicle. Its trunk was already lifted up. It was parked on the right side of the road, opposite the side where the small white car was parked. At the trunk of the white car, a man, a tall, slender fellow, put a suitcase in the trunk of the white car. She felt Gina was in that suitcase. He walked up a hillside to the back, behind the hospital grounds where the cemetery was. Tall graves. The tall, slender fellow was carrying parts of my sister in a small suitcase. And this man she saw was not the young man they had arrested. It was a different one, an older man…taller. And connected to the hospital. Those souls that are buried there, they need peace. She said she saw the hospital person carrying the suitcase. She believes sometimes evidence points in the wrong direction. He walked to the old graveyard that has three tall headstones. They were a hundred or more years old in 1980, really old, and from the same family. She said she believed that only part of Gina was there, but we would need to dig when we find that gravestone. She said she would never be satisfied because of what she had seen.

"Honey, I was born the way I am," she said by way of explaining how she knew these things. "And I believe that you can just teach yourself to douse. Just take yourself a metal clothes hanger, bend it, and use it. Go to St. Albans, stand at the back of the building looking away, and you walk until you find that family graveyard—on a hillside back of the hospital grounds. Those souls that are buried there are a family—they need peace, and part of your sister was placed in one of those graves with one of the family members, the grave farthest from the left when looking at the three headstones. Your sister's grave is a shallow grave down one foot. Only part of her, like just her thigh or leg. And when you find it, you start digging. A grave on top of a grave is not at peace."

She had not forgotten a single detail. And thirty-seven years later, she was still disturbed by this vision.

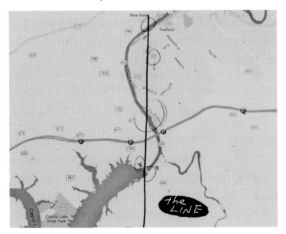

I began wondering if we extended that straight line from Dorothy Allison's notes, in the other direction, toward St. Albans property, what would it cross—an old antique graveyard? Allison had mentioned a white car too. A helper. My first thought of where the graveyard might be was an old farmhouse on the property of St. Albans that I could see in the historical picture. In that era, that could have meant a family graveyard on the premises somewhere, covered over by decades of nature hiding the human footprint. I would remember this line of thinking later when Nola would share his last message of holding the bushes back and people, an adult and a child, with Gina. I even wondered whether, if I found that family graveyard, the far left grave would be a child's. I had received messages about body parts, the scarred leg, and the tall, skinny, white-haired man who kept showing up.

After the visit inside of St. Albans, new thoughts erupted as though they were not my own. Some of these thoughts opposed what had always given me peace, knowing Gina was in heaven. And some opened my mind to question new possibilities of the unknown. It was as though I could look in the mirror, but I was not seeing the person I had always been my entire life. I was seeing a different person with thoughts both contrary and validating to my core beliefs. Some good. Some not. I was in the thick of a spiritual battle.

After Epperly was convicted, and after my sister's memorial service, my family didn't search anymore. *How could we have ever stopped looking for Gina?* A truth twisted into self-blaming and intentional judging—a new guilty thought—was emerging. *Why had we been satisfied with that?* I found myself frustrated and angry—at myself and at my dad.

This anger at my dad came out of nowhere. I really can never, ever remember a time when I was truly ever disappointed with my dad. I even started to wonder whether I was doing all of this for him, *wanting to please Daddy*. A negative thought I had never had about him in this manner. My sudden anger seemed to have intent—camouflaging an underlying purpose that was breaking through. An intentional, redirecting of purpose. Again, I was in the middle of a battle I could not yet see.

I was divergently forgetting my why. A new misdirection implanted intentionally within my mind was guiding me on a new, angry divergent path.

One day soon after, I was on Route 611, traveling with my husband near the property that spanned from the river dumpsite butterfly spot to Route 611. I wanted to find that old road I believed people used in the past that led to the cliffs where they would dump trash from up high to the remote river dumpsite area below. When I saw a couple gathering fresh spring water on the property, I stopped and walked over to them, seeing out of the corner of my eye an old wagon road up to the left, on the hill. I asked them if they owned this property. It was a beautiful, historic log cabin, well-maintained, looking just like it would have more than 100 years earlier. They gave me directions to the home where the deceased owner's son and grandson lived. The directions would take us in the vicinity of another home that for some unknown reason I had been wanting to stop at for the last few passings to talk to whoever lived there. When we got there, it was the same house as the one in the couple's directions.

I knocked on the door. As soon as I mentioned my name was Dlana, the man who answered the door knew I was Gina's sister, just as so many others from my no-coincidence, crossing-of-paths experiences. It seems that even my given name Dlana, uniquely recognizable, is a part of this intricate plan I am starting to see unfold miraculously in my life. The pieces are coming together.

"I was only ten years old when I first heard your name," he said, "but I have never forgotten. I still think about Gina. We all do. I can remember my friends and I would help the police search. They would ask us to lead them to all of our play areas—the places we knew and explored as little boys. The police would tie ropes around us and lower us into the wells to help look for your sister. I often wonder what we missed back then." His caring, sympathetic face changed to one tinged with anger as he continued, "I keep up with Epperly's location through a friend who is a prison guard. I get upset when I hear the stories. Stories that he lives like a king compared to the other inmates."

My sister's murder had happened, essentially, in this man's backyard. He lived not even a half mile from the lake house. I cannot imagine how this impacted him as a young boy. The atypical summer of 1980 was not a season filled with swimming and boating on the lake like most ten-year-olds would have spent that summer. His had been spent searching for the body of a murdered young girl, forging memories that would never leave him.

"There is one memory I wish I could forget," he continued. "The day your dad pulled up in his red Jeep Wagoner. Rolling his window down, he motioned me over. I remember having to stand on my tiptoes to see into the window of his Jeep. I held myself up, placing my arms on the edge of the door, and when I looked in, I saw his shiny gun laying out on the passenger seat. I looked in your father's eyes. I will never, ever forget the deep sadness I saw. Your father said to me, 'Son, are there any other places you can think of that I can look for my girl. Any place?' Your father was so sad. That moment has never left me. I am so sorry that happened to your sister."

I knew right then that this divinely inspired moment was to help me see that my dad had done his very best. He had never stopped all summer, no matter how impossible it all seemed. None of us had. The blame that had started building toward myself, my dad, and others, and the overwhelming guilt I was carrying, disappeared. I knew in this moment that it was best for everyone that we had stopped searching after the trial. Gina would have wanted us to continue living life. Maybe that was why Daddy was shaking his head at me in my August nightmare. Am I to realize that the mortal body does not matter, only the soul that lives within? I needed this moment with a very grownup ten-year-old to help me remember how hard that summer was on my dad so I would be reminded how to keep the bad thoughts from taking hold of the good. I learned this day how to be more conscious of what thoughts I allowed in my head. I needed to recognize when shame, blame, guilt, judgment, and fear were moving into my thoughts in a destructive manner, messing with the goodness of my limited, precious moments. The small, unnoticeable spiritual battles are ever-present, every moment of every day. This day my spiritual army won that battle.

Still, this did not slow me down. I remembered why I was in Radford this day—to find a road, a cave and a pond, the flash-vision from August. I had clearly seen still water, not running water. And something white floating on top-lots of stuff floating on top-and an image on October 21, clear images of glistening water, something scattered on the surface, floating but not moving, separate but close. I had noted, "different pieces."

I asked the young man about ponds in the area. "Do you know about any caves on your grandfather's property?" He did. "And do you remember a road that led to the top of cliffs at the back of your grandfather's property, possibly where people would have dumped trash years ago?" He did not. *The cliffs must be accessed from some other direction.*

As we drove up to the spot, the young man shared that this land was a favorite of many hunters. His grandfather had given hunters permits for many years. He showed me the first spot that came to mind when I asked about caves. I followed him on that old, barely visible remnant of a wagon road to the left of the property, up the steep terrain to a very recognizable concave area. Pointing to it, he said, "It looks just like it did when I was a boy. I discovered it a year or so after your sister was killed." A triangular rock blocked the small entrance. Clearly, it had not been moved for decades. But that could easily be explained by an owner who did not want children to climb inside. The area was distinctly concave, like a sinkhole. If Epperly had known of this place, it would have come to his mind as a very deep place to hide a body.

"May I come back and dig?" I asked, and he agreed.

I asked again if he knew of a pond off a curve on Claytor Dam Road, and out of the blue, he remembered a pond he had not thought of for thirty years, even though he would drive by it every day. The moment I saw it, I

recognized it. The white plastic milk-like carton float-ing on the back of the pond, leaves and debris, all separate, floating on the still water. "This was a pop-ular spot, back in the day, to party," the man recalled.

I flashed on Special Agent W. B. Wilmore's story of evidence from 1980: cattail seed pods in the front grill of my Monte Carlo. How had they gotten there?

I had known the pond was somewhere near there because I had spotted it searching GIS plot maps. The land plot with the little blue circle indicating a water source was on a parcel not numbered on the GIS site. Could it be 8-1-35?

This area had been ignored for years. Even when, weeks later, I found and met with the owner, she indicated she had honestly forgotten about the pond. That was how well-hidden it was, yet it sat right over the edge of Claytor Dam Road. I asked the owner, if I decided to search here, drain the pond, and dig up forty years of pond scum, would she allow it. Looking at the layout, she said, "It's possible."

I believed I had found another place I was to be. A place forgotten in time. At this juncture in my journey, I felt so strongly about this place. But I did start to contemplate whether this clear vision of the pond right down to the white container floating was another premonition for some unknown objective like steering me away from the truth. I was starting to question everything that happened.

Later, as I walked the wooded perimeter of the area around this pond, I found evidence that confirmed it was a party spot—discarded, decade-old pull-tab beer cans were piled beside a campfire site. I remembered one of my night's notes from August: Song in my head. "Boys 'Round Here," by Blake Shelton, the same night I wrote Bog and 3-4 snakes under bush beside the water. I proceeded carefully! A friend with me this day held my hat with my new GPS tracker inside of it while I took a call from my son. As we walked, weaving back and forth in the woods, I talked with my son. When I was finished, I reached for my hat and discovered she had dropped my new GPS tracker. How was I going to find it in these woods? Standing there, I quietly thought in my head...go left...go right...six feet ahead? Back? Ten feet? Twenty? Somehow I found it listening to the truth in my head. In my mind, quietly, I was grateful.

Remnants of an old road leading off Claytor Dam Road went right up to the back edge of the pond's now-overgrown perimeter. I shifted through the possibilities of my Monte Carlo pulling right up to the edge of this marsh thick with cattails. If someone were to walk to the water's edge, the tall cattail pods could have been pushed aside, stroking the front car grill, easily leaving behind hundreds of flowerlike, sticky, feathery seeds adhering to the grill.

As I pondered this place, I wondered whether Epperly was searching for the naked, beaten girl wrapped in a gray blanket. That would explain the 30-40-minute gap in the time between 4:15 a.m. or so when Skipper and his female guest say Epperly left the lake house and David Sauls' report of the Monte Carlo's reckless crossing over the line at 5 a.m., just past the pond entrance. Or did he stop to put something in the pond?

One day in early November while searching near the sinkhole on the grandfather property, I looked up the hill, through the power lines, and saw the bluest sky and fluffy, white cumulus clouds as vivid as I had just seen a few days earlier like a clear picture. I knew I was where I was supposed to be. Even the view at an uphill angle positioned the power lines in the exact place as I had seen: 10/29/2016 Flash Vision. Real sky and view up through the power lines.

Curious, I left the sinkhole area, walked up the mountain, and found the clearing. Finally, I had found the remnants of that old road from 1980 that bordered the top of the high cliff wall that overlooked the river right where the butterfly led us to our first miracle—Gina's face in the water.

We were back at it, Andy and me, probing holes. Andy had arranged to bring the cadaver dogs for the third time to check the accumulating "places of interest," about eight places by now. We started and spent the most time at the RPD rocks, the hidden pond area, and the Route 611 Grandfather Sinkhole Property with its vast woods. The dog handlers were nervous about letting the dogs too close to this sinkhole with its very long drop inside this cavernous small opening. We walked throughout the woods, close to the high cliff area, but never quite reaching it. Last stop—the muck place. The handlers concentrated on an open field on its border. The dogs also walked the dry creek bed. I had hoped the dogs would cover the reeded area up top of the muck place where I had discovered the tree that bore the religious plaques, but we never made it up there to probe holes before the dogs walked it. We never made it to the landfill/museum area either. The dogs had had a full day.

The only place of slight interest all day was an area around the muck place, up near the road. At the end of the day, the dog handlers said it was not substantial enough, but right then, I knew I would be back to dig. That spot of slight interest was exactly where I had been standing with Kevin a few weeks earlier.

Time for a break. I traveled to New York City to celebrate my son's thirty-fifth birthday, sharing with him all that had transpired. He was concerned about how drastically my life had changed in just a few short months. I asked myself the same question each morning as I woke to see words written, contemplating, *What is happening in my life?* Imagine being a fifty-seven-year-old woman, living life within all definitions of normalcy, when suddenly, your view of the world you live in is turned upside down, inside out, literally. I just had to keep having faith and trust that there was a reason behind what was happening.

Returning to Virginia, I learned Andy had another day planned for us. Curious about that sinkhole, he had located a cave expert. The caver would meet us at the Route 611 sinkhole cave on November 11. This kindhearted caver and his spelunking daughter would dive in, head first, to the sinkhole. Soon he popped his head back out, handing my husband and me the large rocks as he removed them.

Before leaving, we walked a part of this property I had not been on before. There was a rock cropping that interested the cave expert. It was steep with years of dead leaves piled deep. I crossed over several dead trees, straddling the large ones that had fallen decades ago, holding back even deeper piles of leaves. I am not sure anyone had walked this section in a very long time. Why would they? Even a hunter would not want to walk that steep hill. A small creek ravine below was always a compass for me to find my way

back down to that cold spring water, taking several drinks before parting ways.

"Please take me by the muck place," I told my husband. "I know it's getting late and will be dark in a couple of hours, but I have to have just one more look before winter." I knew where I wanted to dig. Right where the dog had shown an interest.

When Buz and I returned to the muck place, the place where I saw the miracle of the light on the water, I stood for a moment in awe, remembering the image I had captured just a few months earlier with just my phone camera. I questioned how my mind could have interpreted the miracle as anything but just that—a miracle, a source of energy from a spiritual realm put on the back shelf and eventually ignored. Clearly, that day in August, someone—a someone who has a relationship with me personally—wanted me to know something. This omnipresent power wants us all to know of its existence.

I stood at the edge, staring into black muck.

The pile of rocks I had dug out of there in August were already covered in leaves and grass. How quickly nature covers our tracks! Staring into the dark water, I asked myself, *Why here? Why would*

God's angels choose this exact place to deliver such a powerful image—a very important piece of this journey never to forget—the angels lying on the water, right here in this very spot. They could have lain anywhere, but they laid at the muck place.

A multilayered purpose? The bread crumbs guided me here, and once here, after August, the more intense premonitions and the bad nightmare about St. Albans began. Why?

The muck place is a beautiful place with a cliff bordering the pond, like the back wall cliffs of Pikes Pond, and the tall cliff walls of the dumpsite, and the cliff wall at Dedmon, and even the Vancouver art that captured my attention in the very beginning. A mangrove-like place. The message is pond. The message is a cliff. After one pulls into this hidden area off of Hazel Hollow Road, a gradual slope provides a path easy to walk, up the hill to the right of the pond, that leads to the top of the cliff above the muck place to the field of reeds—a remote section of the historical Ingles Farm that would never be sold or developed, a place with running water trickling down the mountain. A place where someone put a shrine—a shrine of guilt? Was this area my sister's final resting place?

The muck place became relevant when the angels lay on the water, lighting it up to send me a message. This place was significant. If not Gina's final resting place, could the muck place be the place she drew her last breath? Perhaps the muck place was where my sister, barely hanging onto life in the trunk of the car, had died. Out of all of the places, this one struck a chord with me. It was the beginning with the Vancouver mangrove picture and it might be the end. Were we getting close?

It was going to be dark soon. I walked back up to the spot I had come here for. The spot I wanted to dig up by the road. The exact spot where the dog had shown slight interest. The exact spot where Kevin and I had once stood, when I experienced the field of energy. On my Garmin GPS, I verified it was as close as I could get to the latitude/longitude given to me earlier. With my short shovel, I started digging. I dug slowly, and carefully, until I was about three feet down. I wanted to get to four. I grew tired. It was already dark. I laid on the dark ground, stretched out, trying to get just one more foot of dirt carefully removed. I knew I had to finish. I somehow knew I would never be back. "Enough is enough," Buz said, and that was that. It had been a very long day.

That night, on November 11, 2016, I wrote this note, unfortunately, with a few words illegible, but the legible parts would become quite interesting as I rediscovered this message long after it was originally written, not making sense to me until much later. I would have had no idea of its meaning at the time written anyhow.

Something _(at)_ lake _(Penn)_ - _3 of people is _.

One went up in a plane and he was _ a bandit.

_ very high. Into the lake.

And, the reason I missed the above message until later was that I also had this message on the same night on the same messy paper, 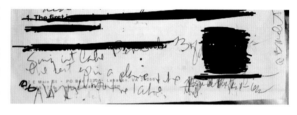 11/11, and I later praised God in gratitude that I had!

Could see red tracking on this place-maybe infection but dreamed I had to tell the doctor.... It would kill me if infection gets to my heart. The doctor said he was the doctor. I kept insisting I needed help. Red was moving....

When I awoke, I remembered the image of me in a doctor's face, yelling. This was an unusual dream message, not like the others. More like the angel dream when I clearly remembered having it. My first thoughts were of my dad.

Once, Daddy had told me that he'd had a football injury that started shooting red streaks up his arm. "Red streaks are bad," he had said. "It means the infection is traveling to the heart." I got up, went to the bathroom, and noticed a quarter-sized purplish area on the inside of my left upper thigh. I showed it to Buz. "You better get yourself to urgent care," he said. "That does not look good."

I went on to the office because I had Saturday morning appointments.

By lunch, it was an eight-inch red oval encircling a blackish, raised area. Red lines extended four inches from the edges of the oval. The immediate thought in my head—sudden and clear as a bell like a voice speaking to me instead of just my own thoughts—brown recluse spider. I went straight to the ER.

Of course, the first thing they ask when you tell them in the ER you have been bitten by a brown recluse spider is "How do you know? Do you have the spider?" And I did not want to share that I had been straddling dead trees in thick piles of dead leaves or stretched out on the ground in the dark digging a hole looking for human bones. They might just send me to another section of the hospital, even though I had to admit it was my own hard-headed, stubborn foolishness. The ER doctor prescribed medicine, and I went home. I felt the poison traveling quickly through me. I did not move from the couch until the ER doctor called the next day to check on me. She said to come back immediately. Buz was gone, so I drove myself back to the ER. "I want to admit you," she said. I knew if we did not get this poison out of me, it was not going to be good. I thought of a rotary friend, a surgeon, Dr. John Kerr. I asked him to come into the ER. He did. He said later that he knew if I needed him, it must be important. I asked him to please just cut the nasty poison out.

My doctor friend agreed and cut it out. I told him I knew I had been bitten by a brown recluse spider.

"This looks reclusal. It could be. What in the world were you doing to get bitten there?"

"You would not believe it if I told you!"

Maybe it was the granddaddy of all spiders. It was more than just making one single bite and then scurrying away. That spider threw everything he had at me. He must have been inside my pants leg fighting for his own life. Ugh! What I do know is I became deathly ill. Had I not received that dream message earlier in the night, just like all of the other many messages, I might not be here to share *the journey*. I would not have gone to the ER—I'm too tough for my own good sometimes. I would have never paid attention to what would have seemed to be just a thought—although *brown recluse spider* did get my attention! Had it been any other thought like a centipede, I probably would have told myself, *That is just silly Dlana.* Had I not had a caring ER doctor call and check on me, I may have never left that couch. And had I not had a surgeon friend who came straightaway on his weekend, I believe I would have died just like I had written. That message saved my life. Do we still think that my premonition, a very clear warning, came only from a bad place and not from a good place? I certainly questioned many theories around this one event. Oh, the thoughts we feed. We just have to learn to pay attention.

The poisonous bite knocked me out of commission, at least from digging duty. It was a blessing in disguise. It got me out of the woods and away from my narrow focus of searching for my sister's bones—winter came, but my experience was far from over.

While recuperating, I spent time looking back through *the journey* photos. I noticed the picture of the spider bite was taken the second day in the ER right at 2:22! I did not know then what I know now.

I had a sudden urge to look through my old family photo albums. For some reason, I was missing my dad. I found my favorite picture of my smiling, happy dad. He was taking me back to Radford after my school winter break. The snow was too deep for my car, but not for his red Jeep Wagoner. He stopped to help someone stuck in the snow. This was before he lost Gina.

CHAPTER 18

LOST INSIDE OF YOU

It's been a long, long way down to here.

During my recovery time from my spider bite, I stayed up until the wee hours while Buz slept so I could gather all my notes. I started to see a narrative emerging—something that made sense of the bits and pieces of my messages. Before November 11, everything came to me like water from a waterhose that quickly turned into a firehose set on continuous full force, an endless stream of powerful water, leaving no time to truly absorb what I had been given. My dad's words of wisdom were echoing in my head—*Time to back up and punt,* to which I would always smile and respond, *Figure it out!* Those two phrases were my life's mantra every time I dealt with a challenge. I began deciphering it all by covering a wall with large paper Post-it easel pad sheets, organizing all I had learned and written in the last six months. It really was quite disturbing to take a step back and really see what I had been experiencing. And it took a spider bite on 11/11 to slow me down so I could start to make sense of it all. The irony of that!

I now had time to contemplate all of the messages. And, it would become more apparent that someone wanted me to know Gina was not alone in her fight. Be still, listen, and learn.

The most challenging line of questioning was: Who were all of these names I kept getting. Sitting in my favorite chair one day, resting from the aftermath of that spider bite, a thought came to me: *Go get your old Radford*

University Beehive annual. I had noticed it earlier when I had retrieved my favorite picture of my dad. I combed through the annual looking for any of the names that had surfaced: Aurora, Beth, Kim, and a beautiful, black-haired girl. My hope was that someone would look familiar to me having met several of Gina's friends during my visits in the spring and the three weeks in June 1980 when we lived together. I was in solemn shock when I came across a picture of a girl, a RU student whose name was spelled V-I-C-K-I K-O-C-H, exactly the same as a girl I knew had been murdered in Ohio in August 1980, just a little over a month after Gina was murdered and a month before Epperly was arrested and charged with Gina's murder—there just are no coincidences in *the journey.*

Vicki Koch's name was significant to me because in August 1980 my family was made aware that Epperly had gone to Ohio, and within days of his arrival there, a girl named Vicki Koch was reported as missing. She lived in the same area where Epperly was known to be. After the missing girl story surfaced and VSP unofficially speculated foul play by Epperly, my dad raised the reward from $10,000 to $12,000 for any information leading to the recovery of Gina's body. My dad knew there needed to be an arrest—we had to find Gina so hopefully Epperly could be taken off the street. The task at hand was daunting, escalating emotions adding layers of more heartache as we grieved for this young Ohio girl.

On September 9, 1980, the Grand Jury handed down an indictment. Epperly was charged with Murder in the First Degree of Gina Renee Hall and arrested. It was mid-September 1980 before Koch's body was found in a remote Ohio cornfield, making it no longer a missing person case but a murder case—and it remains a cold case to this day.

In 1980, some Virginia authorities believed the Ohio Vicki Koch may have "just crossed paths with Epperly" just like Gina. Could it be that these two cold cases were interconnected—something more than wrong place, wrong time? There have been many unexplainable no-coincidence moments since I began *the journey*, so I contemplated whether it could be a coincidence that I had landed on that same name, different person, in the RU Beehive. Seeing the same name in the 1980 RU annual brought on an onslaught of questions.

First, I focused on the Ohio Vicki Koch. Was she an RU student? Had she known Gina or been at the Marriott in Virginia that night? *Could the Ohio Vicki Koch be the escaped, naked, beaten girl?* No. I do not believe so. She was a much loved young teacher in Ohio. Epperly was staying with another teacher from a different school about twenty miles away. Maybe it was wrong place, wrong time. But I still questioned whether I had come across the name Vicki Koch, a different Vicki Koch, in the RU annual just to point me back to Ohio so I would connect Epperly as the murderer of the Ohio Vicki Koch. If I found out more about her murder, would that somehow link back to Gina's murder, Romano's murder, the naked and beaten girl, and that entire night at the lake house? Too many murders to be ignored. This prompted me to dig more. I was now digging for truth, Gina's truth, and the endless, impossible search for her hidden bones now on hold.

Everything was in order in Vicki Koch's apartment, as though no struggle had occurred. That night, she returned to her apartment from watching a play. Kicking off her shoes and turning on music, she logged a note in her diary about the play. Then someone broke into her apartment; the window screen was taken out and laid on top of an overhang. It seemed that these little details align with some of the details in Epperly's previous sexual assault reports. Other local victims had reported that Epperly tapped on the window seeking help or they reported him coming in through a window. Hearing this reminded me of the attempted break-in that our Bergen Pines next-door neighbor reported as occurring the night before Gina was murdered, Friday 27, 1980. He told the police he believed it may have been someone who intended to break into our duplex townhouse. I find it most interesting that right before this break-in occurred, Epperly and Skipper were at Sal's Restaurant where a waitress reported she was being bothered by them. She felt both were responsible for the drama playing out, feeding off the actions of each other. And to note, the trusted buddy had a Bergen Pines address listed when he was deposed in July 1980 by the police. Andy has always believed Gina was targeted by Epperly. Me too.

It is possible Epperly killed the Ohio Vicki Koch, no matter the why behind it. It had similarities to his mode of operation. There are other theories surrounding Vicki's death. I would not rule out Stephen Epperly.

November 24, 2016:

> I was at a large house place sitting on a cliff-like place. I decided to go down these steps on the side of the cliff and sit and look at the river ___ (illegible). Too steep and a snake came out. Did not chase me. I watched it. The snake left, then I went back up, but I almost fell at the top.

Before I was on the cliff, I was at a party in the big house.

I could see the island from the cliff.

Me and another girl hid, but they came in and kept coming-had to fight. One used his belt. I tried to get her to go and she couldn't _____ (illegible, but looks like one man). I went to get help, but I could not even talk and say "Help." More than one bad person.

One leader _____ helped us.

They picked me up and drove away. No one would help us.

Finally, a moment of clarity. The aha moment came. I was beginning to know that there may have been a party at the lake house. Could there have been more bad men than just Epperly, and was there a leader—someone to be feared? Was the tall, skinny man the same as the *one leader*?

On November 28, two other messages written on the same night at different times clearly showed a difference in the same night's handwriting. Often, the handwriting was just not mine and difficult to decipher. It was unique.

Could have been something else but not-only worried about the _____ (illegible) not the boy pair.

Two men driving early in the morning before the (party) or morning. Getting drunk-we were all waiting in there. No respect - Driving Talking bad - Disrespectful Home so I _____ (illegible) _____His _____ In his shirt and the other _____ Man_(Monster?) And cut his shirt in the back.

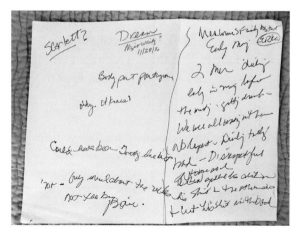

Curious, I tried again to take this message and compare it to my sister's handwriting in her letters and to my dad's letters. The capital "I" is unique like the "I" on her envelope. No words can express how thinking like this made me feel. The thought that something, somewhere has the power to do this should have scared me. But I had begun to believe it was Gina guiding me and that she needed me. Nola told me about automated writing. Something in our world clearly has the power to do this, good or bad—or both, and that should scare the bejeebies out of us. This, whatever this is, was very much out of my control. I was asleep.

And on December 2, my dad's birthday:

> I wrote: I was at a funeral. My left arm was itching.

My loving mother-in-law died peacefully a few weeks later, December 22, 2016.

And that same night I also wrote:

> I drove my car over concrete pillars trying to get here to there.... Fell straight down into the water off of the concrete pillar. From high up. Straight in.

For some reason, this made me wonder about a second car following Gina and Gina looking back at either a car or the backseat. There had been re-ports by neighbors about multiple cars being heard driving down to the lake house at 12:30 a.m..

A lady called me to share information she believed was very relevant to Gina's case. She had lived in the area of the power company's Claytor Lake dam substation most of her life—a place on the shoreline opposite the lake house where my sister was taken and murdered. She shared details she knew from 1980, with this being the most intriguing: On Monday afternoon, June 30, 1980, Epperly's sister came home after work to find her brother sitting on her porch. This frightened her because Epperly had been warned by his brother-in-law to come nowhere near his sister or their home and he had not for three years. Then, that day Epperly was sitting on her porch. Coincidence? An odd place for Epperly to have been thirty-six hours after Gina's death before anyone else even knew she was dead. The sister lived in this same area across the lake from the lake house. This substation area had a cave and a quarry nearby, and because the pow-er company owned the surrounding land, this remote, wooded area was rarely trekked. In 1980, the entire area was accessible through a hole in the fence large enough for a car to drive through. They drove through it all of the time. And, this spot in the fence was very near Epperly's sister's home. The locals knew about it and the very deep, blue water of the quarry with its surrounding rock shelves and creviced high cliffs, a favorite swimming hole. I entered "Quarry Radford, VA" into a search engine knowing that the quarry was right there, very near where Epperly's sister lived. I could not help but think of Pike's Pond and its legends of no-bottom-deepness. The same as the Radford quarry with its high, creviced cliffs. I just thought, *One day I will know.* The lady caller also shared that Skipper's great-grandfather's lake "cabin" was also in this area right across the lake from the lake house. And, one of Epperly's football buddies lived on the point near a small, uninhabited island. All of this straight across from the lake house where my sister was murdered. I cannot help but connect all of this to the boat heard crossing the lake right after Gina would have been killed. I wonder, what secrets does this vast area hold? And that bluff visit Epperly made as soon as he got out of jail November 1980 always bothered me. Why there?

On December 8, I wrote:

Great Escape

This message became relevant when I finally realized the connections of that night, and this next message was sent to make sure I was listening and seeing the connections.

On December 13, I woke to having written this note about a song.

"Wagon Wheel" in my head, the line about Johnson City.

And a separate note, Campground and Music playing. Gary Romano?

The great escape? I am guided back to the naked, beaten girl wrapped in a blanket—the postal worker's report and the Mind Reach clues from 1980 resurfaced in my mind as relevant—Had we only understood remote and Ohio before Ohio happened.

VSP knew Epperly was in the area—Circleville, Ohio—when Vicki Koch was murdered on August 10, 1980. By July 1980, Epperly was the leading suspect in Gina's murder, but not yet charged. He was free to come and go. Epperly told the police he owed money and needed to go to Ohio to work to pay off people—that was most likely Hardie and Cranwell, as confirmed in their own police interviews. Both men said Epperly had not paid much toward the personal loans they had given him back in 1976, so why the sudden urgency?

I do not believe for one moment that Epperly went to Ohio to work. Why would he not keep a watchful eye on the investigation, or miss the unfolding of events, or pass on the enjoyment in the revelry of what was a game to him? He would have only left Virginia if absolutely necessary. He moved an hour away to Roanoke, saying the reason was because he was receiving threats on his life. Epperly! That story always brings a wry snicker. So, why Ohio? Did Epperly go to Ohio to intentionally kill Vicki Koch? And if so, why Vicki Koch?

Did Epperly or others find the name in the 1980 RU annual just as I did, seeing the picture of this person and convinced she looked familiar. Epperly did not know Gina's name when asked at the Sunday Horseshoe Picnic. Who else did not know the name of—the other girls? Did someone surmise that the picture in the annual was the escaped girl, a girl not known? A girl who could still come forward and tell the truth—the missing girl from the lake house night gone wrong.

This RU picture in the annual is a person whose true legal name was Victoria, not the shortened version Vicki as labeled in the RU annual. So a search for that same spelled name, Vicki Koch, would have easily provided a match and the information needed to narrow down where Vicki Koch was—Ohio. The address then given to Epperly.

So then the next obvious question: Who helped Epperly locate Koch if he did indeed go to Ohio intentionally to murder her? Who would have had access in 1980 to a national database of public records to search the name Vicki Koch? I can only think of a few occupations that would have the capability to know this type of information.

Epperly's cohort, Tom Hardie, was a well-known, financially successful real estate developer who had a tarnished reputation, and later, a conviction record for his drug-dealing activities. Hardie, who was referred to as Epperly's former "construction boss," having met Epperly in the mid-1970s, loaned him $5,000 to hire a defense attorney for his 1976 rape trial. In 1980, Hardie came to the Radford police station with Epperly several times during the first week after Gina's murder. A policeman was curious as to whom Hardie was and why he kept coming into the station, escorting Epperly during multiple visits. When the policeman asked Hardie if he were Epperly's attorney, he replied, "No, I am just his sidekick, a friend." The policeman then asked Hardie to leave.

Clearly, the evidence points to more than an employer/employee relationship.

In November 1988, Hardie was arrested and indicted on felony charges of dealing in cocaine. The long list of people charged with Hardie in this group of serious, organized, street drug dealers supplying cocaine to local residents and university students included a former police sergeant with the Montgomery County Sheriff's office. Police have the means to search national databases. Was Epperly's police connection Hardie and his inner circle or that one local police person who kept dropping by trying to convince us Epperly was innocent? Was a DMV or driver's license search how the address for Vicki Koch was obtained and given to Epperly?

And the most disturbing question—who was the naked, beaten girl wrapped in a gray blanket and picked up by the trucker on Interstate 81? The great escape—with only a gray quilt to wrap herself in. I believe that gray heirloom quilt did end up in Johnson City, Tennessee, or Norfolk, Virginia. My heart sank imagining the weight of fear of a girl who might have survived, always remembering, never forgetting that night. Fractured souls—evil spreading its roots into the hearts of so many.

That may be a stretch of a theory, but it was possible.

A message from two months earlier was now starting to become clear.

> The girls tried to get me in the bathroom. We fought. She escaped by running out the door. We hurried to leave, packing everything fast because the man and the woman were coming to get us. The man was fair-skinned, tall, with a small-build and blondish.

And just days earlier, this part in a message:

> Me and another girl hid, but they came in and kept coming—had to fight.

I delved into everything I could find to confirm this sequence of events.

The items found in my Monte Carlo were not there before that night, especially that Orange Tennessee Cup. Maybe the unknown passenger(s) if still alive could help confirm how my sister came to be at that lake house and exactly what happened.

Was the utility room where *they* had hidden together? And from whom?

Consider this: Blood splatters—O positive—were found in the utility room. A common blood type. The splatter pattern had indicated blunt force. There was a fight in the utility room where the beating took place. I believe Gina eventually got away and tried to escape her attackers by attempting to go up the spiral stairs. Gina never made it up the stairs; her leg was grabbed, her broken ankle bracelet falling off at the foot of those stairs during her struggles. A girl made it up the stairs, whether taken there or followed by one of the men. Gina's fight began in the basement rec room and ended there. The large bloody spot was on the carpet between the entrance to the utility room and the spiral stairs. Gina's death became a distraction that maybe freed the girl when the upstairs attacker joined Epperly down in the rec room. The upstairs naked, beaten girl grabbed the gray quilt from the rack and escaped out the upstairs door while the other men were gathered in the basement dealing with Epperly, who, Nola believed, was crying desperately after he had killed Gina. I still believed he might cry initially, but then he snapped out of it and followed a same well-rehearsed routine. No guilt. No remorse.

And I wondered, *Could there be more than one victim we did not even know about?* The black-haired girl resurfaced in my mind.

There is that one mysterious police report from 1980 from a caller who simply said *Call Philadelphia Police.* But when the police called, they inquired only about Gina and how she might connect to Philadelphia. Gina was always believed to be alone, and that one thought always changed any and every line of questioning. There could have been a missing girl reported to Philadelphia police locally, a family not even aware their daughter had been in Radford that weekend or did know, but did not know details—the what, when, and where.

Were other party guests out looking for the escaped witness—the naked, beaten girl wrapped in a blanket? Did they return to the lake house at 4:00 a.m. seeing Skipper's mom's sports car, which he had taken to the Marriott, now parked in the driveway, so they moved on to the trestle waiting on Epperly to drive by? Or, not. A chapter could be devoted to just the 3:00 a.m. slow driver versus the 5:00 a.m. fast, reckless driver theories and the timeline inconsistencies. I learned many stories as I dug through the mountains of "minutia." Too many conflicting details for just one book. These tiniest of details are organized chronologically in a companion book: *Web of Lies Unveiled: A Day Made in Hell.*

So many new questions can arise from one story—the bass fishermen story kept secret for decades or from one report in a big box seemingly irrelevant at the time. My messages provided the direction so that as I searched Gina's files, I paid attention to what I was to know and I found facts that aligned. At first, it was hard to believe the storyline that seemed to surface in the messages I received. Often, during *the journey*, whenever people came into my life, my dreams would come alive. The storyline that emerged would be validated by some hidden report or Epperly's own words. I discovered this revealing fact that aligned with other girls hiding in the utility room: Epperly's letters dated May 17, 2004 and December 19, 2012, appealing to the Clerk of the Court and the Pulaski County Judicial Court. Epperly maintained he was innocent. He is not. What he is, though, is calculatingly manipulative.

In Epperly's 2004 letter sent to R. Glennwood "Woody" Lookabill, then Clerk of the Pulaski County Court, and his former defense attorney, Epperly requests confirmation that items entered into trial that had been returned to the Clerk's office for safekeeping were still in the possession of the clerk's office. He notates only *specific exhibit items from the trial*, 60, 61, 62, 63, and he adds: *the two towels may be needed later to be retested by a lab.* He acknowledges there is other evidence—hair, blood, etc. that was collected, "*but for right now just check to see if you have those six items in storage.*" He specifically lists only the exhibit numbers that are the blood samples that were collected from the utility room, where the splattered blood was found. Epperly implies in his 2012 letter addressed to Judge Colin Gibb of the 27th Judicial Circuit Court Pulaski County that the blood will not match Gina's blood-typing.

The exact wording in his letter of his question to the court: *Does all of the blood found during the investigation belong to the same individual?* He already knows the answer.

As I continued to read Epperly's letter, the arrogance and confidence of his sinister mind was coming through. Epperly already knew the blood would not all match Gina's because another girl or girls and other men had been there. In my opinion, this was confirmed by his own line of thinking, his own written words, and his own questions. Epperly's self-incriminating statements were endless.

I know now that Gina was not alone in the terror of that night. Chances are that all of the blood collected may not have been just her blood. But her blood was there. Her hair was there. And the blue towel covered in matching carpet fibers cleaned up her blood, her hair. The refrigerator was smeared with blood and her hair, and her panties were covered in matching carpet fibers. She was beaten in that lake house. And she laid in the floor of the rec room, her blood spilling out. I pray she did die there—that she was not still holding on to life as she was picked up and placed in the trunk of my car. I know now she was not the only one hiding in the utility room. Girls were taken—taken into a snake pit.

There were other victims.

Who was this naked, beaten girl wrapped in a gray quilt? If she, too, had been taken into that snake pit, whoever she was, I was thankful she escaped. I pray for her to be at peace. And I selfishly hope she comes forward to speak her voice. The truth. Then, maybe, just maybe there could be other victims connected to Epperly whose families could also have truth. Truth is peace.

I always knew this truth for sure—Gina did not go to the lake house of her own free will. Gina would never have gone alone with a man, a stranger ten years older. That was not my sister. I knew my sister. And Kim Jett helped validate that truth. And, Gina was taken to and into that lake house. The broken car door pull paints a clear picture of truth. And, Epperly's own inculpatory 2012 questions helped me prove to others what I now know to be true: Gina was not alone. And, the naked girl wrapped in a blanket report could be connected. I knew more answers would come in time. And they did.

A recent conversation in 2018 with a person I just happened to meet brought the lake house party to light. She shared a conversation she'd had with Skipper in which he told her, "You never want someone like Epperly to find out you are having a party." So, was that reference to *a party* a general reference or was Skipper referring to the specific night Gina was killed?

Who was at that lake house—organized party, inside or just down at the dock? Why would it be important for everyone to believe Epperly and Gina were alone...*to the best of his knowledge*?

A lot happened at that lake house the night of June 29, 1980. None of it pointed to the idea that Gina was alone there with Epperly. But that is the way the story had been told—that Gina went willingly with Epperly to a lake house where they were alone until 4 a.m. I know Epperly killed Gina. So the rising question was: Why would it even be necessary to keep a party at the lake house secret? The secrecy must have had to do with who was actually there. The guests—mystery guests? In my opinion, there was someone there who holds something over everyone. Maybe even a some-one a lot scarier than Epperly—*one leader.*

Sufficient evidence exists in the reports that we cannot ignore, including the multitude of statements of the lake house gun-shooting activities; the boat pulling out from the vicinity of the lake house that was witnessed by different, unrelated people; and car traffic reported as going to the lake house on a residential road with very little traffic. An interesting fact I learned—the background of a nearby neighbor—a sergeant of arms of a local 1%er motorcycle club, the second highest ranking member some-times referred to as the enforcer. He had a party that night at his house just up the hill. He and his wife were interviewed by the police. They shared specific details not because they were associated with what happened down at the lake house, but just as neighbor witnesses—part of several neighbors telling what they had heard. I believe this person qualified as knowing exactly what he said he heard right down to describing what kind of gunshots. And, we can never forget Epperly's drug activities, his fifty trips to Fort Lauderdale indicative of other, unrealized associations. All substantiate a gun-shooting party gone wrong.

How does Romano fit into all of this? Maybe Romano was the villain first, then the victim. Romano had lived beside a 1%er motorcycle club hang-out. Romano was a drug dealer. Could all of this be connected with an-swers found in the minutia of facts buried deep in Gina's file?

Multiple cars were heard at 12:30 a.m., so was an enticing party already taking place at the lake house just down the hill from a 1%er's party 200 yards up from the lake house—all within earshot when the neighbor's party ended at 1:30 a.m. Did some partygoers move down to the dock at the lake? There have been recent stories shared by people living nearby who said a lot of noise went on that night at the lake house, yet in 1980, that scenario never surfaced. Maybe Gary Romano joined these mystery bystanders outside the lake house or inside with Epperly. Maybe he and a friend showed up looking for a party. A powerful friend—the one leader.

Is it possible these partygoers, whether bystanders or not, heard the screams of violence from within the lake house, maybe even drawing some down to the lake house? Or were the screams witnessed by an un-associated group of people at the lake's edge who would not want to be known to have been anywhere near that lake house. Epperly could have escalated tempers by recklessly killing Gina. Or did his actions set off a celebration, guns being shot off in the air? Who shot the two guns? Who was connected to the violence? Who was the mystery person who came to the lake house party in a boat? Maybe in these bystanders' eyes, Gina and others were viewed as innocent young girls—which they were. Or maybe exactly the opposite—girls fighting against worse than we could have ever imagined.

Whoever may have been near or inside that lake house, whether bystand-ers who happened to walk down the hill to the dock to continue their par-ty or invited lake house party guests, someone saw something. And, in my opinion, Skipper may have known who was there at the lake house. Skip-per was afraid of someone, having fearfully visited the police station that first week three days in a row. If my best friend had just murdered a girl in my mama's house, I personally would have run straight to my daddy.

If we believe Skipper and his female guest's statement about what happened at 4:00 a.m. and after, it could be possible that Skipper may not have known then about Epperly arranging his own party—inviting his drug buddies. The guest list I envision is why I do not give much consideration to the known Marriott Wolfpack attendees, at least three of the four, as having ac-tually been there inside the lake house when Gina was murdered. But they knew more than they told. If I am right, then this secrecy is beyond com-prehension, worse than I could have ever imagined. The secrets abound. All seemingly because a lake house party needed to be kept a secret.

That is the only way I can reconcile no one speaking up throughout that summer and all of these years, aside from the fact that they just kept drop-ping dead.

Hearing these stories and learning the smallest of details from 1980 lay-ered more and more murk into my heart. Several factors converged so that details like this were lost, provoking me to see how sinister evil is. Evil is elusive and hides sometimes in plain sight, always at work. Thoughts are influenced. Questions don't get asked. Details never get probed.

I was standing in my bedroom when I finally had this realization beyond any doubt: *There were other people there at the lake house. Other girls too.*

No longer was it just a theory to me. It was the truth that I had silently longed for for decades. Loudly echoing in my head was the song "Hallelujah" as though someone were shouting the chorus in my ear.

At first, I had thought the song "Hallelujah" was just to high-five me for finally figuring it out, and maybe it was. But was it also this message from the lyrics: *I did need proof. But where was this proof coming from? The dark, not the light? No way. I can feel the light?* Or was it to confirm this: *My thoughts, others' thoughts, are being misdirected by someone or something who has not seen the light?* Twisted truths.

How Gina and maybe others got to the lake house may no longer be a mystery. Gina could not leave. No matter whether from the Marriott parking lot or the lake house, I knew this truth from the message I had previously received:

> I was driving, and a car blocked me. Pulled in, and the car pulled in behind me. Blocked me in. I asked him (or them) to let me out.

This was a pivotal message that prompted me to look closer at the beginning of the composed story for the truth of what really happened to my sister that night. I focused on the intricate facts surrounding the Marriott parking lot, reviewing my notes, the Wolfpack's statements, and testimony related to the Marriott and the parking lot. A new storyline emerged that was supported by facts, especially the broken door pull. I was content now confirming in my own mind what I always knew to be the truth—Gina was taken. I believed the violence began in the Marriott parking lot and the composed story was exactly that—composed—made up by the murderer and his friend or friends. But then, the second similar message was shared with me by the ghost hunters and I began to waver again, within my own thoughts, Marriott parking lot or lake house? I landed on the lake house driveway even after having found all of the facts to support the parking lot theory. Influenced thoughts?

Now I can look back and contemplate this sequence of events. Both messages, mine first and then the ghost hunters', differed ever so slightly. That intrigued me. A perplexing thought—the ghost hunters received basically the same message. Was the origin of the second message, *I called after I was blocked*, from the dark or light or Gina? *I do not believe in ghosts as defined by most people, so I questioned the source.*

No matter which place Gina was taken from, the Marriott parking lot or the lake house driveway, both notes can be true. But, the end result after I heard the wording of their second message, *the call happened after being blocked in,* is to be thought about further. The second message led me away from the Marriott parking lot theory to the driveway of the lake house, surmising that Gina was blocked at the lake house because the call happened there. Could the ghost hunters be almost right—a manipulative spirit, not Skipper's granddaddy as they believe, but indeed a deceiver twisting the truth? Initially, after receiving my own first message, I was questioning and theorizing both places as to where and when the door pull was broken. The *facts* led me to conclude the Marriott parking lot. After hearing the exact wording of the second message, my thoughts redirected me to this assumption: Gina must have been blocked in at the lake house. So I stopped questioning which place the struggle happened, my mind seemingly satisfied with only the lake house driveway theory, even though something inside me did not fully accept this as plausible. I now see this experience as an example of a truth we all need to be aware of—the possibility of an external force with an objective—a spiritual battle. The Marriott parking lot facts would certainly be something the Enemy would not want me to know because it could lead to more darkness revealed. The second message, along with my own interpretation of it, almost succeeded at misdirection. Almost two years later, after Kim Jett came to me, I revisited my original theory and questioned again, *Where exactly was my sister blocked in?*

Both messages are true—a call that actually took place after Gina left the Marriott, and after arriving at the lake house. So was the second message a truth, deceptively worded with an objective to misdirect? Was it a twisted truth used to lead me further away from the real truth, twisted ever so slightly to cover the tracks of those involved in the parking lot? Was the second message from the dark? Consider its source—a question and answer session *seeking* the answers from the dead? Who's answering?

Or, I guess it might have been just a more to-the-point answer to the original questions that were asked—How did Gina get to the lake house and how did she call? How could we ever really know anything's true source? And interestingly, the same questions that arose from the "clues" revealed during the ghost hunter's sleuthing thought process were the same questions I had always asked for decades. To really give this deep thought is to question the truth of everything we believe we know.

No matter *The Who* behind it all, I know in my heart the truth.

Andy and I disagreed on my *other people at the lake house* theory. I never dreamed it either, until I literally "dreamed" it. The messages came to me for some reason still to be seen. He holds to the original theory. That Epperly targeted Gina, cunningly manipulated her to go to the lake house, and when she refused his sexual advances, seeing her scarring, he became enraged and killed her. These are logical assumptions and the composed story most believed for decades. I always believed the last part of this story too—that Gina refused his advances. But I would have added this line: My sister fought Epperly, (*or them*), to her death with all of her strength never giving in until she drew her last breath. I used to believe that is why she died—her goodness, morals, and beliefs—knowing she would never have given Epperly what he wanted. She would fight. That is what I had believed all of these years. I was not wrong—I just did not know the rest of the story. I never could reconcile the why behind the foundation of that composed story. And now I know.

But still, who is "them"? We can narrow the list down with these facts.

In 1980, my family did not know about the rumors swirling around Epperly, that he was the "muscle" for a massive drug ring. Much more about the possible drug ring connections came to light between 1986 and 1988.

Charles Jerry DeHart, associated with both Hardie and Epperly, was a suspect in the double carbon monoxide poisoning of two North Carolina men in May 1980, possible drug informants. Charles Jerry DeHart would be murdered eleven months before Hardie's arrest on January 8, 1988. An interesting fact caught my attention from DeHart's murder trial: Two men pulled DeHart from a car to stop him from beating a woman in the car—the nature of his game. His murder investigation yielded an important detail to Shockley, the same prosecuting attorney that handled Gina's case. A key witness, the mother of DeHart's young son at the time of the trial, Lois "Strawberry" Quesenberry, told authorities that DeHart "helped Epperly move the Hall girl's body." *Did he help Epperly carry Gina's body from the lake house to the trunk of the car?*

Just a few weeks before DeHart was killed, he told Strawberry he was going to help the FBI bust some big cocaine dealers. Was DeHart reporting on the Fort Lauderdale-Miami drug funnel to southwestern Virginia that was prevalent at the time?

DeHart had become a drug informant for the FBI in 1986 with one main objective—get Hardie. In 1980 DeHart and Hardie were tight. And both were tight with Epperly. What caused their falling out—Epperly's actions? If so, was only one there at the lake house—both? They separated ties soon after in 1980.

DeHart lived down by the river near the Pepper's Ferry bridge—I wondered, *The same bridge from a story shared with me in 2016 about the mysterious death of a young boy found under that bridge?* When I heard this story, it made me cry. He was rumored to be found wrapped in barbed wire and seemingly thrown off the bridge. The police report noted drowning as the cause of death. This victim in the mid-1970s could be connected to living in close proximity to Epperly, but since the means of the boy's death was just shared with me in 2016 by someone who knew the family, and there were no substantiated facts, I will just refer to it as the neighbor boy story. His grave has a tiny, wooden cross.

And, this same bridge would have been crossed on a trip from the Marriott to the lake house. I did wonder, *Did DeHart get picked up or was he just an invited lake house guest?*

What about Tom Hardie—a lake house guest?

Pulaski County Deputy William Patton had testified that he saw a Cadillac parked beside my Monte Carlo early that Sunday morning. So a van was spotted within yards. And a Cadillac? This intrigued me. Of course, Cadillac owners do go fishing.

In 2018, I crossed paths with a man named Glenn. As soon as he heard the name "Dlana," he remembered the stories of 1980. He said he had been just thirteen when Gina had disappeared. He spent his summer riding his bike up and down Hazel Hollow Road, hoping to help find Gina too. I asked whether he knew Epperly back then. He had. I asked about other bad guys on my list. He responded yes to Tom Hardie, sharing that when he was about fifteen, he used to wash Hardie's cars, and he could never forget that big, silver Cadillac he used to wash. *Cadillac.*

It seemed Hardie liked owning Cadillacs and shooting his gun in the air from his van according to some newspaper accounts regarding his illegal activities.

The question remains: What is the connection to Romano—the guitar-pickin' drug dealer with a mysterious crony at the campground the night of his murder?

One of my messages was: One of the men was leaving and she needed to get him to help. Who was my sister trying to get to help her?

In mid-October, I had written a message I never could figure out until now:

> He would talk so he was a witness. Two guys and a girl witnessed (illegible) two shots (illegible). Witnessing so had to help. Tied up.

O positive blood had been found on a chair leg by the sliding glass door at the lake house. Could someone have been *tied up*? Tied to the chair? A similar clue in the "Hallelujah" lyrics? Maybe another girl, the beautiful, black-haired girl, while the group of men dealt with Gina.

And the witness—could this have been about Gary Romano or the mystery guest? What about Strawberry? Many to choose from. Whoever witnessed had to help. And maybe one of the witnesses was the outsider—Romano.

The execution-style nature of the Romano murder points to this ring of drug connections. The police believed it was his connections to his drug business that got him murdered. And, in a way, it was.

If Romano did show up at the lake house party—invited or not—with a powerful friend who just might have had every reason to distance himself from Epperly's rage-induced problem—a dead girl, it would explain the strong communication sent by Romano's execution, whether Epperly was his murderer or not, warning others not to talk. By killing Romano and dressing him in girl's panties, it could have been a warning sent to all party participants or an attempt to misdirect circumstantial evidence, or both. A leader that had the power to do just that, influencing all of the others to make sure it all just went away. And the person responsible for getting this mysterious one leader into Epperly's rage-created mess, Gary Romano, became the example. That might also explain the late night Ford LTD drive to a mile marker spot on I-81 to receive the communicating gory scene or witness the message being sent: *FIX THIS or you will be next. This party never happened.* Self-preservation kicks in. And in my opinion, Skipper and Hardie are both scared of someone far worse than their good friend Epperly. I now wonder if even Epperly was afraid of this one leader.

This mystery man—a leader—is a powerful, even worse guy, but maybe a bad guy with a personal rule: Don't rape and kill little girls. And especially not while I am present. Message sent. Message received.

But, of course, the most logical theory is Romano was just a loose-end witness, and Epperly killed him. And, we cannot rule out that someone could have witnessed it.

The statement made by Strawberry, to the prosecuting attorney—"Jerry helped Epperly move the Hall girl's body"—substantiates the possibility of who else could have been at the lake house. I believe Strawberry told her story for no self-serving reason. That night, a night that should not have been prevalent in her own mind, still was. Maybe she wanted Shockley to know that DeHart was connected to Epperly and Epperly was connected to Hardie and

Hardie's connection to DeHart's murderer was a viable possibility. Was she telling this because it was the catalyst of their discord? Or maybe she finally could just tell what she knew since DeHart was now dead.

On a whim, I sent DeHart's picture to those who had had the knife dream. Two gasping yeses. "He is the man in my knife dream!" one proclaimed. I believe it is highly possible he was at the lake house that night. There are just no coincidences that the day I received DeHart's photo from a friend who knew I had been searching for a picture of him, and the very night before, the same scary knife dream had resurfaced again. I had told her that if she had the dream again, to write down every detail she could remember about the man with a knife. And then that very same day, I sent DeHart's picture to her. There are no coincidences. Here is that text:

What I have learned is that

these were people capable of murder. People were murdered. Two other known cold cases are most likely connected to this night of violence.

The long history of Hardie and DeHart includes a lot of bad blood, many associations with convicted drug dealers, and violence against women. It also includes Epperly. Epperly's relationship to these men is referenced in the case file, but what do we really know about anyone else's true relationship with any of these men? Epperly had the muscle to offer. Their lives play out like a bad movie. And we must never forget the list of 100 women's names—half listed as being from Fort Lauderdale.

I just do not believe the *one leader* was *Tom or Jerry.*

Another recently shared story led me to wonder if Hardie, DeHart, or Epperly, were associated with Wallace S. Thrasher who was known to frequent the Claytor Lake area. The message *Airplane 1974* was coming to light. Thrasher was a known drug trafficker who used planes to smuggle cocaine and marijuana into the mountains of SWVA from the Caribbean. That would be *a bandit who went up in a plane* from my 11/11 message, written more than two years earlier. Nola was right—in time it will all make sense.

From the mountains of SWVA, distributors smuggled the drugs into the larger US cities. Thrasher was on DEA's radar. He had Fort Lauderdale smuggling connections as would become known in a federal indictment. That would certainly explain the government's involvement and interest in Gina's case. Remote, scattered, *Airplane*. The connections are endless. I find this one interesting. Later, many believed Thrasher faked his death in an airplane crash in 1984, after a decade of drug smuggling with his airplane—*1974.* To avoid drug indictments, his wife Olga became a drug informant, helping the authorities connect the dots. One such dot connected to Gina and my family. Carl McAfee, was the local attorney in our county that my dad called on to hire for help in Gina's case. McAfee's response to my dad was that everything looked as though it were in good shape with Gina's case and that my dad did not need to waste money hiring him. In the mid-1980s, after Thrasher "died" *or not,* the "Black Widow," as Thrasher's wife was nicknamed, provided the government with information of their known associates. Carl McAfee was named as one of Olga Thrasher's attorneys charged with connection to the drug-smuggling business and their money-laundering activities. I can now assume there could have been an underlying reason for telling my dad no because there is really no way to know exactly when the McAfee/Thrasher relationship began. The drug business can have years and years of secrets. The appellate court states Max Jenkins became involved first and then referred Olga to McAfee. The connections are endless. I believe Max and Epperly's paths crossed. And I can take my thoughts a step further—my dad was being watched over, a blessing in disguise. When I saw Thrasher's picture, it seemed familiar—my September 8, 2016 dream message.

It seems most logical that right then, right there, the leader must have been a mystery guest at this party or somewhere nearby. If any higher-up drug connected individuals or a 1%ers were present or nearby, witnessing or participating, that could illicit fear. Either would certainly be someone the other men would fear. One leader. Only one of my many messages that seemed either to point us in the right direction or far away from the truth. I guess we may never know who the *one leader* is. Seems there are many to choose from. But one man could certainly fit the various messages combined: One leader. A Bandit. Plane...Thrasher.

And I must admit, I even wondered if the snake pit was premeditated. Epperly invites a few friends over to a lake house party, with or without Skipper's knowledge, and maybe his drug cronies, even his drug boss or bosses, instruct the lowest man on the totem pole, Epperly, to bring them some young girls for the party. A far-fetched, premeditated theory, but then again, it would not surprise me in the least knowing the additional facts surrounding this night of lake house activities.

And, the messages continued: I would wake and see this full name I did not know:

> Gary Lang, written with an encircled 1981 and Red Door, walked to it-very red.

I had no idea who Gary Lang was or is and why I received this message.

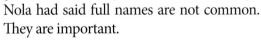

Nola had said full names are not common. They are important.

My mind still contemplated what was missing. What do we not know? Who might have been involved in covering up the before (*the Marriott parking lot*), the during (*that a lake house party had happened*), and the after (*protecting himself or someone else at that party*)? Why would this be necessary? I am back to the extra layer of cunningness. I am back to the parking lot story. The many trips made driving right past my car, and in my opinion, knowing what had happened long before Tuesday morning, as was told. The ridiculous, last-minute, Sunday horseshoe picnic gathering. The later, revised variance in statements given. The Barbell Club gossip gathering—the most telling. The lies began. The composed, manipulated story was taking root. Gina was not alone, so where exactly did the lies of the composed story begin—the parking lot, the lake house, the after—more truth becoming known and not shared—all of the above?

The polygraph given to Skipper only asked ten questions. And they all most likely focused on Gina's murder and the disposal of her body. I do not believe Skipper knew about the specifics of either, so he could answer truthfully. Answers are given based on the questions asked. And no one was really asking the outlying questions. No one had any reason to want answers to those questions except a sister who always believed in her heart that the secrets kept and the composed story was built on lies. A sister who could not stand by and allow her sister's honor to again, decades later, become irrelevant because of the 1980 composed story resurfacing as if it were the complete truth. Gina's voice must be heard.

My daddy taught me once that often in small town "politics," people compromise their principles when they should not. I would venture to say that every little town knows what I am talking about. And this compromise usually revolves around money and power and pride. "Don't touch that with a ten-foot pole" becomes the prevailing mindset.

A retired, RPD policeman told me, "All of the higher ups were relieved when Skipper passed the polygraph." So much seems to point to handling him with kid gloves in a town where his family had power and influence. Ignoring the extenuating details, not looking past the circumstantial evidence of anything but a murder connected to only one person, seems to infer a desire to avoid knowing the whole truth. A truth that included the grandson of a major Radford regional employer—St. Albans.

Andy told me he had sent the 1980 handwritten statements to a behavior handwriting analysis group that reported back to him that there were questionable negative results, possible lies and secrets kept. The line of questioning in the trial was not based on every detail written in the ten-page handwritten statement as told. The focus was always on the actual murder, which Epperly did do, and the location of Gina's hidden body, which again, Epperly did do, not so much what transpired that led to her murder—the composed story, or what happened in the weeks to follow—the hidden truth.

I never could reconcile Skipper and Hardie's multiple visits to the police station until now. Skipper, a large, strong man himself, seemingly afraid of Epperly and Hardie, not a small-time drug dealer, was keeping a watchful eye on the progression of the events. Maybe someone witnessed the shooting of Romano in the head, effortlessly, and woke up to what Epperly was capable of doing. Is this why multiple visits to the police station every day happened? Again, victim of circumstances, or as guilty as the others? *Victims or villains?*

We may never know exactly who witnessed what and who participated in the violence of that night until the person who knows the truth of who was there tells the truth. We may never know the whole reason behind the lies composed that Gina was alone. Epperly's own inculpatory letter confirmed the truth—Gina was not alone. The question remains: Who knew this?

Wow! How did all of these additional facts go unnoticed? Gunshots. Multiple cars. A boat. A naked, beaten girl. Drugs. A murdered drug dealer. And on and on....

How could the possibilities of others at or near the lake house not have been seriously considered by authorities? Everything was so overwhelming in 1980. The search for Gina's body was top of mind, and it and Epperly's conviction were all that mattered. So many hearts were warmed to help and do what was right in 1980. That was God. And not knowing all of the interwoven moving parts of what really happened that night helped those who sought to ensure that the man who murdered my sister was convicted and removed from society so no more victims would fall by his guilty hands.

The overarching question still remains: What is the likelihood that in rural Pulaski County, within twenty-four hours of Gina's murder, Gary Romano would be found nearby with a bullet in his head and a naked, beaten girl wrapped in a blanket would be found on Interstate 81 near the overpass of Claytor Dam Road? And a third murder, Ohio Vicki Koch? And, what else could be discovered?

So why bother now? Justice. Truth. Peace. Fractured souls. And the elephant in my room—my cross to bear—parole.

I asked the VSP to run the partial fingerprint found on the handle of Gary Romano's truck against prints in the national database. Epperly's fingerprints should already be there. And there is that Ford LTD reported as pulled in behind Romano's truck. In January 2017, I stopped by the VSP headquarters in Wytheville to add Hardie and DeHart to my request, all of whom would already have been in the system. I drove to Circleville, Ohio. When I met with a team of several investigators, I asked if there was anything at all in the Koch file that could be DNA tested with today's technology—specifically against what should be on file in Virginia—Epperly's sample. Andy had tried to connect with them. All seemed so simple, but unfortunately, I experienced that one region of the country does not play well with other regions of the country. Some investigators are quite territorial, wanting to be the one who solves the case even within a state's boundaries, county to county!

Not everyone can be the rooster.

We need a team with national authority over all jurisdictions with state regional teams who work together, communicating and combining resources; brilliant minds and efforts focusing in one specialized area—unsolved crime. These interconnected, cooperating teams who have the time, authority, and resources to ask whether a cold case murder of a drug dealer, Gary Romano—within twenty-four hours and less than ten miles away from my sister—could be connected in a place where one unsolved murder in a decade would be unusual. And then connect Ohio and Richmond and Fort Lauderdale, and, and, and...I dream of this powerful, effective team. We could call it Team Gina! And, Gina's Law could be enacted to provide this team with the authority necessary to work across jurisdictions and to provide consequences to those who do not cooperate. Team Gina could begin by focusing on the cold-case murders of children. A society that cannot protect its precious children is one we all need to question. And if a person murders or preys on one child, they will another and another and another. Too many cold cases—too many of them forgotten. The missing and the murdered, with only a few dedicated to solving these cases, and every day, new cases are mounting.

On the spiritual and emotional level, after what I experienced in 2016, I would model Team Gina differently, built on Christian principles. A spiritual army would be at its side that also wants justice to prevail every day; it would be gifted with the ability to work as an adhesive team, each seeing what others might not because all of the spiritual gifts are covered. Not a team built on similar investigative skill sets. This is how I have found success in my own life for many years. A team built from the wise instruction of 1 Corinthians 12 that balances all the gifts—wisdom, knowledge, faith, healing, miracles, prophecy, interpretation, discernment of truths, etc. That would be a powerful team! And I have met many people who could be on Gina's team. People who have been helping me from the kindness and generosity of their hearts. I want to watch what would happen in our society when that team goes into action. I believe God is saying to the evil that escapes us, "Enough is enough."

THERE ARE NO COINCIDENCES IN THE JOURNEY...

THE
MIRACULOUS
JOURNEY
A Day Made in Heaven

CHAPTER 19

SYMPATHY FOR THE DEVIL

This song makes me sad, just like this chapter.

The day Stephen Matteson Epperly was sentenced to life in prison, the appeal process began. As glad as we were for a conviction, Epperly stole our focus away from Gina. For thirty-six years, my family lived in fear of his release—which kept our attention on his continued incarceration. Epperly robbed us of not only her life, but also the best of her memories. I hated him for that. If I had truly healed—truly forgiven him—I would not have missed all of these years of letting the happiest memories of my sister slip away. How quickly the 1980 nightmare of the hunt for justice had become the new normal. How sad that a recollection of Gina, a loving thought or good memory, shared at a family gathering always led to a redirected conversation, "I wonder when the next parole hearing will be?" "I pray he never gets out." "You know he will come after one of us if he ever gets out." These conversations overshadowed our good memories of Gina.

A life sentence then did not necessarily mean life. Every one to three years, Epperly comes up for parole. At the last parole hearing, I included parts of this chapter as my permanent letter for parole denial, requesting that it be kept and reread at every future parole hearing as the official victim's families' parole denial request. The deferrals had recently trended to minimum deferrals probably because of his age. The last parole hearing set the next at the maximum deferral of three years. For decades, I could not have buried all of my bad memories if I had wanted to. They always surfaced on a regularly scheduled basis—when the parole hearing came around. I could see now that by focusing on him for thirty-six years, I had not been at peace.

I knew I still needed to release the burdens of unforgiveness, anger, and hate that filled my heart. That was not an easy task.

SMILING STEPHEN EPPERLY PHOTO COURTESY OF *PULASKI SOUTHWEST TIMES*

This is the evil monster I needed to forgive:

In 1980, local and state police did a thorough job of following the leads that Epperly's acquaintances shared, including information from multiple women. The *hand burned on the stove* story haunted me most: Two sisters, just like us, living in Radford had an encounter with Epperly. Police documented that when one of the sisters refused to have sex with him, he took her hand and held it on the burner of a stove, severely burning her hand. We had heard her hand required emergency medical attention. After this encounter, Epperly went outside of his trailer and shot his gun in the air, scaring the sisters even more than they already were. I wondered when I read this if the gunshots heard at the lake house were part of his and others' pattern—a celebratory shooting in the air, displaying pride for their triumphant power. I also found it interesting that one of Epperly's chosen character witnesses and his June 1980 construction boss and long-time friend, Housel, was questioned by the police in 1980 about these two sisters. The police had found a letter during the search of Epperly's bedroom written to Epperly by the sister who was raped. The letter confirmed and validated the police's suspicions. This friend/boss had dated the older sister. The connections were thought-provoking.

Knowing the pain Gina suffered as a little girl and hearing this story about burning his victim's hand, I could not stop seeing in my mind the image of my sister's scarring and his emotional reaction to discovering her scars. Andy said her scars became Epperly's trigger. I understand. I wondered the same in 1980 when I heard this story about him burning the girl's hand on the eye of the stove. The hate I had felt roared from within in 2016 as I relived this memory, seeing the facts on paper. I wanted to kill him myself. I felt Gina's pain. Did her scars trigger his rage? I don't think so. I have to not think so. My sister's burns might have escalated his own emotions, but they did not cause his actions.

Sadly, my dad knew of this incident. It is unfortunate that these stories became woven into our life story, but they were. When the police shared this story with us in 1980, I realized the evil that had crossed my sister's path. I always knew Gina had fought him with all of her might—the physical evidence made that clear—but this story told me who and what she had really been up against.

A trail of stories followed him, by women who described consistently similar stories: He would ask his victim to give him a massage. When she didn't consent to having sex with him, he would choke her while he raped her. And then he would make the victim give him a massage—"a rubdown." What's striking is the uncanny similarities throughout all of these statements, pointing to his consistent mode of operation.

Until I examined the full file of reports, reading multiple accounts from his rape victims, what I did not know was Epperly's M.O.—the details of his actions against these women. The connecting thread to truth—the massages. When I read Epperly's 1980 statement, his story of the night's events of my sister's last moments, he said my sister went with him to an upstairs bedroom and gave him a—"a rub down"—and I knew then the truth. He had raped her. He had choked her. He had killed her.

Andy told me that he believes Epperly did not rape Gina because of his own arrogance regarding his sexual performance and belief that he was a gift to women, evident by Epperly's statements made to his victims. Epperly's intent was to rape her, but when he saw her physical scarring from her burn accident, it triggered a rage that caused him to kill her instead. I disagreed: the evidence of the downstairs recreation room carpet fibers found on her underwear tells me he definitely had intent. But I believe there is so much more to what actually happened. And again, his own inculpatory words in his own statement tell me all I need to know—rub down. He said, "We went to the upstairs bedroom and Gina gave me a rub down."

But one detail did not align with Epperly's repeating patterns, his mode of operation apparent in many other rape reports. He would choke his victims, not beat them. Gina bled. Gina experienced violence. Gina even had blood on the back shoulder of her jacket. Gina was beaten unmercifully.

We could consider two sides to this man and surmise that we only saw the reports of those mid-'70s girls who survived, not those who died. Yet, his words, "Gina gave me a rub down," seemed to indicate his own truth of what happened to Gina in regards to his actions. It is the combined actions of many, those we never knew about and those that held secrets, that painted a more layered and complex picture of Gina's last terrifying moments in this world.

I promise, Lord, that I am trying. Forgiveness is the hardest thing I have ever done.

To get into Epperly's psyche is to look more closely at these clues about his past that might point to the root of his problems. I believe some of the answers came to me in the autumn of 2016 by another no-coincidence experience.

In mid-October, I had a speaking commitment in West Virginia, at the same hotel I had been to in June. I was pushing my luck, the gas in my car depleted to almost empty, so I got off at Clifton Forge. A sign pointed me right to Selma. *That was the town nearest Pikes Pond, where it had all begun months earlier.* After I filled up, sitting in my truck, I noticed the same number from my early June messages. My dashboard will display how many miles I can drive on the gas in my tank. The display read 696. I just shook my head, snapped a picture, and decided to take that turn again onto Route 696 to Selma, crossing lots of railroad tracks, ending up back at the pond. I believed I was here again for a reason. A very deep pond-full of regrets? I can't believe Pikes Pond happened like this again. Why?

Knowing the myths of the bottomless Pikes Pond, and remembering my very first message, I wondered if Epperly had a relative he would have visited there—a connection to this area. I asked a lady at the hotel if she knew of any Epperlys in the area. She told me that the Epperly family used to own the movie theater in Covington, the county seat of Allegheny County.

Of course, on my way home, I went by the Covington Theatre, but it was not open. Across the street was the office for the local newspaper, *The Virginian Review*. I felt an urge just to walk in and ask what they knew about the theater and its owners. Could they be related to the Radford Epperly family? I met David Crosier, a journalist at the local paper. Ironically, he knew all about Gina and shared that he and his coworker friend Larry O'Rourke thought about Gina's case often. "Let me know if you ever need help," he said. I told him I was most curious if there had been any unsolved murders or missing girls in that area during the '70s. I learned the theater owner's name was Maxine Epperly. A familiar name. Was that why I kept landing back in this area near Pikes Pond?

What was the relevance of Maxine Epperly?

In various reports from July to October 1980, Epperly's mother told police, my family, and others that "Aunt Maxine" was the root of her son's problems.

Recalling this, could the theater owner be his aunt? Could this be *the* Aunt Maxine? No, I do not think so. Aunt Maxine was married to George Taladay when they all lived together on Second Street in Radford in the Epperly homeplace. Taladay was not the name of the Covington Maxine's spouse. I was to pay attention to "Maxine" and her connection to Epperly, and that is exactly what I found in the minutia.

Mrs. Epperly stated, "Steve's psychiatric problems go back a long way to the time when Maxine Epperly lived with us. During this time, Maxine had spoiled Steve. When I disciplined my son, he would be confused who the 'mother-figure' was. I believe he had no respect for women due to the fact that he could manipulate his Aunt Maxine into doing anything that he desired." His good friend Hardie, when asked by the police if he knew why Epperly had such a low opinion of all women, would share, "It was something that occurred in his childhood. An aunt of his spoiled him very badly when he was small. I am certain that this had something to do with the way he felt about women. His mother would whip him for misbehaving when he was small, and according to other family members, this aunt would rub the area where Steve had been beaten by his mother. His aunt would tell him everything will be all right."

So Aunt Maxine would spoil Epperly by *rubbing the area.*

I then questioned, *Was what happened in this family's life more than Mom ever realized? Did she know the extent of Maxine's infiltration into her family?*

Epperly's victims had shared their experience with his rage and anger toward them when he raped them. These statements paint the picture and may be clues to the origin of his nature. His own words spoken to his rape victims include: "You are just a damn virgin," "I am going to train you," and "You could be good if you practice and you have the right one to train you," which is why I believe he targeted young, innocent girls like Gina. He repeated to his victims over and over, "I can't stand liars." He would comment about whether they were good or bad girls. "The kind of girl you would bring home to Mom," he would tell one of his victims. Mom had said, "Another reason for my son's hatred of women was that I tried to teach him about 'good girls' and 'bad girls,' and she felt that anyone who accepted his propositions or went to bed with him would be thought of as being 'bad.'" And the most obvious: telling his victim how lucky she was to "get the opportunity to experience me" and making his victims massage and rub him down. I can only imagine what similar words Aunt Maxine verbalized to him. I can only imagine the harm done to the mind of a child raised in this rigid, religious upbringing where girls were labeled and defined as only good or bad, while simultaneously losing trust in a woman figure because of his own experiences with Aunt Maxine.

A monster was being created with help from Aunt Maxine.

I understand trauma. I understand disappointment as a child in the adults who are supposed to protect and care for us. How can one person respond to child molestation by letting go of the bad that happens to them and becoming stronger while another becomes a monster? What I want to understand better is how to help others who cannot let it go. Forgiving is so very hard.

I was nine when it first happened to me. What is the difference between Epperly and me? Resilience? Strength? God? Or just pure evil taking a stronghold in the life of a child. I thought I had won that battle as a child, burying it away in my heart. But the Enemy never quits. The stronghold came into my life when that same evil crossed into my beloved baby sister's life. Now it had won—a stronghold of hate entered in my life that day when I learned it cannot be buried.

During my first year in college at Radford, I came home one fall weekend. I was seventeen. My roommate, also from Coeburn, had a car, so on the spur of the moment, we decided to go home. As I came into our home, it was quiet. It seemed no one was home. I walked on back to mine and Gina's bedrooms. I found my sister hiding on the floor in my bedroom closet. She would have just turned fifteen. Her nature evident by her actions—genuine pure innocence. I asked, "What are you doing?"

"I thought you were *him*," she said. And I knew.

My heart broke. I had no idea she had experienced what I also had experienced with this man who was trusted by my family. I thought I had stopped it. I never once suspected that my sister would ever be part of the bad experience I had buried in my heart earlier. We both had the same predator in our life. I was always grateful that the bad dream never became a bad nightmare. He was a sick man who liked playing games with little girls. It could have been far worse. I have met many others whose experiences were almost irreparable.

And this is exactly another unknown reason I always knew the willingly composed story was a lie. My sister did not go to be with a man. This part of her life influenced her trusting nature. She was hesitant that she would ever trust and find the right man to love. She confided this fear to her best friend, and it was not her scars that caused her reluctance. It took years for her to rebuild her trust in men, and only one known loving relationship succeeded. And that relationship took years for them to develop. A man she did love and trust. A man Gina would have married before that summer ended.

Sometimes, I believe I was afraid that if I forgave, then I would forget. And it is these moments in the tapestry of our life that make us who we are. Somehow, while I could never forget what happened to me, I had been resilient. I was fortunate. I learned how not to relive those memories. I am grateful for a pajama party at my house when I was almost thirteen and my friends explained what sex was. I learned what was right and what was wrong. Right then, I knew he was a bad man, and what had been happening was wrong. No more offer of quarters so he could touch me. No more pressing of my hand where it should not be. The next time he tried to touch me, confident and strong, I emphatically told him to stop. From that day forward, I stood my ground.

The day I found Gina hiding was the day it all changed. No one messes with Gina. I never buried this anymore. Anger filled my heart. I hated him. I dared him to hurt Gina. If I had had my own car that day, I believe I would have found him and done something I would have regretted my entire life. Instead, I found myself sitting on the floor, hugging my baby sister, holding her in my arms, rocking back and forth. Anger stole some of my heart that day. Every time I had to hear his name mentioned in all the many years to come, anger boiled inside of me, my heart always unforgiving.

One day while making a pecan pie, I had just a little corn syrup left in the bottle. Rather than throw it away, I remembered a favorite childhood treat. We would mix it with peanut butter and spread it on toast. My lips were smacking at this fond memory from years long past. But just as I mixed the syrup and peanut butter, my good happy thoughts were overshadowed by a dark, buried thought: That had been his favorite—our predator. I did not want it anymore. This is the battle of our minds, holding hate and unforgiveness in our hearts. When our hearts hold these bad memories, the small joys try to surface, but the bad will always rear its ugly head. Next time I make a pecan pie, I am going to have that childhood treat we so often enjoyed because my heart is now free of the hate.

When we, not only as parents, but as a society, do not protect our children, we could be unknowingly creating monsters. This is the Enemy at work.

Evil is a hole in a bucket full of water—living water. Eventually, the water all leaks out, and what remains is nothing but a seed within our spirit, something powerful disconnecting us from the internal goodness of our own soul. A soul that knows the truth, yet a spirit that has been drained. A very real part of our realm, sucking the good, the truth right out of us until nothing is left. The heart filled with more hate and unforgiveness, layer by layer. There is only one Way to plug the hole. Forgiveness. Forgiveness sets the heart free.

Epperly's heart was not free. At some point, and perhaps we will never know when, a deep-rooted anger had bloomed into a full-throttled rage.

In the eyes of the law, we cannot call Epperly a rapist because he was never convicted of it. In 1976, Epperly was charged with rape in Montgomery County Circuit Court twice, neither case resulting in a conviction. By this point, he had mastered the counterfeit all-American boy impersonation.

In April 1976, Epperly was charged in Blacksburg with a count of rape, the first known official indictment. The victim, in her rape account given to police at 5 a.m., describes a chilling scene:

> At approximately 3:15 a.m., I heard a tapping noise on the bedroom window and a voice I recognized as Stephen Epperly saying let me in, I am in trouble. I thought he needed help. I let him in and as soon as I did he started raping me. When I screamed he would put his hands around my neck and choke me. My baby started crying and I was able to escape. I do not believe he expected that I would run out of my apartment with no pants on.

She also said he kept repeating, "I hate liars." And told her, "I am going to get even with you."

Epperly, however, described this incident as: "We were just talking and *finally* we had sex 2 to 3 times."

That judge-only, no jury case in the Blacksburg General Court was dismissed because Judge Jordan said he felt "there were two different frames of mind involved" so the evidence in the case was not submitted.

The second rape charge came only four months later, August 15, 1976, also in Montgomery County at the Terrace View Apartments in Blacksburg. Because the first rape charge was still pending, Epperly was arrested without bail. They came to the Hardie House Restaurant to arrest him for his second rape indictment. Another Dorothy Allison clue maybe relevant decades later—*Restaurant remodeled—changed name—1974.* The victim's report was quite terrifyingly detailed. Her reason for agreeing to press charges: She believed he was mentally ill and needed help. She was a kind soul.

"I was so scared when he began to rape me. He kept screaming for me to be quiet and choking me. I blacked out. I thought he was going to kill me. At one point I tried to scream but nothing would come out of my voice." It is no coincidence that a part of one of my messages in 2016 mentioned: I tried to get help, but *it was like I had no voice.* This victim's fear is real. She believed she would not get out of there alive.

A copy of this police statement was sent to me. No coincidence. The sergeant noted that Epperly choked the victim into near unconsciousness. She bit him on the shoulder, but the police never even got a chance to see it because Epperly's lawyer prevented it. The report noted that after he raped her, he cried. Nola said the same: *He cried, desperate scared.* He tried to get her to admit that she would go to the police with him because he knew he had done something very wrong. She knew if she agreed he would kill her. She had survived because she understood Epperly's hidden motives.

It is beyond belief to me that if any jury were allowed to have known what I read. If the jury members had heard her voice, they would not have come to the conclusion they did. The jury found Epperly not guilty. The young girl did not have the privilege to hire a bulldog defense attorney to help her as Epperly did by use of Hardie's millions. Hardie stated to the police that he had been on both bonds for Epperly's two rape charges in 1976.

He also told the police that he had personally loaned Epperly $5,000 so Epperly could hire Richard Lawrence to defend him on his second rape charge. Hardie told police he liked Steve personally and believed he was just a victim of his circumstances. I believe there was so much more. So many trips to Fort Lauderdale—why? While Epperly was in jail after his second rape arrest, he became concerned about the police searching his apartment. He called his mama. She called her son and son-in law to go retrieve his belongings. When they arrived, Epperly's apartment was filled with drugs. According to his brother-in-law, it took almost three hours to flush the drugs down the toilet. During that same visit, two newspaper clippings of two different girls missing in Richmond were observed in a manilla folder. Something better understood by the observer four years later when Epperly became a suspect in Gina's murder. That was why he helped us in 1980. He knew.

The sergeant who arrested Epperly concluded that the verdict was due to a combination of things, including that the victim had "*willingly* gone to the place where Epperly lived." Nothing should excuse violence against a woman, justifying it as acceptable, or deserving. It never is. The jury's conclusion: We cannot call it rape. This was a victim-blaming mentality that we could only hope would not be seen in the future. Unfortunately, it still is prevalent today.

Epperly avoided jail both times. Confidence prevailed. Arrogance was fueled. These are just the rapes that were reported, charged, and tried. These are the girls who survived. Many more victim reports of sexual predatory violence would appear, his repeating patterns consistent in them, aligning truths in the victims' statements. One such alignment was the fear felt that every victim's statement repeated. Epperly's rage against them was extreme. The girls said they thought they would die. They prayed to God just to let them live through it. My sister would have prayed to God not to let her live through it. She would have asked God just to take her on to heaven, the trauma too much to bear. "I pray to God my soul to take," the words of our bedtime childhood prayer, may have gone through her mind.

Understanding the battles within Epperly's mind was a challenge. Esther Epperly did not ignore her son's spirit. She tried, but clearly, the system failed her. On September 21, 1976, his mother followed the attorney's recommendation and had her son committed to St. Albans for psychiatric evaluation.

In July 1980, a psychiatrist, Dr. William Keck, was interviewed by Special

Agent W. B. Wilmore of the VSP to determine if Epperly had been previously diagnosed with any mental disorder when he had been a patient at St. Albans in 1976.

In that evaluation, Keck noted that he could find "no definable psychiatric problem." But he added that he had observed Epperly had a "terrible temper," a "dislike for women," and a "hatred for authority." Keck went on to state that his observation was that Epperly was "not a sentimental or remorseful person."

Keck used the words "dislike for women"; Epperly's own mother used the word "hatred." Esther Epperly met several times with my dad before her son was charged with the murder of my sister. She shared with my dad that her son's violent temper and disrespect for women was displayed even in their own home. Her statement was that her "whole family" had been beaten at one time or another by him. She observed that when the beatings happened, her son's personality changed. That's when she realized her son was a danger to other people as well as to himself.

He killed Gina less than four years later. Four years is very little time unless time becomes ignored. A lot can happen in four years.

I contemplated further how deep his elusive reach could have infiltrated into other peoples' everyday lives? After graduating from Virginia Tech with a business degree, he worked odd jobs, including substitute teaching at Pulaski County High School. Right before he murdered Gina, his days were spent there on the campus of Radford University in construction maintenance. What a perfect job for a murderer—concrete construction. What a hub to be in the middle of if prone to rape and drug dealing.

So here he was, a twenty-eight-year-old, job-skipping male, twice charged with rape with a significant defense price tag attached, and an in-patient committed to a mental asylum by his own mother. Already, he had been slapped with the labels of "mental patient" and "rapist." What would these two factors produce in his mind? I can only imagine.

Beyond my imagination was how anyone could ignore his campfire statement witnessed by others. Did that campfire brag story that surfaced during the investigation of Gina's murder come to fruition after his 1976 financial burdens of defense? Epperly's camping buddies said he boasted around the campfire, "The next girl I rape, I am going to cut her up and throw her off of the Claytor Lake Dam."

What fueled his arrogant and confident nature?

The question that arises in my mind: How many?

Epperly is a sick man, and I believe he was not only a serial rapist, but became a serial killer to hide his future violent tendencies. Most of these victims' rape accounts that surfaced in 1980 were reported around the mid-1970s. I believe the financial burden of defense from those two 1976 rape charges spurred the creation of an even more calculating monster between 1976 and 1980 when my sister ended his trail.

What we do know is that people witnessed Epperly making statements that show instead of reining it in, he was ramping it up: He would become more calculating in his encounters with the women. Instead of just raping them, which would result in their still being able to point the finger at him, he would also kill them. That would silence them. Can we ever really know the far-reaching extent of his evil? I believe we can.

Epperly is a murderer. He is serving a life sentence for Gina's murder. And, when considering the details of other cold cases within his proximity, I think he committed more murders. It's unacceptable that these are still considered cold cases. The start is easy. Connect the cold cases we already know about—Romano and Koch—to Epperly. Then connect Epperly's paths traveled to any missing girls in the '70s. Katie provided Andy with some check stubs and old receipts that might prove useful. As many as one hundred names of girls are on Epperly's sex list, which notes the towns they were each from, many noted as Fort Lauderdale, Florida. Do we think that list of 100 names could just be 100 girlfriends' names, especially those in Fort Lauderdale? Drug runs? I hope some federal authoritative body will look at it closer and consider the possibilities of foul play.

Fort Lauderdale—the city listed for most of the girls on this list—was near one of the largest cocaine-trafficking hubs in the United States during the 1980 reign of Colombian drug lord Pablo Escobar. Right there, just boat docks away, was Wallace S. Thrasher. And Hardie was connected to cocaine distribution, and closely connected to Epperly and DeHart. Everett Shockley told me that while he was the Commonwealth Attorney in Pulaski County, even he was surprised at the drug-related crime he dealt with in this rural area. He said this was not small-town crime. Pulaski County and its surrounding area was the gateway to the northeast. Miami-Fort Lauderdale was the gateway into the United States and the southwest corridor surrounding the connecting interstates 77 with 81, a connector from the south to the north, right through Shockley's area. Right before Thrasher's disappearance, one of his planes crashed in October 1984 in the remote mountains of Fancy Gap, Virginia and was reported to have had drugs on board with a 1984 street value of more than one million dollars. On just that one run!

There is no proof that Epperly really was the muscle for Hardie's drug business or a connection to Wallace Thrasher. There is no proof that Epperly was associated with the drug business other than what locals would tell. But he was. His brother-in-law saw the proof. His connection to Hardie is certainly telling. There was a serious drug problem in this area if the FBI had informants like Jerry DeHart, Olga Thrasher, and even a 1%er involved. And Hardie's association with cocaine dealing that focused on the university campuses, as determined when he was sentenced and charged as guilty in November 1988, substantiates his official connection to drugs. And not just one but other universities close by. We could speculate Epperly's guilt just based on the "*birds of a feather flock together*" theory. But do we really need to know any more than what I saw? The Fort Lauderdale location of many girls on his sex list shows that he frequented that city. These drug-dealing connections and Epperly's list of 100 girls could paint a picture of a trail of violence.

Which brings me back to Epperly's better-than-average prison life, at least before his transfer to Buckingham, and his association with Hardie and DeHart. The 1980 police reports indicate that many speculated that Hardie was being blackmailed by Epperly. Were his favorable cell arrangements due to what or whom Epperly knew after June 29, 1980? Is he associated or protected by someone within the system with the power to make all this happen? Or was it simply a woman. Perhaps a combination of all of the above. And many always ask, "Why would Epperly not talk if others were involved?" Someone out there knows his secrets—He is a coward. Trophy graveyard. Death sentence.

All of these shared details are not to redirect fault. It does not change that Epperly killed Gina. The new layers of this story tell us this—the composed story was not the whole truth. And maybe there is more truth still yet to be known. There is still time to make amends, to set it right. If Epperly does get to heaven, and I believe strongly that there really is only one Way to get there, it still gives me comfort and peace that there will be accountability. So believing that God, a loving God, will be a righteous

God, and a just God, then why should I live my amazing small dot of this human life carrying the heavy burdens of hate, anger, vengefulness, sadness, and fear in my heart? Easier said than done. Hence, the challenge.

I am comforted that evil and injustice are not without consequence. A popular movie *The Shack* illustrates the reality of evil in our world and the heart-wrenching results of hate, anger, and unforgiveness. From experience, I know forgiveness is an uphill, endless battle without God. That is a truth. And it is a truth that the same God who loves me, loves Epperly. As I recently watched this emotional movie that tugs at every heartstring, I gasped, maybe because of my own personal experiences, and interpreted it as implying there would be no judgment for the actions of the wicked, as though God will not choose one child over the other because he loves us all—Is that the whole truth? Or a thought that can become a twisted truth—a misdirected path paved with subtle deception? We must start paying attention to what comes into our heads! It is the subtle twists that create new realities that become beliefs, and often these new beliefs do not align with God's word. We can't just pick and choose the parts that make us feel good. I reminded myself it is a fictional movie, but people change beliefs everyday, based on many subtle, deceptive non-truths that give rise to new thoughts.

Sometimes extra layers of new interpretations get mixed in with strong core beliefs, twisting until new beliefs emerge—in one direction or the other, right or wrong. Nola said to know the difference. Just by watching a movie, a subtle new thought, *If God does not judge and only loves, then we must all go to Heaven in the end,* can become a new belief. A belief that can have eternal consequences. Can we even begin to imagine what could happen to our already challenging chaotic world if enough people really began to believe they can do whatever they want?

Gina's life story is a real life nonfiction *"shack story"*: a heinous evil act committed, leaving a family with no body to bring home, unforgiveness and hate burdening the hearts of many. There are many other real life stories of pure evil acts visible and non-visible in our world every day. Love, forgiveness, and compassion are all in the presence of our righteous God, but so is justice. We will account for our life and everything will be known. Epperly will have to give an account for his life, as we all will. It gives me peace to know God will have the final justice for the taking of Gina's life and for the many secrets kept. Lies are lies. We either serve God or we serve the Enemy. There is no in between. God wants us to hear Him.

I think of Jesus' words referred to as the parable of the tares:

> The field is the world, the good seeds are the sons of the kingdom, but the tares are the sons of the wicked *one*. The enemy who sowed them is the devil, the harvest is the end of the age, and the reapers are the angels. Therefore as the tares are gathered and burned in the fires, so will it be at the end of this age. The Son of Man will send out His angels, and they will gather out of His kingdom all things that offend, and those who practice lawlessness, and will cast them into the furnace of fire. There will be wailing and gnashing of teeth. Then the righteous will shine forth as the sun in the kingdom of their Father. He who has ears to hear, Let him hear! (Matthew 13:38-43 NKJV).

There are many in this world who do not hear. They are the wicked. And the soul of the wicked desires evil.

Even Epperly's own mother, who loved him, understood justice. Epperly's own mother knew he had murdered my sister. Mothers have a way of seeing truth. She told us she always knew when her son lied to her because he would hang his head down and look down at the floor, not directly at her, when he would lie. When she asked him if he had killed that girl, his actions told her the truth. "I know my son killed the Hall girl," she had said. My heart ached for his mother, who must have felt the pain of not being able to give him what he needed. A letter Epperly wrote in 1974 fell into Andy's hands. Andy determined that Stephen Epperly had written and signed this letter, put it in a bottle, and thrown the bottle into the New River where it would wash up to the shore years later. It made its way to Andy just as he started investigating what he called The Gina Hall Body cold case. Coincidence?

Andy showed me this letter the day my brother and I first met him in person at his office at RPD in May 2013. This letter angered me to the core. I hated Epperly. My emotions escalated when I saw his tagline signature—The Stud. It enraged me.

Here is a translation from the damp, aged pages:

> To whoever finds this,
>
> It is FEB. 6, 1974

1:25 A.M.

I'm all alone, very oppressed [oppressed], and I am one of the few people in the Universe that that know I have <u>super potential!!!</u> I don't know what exactly I want to do in <u>this</u> <u>life</u>, but when I find out, you'll read about me and hear and see me everywhere. And brother, if you [illegible - see] this message, bring it to me and it will be worth a lifetime.

HOSS.

Stephen M. Epperly,

198 lbs 5'11",

Blonde, Green Eyes

Radford, VA

The Stud

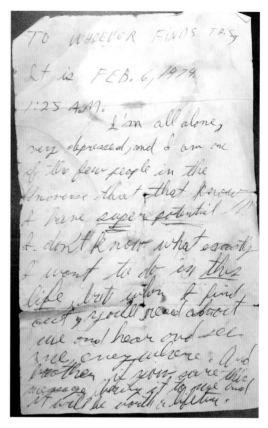

And this was the person I was to forgive. I still had to find my way to forgiveness.

It has been almost four decades, and I can still tell you the exact spot where I was sitting on a long wooden front pew on December 28, 1980 six months after my sister had been murdered. After the trial ended and Epperly's life conviction was rendered on December 19, 1980, my family returned home to the reality of Gina's empty bedroom. There would be no Gina with us on Christmas Day. We planned her funeral that Christmas weekend.

The Memorial Service was set for the Sunday afternoon after Christmas. Gina's favorite hymns, "In The Garden" and "What a Friend We Have in Jesus," were carefully chosen. We needed to have closure, and we knew we were to honor her goodness. Long before the 2 p.m. start time, every pew of the Coeburn United Methodist Church was filled. Community members had come to pay their respects to my family and honor Gina. Folding chairs added in the empty spaces of the church filled quickly with only standing room left. The church reached its capacity and latecomers had no room to stand. A lady journalist Sharon Hatfield from our local newspaper, *The Coalfield Progress*, wrote in a news article titled "Family, friends celebrate the goodness of Gina Hall":

> ...the winter sunlight poured through the stained glass windows and fell upon the sanctuary. The saffron robed choir just finishing the benediction...May peace be with you. The crowd of people gathered seeking peace—some kind of explanation for the senseless death of Gina Renee Hall.

I looked up at the large, yet simple wooden cross that hangs in the front alcove of our youth sanctuary with an overwhelming sadness. I had never been to a funeral. Gina's memorial service was scheduled to begin within the hour. There was no way to reconcile in my mind what should have been the beginning of closure and healing, but in actuality, was the continuation of living with the reality of her brutal murder. Three days earlier, she had not been there with us opening her presents, joyfully filling our living room with her laughter. It was the beginning of a new prayer dominating my thoughts: I pray, as does my family, that justice will always prevail, and Epperly will never be released. And I ask that we can know the truth, so if there are others who need peace, they too will find it.

After Gina's favorite hymns had been sung, Reverend Frank Bauman began his eulogy in the solemn sanctuary, the tears echoing through the air became smiles when he focused on Gina's goodness: "Gina was a happy young lady. One indication of her happiness was that she lived to dance, her purpose in dancing was one of a creative nature. And her talent was an expression of her beauty." He shared with everyone that Gina's favorite chapter in the Bible was Psalms 1. He quoted a verse that says not to keep the company of sinners. He asked the congregation, "If she believed this, if she was this kind of woman, why would she have ever gone with a man like Steve Epperly?" The answer he said was that Gina's killer was "a master of impressions." He added, "Epperly was in the company of a friend whom Gina trusted." I just sighed. Threads of the composed story, their lies, even followed my sister to her memorial service. And almost four decades later, her best friend recalled the exact words spoken, and the anger she felt during parts of the service. She wanted to stand up and scream out right in the middle, "No! Gina did not do that." I understood. We knew her. We knew always that she had never gone to be *with* him. Everyone settled on believing that her naive goodness caused her to be deceived by this manipulative, cunning man. It was what we all *believed* but could not reconcile. Gina, no way, never. But I settled too. It all did not seem to matter anymore. I did just as I had always done—buried the bad deep within.

Reverend Bauman continued, reminding us that Jesus had also been the victim of a violent death. He added that he was not comparing Gina's life to that of Jesus, but just noting that good could emerge from her death just as it had from Jesus' death. Her life had not been in vain, because, like in her favorite Psalm, we, her loved ones, *could be like trees along the riverbank, bearing fruit. "May there be no end to the growth."* I now think of these exact words and their relevance in *the journey* I have experienced.

We were celebrating Gina's life. Reverend Bauman ended her memorial service with this reality, "After all, the family has been denied the comfort of a funeral burial for Gina Renee Hall." This was the sad reality that haunted us—no body, an empty grave. Where was she?

I so understand now. Graves are already empty. The body is just a physical body and only a part of us. The soul can have eternal life. We were not seeing the larger message that her life had shouted loudly and clearly—to embrace life, to love, and to live every day that we have with purpose. To remember to sing with her in the laughter and in the tears because she was right there with us, always forever. *Live life because you never know when the good Lord will take us away.* So yes, for thirty-seven years I visited an empty grave, always saddened that she was not there, as though she should have been. I was always angry that Epperly had taken her from us. He hid her from her family, but not from God. And now, not from me ever again.

Nola had said, "You need to forgive him."

I told myself I needed to forgive Epperly. But I wasn't quite there. I was almost ready, but the task felt too large. Thoughts of hate and anger still lingered in my heart. Fully forgiving him would take three more months of healing my heart, currently a murky swamp, and he was not the only one residing there. There have been others in my life that I just could not ever forgive. I really was very good at burying the bad, but the anger and the hate always surfaced. Those bad memories were holding on tightly. It was as if the bad within knew it was losing the battle, so it stepped up its game.

It was no coincidence that I had felt the urge the last day of July to find my study Bible. I was going to need it. I knew, beyond a doubt, because I had experienced it earlier in life, that my heart could be filled with God's love. But at this point, I still harbored hate for the evil. An evil heart had taken my sister away from us. And evil was giving rise to new thought. And this evil was getting a tighter stronghold on my heart. And I know exactly when these deceiving thoughts gained their unrelenting powerful grip.

After Gina's death, hate and anger took root, buried in my heart, just waiting for the event that would tip my scale, the water that would cause the root to grow into a full-blown stronghold, smothering my heart to the point of no return. It happened—a night in 2014 when evil entered my life. After that night, I began questioning, *Why me? Why did God let this happen to me?* My view of God began to divert from a loving, wise, merciful God to a divergent view: a God who was indifferent to me, permitting of evil, and punitive. My Spirit of Life was being suppressed. My path was now a lower level of conscious energy orchestrated by the Enemy himself—shame, blame, guilt, anger, hate. That one event in my life—that was when the divergent thoughts gained their stronghold. Two years before *the journey*. One thought at a time. One tipping crossroad in my life's path, created and designed by the Enemy, the root already there. The further I veered from a path of goodness, the more and more my life purpose went off course, a stumbling block causing me to be unaware of God's love. Indifferent. And the further away I got, the more my thoughts changed. I could not easily find my spark, but it was always there. It never leaves us.

It was the same in Epperly's life. Aunt Maxine was his root planted by evil. But his root grew into a giant tree with branches reaching out everywhere. And as his letter said, "I'm all alone, very oppressed"—a lonely tree in the middle of the field that had to be cut down. Something was missing—he did not know his spiritual army. I somehow knew this when I was a teen: "No one ever needs to feel alone, like that tree all by itself, because Jesus is always with us, especially when we feel alone. All anyone has to have is a tiny little seed of God, and it will grow into a big, strong tree, never being alone. God is all around us, and that majestic tree must make Him smile."

Life's stories are certainly perplexing. There are no coincidences. Just knowing this makes *letting go and letting life happen* a little easier, but not so easy to do while living it.

Now I understand that the spirit within us can be literally ripped open; the seed of darkness had a tightening stronghold on my soul for two years. The subtle changes began. I can look back on my life now and see clearly what I was to see. Nola saw it the night he met me. That was his purpose in my life. And he was right. I had to find my own way. We all have our own individual paths. Thank heavens God lovingly apprehended me so I could see the truths. Jesus did not give up on me. While the root of evil was being watered, my spiritual army watered the tiny mustard seed still present deep in my soul. But it was a process, a plan—*the journey*.

CHAPTER 20

HAIR OF THE DOG

I know now who I was messin' with. And fire is his favorite friend.

Breaking through was the truth that I had always known before *the journey*—that my sister was in Heaven, not somewhere hidden from us. But the peace did not last. There was still more I was to experience, lessons to learn so that I would come to a better understanding of what I was to know and what I am to share.

I finally got to meet Natasha face to face, and I immediately felt her genuine love for Gina. Natasha is a beautiful woman with hair black as coal. Knowing of my skepticism about ghost hunting, she shared that she realized many people in the ghost hunting field chose false directions.

"I rely on my Father in Heaven every day, and I always ask for his guidance," she said. "I feel we are close to the finish line."

Natasha believed there was a plan at work for Gina. She explained how she uses dousing rods to guide her just as the eighty-three-year-old woman had told me about. Her deep desire to find Gina was evident. Her connection to me felt real, emotionally connected. I quickly began calling her Tash. It just seemed right to me.

Natasha had a treasure trove of unexplainable experiences. "For months after first going into St. Albans, before I knew the details of Gina's murder, I was drawn to drive up the road beside St. Albans, Hazel Hollow Road. I finally just went one day, and when I got to the trestle, I stopped. I felt Gina."

I understood what she was saying. I felt the same.

By December 2016, I began believing that all leads led to one place—St. Albans. The river and the muck were places where body parts must be buried. My focus narrowed. The miracles became just clues, each a stepping stone to the next place and the next after that. The museum area was an old landfill, under a parking lot, a graveyard for victims. Large flat rocks behind the box factory were makeshift beds, places where Epperly took his rape victims. I was seeing a very dark world. My mind spun around this dark center. It was not God-centered. The darkness seemed to come from within. I compiled a new story in my mind—a theory, seeming to be written by someone besides the Dlana I had known my entire life.

And Nola's messages continued to align with this emerging theory.

> There is somewhere like bushes or landscape with white and blue little flowers. I also went to a hill with a girl pointing down.
>
> A large hill at top.
>
> Not a high hill.
>
> A hill with grass.
>
> A hill where you can walk normal no problem.

I told Nola that the museum sits on a grassy hill not too high up.

Nola continued:

> But we saw down like we were high.
>
> The important message here is a hill no matter what it is.
>
> And her pointing down.
>
> It was real flowers.
>
> I was walking with a girl and somebody dark-haired—an adult—was with her.
>
> The girl is 8 or 10 years old.
>
> It was a short hill.
>
> At some point they were waiting for me, opening some branches of some trees or bushes for me to pass.
>
> They pulled the bushes back and opened a way and waved me to come in.

In the photo I had taken of the museum, white African violets were visible through the window. Purple African violets had been in Gina's photo that I found in my Bible. The picture of the two-story brick Civil War house covered in thick brush seemed to match what Nola was seeing, sitting up on the grassy knoll.

And then he texted:

> I also saw a tub like a white, old-style bath.
>
> Wasn't clean. Walls were grayish, and it was attached to the wall.

Nola would tell me:

> Don't look at the message in a perfect way. That doesn't happen. Look for similarities like tub, hill, girl. But names have to be the same.
>
> Consider my tub or your tub does not matter. What is important is tub.
>
> Something happened in a tub.

I sent Nola photos of Glencoe. The museum matched what he had seen in his visions. *Very similar.*

This was becoming quite disturbing.

I drew a strange oval picture in the middle of the night. I even tried to redraw such a perfect oval. I could not.

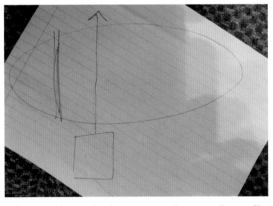

The ghost hunters at St. Albans believed the bathtub was used to dismember my sister—and not just my sister, others. Maybe the messages just got mixed up or had multiple meanings. I believe what I drew may have been the tub I would see again, a closer view, in just a few weeks with the square plate on the wall. But I cannot know for sure.

The dismemberment story was emerging into a pattern that fit the farmer's account. I had gone on a tangent back in August wondering if the farmer was a gifted person, a seer like all the other people I had met. Being an old

farmer with an honest reputation, according to those who knew him, he would have likely kept quiet about his abilities if he did have them. Like Nola said, "People don't understand, so not very many people know about me." And that is now. Imagine 1980.

A section of the older St. Albans building had just been recently closed off—the entrance to the boiler room and the tub room. Someone could have made Epperly aware of the closing of that old section of the building. The new site had just been constructed and the old area disrupted, the coming and going less noticeable. It might not be so far-fetched to consider a tub in the basement boiler room area of the mental asylum as an actual place for dismemberment. Or is the message to be known just the concept of dismemberment? The shed. Meadow Creek. The muck place. The dump site at the bottom of the high cliff. But then why a tub? As Nola explained earlier, "Don't look at the message in a perfect way."

I still cannot help but wonder why long ago in this large building, a completely tiled room with a single bathtub was built in a section that also housed the boiler room. No words could describe the anguish of the souls who endured this place.

On December 16, ghost hunters Ken and Natasha and I got into another conversation about the boiler room, and Ken decided to show me his screensaver on his phone. "I was just messing around back when we were decorating this place for the Halloween tours," he said. His screen-saver photo showed a hand reaching through a hole in the brick of the St. Albans boiler room.

I told them both Nola and I had also seen a vision of a hand reaching through bricks—months earlier. "I saw a hand coming up through the floor," I said. "Nola saw it coming through bricks."

Ken had shot the photo months before, about the same time. All three of us had been on the same wavelength. How could this be?

Natasha shared with me that she had been having the same repeating dream: a vision of a place near the trestle. She described seeing a dark-haired woman with Gina. This girl was pretty. She was in a long, white gown, torn and old. They were in a field on top of a big hill. Gina was pointing to the ground.

Nola had described the same thing. He saw the dark-haired girl with Gina on a hill, pointing to the ground, pulling back the brush. I remembered the Polaroid pictures the curator showed me, the mansion completely covered in brush.

Were they both seeing the museum sitting on the hill near the trestle? Frankly, there were just too many hills: the field at the high cliff above the butterfly spot, the reed place would be a field up a hill above the muck place cliff. St. Albans was surrounded by fields and grassy hills. The museum sits atop a grassy knoll. *Maybe I am just supposed to take Natasha to all of these places.*

We were due to return to St. Albans the next day.

"St. Albans is not the place for you," Nola had warned, but I did not heed his words of wisdom. He was referring to a spiritual world that, at this point, I still did not fully grasp. My heart, my love for my sister, was overruling my head. I believed someone good was communicating with me. Natasha said my spirit connection with Gina was real. Andy did, too. Everyone around me believed it. I thought it was my heart that told me my sister *needed* me to do this. I still had so many unanswered questions. I was headed back to St. Albans again with a single-minded intention of finding truth. I had no earthly idea about the reality of what hides in this world. My strong-willed head ruled. Others had the same conviction— just find Gina. Natasha's passion fueled the same, intense emotions. Ken, too. Seeing with my own eyes these very real emotions coming into play in so many people's lives intensified my desire to finish what we had started. They all believed, like me, that if we could find the answers, all the fractured souls around this tragedy could have peace. I could not let it go.

Nola had told me a few weeks earlier, "Only think what you need or want quietly. Do not verbalize your wishes. *They* can hear you," referring to the dark forces I was not understanding. He would tell me, "You want only God to hear you." I was still not remembering what I knew before—the place of truth from where all answers can come, and I was still not discerningly questioning "Exactly who is *they*?"

Have you ever questioned the feats of the ancient civilizations? Ancient, congruent similarities are found in all corners of our earth. I will never forget the day I stood in front of an ancient temple, El Castillo at Chichen Itza in Mexico, clapping my hands, and the echo that returned to my ears came in the sound of a chirping bird. The Mayan legend says it is the soft song of the quetzal. To this day, engineers do not know exactly how this temple was designed to do this or how perfectly placed enormous stones allow sound to travel in a specific manner—some believe designed as chambers that create specific frequencies to enhance healing. Their legends might provide some clarity. Just like in 1980, stories often are built from personal past experiences. There are usually facts somewhere that reveal truth just like the enormous monolithic stone walls of Peru just might be the factual basis for Genesis 6 in the Bible. What did these ancient people know then and who knew it? Even today, with all of our technology, and self-centered confidence in our human abilities to know everything, we really do not know that much! Or, do we?

In the Bible is a story not often told in Sunday school. Genesis 6 tells us of a time when giants ruled. I believe verses in the Bible—from Numbers, Ezekiel, Jude, Job, etc.—all paint a clear picture of horrific times long past and who just might be the builders of these ancient places.

Some refer to these giants as the Nephilim:

> There we saw the giants (Hebrew: Nephilim) and we were like grasshoppers, in our own sight, and so we were in their sight. (Numbers 13:33, NKJV)

This story is like the scariest movie ever made. It goes like this: The angels that at one time were here to help us on earth, in our realm, became rogue angels. It seems a lust for power was at the center of it all. That sounds like this earthly realm! They took a liking to human women, producing half-human, half-angel hybrids. The world was beyond repair, "Because of the terror of the mighty in the land of the living." Some texts say man could not sustain them and the giants began to devour man. Really? That is just a terrible image. Definitely not a Sunday school story. So this is how we got the story of Noah's flood—God wanted to annihilate this wickedness. Some say that God sent the disobeying angels away, but not their offspring. God spared the ark and its collection of life. Some believe these half-human, half-angels were also not destroyed by the flood. This world was left with some not so happy spirits—demons. Their spirits had one objective—to mess with us. These spirits are different from the original fallen angels and their ruler Lucifer—Satan—the Enemy, the source of pure evil, a dark power that exists in our world. These are the spirits of unrest in the spiritual world that exist right alongside us, now ruled by The Enemy, the Prince of Darkness.

And now I understood who "they" were and what Nola meant when he said, "You only want God to hear you."

I did not really know this whole story the day I visited St. Albans. I wish I had. I came to believe Gina must be connected to this terrible place somehow, and I needed to free her. There was no stopping me from searching for my sister's remains as if that was all that mattered. I began to believe she must be hidden somewhere there in St. Albans. It was my choice, and I was not listening to the whispers, the subtle clues trying to help me choose wisely. I did not remember about prayer as God's armor because I did not yet fully understand why I needed it. I did not really know evil. Upon my second visit into the dark halls of St. Albans, I met this evil.

That morning, I sprung up when I woke, eager to conquer this place. Outside, the air was chilly. As I walked to my truck, my thoughts were upbeat. I believed we were going to have an end to it all; I just knew it was all going to become clear, and we would have answers. We were going to find Gina. I sat in my truck and said out loud, "Gina, if you are there, guide us to where we are to search today. Help us to finish this. We are going to get you outta there, baby sis. Let's listen to a song. Play me a song." My truck started and the music played; the first song was "Radar Love." I smiled. "Yes, that is exactly what we have, radar love." I laughed from within, thinking someone had a sense of humor. Nodding my head, I said out loud, "Yes! We've got this."

But the real chills came the moment the next song played: "Hair of the Dog" by Nazareth. I didn't even know the song was in my playlist. It had never played before—it was part of a classic rock collection I had downloaded. I heard the one line, over and over, and I knew I was getting ready for a fight with a son of a bitch. My honest, first thought—*the Doctor?* The ghost hunters all believed he was the one who makes Gina whisper. I even wondered, *Is he the tall, skinny, white-haired man from my dreams?* I knew now whom not to mess with, and it was something far worse than just one man's ghost! I was warned by someone who cared enough to try to tell me.

I expected to search all of the nooks and crannies that had been closed off in 1980. I wanted to know what secrets this place held. As soon as Natasha and I walked in, we laid out a plan to where we wanted to just walk quietly, searching not only with our eyes but with our hearts, and she with her senses. We headed to a stairwell that led to a different section of the basement where I had not been the first time Ken took me inside. The graffiti on the wall stopped me in my steps. There on the wall is "1 Doo" spray painted in black. *Could this be "one door" and the vandal did not finish it?* In shock, I thought, *How could this be? Even the little crook, similar to what I had written in the night.*

Natasha, seeing my dismay, said, "The graffiti in the building has been here a really long time. Probably happened when the building was abandoned." But she shared later she had never really noticed that particular graffiti, and seeing it, just like me, had brought chills down her spine for some unidentifiable reason. Even the little crook at the top of the "O" from my October 1 message seemed to match what was spray-painted on the inner walls of St. Albans.

The beat in my step was gone.

My mind raced with questions: *Is this the "one door" place and not the museum? Or is this a message directing me back to the museum? First, I discover the connections in my messages to the eerie, exterior of the St. Albans brick mansion, then I land at the Civil War mansion museum right across the river, believing it is relevant, and now I find myself back inside the*

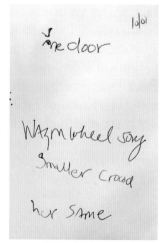

brick walls of St. Albans. Which big house? What are the secrets of this big house? Why am I led to this haunting place? Could it all just be premonitions so I would trust and believe and remain resolute?

Stay with the plan, Dlana. No time to ponder. Keep up.

A panel on the staircase was loose. One hundred years of paint thickened in the crevices except for one panel. I wondered, *What is under the steps of these wooden stairs?* If the bathtub story were true, body parts could have been hidden in many different places of this abandoned building. Certainly, someone who would do such an unimaginable act would not stop at anything. Hiding the proof would become just another game. That is how terrible the thoughts in my head were.

I knew I wanted to find an office—the left wall in an office. I wanted to find the spot where if I pulled the carpet back, I would find the half-moon-shaped hole in the foundation. I watched as Natasha walked through the upstairs, dousing rods in her hand, following the unconscious connection that seemed to be in her mind, step by step, walking into one of the many rooms, right over to the left wall, and stopping. The left wall to the opposing corner of the room. Just like my mental note. I did not even stop to wonder; I just started ripping the baseboard off and peeling the carpet back. I knew I would find a hole there. How I knew this I did not really know. There was a hole—a big one. Not exactly what I had written, but close enough. An old section of building had been added on here to an even older one, creating a chasm between the building's two sections. Seemingly out of the blue, a thought entered my mind: *Bracelet.* I had written down an earlier message—*bracelet.* I first had thought that the bracelet message referred to the bracelet I had been asked to identify during the trial, as though it might have been Gina's, having been found inside the lake house. I had never seen that bracelet. It was not Gina's. But no one ever seemed to question: If it were not Gina's, then whose bracelet was it? Later, I would surmise it must have belonged to a different girl—maybe someone else there at the lake house that night. Now, I went off on another tangent, wondering if the half-moon hole somehow connected to jewelry.

Ken fixed my mess! Then, behind this wall, in the connecting room from the older building section, was a bathtub, connected to the same wall, with a wooden box seat built over it, covering it from view. Now I was asking, *Which tub did Nola see? And what happened in a tub? Why were so many people seeing bad images of a bathtub? Especially that tub in the boiler room.*

We continued searching in the bowling alley, the graffiti still daunting to see remembering *my artwork* from my messages. I watched a young girl who came with Natasha and Ken, plus my husband, climb back behind the mechanics of the bowling setup to see if there was anything to be seen. Someone had talked about the sealed off tunnels—sealed because they had filled with water. My thoughts burdened as I recalled all of my messages about swimming and the dark tunnels. And then the green-tiled room, the bathtub with a plate on the wall, a room within close proximity of the old boiler room. Why were so many people drawn to this place?

We spent all day searching for my sister's body to no avail. It was time to go home. That night, I could not shake the terror I felt after leaving St. Albans. What had happened to me in there? Where had the amazing feeling of love and peace I had come to know on *the journey* gone? I felt as though something was attacking me. Something unseen. Nothing I tried would bring me back to the state I knew I could be in. I had experienced bliss, so I knew it existed. I would sit quietly, but there was no quiet. I knew what I was feeling, this inner feeling of being literally captured, and it was be-

yond my control. I know now that the closer one gets to God, and in my case, the truth about evil, the more the Enemy will step up his game with his demonic forces. Because my premonitions were abundant, I knew I had been guided to this place, but exactly by whom I did not know.

I know now. I was messin' with the true son of a bitch just like the song had warned me early that morning.

Memories of the summer's miracles—the divine image in the water, the butterfly, my sister's face—were far from my mind.

When I sent Nola a note, he suggested I immediately see a healer. It was no coincidence that I had crossed paths earlier in October with an amazing lady. Just like the night I had met Nola, sensing her goodness, I had said, "I feel I am to get to know you more," to which she answered, "I knew you would be coming into my life." I just smiled. I did not ask her how, but months later, I knew. It was for this very moment. I ended up on a table within a few hours, listening to her pray over me, "In Jesus' name, God guide me to help Dlana. You are the only one who knows what she needs." Afterward, she told me I had an unbelievable bad energy presence, my energy fields were a mess, spinning counter-clockwise in my sacral area, "as wide as any I have ever seen." Adding, "Your spiritual GPS is spinning out of control. You are being threatened." Her message didn't stop there. She said I was in serious need of balancing. She warned me that every single thing in my life that needed healing would begin to surface, and this would be my road to peace. This was the thought in her head that she somehow knew she was to share with me. She cautioned me to be ready for some difficult times ahead.

Was it all just breadcrumbs to get me from there to here where I needed to be to jumpstart a healing process? Did I really meet the devil, the Enemy, in St. Albans? Did my guardian angels step in to ensure this battle would be won? No one will ever convince me, ever, that the demons are not real. Literally, I experienced it. And I experienced my Lord's power over them. It was necessary for me to truly absorb this reality so I could be fully awakened to the truth of the world we live in.

After my husband picked me up, I saw a dozen or so doves in the woods at the edge of this woman's driveway. I felt peace. My bliss had returned. I was ready.

I learned this: If a person enters any evil space—the places where evil lingers and very real dark entities, the wicked, congregate—the wicked will not waste their time on the nonbelievers. I walked right into the battlefield unarmed. I was like candy in a candy store to this very real presence whose only objective was to steal my soul and expand its reach into the very goodness of whom I was born to be. The bad comes from a very powerful, influential reality that exists here in this realm, and there truly is only one way to win these battles—Believe. I now know to say three little words quite often, *In Jesus' name*....And ironically, even though we win the battles, we do not stop the war. We then become an even more desirable target. If one dark spirit fails, it will return with seven more. The battles are very, very real. My daddy nightmare in August had warned me to stay away from St. Albans. Nola had warned me to stay away. Even the song warned me I was messin' with evil. My head had not listened. And the Enemy knew my love for my sister would bring me right where he wanted me to be. And that was what I was to see—to learn, to know, before I would head into the biggest battle of my life.

But that was not the end. Nowhere near. The next day, Natasha texted me, very upset. She and Ken had left St. Albans to go to a different video shoot two hours away. She said the shoot was shanghaied by a ghost who said he had come along with them from St. Albans—attached to her. She felt the attachment and was disturbed greatly by its presence. Unfortunately, I better understood now what she was talking about.

Natasha asked, "Who are you?" The answer: "I am Mitch, the orderly. I am Gina's buddy." Mitch told them that he'd walked in on the dismemberment, and it had cost him his life. He told them the drug ketamine had been used. The ghost hunters used a "spirit box" when talking to Mitch.

It cranked out these words:

> Steven
>
> Ellie
>
> decompose
>
> trinity
>
> soil
>
> marker
>
> mutilate
>
> so sorry

Natasha assured me that Mitch had revealed way too much for it not to be valid—he had described places in detail. Mitch had mentioned the name *Scarlett*, another name I had written down. The word "bloodletting" that he used was quite disturbing. Mitch had also said three headstones. Mitch confirmed the "rape party," with the words "needles," "friends," "screw," "ketamine," and "weapon." And Natasha and Ken believed the word Ellie was the closest word to Epperly. Smiling Steven Epperly.

When asked what he saw he said bloodletting

SPIRIT BOX WITH BLOODLETTING TEXT. PHOTO COURTESY OF COOL KIDS PARANORMAL

My first thought was not to question who was talking to them but instead *Could Mitch be a nickname for Gary Lang? Could Mitch be the male whose clavicle and femur were found in 1985? Two guys and a girl—perpetrators or victims? Two guys: Romano and Mitch? And Gina, the girl—justice for two guys and a girl. Who was the friend dancing with Gina who wore glasses—broken glasses, muddy with leaves on them? Was there ever an employee at St. Albans who had just gone missing? Like a runaway?* My mind took off in so many directions, landing on the possibility that others besides Gary Romano and Gina had also been murdered.

I wondered, *Did I mention that day while inside St. Albans, out loud, to someone, anyone about the eighty-three-year-old lady and her visions of the three headstones there in St. Albans' property?* No. I had not. These words—soil, marker, mutilate—and three headstones align with the woman's story from 1980 about Gina being buried under one of the three headstones.

For emphasis, Natasha added, "I am a believer that God has got this, and in time, we are going to find the truth."

That night, Nola would warn me that I'd crossed the line. I was messing with evil.

> Remember that we live in another plane, but we live together *en tierra* (on earth) with those from a different plane. We don't see them, but they can see you. They have been around us all of our lives, and they know any single detail about you and Gina, even things you think just Gina and you know.

> If you make it public, they can join and tell you things that are true and other things to confuse you and get you to another direction.
>
> They can't read your mind, but even like that, they can tell what you are asking by your actions. So you have got to be careful with that and be smart.

Familiar spirits controlled by evil spirits mixed with good spirits, angels or demons, lost souls. Something was communicating with them. I saw the recordings. I still did not know who, for sure. Or even why or how. I pondered what Nola had told me, "Only think what you want or need quietly. Never verbalize your wishes. They can hear you."

I was still questioning, "Exactly who is this *they*?"

Nola's reply: "You want only God to hear you."

It seems *they* know what they should not know. And what they share are truths. The name of our cat, our dog, Gina's favorite color, our secrets no other human present knows. And how in this human world could we ever begin to know the difference. Angels or demons? Souls? People need to understand this: *No matter who is communicating, if they are not from a good place, they could be communicating the truth, twisted truths that become lies, but still truths used against us.*

Is it even possible for humans to discern the power of this? If our minds are open to the possibilities of our existence being connected to a spiritual, conscious realm where Light and Dark exist, then what? God does speak to us—we just have to *listen and learn* who is talking to us. A thought from within myself—the same words written on the bowling alley wall. Listen. Learn. Love. But it is more—discernment comes with a personal relationship with God, through His words, prayer, and love.

I was deeply troubled that so many people believed Gina was communicating with them. And now, Gina had a "buddy"?

I was in danger of becoming my thoughts. Something in me resisted this mightily, as a deception. We always seem to allow our minds to focus on the direction that validates our preconceived ideas, conditioned beliefs that become who we are. Our thoughts define us. And these thoughts are created by our experiences. And these experiences become our perceptions, which then become our reality—our beliefs. We become our thoughts. So it all begins with our thoughts. Thoughts that are known.

Truths that are known. Thoughts influenced not just by the dark—fallen angels, but also the Light—our angels.

A message that had come earlier, on December 1, 2016, was now clearer. Understanding the battles became pivotal in helping me answer the questions I still had about what had happened that night to Gina at the lake house and, most importantly, who was communicating with me.

Girls fighting, left behind, had to go back and help, fighting the bad men, three men. Choking, nothing helped.

Then these words:

Baby clothes made.

Why choose these words to describe what had happened? If this message came from a dark, deceiving enemy, why not just use the phrase *girls raped*? Or other common words used here in this realm where the Enemy reigns, like *sex*. This message came from a place of innocence. The only words that an angel might use to explain this act of violence—Baby clothes made—came from a realm where only goodness, pure love exists. I could not imagine why these words would be used to describe sex. Sex makes babies, so I just cannot believe the Enemy or his demonic forces would not just use the word "sex."

These words broke my heart: Baby clothes made. I knew what the message meant—the girls were raped. And later, this disturbing thought came, *Was life conceived during that night of terror?* An onslaught of questions entered my mind. Again, my heart was overwhelmed with sadness. *Could it be twisted truth? I will just twist it right back.*

I now understand what Nola meant, "Gina is pure love now." I would add, "Peace, Joy, Pure love is God's Love in the heart of her soul." *Hallelujah!*

I believe I have been given the answer to the question that I'd been asking for thirty-six years: What really happened at that lake house? I knew my sister. I knew she had never gone *to be with him*. The Wolfpack-composed story had added murkiness to my already-broken heart. I always knew the composed story was not true, but I never once in all of those years expected what I know now. I could never have even dreamed up this scenario, until I dreamed it, the nightmare unfolding piece by piece. Defending Gina's honor was always so very important to me because it was *Gina*. To me, she really was an angel on earth.

What really happened there? The answers had come already—layered within the messages from someone who loved me enough to help me know the truth.

> I was driving, and a car blocked me. Pulled in, and the car pulled in behind me. Blocked me in. I asked him (them) to let me out. Before I was on the cliff, I was at a party at the big house. Girls were fighting-trying to get away, had to go back and help fight the bad men. Baby clothes made. Fighting the men. Nothing helped-choking. Three men. We escaped. Another girl and I hid, but they came in and kept coming-had to fight. One used his belt. I tried to get her to go and she couldn't. I went to get help, but I could not even talk and say help. More than one bad person-one leader. They picked me up and drove away. No one would help us.

Is it hard to believe that someone somewhere might just want us to know something? And because God is God and nothing is impossible, is it inconceivable that a soul family can still be connected to us in this realm from another? I do not know this answer, but I do believe we just have not received all of the answers, yet.

Before I was on the cliff...the cliffs around Pikes Pond, the High Cliff above the butterfly spot. The message was *cliff*. Sis, I finally see it. The muck place cliff. Right there—under my nose—Hazel Hollow Road. The beautiful cliff bordering the muck place where the angels laid down in the water. Was this the place where you drew your last breath and your soul went to be with Jesus?

And *I was at a party at the big house*...

I know now, Sis. I'm so sorry.

I know now you were not alone and neither was Epperly.

After this moment of seeing the story from the bits and pieces within my messages, and aligning the facts, I compiled possible theories. Some very disturbing. It was time to have closure. Any closure. I wanted one certain line of truth about what had happened to my sister. Andy really wanted the ending wrapped up neatly like a fictional murder mystery where the hero points a finger to the ground in a cave, revealing where my sister's murdered body could be found. We both wanted a *real-life story* that ended with truth and justice. A story where those who commit evil acts are punished—where all who put Gina there are punished. I wanted the Light to shine in the darkness. I still had not found my way to freedom—to forgiveness.

If the messages are from a place of truth, then this wickedness is deeply rooted. This was not a coincidence of wrong place, wrong time. Evil never is. And it is always actively at work, covering its path, hiding and protecting its own—the wicked.

The thought that always brought me peace, not anger or stress, was the muck place. But that shed did not give me a peaceful feeling, the quarry questionable, and St. Albans far from peace. The question still remains: What is the relevance of all of these places? How can we really get into the mind of a killer? Killers all have their own repeating patterns, their own demons, their own secrets.

So why share so many of my messages and experiences in this manuscript? I haven't shared all of the messages—just the ones that seemed to be breadcrumbs in an unexplainable journey. I've shared the messages that I believe illustrate a point. It is always easier to look back at something and see the minutia than it is when you are living in the minutia. Sometimes I did feel as though I was chasing my tail just as Epperly had everyone else chasing theirs throughout the years. I know now, looking back on 2016, there were many more paths to learn and understand. One being that the messages were not the only reason and purpose of *the journey.*

To better illustrate this thought, I will fast forward to August 2018 when I finally saw what I believed to be the half-moon hole in the foundation where the wall connects and the one door and the *purple flowers* and maybe even this message: the Wall is important. And this may also be of relevance—a family, children, all helping to build a wall.

In mid-August 2018, Andy texted, "Dlana, you have to go see the basement of the Epperly house. I know you have always wanted to see inside that shed. Here's your chance. Here's the number. Call and go see for yourself. Tell me what you think after."

This suggestion weighed heavily on my heart. I had been at peace. I had stopped trying to find Gina's body. I did not want to keep searching, but this was a place I had felt so strongly about during the 2016 progression of events. I struggled with what I knew would come in the next few months.

But I also knew there were absolutely no coincidences in my life. And this was the Epperly homeplace. A place where I had sat by the road, staring at a shed as if it held a secret, and I just knew I had to see for myself. Who am I to question the path—a path I cannot yet see?

So I called the realtor, Katie Monroe, who was managing the Epperly homeplace for the new owner. What a wonderful lady. As soon as I met her, I could see her heart had very quickly connected to Gina's goodness. I walked the row of pine trees that lined the alley. Katie took me through the house and the 1980 stories and the 2016 messages came alive. The moment I stepped down into the basement, as soon as I crossed the threshold, I felt something indescribable. That basement made the hairs on my arms stand. What I saw in the basement was certainly perplexing. A brick vault-like wall built in a manner that seemed to have no logical basis, built, by my guess, in the last four decades. Examining it closer, I could see newer concrete poured on top that appeared to have been completed more recently than would be expected, considering who had lived there and when Epperly's parents had passed. And the location of this wall, no doubt in a basement full of stuff, would have been an undertaking to accomplish with the mixing and carrying that concrete by hand. When I told Andy, he had just thought someone had laid a piece of something on top of the wall. I told him, "No! Look closer. That is new concrete. I know. I have done a lot of projects with my husband throughout the years." Quite curious.

It would be the shed that took me to my knees. Inside, *one door* was propped up in the corner. *One door* was stored in the ceiling rafters from a very long time ago. And there, finally, after two years, was the half-moon hole I had so clearly seen in my visions that had haunted me throughout the fall of 2016. We can never really know the messages' true meanings because of the spiritual battles within our own thoughts—a battle that guides us in one direction or the other just like in the one door message. There was just no way to know for sure the purpose of it all or to discern the source. Or is there?

What is the relevance of this place?

My mind was battling to come up with an interpretation. Is this where Epperly has buried his collection of something that belonged to each of his victims? Then my mind went to a much darker place.

The dirt floor of the shed made me feel like

nature itself was talking to me, trying to tell me what I was to know. I could see it so clearly. Can you?

A series of events began to unfold after that mid-August 2018 visit. Andy brought in the radar-detecting machines. And, of course, the paranormal enthusiasts immediately asked Andy for time in the home. There was no stopping it. This was the home of my sister's killer. I remembered Ken and Natasha and their love for Gina: "We protect Gina and keep others from bothering her." I talked with the property manager Katie, also

a caring advocate for Gina. I gave her Ken's name and expressed my opinion, "If someone were going to go in, then let it be Ken and Tash," Ironically, that day when Katie called, Ken was right up the street working a job in Radford, not knowing

he was near the Epperly house! She arranged for Ken to visit first. He came with some friends who doused the yard and walked inside of the house. I was there that day. I watched as a young girl walked into that basement and fear consumed her face. She came outside and would not go back into that house. She described a chilling movie-like scene that played out in her head—two men, one smaller than the other. The smaller one wore something similar to overalls. The larger one was beating him severely. Her face told the story of the visions she saw. They call it residual energy from the past. All I know is that I saw her face and what she saw was very real to her. Ken set up a time with Katie to return to the house. I did not want to be there. Neither did Natasha. She believed her role was finished. I am appreciative to Ken and Natasha for their respect and love of Gina and understanding that I was the girl who could just never believe in ghosts as others viewed them.

That night, I was sitting at home when I received a text from Ken: "It's Gina—We got Princess" (the name of our childhood dog). It did not surprise me. But what was captured on video that night from a camera left running all night in the basement is what would take my breath away. There is simply no way to provide a true answer to its origin and meaning. I choose to see it as the same concentrated ball of energy that lay on the water. The energy of our angels. And someone somewhere wanted us to see this. That was the reason I met Ken. When I look at this unexplainable footage, for some reason I feel at peace—a happy feeling. I do not believe any one could ever say exactly what it is—angelic, demonic, a spirit, or—a soul. But *it*, whatever *it* is, exists. And my gut tells me *it* does not want to be bothered. Which is exactly how Ken came to capture its footage. *It* chose this path of validation that *it* exists. Ken was not obtrusive. Ken was not disruptive. Watch for yourself: TheMiraculousJourney.com.

STILL SHOT OF VIDEO PROGRESSION 1

STILL SHOT OF VIDEO PROGRESSION 2

STILL SHOT OF VIDEO PROGRESSION 3

I know angels can communicate. Angels announced the birth of Jesus. I know they can be among us. The Bible tells us, *"Do not forget to entertain strangers, for by so doing some have unwittingly entertained angels"* (Hebrews 13:2). Some will say the origin of the amazing little ball of energy gracefully moving on the video is of the Enemy—demonic. Oh, the thoughts we feed. And of course many will believe it is Gina's spirit—her ghost. We cannot know beyond a human doubt the answer to its source. I do not know. What I do know is that God's angels are always nearby, maybe just like what the video captured—an orb of light energy. I choose to accept that I can never fully understand or know the truth of everything, and I do not need to. I know I am to have faith and believe in the power of God and maybe it is just the spiritual army's marketing plan for this book so that the ultimate message of God's love and power revealed in the end will reach more people!

But I can keep pondering!

During the last days of September, we poked 2,000 or more holes everywhere

for the cadaver dogs. Reggie Pinkerton, a dear friend of mine, made long drill bits to make the job easier. I wish I had known him before the 2016 hole-prodding cadaver dog days. I must have drilled a hundred holes in that shed floor. He and my husband drilled into the wall, hoping it would provide enough of a hole for the dogs to sniff.

The dogs arrived to do what they do. I said my prayers as I hugged these amazing animals. I knew if it were God's will, then something would happen.

Both cadaver dogs identified one spot. The spot in the dirt in the shed right

where I saw the eerie image of the skull in the dirt floor of the shed. That was the exact spot encircled for later consideration. Andy said they would bring in a machine and excavate the dirt floor.

For some reason, this troubled me. Echoing in my head were the words spoken at my sister's funeral, her blood crying from the ground. I remembered what Rev. Bauman had said, "The blood in the ground cries out for justice, for truth." Prophetic words?

I had learned that the shed was where Epperly, an experienced hunter, would hang his deer, gutting them, and letting the blood drain as hunters do. Reverend Bauman compared all of our pleas for justice to the Bible story of Abel, whose blood cried from the ground. And he charged everyone with continued prayers to ensure justice would continue. "Her blood cries from the ground." Were words spoken in 1980 becoming relevant to me decades later?

Had Gina been taken to that shed?

If that had happened, then my sister's soul was screaming for the truth to be known. Nola said that when he felt Gina's pain, he kept feeling this message: *Why did you do this to me?* I felt the same sadness God must have felt when he told Cain, "The voice of your brother's blood cries out to Me from the ground" (Genesis 4:10, NKJ). That is how I felt: *Gina's blood has been here, somewhere. And her blood is crying to God and He can hear it.*

And, I also thought of Natasha and Ken's experience with the ghost of Mitch and his word "bloodletting."

That was the thought in my head. So I asked Andy and the handlers, "Can the dogs tell the difference between animal blood and human?"

"Yes," she replied. Curious, I asked, "Can the dogs identify only human blood without bones or remains—just blood?"

"It is organic, so I imagine if there is enough of it, then, yes."

I simply knew I needed to have some of that dirt from that exact spot just in case nothing tangible showed up when they excavated. If my thoughts were correct, and the ground had only remnants of an organic material like blood, I would need the blood-soaked dirt to test it for the presence of human DNA. The dog trainer suggested, "Why not just get some of the dirt?" And that is what I did—an empty drill box full. And one day, if even possible, I may have that dirt tested for any human DNA.

As I dug deep down into the ground in the exact spot in the shed's dirt floor, there in the ground was something that caught my eye. It was stuck in the ground at least sixteen-feet deep, right where the dog had identified. I thought it could be hair. Katie and I just looked at each other, a dazed and confused moment.

One end was matted with mud, but the other end was a perfectly straight cut. I thought of Gina's perfectly cut hair and wondered, *Could this be Gina's hair? Does hair lose its color?* Andy had just left about 3:00 p.m. He had a funeral later that night, so when I called him, he said he could not come back and instructed me just to put what I had dug up in a plastic bag and leave it in the shed on the tractor trailer. He was not happy that I really had done what I said I was going to do—dig up some of the dirt, as was evident by his verbal response. Katie was worried about leaving what we had found just lying there in the shed.

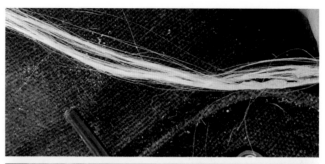

After two days, I decided to text VSP Investigator Santolla and ask him if Katie could bring it to him for safekeeping so he and Andy could later take it to the lab to determine what I had dug up. I already expected it would not be Gina's human hair, but not at first. It would be no coincidence that I would soon after watch a documentary about Peru, a place on my bucket list, and learn that an elongated skull found in Peru still had hair on it, red hair. (Some believe that that skull belonged to a member of the Nephilim.) This knowledge gave me peace because I could no longer believe whatever I had found was Gina's hair after seeing that elongated skull still had red hair on it.

So then I still wondered, *If it is not Gina's brunette hair, could it still be human hair? Blonde hair?* The VSP Investigator Santolla told me the report came back as non-human, possibly just twine. Others called it animal hair. There was another reason behind how the events transpired that day. I would write this message:

"Rough edges of life lovingly soothed away by God."

Earlier on the same day that I had dug up the "non-human hair-like strand," I had been told that Gina's personal items I had entrusted to a dear friend had been shared with people I did not know for use in a spirit gathering held in the Epperly basement. I felt such anger in the fall of 2016 learning that almost every week it seemed someone was trying to talk with my sister's spirit. I know this: The spiritual realm is just not to be messed with. Let life just happen and the rough edges will be taken care of. The tiniest twists are close to impossible to discern without prayer.

The last song on Gina's playlist was "Woodstock" by Crosby, Stills, Nash, and Young. They were a favorite group of my college years. I had never paid attention to the meaning of this song's lyrics. I missed Woodstock by a few years! The event is not the message. The message was in the lyrics, and I now better understood its meaning. We really do just have to get back to the garden, biblically speaking.

It was the day's silent but glorious message that I noticed. When I was first at the Epperly house in mid-August, 2018, I took a picture of the half-moon hole in the shed. When I was there six weeks later with the cadaver dogs, no surprise—I took more pictures. Purple flowers adorned this yard everywhere. Purple. The purple flowers were in the gardens. The purple morning glories had blossomed, trailing inside and out of this shed, up through the half-moon hole. I know what I am to know. There are no coincidences in my life. I will just let life unfold, having faith in God's justice. My spiritual army always has its own plans still yet to be seen.

AUGUST 13, 2018

When I experienced faith beyond any stretch of my imagination in June 2017, the climactic moment in *the journey*, I reconnected to God with every breath. I not only sing the song *Stop and Smell the Roses*, but I now do it more often. I create my own life experiences by taking time to stop and breathe in God's canvas. Better yet—"making *time* let me." But I was not there just yet.

SEPTEMBER 29, 2018

Peace was almost within reach, but *the journey* was not complete. The battles still to come culminated into a full-blown spiritual war.

In the first days of the New Year, January 2017, I had sought help from a NoVa investigative PI firm. This action was multi-purposed. In the forefront of my mind was still the question: Who else was with Gina that night? If we could just find those other girls, if any one of them were still alive…we would have the truth. And that might lead to who helped. And then, we might find her body. And, there must be others who needed closure. He would advise me to "Call this person—a nationally known crime profiler I just heard speak at a law enforcement educational conference. She might help you profile Epperly." So not hesitating, knowing that I have no coincidences in my life, I sent this person an email. This criminal profiler had years of experience in serial killer cases. When I received a reply to my email, there was only one line, asking me to verify my identity.

"Okay, now that I know who I'm talking to," the satisfied crime profiler continued, "as I was reading your email, I kept getting images of bones being destroyed, like at a construction site, at what looks similar to a conveyor belt. Makes no sense to me. Maybe it will you."

I just sat on the other end of this correspondence, shaking my head. How could she see this by my initial email? In essence, just my name gave her this vision. And the words "construction site" got my attention. That could certainly be a possibility. The quarry a few miles up the road on Route 611 crushed stone for road maintenance. But the more questionable quarry in the west end beside the river near where he was said to have been Monday afternoon seems more obvious. Was it operational June 1980? All I could think of was Epperly's chanted statement made with no remorse to his cellmate, "people are driving over…." It brought images to my mind that I did not welcome.

"There is a girl with your sister," the profiler wrote. "A dark-haired girl, late teens, early twenties, in a light-colored dress resembling a nightgown, pretty, with big front teeth."

This was just as both Nola and Natasha had seen—with one difference. The girl seen in this vision was a hitchhiker picked up after having had car trouble.

The criminal profiler added, "Beyond trying to find Gina's body, maybe this is all to bring attention to another case, maybe not even related."

The next thing she asked made me surmise that her title of crime profiler also meant psychic. She asked if I was thinking of changing something in my life, like a job or a hobby. "You will be teaching something," she said. "There are some things you need to let go of."

Then I was asked a perplexing question. "Have you heard Gina hum in spirit?" I wondered, *Is that what some people call "the white noise" I hear? Can we hear energy—energy of a higher frequency?*

"As I am writing this, I'm hearing her hum. I am positive *she left something for you, whether you found it or not. It was a very small item.*"

A second email came. This profiler was persistent:

> Have you found a little trinket/item that seems to have appeared out of the blue? I get a sense that Gina has left something for you to let you know she is around.
>
> I also get the sense that Gina is worried about you. There's definitely concern for your wellbeing from the other side. You have been visited by more than one spirit. There is another young female who passed early who also comes around you. I don't know if this is someone you are familiar with or another victim.

I did not think too long on all of this, in light of all else that had already happened. I just assumed I would run across some small item of Gina's that I had simply put away somewhere.

What I did want to know was: Who is the black-haired girl that Nola, Natasha, and now a third person all say they see with Gina? The description was the same from all of them.

I remembered Andy had mentioned two hitchhikers who had disappeared in the late '70s believing Epperly could have been involved. A picture of a young, missing woman had been posted on NamUs. After seeing her picture, I do believe she could very well match the visions that were described similarly by three unassociated people from three different places. All say black hair, but one says long hair, *two say larger front teeth*, all say pretty, two say white tattered nightgown, one says a light-colored dress that resembles a nightgown, and two see her pointing to the ground from a grassy knoll on a hill. One says she is with Gina, pulling back the brush that surrounds a large brick house and waving him in, and one says the girl she sees was a hitchhiker or was picked up on the side of the road after she had car trouble. And if we assume spirits can be seen by these gifted, connected people, this person seems to match the descriptions.

Looking at this picture, I want to ask: Why is this spirit in Radford believed by others to be with my sister's spirit, pointing to the ground? What is the connecting factor? Two unrelated murdered victims, maybe. The hitchhiker named Angela was reported missing in 1977 from the Roanoke area.

February 08, 1977
MISSING WOMAN— PHOTO COURTESY OF NAMUS

Angela is a name relevant to me during my experiences. So who is the mysterious black-haired woman? Could it be this hitchhiker?

If not Angela, then could it be Beth, Scarlett? The possibilities go on and on and on. I believe Epperly is a serial killer, so there are many fractured souls in his trail of violence. There are other families just like mine who have walked the dark path of unknowingness, their hearts heavy laden with hate, anger, and unforgiveness just like mine.

As the new year began, I believed my journey had ended. The feeling of urgency left me, and I felt the weight of the world I had carried for six months lift from my shoulders. I was almost at peace, the message clear: I don't need to find her body. She is in a good place. She is breathing fine and she has gone into the light—there forever. But still a darkness held on as I looked back through everything that had happened, every detail, seeing what I was to see. My theories arose from a very dark place.

I am still unsure about the true source of some of these experiences, even though I now understand the power of the dark, but I also know the power of Light, wanting good to triumph over evil. I'm sticking to the theory that evil would want to cover its tracks and not reveal the truth of its wrongdoings. Confusion and chaos arise from the dark. God's Light calms the storms of darkness so that truth can be seen.

Now, every morning, I talk to God, silently in my head from my heart. *Let me see only you the clearest, hear you the loudest, and love you the most with all of my heart.* But I still did not know to do this, not yet. I was still finding my way back to the heart of my soul. I knew something from a few years earlier needed healing, but I had buried it. I ignored it. What I did not know is that there was a seed of evil literally left inside my spirit, waiting to raise its ugly head in hopes of winning the final battle. A plan to derail me, break me, so that I would never find my way back to God's love. Knowing, acknowledging, and really understanding this was the path to my peace.

The healer had told me, "Hang on; it's coming." It did, like an erupting volcano. Everything in my past that needed healing began surfacing. I only thought I needed to heal one thing in my life—the unrelenting hate and unforgiveness of my sister's murderer. But more than just forgiving Epperly needed to be dealt with. I had no idea how much more was buried in my heart, piece by piece, over time. And it wasn't only the events of my childhood I needed to forgive.

Something I had buried was raising its ugly head.

TRUTH? HOW CAN WE EVER REALLY KNOW...OH YEAH!
LOVE IS NEVER GLAD ABOUT INJUSTICE, BUT REJOICES
WHENEVER TRUTH WINS OUT.

CHAPTER 21

I'LL FOLLOW YOU

There is assurance in knowing that God is the God of all creation.
And that includes our souls made in his image that man cannot kill.
So, too, then, is it possible that God listens
to the prayers of the hearts of those eternal souls always connected to me?
She's not heavy; she's my sister—a profound thought to ponder.

T he first nightmare came the night I returned home from St. Albans—after I saw the healer. I had the same dream twice in the same night. I wrote:

Terrible scary visions. Different than all other dreams. Could see the rape party.

No more St. Albans.

And, one disturbing word:

devilish

A few days later, I had the same terrible vision. I could see myself in the repeating nightmare vision. As the vision repeated, again and again, it became clear it was something still very much a part of my recent past that needed healing just as I had been warned would come. Something I had buried. A heinous cowardly act committed against me. And my visions with me in the center mirrored what I knew to be true from one of the darkest nights of my life, spring 2014. Dreams that were, in reality, not dreams, but flashbacks breaking through—with a vengeance as if attempting to break me.

The messages were still coming, and I suspected this one that came December 29, 2016 was about my own life's story from 2014.

> I was going to be in a show. Risky to get ready.
>
> Used men's bathroom. Man and a boy came out rushed to get dress on.
>
> $ cost a lot. ladies??
>
> Me and up my fist. Never could?
>
> If late in not one hour kept looking at time did not seem to move. So late? Or not?

Music played in my head—the chorus of a song playing over and over—"Victim of Love" by the Eagles. My heart did break. I was listening. They were not wrong—I knew what I knew. The content of the flashbacks were for sure from my own traumatic event that had occurred two years earlier, but with a few extra details that did not fit what I already knew to be true. What I did not know yet would become the one last piece that would tilt the scale of my inner resolve and resilience. The straw that would have broken the camel's back had I not just experienced *the journey* full of miracles. My heart could hold no more. I now see God knew this. He knows everything. But I was not thinking about God. Not yet. *Thank heavens the heart of my soul remembered.*

My soul knew I needed to be brought from unconsciousness to consciousness.

I decided to contact a person who practiced applied kinesiology—muscle testing for truth. He had proven himself a few months earlier during our search for Gina's body by helping me identify matching latitudes and longitudes, the positives aligning with the many places of interest we already had. Eight locations aligned with our places of interest. The task was just too big, so I was trying to narrow these eight vast areas down to within six inches using only a handheld GPS. His notes were always encouraging as he eliminated location after location. "Okay, now that you know where she is *not*, [you are] one step closer to where she is. You know you're meant to do this; you would not be doing it if you weren't. The question is why?"

I trusted in his pure soul and his abundant goodness from my earlier autumn experiences. I needed to understand the content of my flashbacks—

flashbacks with more than one man, with only me, and the actions of that night, not a part of my life, so in desperation to know truth, I texted him:

> Can you determine truth about something that happened to me? I know I was drugged and I believe I was raped by [man named]. I'm not sure of all of the details because I have no memories of the night. I need to know the truth so I can deal with it, heal, and forgive.

Radford in morning. Andy wants to use drone. I want to go to the actual places and try   If you get a few minutes can you check the following longitudes

> 37 05'38".21n
> 37 05'16".71n
> 37 06'34".10n
> 37 08'00.03n
> 37 08'19".52n
> 37 05'37".88n

His answer confirmed my suspicions that had been stirred by my recent flashbacks, throwing me into a darker place than I could have ever imagined.

> I am so sorry DIana. There were four men, premeditated rape. Three of these men raped you. The fourth man's room may have been a connecting room. He did not rape you—he watched.

I am trying 😊

DIana, remember that you are stronger than the thief who tries to steal your dignity, your power, your feeling of safety. You are stronger....

My last memory of that night, two blurry doors side by side, now made sense. The two rooms were set back in small alcoves from the main hall. *Who was in that room beside my room? They knew where my room was.*

And days later, he comforted me with this message:

> You absolutely have a lot of people...who believe in you, who are here to support you and protect you, including me. One thing I have learned is that to release is to heal. Your body, your spirit, your time, it can't hold on to things and be healthy. Just like breath is life...going in and going out....

> You love so strong that your heart doesn't release. It's okay to release.

I would ask him: *I wonder if this is why Gina came into my life?*

I was now fully believing that it was her saving me. And, in a way, it was.

Wonder if this is why Gina came into my life.

I loved to travel with my family and friends. Quickly, I learned the more places I got to go—the more people I got to meet. I loved it. My aunts had always called me the "go-go girl" and said "No moss grows under Dlana's feet." Getting together with other like-minded people, developing trusted friendships, sharing and learning from each other, was my normal reality. That is how I crossed paths with my one known rapist. Eight months earlier, I had kindly offered to take a picture for him of him and his two little girls. A one-minute crossing of paths.

Away from this safe space, I trusted no one. I always understood the realities of evil lurking around every corner, experiencing enough in 1980 to last a lifetime. I lived life not in fear, just with a sense of realistic caution. I always understood *"See Something, Say Something."* I imagined someone saw something in 1980, and I was right. Kim Jett came forward. She had seen something and she had said something. And with me, in 2014, in a public place, surrounded by my friends and acquaintances, someone must have seen something. Their mind maybe questioned what they were seeing for a flashing moment—*that does not seem right, knowing Dlana*—but then perceptions changed maybe because of a presumed, judging thought, leading to not recognizing that evil was at play—not saying something.

First, I know my reason for being in the place where I was in the spring of 2014—*$ cost a lot - ladies.* That line and others of the December 29, 2016 message validated my repeating nightmares were actually flashbacks about my own life. I always remembered the before and after details. I just had no memory of the in-between—None. Flashbacks can be common from traumatic experiences—PTSD. The unconscious memories were surfacing. Maybe my inner soul, my own consciousness, told me what I needed to know. Maybe my soul had help from my sister...my angels... God. Maybe all of the above—my spiritual army. All I know is there is more behind this than what it seemed—God had a plan. God is not the author of evil, but He will use it for good.

"And we know that all things work together for good to those who love God, to those who are the called according to His purpose."

— Romans 8:28 (NKJV)

What I remember most sharply from that night is taking my first drink from the glass handed to me. The taste was terrible, with chemical-like strength. That concoction was a very powerful drug. And the power of that drug kicked in very quickly. I came to consciousness the next morning, lying on my stomach, my eyes opening to a naked man sitting on my toilet in my hotel bathroom. I recognized him from the night before. It never once occurred to me that anyone within my trusted circles would ever do me harm. Had he gotten out of my room before I regained consciousness, I would have never known anything. I only told a few people what I believed had happened to me. I called my best friend the day I got home. She was there for me when I needed her most, and I will be forever appreciative. I buried what I knew from that night—one man. I just moved on with my life. I had no proof. I knew my circumstances, and I knew I would not win that fight, so I became one of the many women in the statistics today who live with the shame and blame of rape. Seemed the right decision at the time. I would have never known there was more than one man that night had my unconscious flashback memories never surfaced. I would have never understood the content of the flashbacks. What I was now seeing in my flashbacks aligned with the physical condition I had found myself in that morning. Flashbacks from my consciousness of the acts my rapist or rapists engaged in—images I now wanted to suppress but could not. A haunting nightmare.

I now knew truth. And more would come to validate this truth.

The afternoon after the rape, while still coming out of my drugged state of mind, a photo was taken of me by a friend with my phone. Not because she knew I had been raped, but because she just happened to grab my phone and take it. There are no coincidences in my life. That one photo visibly confirmed the same truth my flashbacks had now showed me— the bruising of my face especially above my upper lips clearly visible. I never even saw this picture in my photo library until I was writing this book. No reason to have ever looked close had the moments of consciousness not broken through in those nightmare flashbacks. A picture really can paint a thousand words.

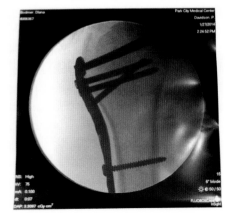

This one too.

This picture shows the physical

state of my body before my rapist targeted me, drugged me, and raped me.

Just a few months earlier, I had had a serious snowboarding accident that required extensive surgery. I had broken my humerus in pieces, shattered my shoulder, and torn my rotator cuff all "in one fell swoop"—literally! I had just gotten to where I could lift my arm and wash my own hair a few weeks earlier. I was still babying my shoulder and using my arm cautiously. I had not taken pain medications after the first few weeks of surgery because they make me extremely sick. I never sleep on my stomach. And it would have been almost physically impossible for me to get up off of my stomach with my injury. The pain was intense when I first opened my eyes that morning with no memory of why.

To make one thing very clear, allow me to set the record straight: Even if I had been a single woman, I never would have even *wanted* to be with this man, ever. Hell would freeze over before that would have happened.

After my rape, my soul seemed to be insisting that I not let this man take any more from me—the cost was already high. I had stopped the self-inflicted guilt. I had stopped worrying about a video I later surmised to be out in the dark underground world, having seen him retrieve his out-of-place phone from where it had been left propped up on the windowsill. *I was going to be in a show,* another confirming part of my message. No more shame. I chose to be grateful that I was not conscious of the acts. No more blame. I had not died and never come to consciousness again. I survived. My sister did not.

We all, men and women, need to know and understand the realities of this new age of rape: When it happens, you will never suspect anything. The thought that you are being drugged will never cross your mind. You will not even remember, once you regain consciousness, anything that transpired—not one single memory. Time will have been lost—*kept looking at time did not seem to move.* You will not call the police because you will not know. And even if you could know, the suspicions of rape would come too late. I never would have suspected or known anything had my rapist made it out of my room before I regained consciousness. The drug's effects continue far into the day, creating an unrecognizable state of mind. I never even had anger until fourteen hours after I first opened my eyes. And anger was always an easily roused, dominant emotion for me—that eastern Kentucky mountain blood flowing through my veins. Anger was suppressed, as was the truth of the night. Not by me, by the drug's effects.

After the drug waned, the emotional nightmare kicked in. The shame was unbearable. Fear won. The Enemy gloats.

And if the memories do surface years later or the flashbacks come, you may not know why. The supposed nightmares will haunt you because you will not understand them unless you were lucky like me and came to consciousness with the rapist still in the room. Only then could you become aware that your nightmares are actual flashbacks. It would be like having a military PTSD flashback from the battleground, not having ever experienced a battle to give understanding to the nightmares. Knowing of having fought in a war provides the foundational knowledge of why and from where the flashbacks occurred. Not even knowing you have been raped, the flashbacks will make no sense. How tragic for so many not to know the why behind them.

It was disturbing enough, then, to come to grips with having been drugged and raped by one sleazy man, a coward, but now to also struggle with the thoughts that I could have been raped by more than one—that was a soul-breaking reality.

The Enemy taunted God to test his faithful servant Job, "…*stretch out your hand and strike everything he has and he will surely curse you*" (Job **1:11**).

No. We did not. We were broken together, and together we found God's strength. And together, we will never give up the fight. This is a sisters' journey to truth—heart and head together—two interlocked hearts of sisters' eternal love. A clear message: *All sisters unite.*

People, all people, not just a few, need to give actionable thought to this new "tolerated" world and what we really are up against. We must realize that even our closest circles may not be safe environments. This is the new reality we now live in. How can we hear the recent stories of our young girls who tell us their respected doctor did what he did and not believe we have a serious problem? I understand what the phrase "War on Drugs" was intended to mean when President Nixon first coined the term in 1971, maybe even initially used with a misdirected, ulterior motive. Today, the phrase has a different meaning, yet remains very relevant. These new drugs are being criminally used against us. *Against our will.* And these mind-altering drugs are being improved upon daily. Many women, men, teenage girls and boys, and others have been affected by these powerful drugs with no memory of what happened. Recently hundreds of unknowing women are suspected of having been drugged and raped by one man, a doctor, and his accomplice. Many of these women are not even aware, as authorities learned from the videos in the doctor's phone. And in that same area, the recent bust of the bartenders ring by the police should paint a picture of what we are up against. These bartenders were paid by "white-collared businessmen" who point a finger at the woman or man in the room they choose, the drink delivered to the unknowing victim by the trusted bartenders. Neither incident surprises me, but it should ignite a fire in us from deep within. This is only part of the iceberg. And the tip of the iceberg is in clear view and we still cannot see it—How can a civilized society, yes us, not stop sex trafficking?

We need to teach our daughters and granddaughters how to protect themselves. Our sons, too, for that matter. There are programs that help educate our youth to these undeniable realities. The national nonprofit, Help Save the Next Girl, was started by a mother whose daughter was raped and murdered in Virginia. It is a grassroots program I applaud. I hope to see this concentrated educational focus spring forth in every community. It is my dream, maybe even part of God's plan, that we just might change this extreme problem from a tolerated reality to a better, different reality.

I recently read the following quote: "May we be strong women, may we know strong women, and may we raise strong women."

I know God loves us. I know God is saying, "Enough is enough." It is time for a revolution, of sorts.

Women, wake up. Let's fight and have the story the way we want it to be. Let's write a different story devoted to women and our truth. And not just women—we *all* can begin to promote change together and tackle the reality of these challenges with solutions. And it begins by supporting each other. It begins by respecting each other. No more victim blaming. It begins by spreading light. It is a battle, and we can never forget that. No, it is not just a battle....

It is a war. *We all need to wake up.*

We are to wage a war on behalf of all women against those who take what is not theirs to take.

I would have never shared the private details of my life if I had not realized that *The Miraculous Journey* had many simultaneous purposes and was not intended to be just for me. How can I convey the truth of a personal, loving relationship—the why behind the why—without the whole story, without explaining every single moment, the good and the bad? So, too, with Gina's life story—the truth to be shared. The realization of this helped me know and understand my purpose—my newly ignited passion to help women heal from the trauma of rape, domestic violence, child molestation, trafficking, and multiple other challenges.

Wisdom came after I answered *How did my rape serve me*? Life happens for you, not to you.

This is what I now can see so clearly:

I looked back on my life and recognized exactly what transpired in my life *after the rape*. Although I was unconscious to the complete truth, I could see that there were differences in the Dlana I had known all of my life. It was like a thief in the night, evolving, stealing away moments of my good life. I was discontent and not as patient with my husband. I seemed to have new and different interests. Shame, fear, and guilt were all taking root, affecting my self-worth. I seemed to be attracting more bad than good, and it was getting worse. My spirit had been infected. The effects on my life were visible. A lovely lady in town whom I had known for years, a godly lady, came up to me in 2017 and said, "Praise God. I can see your light again." She told me that a few years before she had seen darkness hanging in my hair, like a weight pulling me down. I am still taken aback at what some people actually can see with their open minds. Nola had seen that my heart needed healing straight away when we met in June 2015. Though I was not conscious of the foothold the events of 2014 had had upon me, he knew—maybe he even saw the violence like others can see—the moment he met me. He also could see the heavy burden I had carried for thirty-seven years about what had happened to Gina. If you had asked me then, I could not have told you what happens to a person's spirit when evil invades it. Now I know. What it was to me was a hole—a rip. I just did not know it yet. This hole allowed evil to infiltrate my spirit and I could not see it. This tear in my soul had nearly ripped me apart and is a reality that cannot be ignored. Now I see clearly the hidden, underlying agenda of the Enemy.

A great lady once told me, "You loving you is what's best for everyone." But I was not loving me any longer.

Rape is not just about someone taking what is not theirs to take. It is also about a web of darkness, spreading its power into your very being. It is about a soul that needs to be healed. A rip to be sewn up by your good spirit, the needle and thread coming from a place of love. A big tear that must be healed so that the Light can be contained and the seeds of that evil not sewn up inside your beautiful self.

Now, thirty months later, the unknown truths of that night were being awakened so I could heal again, really heal. But this time the thoughts of more than one man were much harder to accept. This shocking, additional information sent me into two weeks of deep prayer and meditation. I was determined to work on healing what I had come to learn about my life. It felt like I had a loving soul family in my heart helping to bring me from unconsciousness to consciousness so I could know the real truth behind my greatest battle and fully heal. I felt their strengths coming through. My spiritual army already knew what was coming into my life. And so, too, did the Enemy.

I am a good, smart woman—really, a superwoman-type like we all are—and yet "they," and I do mean "they," got me. I even questioned, *Have I invited this evil, somehow?* so I asked the healer. A while later, she replied, "No you did not." It is simply insane, unexplainable, that I would have, even for one minute, had this thought in my mind, questioning that I had somehow caused this heinous act of cowardly violence against me. Why do we do that? And that question leads to this next question to contemplate.

What was the true origin of this act committed against me in 2014? Can we say my rape became part of a plan? Not God's—The Enemy's? Why had this happened in my life? Can we say it is free will and destiny if all I did was accept a drink in a split second from a person viewed as a part of my trusted circle? Is it possible evil had its own plan? The Enemy knows everything—all of the intricate connections, the past, the present, and the future, always at work, spreading and connecting without notice. Even covering and hiding the acts of his own—the wicked. 2016-2017 was coming, and the Enemy would not like that path. I was moving closer to truth and to God's message of love, so he stepped up his game. His plan was to thwart the message that was to come. Thoughts of shame and blame caused me initially to bury the heinous act committed against me by the one known man. *Influenced thoughts.* Fear of what others would think prevailed. The created self-judging endless. The Enemy was smiling, but he still needed more to ensure I would not heal. And that is why what happened next, in just a few weeks, happened—Fear.

Seeing the details of that night, the repeating flashbacks, most definitely could have been the final hurdle. It should have broken me. It could have won. But it backfired. How could I let *them* win? That was not going to happen. Now it had become free will. What was happening instead was that the warrior in me was waking up.

But first I cried. I cried until I could cry no more. I emerged stronger. I would not let discouragement win. I would not let "them" win. I drew on the unconditional love surrounding me. Joy trumps discouragement every time when love is present. I knew Nola was right. And so was Gina: Listen to your heart. Every day, we choose the path that creates our story. I now choose to remember the other amazing picture that captured the only truth I will ever need to know. The angels lying on the water. I chose God's love, and I healed. God helped me completely sew up that rip. I am reminded every day how much God loves me. I now know that "Love your neighbor as you love yourself" is also telling us to love ourselves. Once we learn to love ourselves, that love will catapult change to the dot of our life. The Enemy will not win one little speck here and one little speck there. He used this event to try to break me. They all followed me down into the eye of my darkest storm, but the Enemy could not win against my spiritual army, which would not leave me behind.

I made the tough decision that I could not stay silent. When your values are clear, decisions are easier. This choice brought a palpable fear into my life. Whether one or more had raped me, it had to be stopped. I knew I had not been the first and only victim. Others could have been hurt this way, too, and that others might be in the future was something I could not ignore. If I again just buried what had happened, I could be allowing the same to happen to other women. I could not do that.

The darkest storm was the system. The system failed me. The system created Epperly. It failed him, too. Our entire world is a hierarchy of systems. Systems that are self-focused, not God-focused, designed to maintain power and control, pride and ego prevailing. *Who is the orchestrator of these systems?* We are a part of a hierarchal, power-focused system evolving from humans' innate desire to be in control over something that cannot be controlled—life! We could just live life from a mindset not focused on power over others, but focused on individual relationships one with another built on love, truth, compassion, kindness, respect, and never forgetting who is really in charge: God!

The system broke me in 2014. And, it won again in early 2017. Secrecy its objective. Legalities halted transparency. But the remainder of *the journey* that would come in the next few months created and united the Spirit of Life from God's power. Rape cannot be buried, no matter how hard we try. You are in the eye of the storm and you must come out. My head was trying to win the battle, but it was my heart that came through.

The hardest moment was yet to come—I had to tell my sons the whole story. In February 2017, we had a family meeting. Now that I had come forward with only my integrity in hand, to report my known rapist and his actions of having drugged and raped me, I knew I would be living in a new reality. And I knew the changes in my life would become changes in their lives too. My sons and my husband were now dealing with the same hate and vengeance I had carried for decades. I did not want these feelings taking root, lingering in my family's life. Through both my recent and my past walk into the dark eye of the storm, I had learned what life is like when we carry the burden of a heavy heart. We trade away moments of joy for anger, hate, and unforgiveness. I knew they, too, would need to set their hearts free. That was my priority.

Several weeks later, I had had an incident when I came around the corner into an elevator and there stood my rapist. I did not expect this so my mind—not knowing, not anticipating, not preparing—could not control my reaction. My body involuntarily reacted in a most physical way. I could not breathe. Real panic, terror, was visible to my husband, who swiftly took me out of the elevator and back to our room. I am positive he would have preferred to administer cowboy justice right then and there, but just like my dad had chosen righteousness and his family when he did not kill his daughter's murderer, so too, my husband chose his family and me. My physical state was top priority, and it was not good. That elevator incident brought back subconscious emotions. One of my last memories that night my rapist took me, before the last memory of two blurry doors, was of a security guard station right before the elevator. I vaguely remembered something deep within me wanted to say something as I passed him, pleading with my eyes, but I had no voice. Now I know why... that night I was drugged, my last bit of consciousness deep within knew something was wrong. I understood what this meant—*Me and up my fist. Never could?* What really happened in that elevator that night? Who was there? That elevator event triggered the beginning of my unconsciousness to consciousness.

And, I know beyond a doubt that prayers are answered! Shortly thereafter, right before *the journey* began, my husband and I celebrated Easter at sunrise in the bush, fulfilling a lifelong dream to see Africa. That year, Easter had fallen on my birthday. I sat on the ground and prayed in the most personal way I had ever talked to God. Silently, in my mind I asked for His help. I knew I still needed to heal fully. That glorious Sunday morning in Africa, I praised God for the gift of Easter and the gift of my blessed life. This was simply a better mindset to be in—my story as I wanted it to be. And now, looking back, I believe the last half of 2016 and 2017 was God's way of answering my pleading silent prayer from the heart of my soul. God is all knowing and His multi-purposed, multilayered, intricately designed plans always perfect.

He was answering my prayers when I sought His help with all of my heart. He always knew what was going to happen before it happened.

> *"For I know the plans I have for you...Then you will call on me and come and pray to me, and I will listen to you. You will seek me and find me when you seek me with all your heart."*
>
> *— Jeremiah 29:11-13 NIV*

Promise kept!

But I now also wonder about the night after I heard the farmer's story when I fell to my knees, praying and wailing desperately out loud to God for his help. I know God heard my prayers, but who else heard my pleas in my weakest, most vulnerable moment?

I remembered what Nola had said, "You only want God to hear you. If you make it public, *they* can join and tell you things that are true and misguide and confuse you. They cannot read your mind, but *they* can even tell by your actions, and then *they* will go into action."

From this day forward, I am only talking to God through the heart of my soul. As Nola told me, asking somebody to pray for you means, deep inside, a lack of faith. You do not *really believe* that just one prayer by yourself…is enough to make God help you. I know this. I had faith that morning in Africa. I asked God with all of my heart. And so too after the farmer story. God already knew what was coming.

On March 2, 2017, another message came:

> Gina. One man was there I did not know if I could trust.
>
> Dreamed someone kept adding weight-extra pieces to a pendulum.
>
> Another man came by and gave us bread to eat. Shared other food with everyone. Girls loved the dessert. And a high school blue and white band went by and played for us. The man who gave the bread did so for the band, but he also gave bread in God's name.

I did not recognize the similarity to Jesus' miracle of feeding the multitudes until much later. Our high school colors had been blue and white, and Gina was in this message. I had only had one other message with Gina in it: The August Nightmare—the dream in a dream. Now, she was there for me again. Almost as if it were somehow known what was coming next. The origin of the pendulum's weight from someone I could not trust warned me from where it would come, but I still did not understand because I was in the thick of my storm.

Two days later, as I was preparing to go west to visit my youngest son, a sudden intense fear entered my mind. I could literally not put one foot in front of the other to take steps to leave my home, to just get in the truck and ride out west to see my son. Anyone really acquainted with me knows that seems unimaginable. I would climb the highest mountains for my sons. And probably would have to just to find my mountain-loving son! But out of fear, I would not leave. It was real. A movie-like scenario was playing out in my head, the fear coming from within my own mind ignited by four little words that had surfaced to my consciousness months earlier during the initial flashbacks. A clear voice echoing in my head words I could not have known. The same four words I then gave to the DEA. And now, out of the blue, I was afraid. The emotion I experienced was real: Fear is the enemy's sharpest tool, and this experience was the sharpest. The battles are real and are not easily recognized or controlled.

Later that afternoon, my son called, "Ma, snap out of it. What the **** is your problem. Get your *** in the truck, and come on out here."

So I did. Love was winning. But it was hard even to walk to the truck. The fear was paralyzing. Those four little words I heard so clearly were twisting, spurring thoughts that were creating intense, very real fear in my life. The Enemy was not giving up on me. He was coming after me full force. And he was using a truth, twisted into a lie of fear.

The Enemy's playground of choice is our own heads. I did not really understand this when I first wrote the message: the mind is the enemy's playground. What I now know is that the spirit world is at work all of the time—not just the bad, but also the good. And I understand now just how hard it is to discern what comes from where.

The Enemy employs deceptive perception every day to lead us further from the truth.

The first lie, "...you will not surely die...and you will be like God, knowing good and evil" (Genesis 3:4-5). A deceptive twist on truth, masterminded in a powerful way. That is when the relationship with the Enemy began— thoughts being influenced.

In the beginning, Love was all we knew. Fear came about not through a literal bite of an apple, but as a thought planted by the Enemy and his twisted lies, *an influenced thought*, that maybe God was hiding something from us so we should eat of the forbidden fruit so we would be smart like God. A twist on truth—the lie that we may not know everything—resulted in the very fear of not knowing coming into existence in our minds. The Enemy *brought fear into our lives.* God knew it would happen, though he never wanted us to experience it. The Bible says God did not give us the spirit of fear. God told us we would die and we did; spiritually and physically our life changed. Fear was at the root of the beginning of the human relationship with the Enemy. We had now experienced evil, fear, lies, and the twisted truth. And just by experiencing it, it became a perception, a belief, a reality in our human life. Fear literally became a part of our world, a part of us, leading to power and control—there is no end to it. Confusion and chaos, pride and arrogance, shame and blame—they all traffic in fear, the Enemy's specialty. We have got to get back to the garden, and we can start by recognizing when the sharpest tool, fear, is being used in the playground of our minds.

Jesus said of the Enemy:

> "*He was a murderer from the beginning, and does not stand in the truth, because there is no truth in him. When he speaks a lie, he speaks*

from his own resources, for he is a liar and the father of it."

— Matthew 8:44

Our own life's story, all of my life's experiences, can become the Enemy's resource. *Taffy....Princess...twisted truths?* How do we reconcile that *someone or something* knew the name of our childhood cat and our childhood dog. Maybe it is Gina, but then I would simply ask, "Why?" We might also consider this: an external force with the power to mess with us misdirecting truth, wanting us to believe in communication with the dead by using our personal truths. The Bible says, not to seek answers from the dead, so maybe it is possible. But still, how can we ever know for sure who *The Who* is? This is too important to ignore. What is the real *why* behind it all?

Jesus also shared these words of wisdom to take to heart:

"And do not fear those who kill the body but cannot kill the soul. But rather fear Him who is able to destroy both soul and body in hell."

— Matthew 10:28 NKJV

So yes, our souls will not die by man. But our souls can be destroyed.

Twisted Truths = The Enemy's Lies. "... you will not surely die..."

The power of it all is just to be realized; then the truth can be untwisted. Love trumps fear every time. So the ultimate question becomes: How do we win? We answer the question with a question. Where will my soul spend eternity?

If the Enemy wants my soul, then why would my spiritual army not step in to save my soul? If the Enemy can use our loved ones, familiar spirits against us, then why cannot God also use my love of my soul family, especially when I asked on my knees in the privacy of my bedroom that night after hearing the farmer story? I believe both heard my desperate prayer about Gina. It seems that my experiences came from the Light and the dark. The Enemy's objective is always to rule, and to do that, he needs us to not believe in God. The joy of God's loving relationship is real. The Enemy wants to steal the credit away from this joy. So when the Holy Spirit, Jesus, or the Angels comfort us, the Enemy steps in quickly to redirect, misguide the truth, and influence our thoughts. His power is camouflaged even within our minds. He will stop at nothing even to the extent of evil playing out in our lives. I finally figured it out. It is a spiritual battle.

"...Put on the whole armor of God, that you may be able to stand against the wiles of the devil. For we do not wrestle against flesh and blood, but against principalities, against powers, against the rulers of the darkness of this age, against spiritual hosts of wickedness in the heavenly places..."

— Ephesians 6:10-17

"Jesus was manifested that he might destroy the works of the devil."

— 1 John 3:8

Why was this even necessary?

There must be a reason we humans need this power and strength on our side. Jesus himself knows because he too was tempted three times by the Enemy, a very real force at work every moment of every day. And the real question to contemplate: What did the Enemy know that caused him to try so hard to influence Jesus? The Enemy recognized the weapon he was up against. Jesus was going to change his world.

And like Jesus said when he was preparing to face his physical death— human pain and suffering we cannot begin to fathom—"Get behind me Satan!" (Matthew 16:23), so I too will now say, "Get outta here. Get behind me. In Jesus' name, you, the Enemy, are not welcome in my life."

I still did not know all of this, not yet, but I would soon!

Even the Enemy had to succumb to God's Will.

After the first night in the hotel along the route, I awoke to a song message "I'll Follow You" by Shinedown. I had listened to this song once before. A friend, Sheila, had played it for me, sharing from her heart that that song happened to play every time she would walk out to her car from her husband's hospital bed, seeking a moment of peace. These lyrics personally meant the most of all of *Gina's playlist.* I had been in the eye of the storm and someone was always with me. I believe. I have assurance. And *the journey* has certainly been profound.

All fear left me. When my husband and I arrived at my son's home, I was at peace again. That first night, sleeping on my son's living room floor on a blow-up mattress, I experienced my greatest personal miracle.

I saw Jesus, as clear as I saw everything else all the months before. Vividly clear. His face, a side view, like a silhouetted, mosaic bust of small squares of chiseled rock, pieced together in a three-dimensional outline, like a beautiful piece of art, the face recognizable—it was how I had seen Jesus as a young child. I felt His strength. I felt His love.

And I wrote this in the middle of the night, again clearly remembering my experience just like the night the angel visited:

> March 6, 2017
>
> Dreamed I was being helped, but then a man's hard face, just his head, was in my mind—distinct and maybe even like made of rock-hard edges.
>
> He is the real one who is going to help me.
>
> Strong face like a statue bust. Jesus' face.

Months before I saw Jesus, I had been visiting my son for Thanksgiving, still recuperating from my 11/11 spider bite, sleeping on the same air mattress on the same floor, when I had received this message:

> November 23, 2016
>
> The Great I Am

I know now why I felt such intense fear in March 2017. Something did not want what happened next to happen. While visiting my son, I crossed paths with three women who helped me in my healing process. And, *it is a process*, another message written. These three women had very different beliefs from me, which was okay! Each provided pearls of wisdom that helped in my healing process.

Maureen, the first of the three, helped as I questioned how Gina's life and mine could have the same thread of evil woven into them—something that bothered me deeply as I struggled with *why?* It was not lost on me that the narrative of 1980 around my sister's encounter with a rapist was echoing in my own life. Maureen brought to my attention how generations of my family had experienced so much violence and hardships in their lives, especially the women. The violence insurmountable in Gina's last hours on earth. Even my own mother, so young when taken away to St. Albans. I later contemplated if that was somehow the connection and reason behind all of my premonitions about St. Albans? Was there some truth there still to be known? It is as if we are all three in some way connected, sharing similar life patterns, overlaying throughout time. It is like those little wooden Russian nesting dolls, Matryoshka, following a theme, a similar story told throughout by each nesting doll. Connected souls. This is why I felt that it was as if Gina were in the eye of the storm right there with me. Maybe God knew I needed her heart, her goodness, her strengths, to find my way.

Life is certainly perplexing.

The second lady, Julie, had had an experience similar to my 2016 journey and shared how hypnosis had helped her. She asked me as soon as I met her, "Do you know that you are a lightworker?" I had not heard the word lightworker before, but no matter the world's interpretation, I now know my truth from what happened next in my life. The coming June 2017 experience would be life changing. And I now can say with a heart full of love, if a lightworker's job is to spread God's Light, then I can do that! With our sister strengths—heart and head—Gina's goodness, and my Lord's strength, compassion, wisdom, mercy, and truth, and on and on, and on, I will. We all can, connecting one to each other like a web of goodness shining light throughout. Imagine a world where our random acts of kindness, just a little Light every day, would brighten our world, one person at a time.

Julie texted me later that night: "I received a message for you. One thousand years of peace. I do not know what this means, but for some reason, I believe it has something to do with the Bible."

A person asked me during this healing time if I had ever had a near-death experience, being curious about the source of my new experiences that came in 2016. I can honestly answer that I do not know. I would not rule it out. I do believe if someone survives to tell a story about a near-death experience, they will remain steadfast in a God-centered focus, reverent in His Word, and not become a story with a self-centered philosophy. That in itself could be indicative of the source from which the experience truly originated.

The third amazing lady, Jolina, taught me to ask the hardest question: How did this rape, this heinous act, serve me? She taught me how to love myself. Together, we recreated my own story the way I wanted it to be. Life happens for you, not to you. And later, I expanded: *How did it serve God? How did it serve me, the bad becoming good?* There are threads of goodness to be found somewhere in everything. It is hard, but it can be done.

In the next weeks, I continued a process to completely heal. I spent hours in quiet, prayerful moments walking through the snowy woods. I listened to God. I felt my sister's heart. I felt my daddy's love-energy hugs that my boys so loved. I felt my husband's strength. I looked into the eyes of my sons, knowing pure love. Life is amazing. My dot is my dot.

Is it incomprehensible that God has an army of angels here every day helping us fight these battles? It is a really big job for our angels. Even Jesus wept while living here in this earthly realm. He knows our battles. He lived them too. And He did not leave us here alone. Jesus told the Father, they (us) are going to need a helper—The Holy Spirit. He knew we would need it!

> *"I will ask the Father to give you another Helper, to be with you always. He is the Spirit of truth whom the world cannot receive, because it neither sees him nor recognizes him. But you recognize him, because he lives with you and will be in you."*
>
> — John 14:16-17, ISV

The Spirit of truth lives in all of us; it is always at work, everywhere, spreading love, shining light on the dark realities of the Enemy. I believe Jesus and God's angels communicate within our consciousness—our soul where we know the Spirit of Truth.

I do still wonder, *Are my loved ones watching us from the grandstands of Heaven, like angels? Did my soul family somehow know the full extent of my trauma when I did not yet know myself? I know my soul did.*

Nola had once told me that Gina was in the third heaven. I had never heard of this, but my eyes landed on it on a page in the Bible. Paul had written to the Corinthians that *"I know a man in Christ who fourteen years ago (whether in the body I cannot tell; or out of the body, I cannot tell) was caught up to the third heaven"* (2 Corinthians 12:2).

Surprised, I thought, *Really—Heaven is numbered like different places within a spiritual realm? And what exactly did Paul see?*

Could our souls be like that same concentrated ball of energy captured in the video from the Epperly basement, or like the same concentrated light Energy captured in the muck place photo when the angels lit up the water to send us a beautiful message? Not the exact same, just similar. Angels are angels. Jesus said when we die we will be *like angels of God in Heaven*. What part of us becomes *like* an angel? Not our physical body because it returns to dust. Is our soul a spark of light energy deep inside all of us, created the moment life is conceived? God's all powerful breath from the very beginning—*is that our soul*? That spark that ignites inside when it is in the presence of good. That Spirit that I can feel move inside of me—Life.

"Jesus answered them and said to them, "You are mistaken not knowing the scriptures nor the power of God. For in the resurrection, they neither marry nor are given in marriage, but are like angels of God in heaven."

— Matthew 22:29-30

I reveled in the story in 2015 of Baby Lilly. This is a story to remember always, not to be forgotten and put on the back shelves of our minds. This tiny baby hanging upside down for fourteen hours in a wrecked car, partially submerged in a river in Spanish Fork, Utah. This fact alone defies the rules of the human body. Icy, cold water flowed through the car windows directly underneath her head. I believe the angels helped save the baby. A clear voice was heard by a rescue worker—the voice of an angel, a part of God's army. Can we really rule out that it could have been her own mother's spirit keeping her warm as her soul left her dead body? Maybe it took an army of angels or maybe only one to make the day end as it did. Baby Lilly was saved. This is a miracle, not a coincidence. How did it happen? Simple—it's God!

Jesus said that in resurrection we will be *like* angels. When exactly does resurrection happen? So many interpretations. Does it really matter? Immediately or later? I do believe our soul, that inner spark of life energy from God's breath, once created, will live forever. Where it will live is another chapter.

Our angels always know God's will....

"Take heed that you do not despise one of these little ones,

for I say to you that in Heaven their angels always see the
face of My father who is in heaven."

— Matthew 18:10, NKJV

God's angels were there with me every step of the way. They are here to help us. To guide us. To protect us. To direct us. They do not hurt us or play games with us, or lie to us. That would be the Enemy and his fallen angels.

"But to which of the angels has He ever said:
'Sit at my right hand, till I make Your enemies your footstool?'"
And of God's angels:
"Are they not all ministering spirits sent forth to minister
for those who will inherit salvation?"

—Hebrews 1:13-14 NKJV

That's us. Our angels are hard at work every day. And my angels were very busy. Both angelic and demonic forces are always busy at work in our lives. The battles are just that—*life*. We simply just need to do the best we can. Embrace the good and live *life*.

God wants us to have joy, happiness, forgiveness, and love. And yes, so, too, could the Enemy disguise himself in this way. But do we think God sits back and lets his angels prop their feet up and not get to work helping us fight against this power? I believe this spiritual army intervenes in our lives. Sometimes we just do not listen. And that was what was happening in my life. Some of my messages, especially the ones in June, were given so I could awaken. My heart tells me it was Gina's friend Jesus and the angels in orchestration with a plan larger than I can ever fully comprehend within my own head who helped me. God's plan.

Awakening means to me—*alive, not dead*. It is not to be interpreted literally like being physically dead, but knowing that we can be and will be alive spiritually forever:

"But concerning the resurrection of the dead, have you not read what was
spoken to you by God, saying I am the God of Abraham, the God of Isaac,
and the God of Jacob? God is not the God of the dead, but of the living."

— Matthew 22:31-32

In Jesus' day, the patriarchs Abraham, Isaac, and Jacob had already died a human, physical death. But Jesus tells us that God is the God of these men in a present tense. They are not dead. They live. God is an eternal God.

Jesus said:

> *"Most assuredly I say to you, if anyone keeps*
> *My word he shall never see death."*

— Matthew 8:51

All of those years when I peacefully thought of Gina as being like an angel in heaven, I did not really understand that Gina "lives" and that God is still her God in a present, loving relationship. And so, if I can ask God for help, then, so too can't Gina or Daddy or any souls "living" in a wondrous eternal relationship with God?

For much of 2016, I had believed I was looking to bring my sister to a place of peace. But now I wondered, *Was she helping to bring me to peace?* God knew the way to my heart was my sister. I was being saved. My spiritual army already knew the flashbacks would come with no room left in my heart to bury anything else, so I had to come from unconsciousness to consciousness to gain the peace that passes all understanding—a peace that only comes from one place. I experienced everything I was to experience during *the journey*—trusting and believing, unconditional love, and God's miracles—so that I would have the faith that would not waver in my darkest moment. My faith was a tiny mustard seed. It had always been present, but now it was blossoming from deep within, just when I needed it most.

We cannot know exactly how the spirit world really works. *No human can.* We do not have the answers to all of our questions. Jesus wanted us to know so much. The last verse of the Gospel of John tells us there is even more to know:

> *"And there also are many other things that Jesus did, which if they*
> *were written one by one, I suppose that even the world itself could*
> *not contain the books that would be written. Amen."*

— John 21:25

My friend Annie gave me a book about women reconnecting to their purposes. In its beginning pages, it references life being "circular not linear"—the same words I wrote in an earlier message. A soul can live an eternal life; life is not just a dot on a linear line; it is not just a dot on a circular line. It is a beginning dot with no end.

Annie's gift prompted me to go back again and see all the beginning messages differently. Now, I understand the angel's visit and that beautiful finger pointing to the top of the notebook—*Look back at the important messages in June.* In the beginning, the angelic messages were telling me what I needed to be told—an answer to prayer—but I did not realize it then because of my own narrow-focused mind. For months, I had been looking for something circular, not understanding that the message was pointing me to eternity, everlasting life, and not literally a circle. Wherever I saw manhole covers, circles of differently shaded grass (the Dedmon soccer field), or ponds, my narrow focus was on finding the circle that marked where I could find Gina. I wasn't seeing the eternal, where she could be found.

> *"Most assuredly. I say to you, he who hears My word and believes in Him who sent Me has everlasting life, and shall not come into judgement, but has passed from death into life."*
>
> *— John 5:24, NKJV*

Remember that gigantic ornament I made with Gina for our church Christmas tree when we were teens? The Christmas tree was always front and center in the sanctuary, adorned with all the beautiful ornaments we had made. For years, I would see my eternity ornament and feel proud I had made the largest one on the tree—completely missing its lesson, of course. That was pride I was feeling then, but its true meaning was the opposite of pride—humility. I wondered, *Was that tree still poised in its same place that solemn 1980 December day after Christmas—that very sad day when we reflected on Gina's life?* They called her memorial service a celebration. Had I understood the meaning of eternity then, I would still be sad, but I might have celebrated, understanding about the circular instead of feeling overwhelmed by grief because I had a linear mindset that could only see a beginning and an end—the dash between birth and death—the straight line, like it is the only thing that matters, instead of realizing once life's dot begins, it is a forever circle. And the dot of our life does still matter. We are born to live an amazingly wonderful life, but that does not always happen easily in this world. But there is a Way to make life as amazing as it can be!

One can always choose to see the good—the light—The Spirit of Life. Even in an unconscious sleep state, the spiritual army is at work:

I saw an angel

I am positive had I seen an angel, like in September 2016, I would have remembered it! But then again, I did not remember most of the writings of the messages when they were being written. That message was on October 21, 2016. Maybe it was just reminding me never to forget what had really happened the first week of September!

On November 27, while out west visiting my son, this picture was taken. Probably not what the message meant, but fun thinking so!

LIKE ANGELS IN THE GRANDSTANDS OF HEAVEN...

CHAPTER 22

IS SOMEBODY OUT THERE, ANYBODY TO LOVE?

Yes—there always is!

Soul families' lives are interwoven, connected not only by our memories, but by a love that comes from deep within the heart of our soul—connected in timeless eternity.

By this time, I had experienced just about everything I could have ever imagined. My only solace was there must be a reason I did not yet see. And, I was ready to try anything, even hypnosis, to see if I could reach into the recesses of my mind. Could a hypnotist bring forth from my own unconscious memory or consciousness—from the heart of my own soul—details about 2014, like the identity of the others? Also, I wanted to know if some tiny detail from 1980, forgotten in time, might confirm my 2016 end-of-the-year theories about Gina's murder?

The experience would be far from what I expected.

When I arrived at the hypnotist's home, I realized her nature was loving and empathetic. Patti wanted to help me have closure. I quickly believed I was there for a reason. Today, I know God had a plan for my life. It's a divine mystery. There can never be a simple, logical human answer for the unexplainable. Many try with many theories. Some minds are willing to open to the possibilities of the power of God working in people's lives, but others are unwilling, and many are only regurgitating what they have been taught. We always try to give everything a logical, human meaning. Doing so can be like trying to fit a square peg in a round hole—using human logic, the meaning never to be fully understood. It is the mystery of our lives. Sometimes there is no answer—a *round peg in the round hole,* but we still try.

While under hypnosis, I clearly saw images of what seemed to be past lives, images so vivid that they were like a movie. I described each scene, the recording capturing the surreality of it all. First, I saw a girl in a blue-and-white gingham dress playing with a little boy in a field of tall grass, the wind swaying the shafts back and forth as the girl looked up at a beautiful sky. I would also later see my feet, now as a man, standing barefoot in a river on the smooth, multi-colored rocks, fishing. I was fishing with my son. Fast forward, and I was the same man wearing different clothes, church clothes, looking up the hill at a white steepled clapboard church, not wanting to go in. I felt an intense sadness. I was going to a funeral. A small boy was lying inside. Then I flashed to a past moment when I was holding this same small boy, and further back, we were all sitting at a dinner table—the girl in the gingham dress, the little boy's sister, the father at the head of the table—everyone laughing and enjoying the meal. Later, I held the son in my arms as he died. I would hear Patti ask me, "Why show this life? What is the lesson she is to learn? Has she got it?"

In a different scene, I was a proper, young girl, standing on a train platform dressed to perfection. I wore a hoop dress, tight at my waist, with shoes that laced up to my ankles, and I held a parasol. As the train approached, I saw people leaning out the windows. One young man caught my eye. He seemed so happy, smiling, wind blowing his hair. His eyes connected with mine, and as the train stopped, he exited quickly past me. His clothing indicated poverty, the pants and shirt the same brown, wool-like fabric, perhaps a uniform. He smiled as he passed, and it was as though I wanted to go with him on his adventures rather than live as I was, a young lady waiting for her father to exit the train. The way my father dressed signified wealth. I was suddenly not happy to be who I was. I wanted to go with the young man, but I knew I could not.

Of all the scenes that seemed to unfold during this process, these two aroused the most curiosity. My scientific mind does not easily accept views without questioning. My Christian heart seeks truth. My experiences = my perceptions = my beliefs! So as a Christian, I was troubled with being told these were past lives, and from my human, scientific, validating mind,

I was challenged to understand what I had just experienced that seemed so easily to validate the theory of reincarnation. I wanted the round peg in the round hole. So I kept thinking, *What was it that I could see so clearly if it was not a prior life? When exactly does the Spirit knit together with our physical bodies to create a soul, thus in that very moment completing this amazing miracle of life?*

Why does it really matter that we know exactly how or why? I only know for sure what I actually experienced, and maybe I experienced all that I did in *the journey* so I could know that I do not have to know the answers to the truth of everything.

But I still asked, "How did this happen?" And I can still contemplate the possibilities. So what was the truth behind what I actually experienced? I saw the images. They were real. This process is clearly subject to human interpretation as to the how or why.

We have conception—a scientific basis for reproduction. *For life.* I do not easily accept that we just get recycled. Yet I saw something as clear as can be, as though it were me, but in a different life. I believe in eternal life, but not recycled here on earth trying to learn a lesson not learned in some prior life or this life. What would the lesson be for the soul of a baby who died before birth? Or, an aborted baby? What would that lesson be? I do not believe Gina dying as she did was part of God's plan. Gina did not choose this path for her life because she had some lesson to learn, predetermined before getting here like a deal made between her soul and Epperly's soul. What would that lesson be? Forgiveness? Do we think she had time to forgive? She did not need to learn that lesson. Her life exuded forgiveness and goodness to so many. Gina's death was the result of an evil monster that crossed my sister's path, created by an Enemy living here in this world. We do learn lessons *here* while living life, and they often are not always by choice. Gina's untimely death taught us many lessons, unfortunately, but I cannot accept that her rape and murder were a lesson for her own soul as if God were part of that plan. Not my God. But that is what the Enemy wants us to think because then we would believe there is no definitive end to life on earth. And if he gets us to believe that we just keep getting recycled with no definitive end to life on earth, then the Enemy kicks his heels up because there would be no reason for us to then question, as we live this life, how to have eternal, everlasting life. A twist on truth. He is grinning from ear to ear.

Many religious-minded people might interpret this hypnotic experience as having been controlled by only a dark, evil force because it does not fit within the boundaries of our normal, limited human interpretations. That simply shows me a lack of true faith in the power of God. Often, beliefs form from what has been taught to us by others, not experienced. What would Nola's childhood have been like had he not self-interpreted his own experience—when he believed he heard the voice of God? I am glad Nola chose a God-centered mindset. What if others had told him, especially as a child, that it was not possible, or worse, that it's a familiar spirit, demons, the devil, and not God? Who are we to know the why or the how and judge him from a one-sided perception? Judgment seems to come into play too often when it is not our place or religion's place to judge. Jesus faced his judging foes whose limited thinking could not see the truth. Their one-sided thinking stemmed from beliefs based on human interpretations when they said to Jesus, *"Do we not say rightly that You are a Samaritan and have a demon?" Jesus answered, "I do not have a demon..."* (Mark 8:48-49). A question to evaluate: How many different interpretations would I have been given had I sought answers to what I was experiencing?

Our experiences are the foundation of everything—they affect how we live, think, pray, interpret, and make decisions—everything. And it is the same with everyone. Change your experiences—change your beliefs. I do not know how what I experienced happened, but I am at least willing to consider all possibilities—not just one side.

So I considered a possibility that the source from this hypnotic experience could be my own consciousness—my soul communicating with me. What I experienced under hypnosis, what I saw unfold as if I were watching a movie with me as its main character, might have to do with genetic memory ever-present in my own soul's consciousness. Why? These very clear visions align with my ancestors' true life stories. My grandfather had lost a child, a son from a brain tumor. I can only imagine the scene of him holding his dying son in his arms. The church looked like it could be in Appalachia America. The gingham dress could be from that era. And I will always remember the story my grandmother shared with me when I was a little girl. She told me she had met her husband-to-be on a train platform. He was heading off to World War I, dressed in an Army uniform. She said when she saw him, "He looked so handsome!" His father—my great-grandfather—was sheriff. Being a sheriff in those days meant dispensing justice by hanging the guilty ones. This would be a heavy burden to carry, maybe altering something deep inside one's consciousness—inside the soul. Was I experiencing my ancestors' memories? There is really no human means to fully understand how consciousness—the soul—really operates. Therefore, many simply conclude there is no soul. My ancestors' experiences were becoming relevant in my life and it seemed my own inner soul knew of these experiences. Could this be—soul families, connected forever?

Could we inherit from our ancestors not just our physical attributes, but also attributes within our consciousness? Genetic memory inherited from my ancestors. This is where the tsunami dream I had repeatedly as a young child, having never seen the ocean, can also make sense. Reincarnation or genetic memory? My belief, my own interpretation, is that we are connected to the genetic imprint from our soul families' tapestries of life, those associated with our genetic DNA, generation to generation. That makes the most sense to me. And these soul families' life lessons become our lessons. Let's consider: 4 grandparents, 8 great-grandparents, 16 great-great grandparents, 32, 64, 128....memories imprinted into our genetic imprint. And to take this thought deeper: If we remove just one of these ancestors from the equation, then I, my soul, the me that is created at conception, never would have existed. Our consciousness, our soul is created at conception just like all of our attributes. Life is created and it's so much more than just a physical body.

Jesus said the greatest commandment is, "You shall love the Lord your God with all of your heart, with all of your soul, and with all of your mind." He would not have named three separate parts if there were not three separate parts we need to be aware of. Heart is not to be ignored. It is the connector. The eyes of our soul. The Soul is our eternal self. It is the "you" that is created that will never cease to exist. And the mind is the hardest to love God with because it is the physical part of us—a playground for the Enemy. But it is also an amazing, beautiful part of us that we cannot be afraid to open to the extraordinary possibilities of our world.

Aside from the alignment to my ancestor's true life stories, this is also why I considered genetic memory:

The alignment of the Bible to science for the theory of genetic memory comes from this verse about third and fourth generations. In my Bible when a word is italicized, it indicates words that are not found in the original languages, but are needed for clarity in English. *Hmm.* So a human mind had to pick a word, *the guilty,* that came closest to the original word that only the scholars might know. *"The Lord is longsuffering [slow to anger (ESV)] and abundant in mercy and transgression but He by no means clears the guilty, visiting the iniquity of the fathers on the children, to the third and the fourth generation"* (Numbers 14:18, NKJV).

I do not believe as some that this verse means we will pay for our ancestors' deeds as if God will be wrathful toward us because of our father or grandfathers' sins. Something got lost in the literal translation if we only interpret its meaning as because my great-grandfather hung people or my grandfather killed people in a war, God intentionally punished me and Gina by bringing bad into our lives—to pay for their sins, subject to interpretation of what sin really is. Playing the guilt card creates fear. I want to try to think and feel on my own—not what someone else tells me to think and feel. I believe this verse could be a clue as to how non-physical attributes genetically come into our lives. The past ancestral challenges, the tapestry of the lives of our connected soul families, genetically become part of who we are—inherited deep within. So yes, it will affect us, not because of God's wrath but maybe because it is the reality of how we are genetically designed. God may also be telling us in that verse what we need to know so we can spiritually heal those emotional traumas from within.

My eldest son has a PhD in neuroscience from Johns Hopkins and a medical degree from Mt. Sinai and my youngest son, a chemistry degree with a biochemistry focus from the University of Virginia. Both sons would have studied the basics of genetics in their pursuits! I would bet their eyes will roll and their jaws drop when they read what their mother has written. I understand. I would have too a few years ago. *Figure it out* has always been my motto, and maybe one day someone will. But for now, I can contemplate and theorize just for fun and, of course, my own edification!

Recent studies propose that fear can be passed from generation to generation through genetic memory. If God did not give us fear, but fear can be inherited, then why not also consider our ancestors' emotional trauma or challenges? Also their lives' lessons? Maybe that aspect of our inheritance is not in the physical aspects of DNA, but in the genetic inherited memory, the *"DNA"* of our consciousness—our soul when it is created. The genetics of individual souls, consciousness, influenced by these many evolving factors as time passes just as our physical attributes can evolve and change. And why not then consider that consciousness—a soul—could be forever connected to another because consciousness—our soul—does not die? After you read just a few more pages, you will understand why I puzzled over this!

Or we could just take the easy route of non-thinking and regurgitate that the devil made me do it. My experience being unexplainable, let's blame it on the Enemy.

We are always learning and growing, so why would our own soul—our consciousness—not assist? And an even better question—why would God not assist? If our thoughts can be affected by the Enemy, then so too can they be influenced by God and his spiritual army.

I listened to the recording of my first session with Patti. In it, I answered her in third person. Here are some excerpts:

Hypnotist: What is the highest use of the gathered information about Gina?

Dlana: *To end it. The information will end it.*

Hypnotist: She already has the answers where Gina is?

Dlana: *"I've been there. I've touched this place before."* (Was this a line from a song the summer before, coming from my subconscious or the answer?)

Hypnotist: I would like to request strength for Dlana to forgive all of the men in her life.

Dlana: *She had to learn.*

Hypnotist: Learn what?

Dlana: *Strength. So she has it in her.*

Hypnotist: Please enhance God's strength within her, truly helping her to forgive—wholeheartedly.

Dlana: *When we forgive we are not doing it for others. We are doing it for ourselves.*

At the end of my long session, I did something that shocked Patti. While still under hypnosis, with my body shaking, I yelled, "*Mother Earth wants those bodies out of the ground!*"

"Why did you say that?" she asked when my session had ended. "We have to explore why you are referencing Mother Earth."

Her curiosity heightened, she wanted me to come back the following day. She explained that she had inadvertently discovered that she could use a surrogate. One day she used a mother as a surrogate for the son, and it worked. So since then, on a few rare occasions, when her subject was hard-headed like me, she used a surrogate to hypnotize and ask questions regarding that subject's life. Leave it to me to be complicated. I agreed to return, arriving back early the next Sunday morning. Shortly after me, an everyday soccer mom showed up to be a surrogate in my place. The process is not like that of the entertainment hypnotists. The routine was the same as I had experienced the morning before, the actual act of hypnosis not even recognizable right in front of my eyes. The surrogate, already in a hypnotic state, followed the same instructions as I had heard the morning before—to go to the bathroom and then come back and lie down.

In this second recorded session, I sat in a chair in a small, darkened room, and watched and listened as the same movie-like vivid pictures were being described as Patti guided the hypnotized surrogate through the scenes of what was assumed to be my past lives, just as I had done the day before.

In a nutshell, Patti asked questions about my life to the hypnotized surrogate as though she were me. The underlying messages I heard roused my curiosity:

Hypnotist: What was the purpose of showing Dlana this life?

Surrogate: *God doesn't make mistakes. If God doesn't judge them, then why should they judge themselves? Just trust that you are made perfect.*

Hypnotist: Feel the good in myself—not judge myself?

Surrogate: *The exercise would be to look in the mirror, not see the physical body, not see what the ego says is not pleasant, but to look and see that what is looking back is what God created in love, full of love.*

When I heard this, I questioned silently, *God doesn't judge?* Later, as I listened to my recordings, I went to where I could find the answer...

"For the Father judges no one, but has committed all judgment to the Son."

— John 5: 22 NKJV

Those are Jesus' words about His Father. And here are Jesus' words about Himself:

"And if anyone hears My words and does not believe, I do not judge him; for I did not come to judge the world but to save the world."

— John 12:46-48, NKJV

I did not expect to find those answers about judging. We live in an environment where often we come to believe we are judged for everything we do.

But I also know of the great white throne. There will be an ending judgment when the Book of Life will be opened, so maybe while we are in the dot of our lives here, we are not being judged—yet. We make choices, changing our paths and directions every day. This is free will. This is life.

What *exactly* is the ego? Synonyms for ego have to do with the self—self-esteem, self-worth, self-respect, self.... Self thoughts. The detriment comes from self-judgment, and influenced self-judgment that results in a self-inflicted weight of shame, blame, and guilt that we can never seem to free ourselves from. So while living this life, maybe we are to try to stop the act of judgment of self and others just like the Bible tells us, *"Judge not, that you be not judged"* (Matthew 7:1).

I get it! The moment your head intentionally tears down (judges) yourself or someone else, stop it. The moment your head thinks an intentionally, unjustified negative thought toward yourself or someone, just stop it. Pay attention to thoughts—all thoughts that seem not to be good for you. The moment you catch yourself feeling less exuberant, take time to praise God and see his canvas. Change begins with self and will spread, like light in the darkness.

As I witnessed the hypnotized surrogate provide answers about myself and individual family members that were right on par with my life, and even details from my initial conversations with Nola the night we crossed paths, I became more perplexed than ever. There is no way these two people, the surrogate stranger or Patti the hypnotist, knew these answers and their specific relevance to my life.

Just like what I heard next—my sister's last words about living from my heart, not my head. I just about fell out of my seat. It seemed my own soul was communicating with me. And if not me, someone or something that knew me. Maybe what I had needed all along was a means to listen better. I needed to turn off my head just long enough so I could listen with my heart. The heart of my soul where the Spirit of Truth dwells, which Jesus said I would recognize because he lives with you and will be in you.

Hypnotist: Dlana needs closure. Will she have it?

Surrogate: *It's not a closure; it's a beginning. To live from the heart, not from the head.*

Hypnotist: Has she been able to do that?

Surrogate: *She's getting in her own way.*

Hypnotist: What can we do to help her?

Surrogate: *Trust her own soul. Only understanding required is to just be. Not interfering with being by thinking.*

Hypnotist: What is her lesson in this life?

Surrogate: *Ultimate lesson in all life is self-love and expressing that love to others so that they can be lifted up. So they can love themselves.*

Hypnotist: Love herself? Self-love—the most important?

Surrogate: *There should be tears of joy because of such freedom.*

Hypnotist: No one can restrict you—only yourself?

Surrogate: *Love is Heaven on earth. To know and to love yourself.*

I contemplated, *Can a soul communicate?* Not like ghosts, séances, spirit boxes, etc. A different way. A way we cannot yet understand. And, then, if so, *Can my consciousness be forever connected to my sister's consciousness?* And a step further, if all this could happen, then *Can a soul's consciousness be connected one with another* like the visible web of life energy found in nature? Living human souls, touching and influencing one another through the tiniest life connections—love being the best conduit, lifting each other.

A reminder of a favorite hymn from my youth: "Love Lifted Me."

Hypnotist: What about her dad, John?

Surrogate: A lesson of love recognizing that he has done his best.

I had learned this exact lesson six months earlier. It is apparent *the journey* was multilayered in its purposes. My soul had known I learned this lesson.

Hypnotist: What about her sister Gina?

Surrogate: To teach her to stop fighting life and just live and enjoy and embrace life. Embrace what you have been given...love every day she is given.

Hypnotist: How is she doing?

Surrogate: She is cracking the shell trying to break through. Trying to break free. Just about there.

There were just no words for what I was witnessing.

I had given Patti some questions I was curious about after my first day, like the next question I kept asking throughout *the journey*. A question about a man neither of them could have known anything about.

Hypnotist: What was *Nola's [his name]* purpose in her life?

Surrogate: *Glimpses of her true worth. He appreciates her more than she appreciates herself. Help her get more in touch with her heart to claim **self-worth**.*

Hypnotist: Is she successful?

Surrogate: *She's getting it!*

Hypnotist: Tomorrow is her birthday. What is her gift?

Surrogate: *To be reborn as the soul she can be....*

Hypnotist: What is her life purpose?

Surrogate: *To learn love and lift others in love.*

Hypnotist: How's Gina doing?

Surrogate: *Surrounded by love and trying to get that message to her sister. She should feel it all the way down to her toes!*

Patti did not understand this saying, and asked "Down to her toes?" but I knew right away. It was what Gina and I always said to one another when we were little girls, scratching each other's backs as we snuggled and fell asleep.

Hypnotist: Yesterday, she felt something sad. A connection to Mother Earth. Was it about what happened to Gina and others? (Patti's question was general. The surrogate's answer—detailed as if she knew my body had shaken the day before.)

Surrogate: *It was actually shaking off the sadness—throwing off the sadness and giving her love.*

Hypnotist: She saw twelve doves and someone told her one thousand years of peace. What did this mean?

Surrogate: *Exactly what it is: Peace.*

Hypnotist: Does she need to find peace?

Surrogate: *No. She is at peace.*

A blessing, not a meaning. It's a blessing to be at peace.

Hypnotist: Her ultimate message?

Surrogate: *Wake up. Being born again. This time it will be tears of happiness, not tears of fear. And to learn love and lift others in love.*

Hypnotist: Her birthday will be really joyous—Final message?

Surrogate: *Love you as we love you. This will be the gift.*

Hypnotist: To her and the world?

Surrogate: *God is Love.*

Is this how my many somehow communicated messages came about—through a soul's connection to a Spiritual Realm? So the question could become the answer.

Here are some of the notes I made as I listened.

Breathe. I need more oxygen. Move.

A beginning—Heart not head.

Forgive yourself. Forgive others. Set yourself free. To know thyself. To love thyself. To love others. *Love me as they love me.*

Let go! All of your life is stepping stones to now.

Jesus wants us to know unconditional love. It is a gift.

Success is when you know who you are. What you are. And how you serve.

We are what we believe. Just be. See the light. See God's power.

Be grateful every day and just live life knowing God's got this.

And He just does not give love—God is Love.

I pondered reverently, *Does any of what I was told contradict God's Word?* I had just witnessed a hypnotized stranger give answers specific to the details of my life.

I shared only a very small portion of the recordings. It was hard to get my own head around the possibilities of what I had experienced and witnessed. What felt absolutely assured to me after my first day was that I had just experienced communication from some part of me that is connected to a place that seems to want the best for me—from within myself—my own consciousness—the part of me where Jesus said the Spirit of Truth would live. Maybe that is the heart of my soul. It was as though I was talking to myself—a deeper part of me that knows what I need to know. A place that cannot be influenced by thoughts, or controlled because while under hypnosis, my voice from within can be heard. These answers were interpreted by me to be from a good place, my own soul. A soul connected to God's love. And how my experience on the second day with a surrogate happened I do not fully understand.

If this was deception from a dark place, then we, humanity, are all totally up the creek without a paddle. We have absolutely no control within the boundaries of our mind's consciousness. The power of this experience was unsettling. It challenged everything I thought I ever knew. I was to experience it so I could learn just like everything else during *the journey*. I watched this process—this woman was under hypnosis. The logical human interpretation is to assume these two people were deceiving me—they had no reason to! But there is always a power at work that could deceive. And I believe that power works in the mind's interpretations. I strongly believe exactly what I was told in a message, "The mind is the Enemy's playground." That message has so many meanings, ranging from the simplest example of just letting your everyday thoughts affect you, to the hypnotist's beliefs coming through in her responses, to this example of thoughts seemingly from my own mind being spoken to me through another. This was a very verbal process. I cannot condone doing it. God's protection is essential. It was impossible to know beyond a doubt that the answers came from my self—my own soul. The only way I could begin to discern my own personal experience was to ask: Did these answers serve God, or did they try to steer me away from God to a self-serving mindset? I now ask this about every new thought and theory that comes my way and I still might not get it right. What seemed to be a means to connect to my own soul changed my life, but only because I interpreted the answers' relevance to my life always with God in my heart. What was the end result? I forgave everyone.

The proof for me was validated by the healing. I believed God always knew that forgiveness was what was needed most in my life. I saw it all as part of a plan. I experienced the muck places of my life being drained forever like a floodgate had been opened from within my heart. This experience that freed my heart from the Enemy's clutches came on my birthday, one year to the day when I had sat in Africa, reminding myself of God's awesome power, and asking for His healing—the best gift I could have received. I felt God's love rush through me like a river flowing in goodness, cleansing my heart forever. Maybe because the faith of a mustard seed was already within me and God was at work in my life. And most definitely, if God wanted to make sure I had the answers I needed to hear, then that would be what would happen.

The answer I heard was: "When we forgive, we are not doing it for others. We are doing it for ourselves." It was the same message a stranger, Nola, had given me: "You need to love yourself. You need to heal your heart...You need to forgive." I was finally getting it! God only wants what is best for me because I am loved. And to forgive others is to love others, which is also loving myself when I forgive—just as Jesus loved me. His greatest commandment:

"This is my commandment, that you love one another as I have loved you."

— John 15:12, NKJV

And His power:

> *"I have come as a Light into the world, that whoever*
> *believes in me shall not abide in darkness."*

— John 12:46, NKJV

That is what this message from a few weeks earlier had meant. Jesus was the real one who was going to help me. And he did—promise kept.

Nothing is impossible with God.

On the drive back home that day, I felt an exuberant energy, as though the Holy Spirit was flowing within me. That was not the intended purpose of my visit, but it was the end result. I did not think so much right then about what I had witnessed or the entire experience. It was too much to absorb. I just know how my life changed in that very moment, and how all of the experiences that led to that moment were part of God's well-orchestrated plan, as I would come to know in just a few more months. As my music played, the same song kept repeating itself, as if my ever-present Angels wanted to celebrate and sing with me. The song was *"Let It Go."* I sang at the top of my lungs. No more fear. No more control. Bring it on. Forgiveness is a mountain of a battle to be climbed. I let go and I let God flatten that mountain. But I had to help him. I had to take action myself to forgive.

I reread Epperly's letter in the bottle. I was flooded with a deep sadness for him. I know now why I felt that Gina wanted me to forgive him. I forgave him. Not for him, for me. I now understood that it is okay to be angry unless that anger leads to hate and unforgiveness. In my mind, I put the letter back into a bottle, sealed it, and threw it back into the river. I let the river carry the unforgiveness and the hate away. I trusted in God's righteousness. His justice. The ultimate win: true forgiveness. I forgave my sister's murderer in March 2017. *The Miraculous Journey* showed me how. Stephen Epperly no longer steals my joy—my good memories of my sister. And I learned to stop allowing Epperly's dot to affect my dot—my own individual path to peace. I stopped the intense narrow focus of wanting to find Gina's body. What helped was simply knowing: This life is just a dot on a circular eternal life. I still wanted truth, but I finally realized the truth was there all along, and I was just missing the true messages. I now know that Gina's final resting place is not what really matters. May Epperly find it in his heart one day to tell us where his victims' final resting places might be, not for us, but for himself. More fractured souls need peace. Epperly may choose to speak the truth—what he, of course, would allude to as being truth—but until then, the many leads will be followed that keep coming our way, even as these words are being written. Maybe if Epperly reads *The Miraculous Journey*, he will hear my sister's voice, his mother's voice. God's message. The story rewritten in truth, the many facts of what we now know aligning to his and others' secrets. He will then know that he holds no secrets. He has no power over us any longer. I have a feeling so much more will come to light. And we will know what we are to know. I choose God. I hope one day Epperly will too. That would be his mother's wish. May light always shine over the dark.

My spiritual army, maybe even my soul family, was cheering in the grandstands. My faith was now stronger than ever, my strength coming from a true source of power—pure unconditional love. Whichever thoughts get fed are the ones that win the battles within our minds. I know I am loved beyond measure for this divine power to care so much about my soul as to walk this path with me. That is a powerful thought. And, I still had more paths to walk. It was part of the plan.

I believed, I came to interpret, that the experiences of *the journey* were from my loved ones and my angels guiding me to justice for Gina and helping me to find her body and others. My thoughts progressed to the belief that Gina's soul was in some in-between world where she could not get to the Light, validated when I experienced the very dark world inside of St. Albans. I did pause and ask myself, *Really Dlana? Why would someone who loves you play games with you...? If they can do all of this, then why not just tell you Gina is under the Allen building, or in the landfill under the parking lot, or in a vertical grave up above the muck cliffs, or in the crevices in the rock walls above the quarry, or, or...?* My question had always been: Why would Gina need to tell us where she is hidden? It is just a body. She is in heaven. Nola said it was because I wanted it. Not really. At first, I wanted truth. I wanted justice. And I do still believe someone somewhere wanted truth known.

The discovered facts in Gina's case seem to align with the spiritual messages. And not just mine.

In the preacher's 2013 message given to Andy was an intriguing layer: *Gina wanted us to tell someone named Kim it was not her fault.* Kim Jett told me in 2019 that not a week went by in her entire life that she did not wonder what Gina would be doing had she just walked her out of the Marriott. What a heavy burden to live with. Knowing Gina's heart, she really would want Kim to know it was not her fault. A truth that none of us could have been aware of, so from where did that message come? Is it just how the angels operate—part of a big orchestrated plan to help all involved? Did Kim need to share all she knew with Gina's family before she died? Can an eternal soul when it is in that eternal spiritual realm somehow know the burdens of those souls once connected by a crossing of paths in this dimension's life? It all seems so interconnected. How can we ever know? I still wanted to know if a soul, my sister, could communicate with me. I kept searching. I wanted to find what Jesus said while He was here—His words—in red. I landed on two different stories that Jesus told about two different men, both called Lazarus.

In Luke 16:19-31, Jesus told about the rich man and Lazarus. One verse stood out:

> And besides all this, between us (Heaven) and you (Hades), there is a great gulf fixed, so that those who want to pass from here to you cannot, nor can those from there pass to us.

It felt like I was making progress. Here it told me that there was no going between heaven and hell. But what about the in-between—earth? Jesus was saying that the rich man knew Lazarus was in the bosom of Abraham as though he could see heaven from where he was—Hades. And it seemed there was a memory, an ability to still care about the loved ones he had left behind when the rich man was asking Abraham to let Lazarus, the poor man, go warn the rich man's brothers still alive on earth so they would know what they needed to know before they died and joined him in the same terrible place—Hades. They needed help. The rich man thought if his family could just see someone come back from the dead to testify, they would listen. Abraham replied that if they did not hear what was already available to hear, they would not be persuaded *even if one rose from the dead.* Pay attention to the words like the tipster talked about. *Heart not Head, Sis!* Jesus is telling this story and He knew what was still yet to come in His own life weaving the miracle of his own resurrection into his dual storyline—amazing! The story is telling us we have to find the answers ourselves and the answers are already here to hear. I was still curious if Lazarus could see earth from heaven, and if so, would Lazarus' soul be connected to his loved ones still knowing, *feeling* their needs from within their souls? Does God hear Lazarus' prayers from the heart of his soul? Then, I remembered: God is the God of the living, including those in Heaven eternal, so was it my angels guiding my soul, thereby helping God answer my dad's last wish for me, or was God answering my prayers? Or many simultaneously interconnected plans? Perplexing.

Then I read about another Lazarus who was raised from the dead by Jesus in John 11:1-44. (There are 44 verses in Chapter 11—my synchronicity numbers.) This Lazarus was dead for four days. John 11:11 tells us that Jesus said, "Our friend Lazarus sleeps, but I go that I may wake him up." And he does. Every word has relevance—*I go that I may wake him up*.... Jesus thanked God, His father, and then He put Lazarus' spirit right back in him. This was Jesus' last miracle before he was crucified so people could trust, believe, and know that God had sent Him. But all people still did not believe, even when He raised Lazarus from the dead. Even when He himself was risen. Exactly what He had talked about in that other Lazarus story. They too will not be persuaded though one rise from the dead. But many did. God had a plan.

> *Jesus said, "I am the resurrection and the life. He who believes in me, though he shall die, he shall live.... And whoever lives and believes in Me shall never die...."*
>
> — *John 11:25-26. (NKJV)*

All this brought me comfort. I know my sister believed. And I now know she lives. But I still do not know who was communicating with me while I slept. I know Gina did not communicate with me like a ghost, her spirit flying around whispering in my ear trying to show me or others where her physical remains were hidden, yet there were "whispers." Not a literal whisper, but still, a "loving whisper." Why would a bad spirit pretending to be Gina tell me good things—tell me factual information—truths? Why would it want evil revealed, which is certainly evident in these messages? I am not sure I will ever know the answer to my most burning question: Could this be my sister's soul connected to my soul whispering the truth? Or was it simply part of a plan to heal my heart with truth so my soul could be set free? Was the purpose of all of my experiences to guide me on a journey so I would have unwavering faith in my spiritual army and the absolute true existence of the spiritual realm so I would be resolute in my beliefs?

Maybe one day I will know what I need to know.

That seems to be a perfect daily prayer. *Lord, help me to know what You want me to know.*

A simple question: Could my experiences have gone in two different opposing directions? Yes. And, fortunately, God's direction won the battle. But we must realize it could have gone in a different, deceptive direction. I believe what I experienced throughout *the journey* came from various sources all intermingled together—direction, misdirection. And if an absolute spiritual battle, which is what it seemed to be, then with which message did the battle begin? And even so, if some of the communications were from a non-angelic source—a demonic, enemy-driven purpose—did the Enemy still use truth—twisted truths in the games that were played? So then, is truth layered in all of my messages? It seems often it is the interpretation or misinterpretation that he relishes in that becomes the lie.

Is it ever really possible to know the true origin of any of our experiences or even to grasp the enormity of this question within the limits of our human mind? No matter the origin of my messages, the lessons were abundant. The bottom line—the power of it all is in my humble opinion a lesson worthy of attention. My experiences were no doubt mind-blowing. I am not an expert, but really, is any one? I believe no human in this world can say what God's plan is or is not. Please do not let me or anyone else's opinions and interpretations define who God is for you. I have chosen to let God in His word and through The Word—His Son, and the Holy Spirit show me who God is. I have chosen to at least try to measure what I hear by testing it against scripture. It is still only my interpretation, and there are many, many interpretations in our world from one side of the scale to the other. I hope *the journey* awakens truth from within your heart, a personal truth not to be searched for down the endless rabbit holes prevalent in today's influenced world.

Finding truth is a personal journey. Thinking for yourself crucial—with heart, not just head!

I received messages that I would consider complex. I believe this message was for the times of today. I have tried throughout to not strongly emphasize my own beliefs, desiring for everyone to discover from their own heart, just as I did. I could not in good conscience leave this one out:

In the beginning I was so excited to just know there was this conscious state of spirit.

It seemed to be a huge playground.

Excited to know more.

Then I realized the separateness of the sides within... [Illegible: our mind? relationship?]

The realization wasn't enough.

Fear came into the headspace.

Why? Sin is the unawakened state.

It was in this space that I learned the unknown reality of existence.

WOW!

It took months to fully absorb the many layers of complexity from that message written at night to be delightfully discovered in the morning.

My interpretation:

Truth lies in the science of our existence—mind, body, and spirit. Understanding consciousness from a spiritual *and* scientific basis, while simultaneously being built on the foundation of The Word—Jesus Christ—is imperative for understanding just how amazing our world is and the reality of our very existence—to be in a relationship with God.

In the beginning, it was intriguing to discover there was this conscious state of spirit. I was excited and happy about the prospects that Gina just might be communicating with me. And that spiritual realm, like a huge playground. We are all participants in consciousness and seeing consciousness as only the power of self, a self-centered mindset instead of a God-centered one, presents a huge playground where the Enemy can easily condition us to believe what he wants us to believe—his ultimate objective to get us to believe that there is no real power influencing us. The deceiver makes it all seem so perfect in the playground of consciousness that you start to believe you not only have tapped into the nuclear reactor, but that you are the nuclear reactor! And some call this being awakened— New Thought! No, just toasters plugging into a power unfathomable.

Current thought leaders—in areas like collective consciousness, the spirit within concepts, alternative meditative practices, and on and on—seem to have threads of truth, yet, in my opinion, have truths that often become twisted, manipulated, and omitted. And many of these influential concepts are missing this truth—the connecting thread of all—God—The Father, The Son, and The Holy Spirit.

When I began to question the source of my experiences, I realized my own thoughts could have easily crossed that thin line of human interpretation that happens every day without notice. Influenced thoughts that could have changed my lifelong beliefs to an actual *new thought* taking hold.

During the initial writing of this book, I experienced exactly what God wanted me to see, to learn, to know. No coincidences. One day while having lunch in Arizona, I met a minister of a "New Age Christian Church" who shared the church's beliefs, and because of my own beliefs, my jaw literally dropped. In that very moment, so much became clearer to me. I questioned how could a "church" not aligned with God's Word, or the cross and its powerful message, refer to itself as a "Christian Church?" This person shared that the foundation of their church's beliefs are based on their own metaphysical abilities to connect using the spiritual laws of the Universe to unfold their *own sense of divinity*. Wow! Clarity, a very clear message, is in the picture I captured during *The Miraculous Journey*. A direct message of such dire importance that it warranted the angels to light up the water to make sure we get it right.

To emphasize exactly the brevity of this New Age Church concept: A lead in Gina's case recently surfaced from a "church" in the Radford area where mediumship, an accepted practice within this "church's affiliation," was used to try to determine the location of my sister's body. I was told that the message delivered to the authorities was that there are seventeen bodies buried with Gina's. There is simply no human way to know beyond a doubt the origin of any communication. In *the journey*, there were many receivers, and there were seekers, like this group. There is a distinct difference. There were many people who shared their unsought experiences that obviously came from a spiritual realm. It is real. Angelic and demonic, both exist side by side in our world, and it is humanly impossible always to discern the difference. We must never forget the many, many examples of *the journey* that illustrate exactly that. Remember, "Taffy, our childhood cat"?

Natasha came to the conclusion she was not brought into *the journey* to find Gina, but to bring peace. It was a journey for her too. It was as if the veil were raised and she could see better the truth behind the spirit world, realizing it is impossible to know 100 percent for sure who communicated. She could look back and pinpoint when the drama of her life began and it aligned to crossing that threshold. Natasha is at peace now. Her eyes had been opened and she said it was as if God were always knocking on her heart, but now she was really listening. I imagine God knocks on every heart that crosses the threshold of a place where portals are opened. A place where demons relish in the games of deceit. Certainly a place God's angels would try to break through to guide and protect. My knock came from a radio blasting "you're messin' with a son of a bitch."

I wonder if the many visitors to an active paranormal place like St. Albans are aware of the realities of what really goes on inside those walls. Jesus tells us stories about these demons. Seems they like to hitch a ride inside a human. And it is not a symbiotic relationship. What if the demon likes you and decides to stay with you? All of a sudden new, difficult challenges seem to erupt in the unsuspecting host's life, with absolutely no way even to begin to understand why. Wonder if all of the curious, unaware visitors help spread the demons to far reaches, unknowingly to the hosts who think it is just a game in a big haunted house.

Once Jesus kicked a demon out of one man, asking it, "What is your name?" The response was "Legion, for we are many." So Jesus sent the demons into a herd of swine and two thousand pigs ran violently down the steep place into the sea where they drowned. The word spread quickly. The image of this very real power here in this world is frightening. The vast numbers of these wicked should bring us to our knees.

Another recent story that drives home this point quite clearly came from a childhood friend of Gina. Her story amazed me. God must have wanted it in this book for a reason. One day some of her friends from Roanoke were planning a trip to St. Albans. She knew nothing about the place, and like many, thought a ghost tour sounded thrilling. A few days later, a stranger approached her and shared this message: "I know you do not know me, but I have something to say you need to hear. You are planning to go somewhere and when you get there you are going to believe that someone you love is there, but she is not. You will not know this. And when you leave there, a young boy will become attached and will come home with you. It will not be good."

Of course, Gina's friend did not know what any of this meant. She at first discounted it as many would, but then wrestled back and forth with the only place she had planned to go—St. Albans, and ultimately made the decision not to go. *God was knocking at her heart and she listened.* She would later learn in another book of the connection of her childhood friend Gina to St. Albans. She was in awe that someone somewhere cared enough to make sure she knew not to go into St. Albans. Our angels are always so busy.

I finally got it! The urgency behind St. Albans. My spiritual army is working more angles than I could ever keep up with. Throughout *the journey*, I kept questioning whether my sister could communicate with me in the manner that many believe she can. Why can I not shake the feeling that my sister needs me? Why would she leave Heaven to worry about this place? Then it just came to me. A chapter in 1 Samuel told me my answer. And one verse tells me why I have not been able to shake my sense of concern.

> "Now Samuel said to Saul, 'Why have you *disturbed me* by bringing me up?'"
>
> — 1 Samuel 28:15 (NKJV-Emphasis mine)

I must add my two cents' worth: **Leave My Sister Alone**.

Nola was right. Gina did not want that. If mediums can really bring forth her spirit, then no wonder she whispers surrounded by the evil that congregates in St. Albans. Samuel was aggravated about being *disturbed* one time. If this is possible, and the Bible seems to say in this verse that it is, then Gina could be being *disturbed* continuously in these types of paranormally active places where the same person's spirit is called upon over and over, maybe every weekend. My heart broke at just the thought of this. Simple question—how can we know beyond a doubt who is talking: demons or lost souls or in Gina's case, a soul from the spiritual realm we call heaven. And yes, in that chapter, 1 Samuel 28, it seemed as though Samuel knew what had transpired in this realm after he died. I am not saying it is the answer, but I certainly can see the problem.

How can I ever know for sure if this is part of the why behind it all? Years and years of psychics, mediums, ghost hunters, so many attempting to know answers by trying to communicate with my sister. Maybe Nola was right—the purpose was to end it all. Is the spiritual realm trying to end it for a reason we still cannot yet see? I know this: God is multi-purposed and it is always His plan. The message is clear: There is no way to know beyond a doubt from where the communication comes. Humans cannot. It does not take much to surmise this truth: *The who, the they,* the twisted truths, the source behind the seances and the ouija boards cannot be verified. Demons are not our loved ones, but they will relish in making you believe so. Will there ever be an end to this? No wonder this activity is clearly against God's will. It is utter blindness not to be awakened to the darkness that will creep into your very soul. In all seriousness, this is not a game.

It disturbingly intrigued me that on two occasions people who participated in the public ghost tours called me to let me know that my sister was right there in St. Albans. One knew me from my high school years and already knew about Gina's murder, never expecting what was actually experienced during their visit, surprised when they witnessed what everyone believed was Gina's spirit communicating with the group. Remember that paranormal TV show Andy participated with inside St. Albans—the spirit box seemingly giving clues about Gina? It happens! Evil spirits will try to be just as familiar to you as good spirits—a truth—and they will use that familiarity to deceive, manipulate, entice, and even disguise themselves as the light—a truth. *"They"* know the name of our dog, our cat, and even that our mother was there in that terrible place, hauntingly surprising facts Natasha and Ken already knew before I ever met them. How did Natasha know that our mother had been in St. Albans? Gina did not. It is deception in the highest degree. That is my exact point! I am sure there is human fraudulent trickery in this paranormal world as is everywhere. But what I am referring to is the non-fraudulent communication. And it comes mostly from the demonic world. Whether deception or not, demonic or not, it is not from a human origin, and there is absolutely no way to know who or what you are messing with. Do not seek answers from the dead is a clear warning in the Bible for a good reason.

And another concern screaming at me: If God needs us to find Gina's remains we will. And it will not be because someone froo-frooed into the spiritual realm of consciousness with their own self-perceived power of divinity. If ever any of these types of paranormal, metaphysical, psychic activities actually led to finding Gina's remains, including my own mysterious experiences, we must still always discern the why behind it with reverence to God and His power, and not allow some divergent path twisted into validation of proof of communication with the dead. Especially not some message delivered from that den of demons perched on the hill in Radford. I now know why I had to experience St. Albans. Simple question: If it was Gina's spirit literally there in St. Albans, we must ask, what would be her objective? There is no good reason.

If truth is to be known, it will come to us by God's power. People are not to seek it from the dead. And mediumship is not God's will. Hence my concern: The Enemy could even disclose her hidden body for advancement of his own agenda. Please do not let this be my sister's legacy.

If Gina is found, no matter by what means, it is imperative that God be given the glory. Gina's life is to be remembered for what she always knew to be truth and the miracle of the glorious image in the water reminds us of that same truth we are never to forget. A truth that is not to be twisted into a new thought so the Enemy can gloat at the manipulative use of my sister and her life. He smiles every time the doors of St. Albans open when people are entertained by the communication with the dead. It is a dangerous game. We cannot let the Enemy smile, so please leave my sister's beautiful essence alone. This must end. The exploitation of my sister's life is wrong. Her soul, her spirit, her life—deserves peace.

In terms of trying to know the truth of everything, we just need to keep it simple. Live life and not worry because we cannot know all of the answers, and cannot is okay. And it is okay that I cannot rule out some kind of eternal conscious connection. I felt Gina's love and guidance and a sense that my angels were protecting me. It is okay for me to believe that my loved ones—my sister, my daddy, my NaNa—are all connected to me throughout eternity, forever a part of me. I feel their love. That is how they communicate with me—through the heart of my soul. That is enough. And I believe my own soul can communicate with me, just like the Light and the dark communicates with us through a conscious realm we will never fully comprehend. It was my soul that helped me remember the true message sent from the real one who was going to help me. And my soul never forgot the Light.

> "Then Jesus spoke to them again saying, 'I am the light of the world. He who follows Me shall not walk in darkness, but have the light of life.'"

> — John 8:12

Light had shone on the darkness and won, no matter the many attempts along the way to rewrite the story—the spiritual battle. It's a battle I now can see so clearly—a dark presence, unknown to all involved, at times deceivingly guiding the story in many different directions, but all the while, a powerful presence of Light, in abundant, infinite love, always guiding me back with Divine intervention. I believe it will always be God's will, His plan, that prevails, still yet to be revealed *in The Miraculous Journey.*

It is imperative in our times to see through all of the New Age, New Thought quackery that has taken a stronghold in people's lives and in some ways has spurred a redefining of Christianity. Humans always are looking for the new. When it comes to spirituality, tell me the old, old story. That is enough for me. The questions I now know to ask: What is the *Why* behind it all? And, *How* does this happen? A powerful external influence used for the overall objective of changing thoughts and creating beliefs to win my soul. The influence can be good leading us closer to God if we let it, or if not, the influence will be like a thief in the night.

Not knowing the threat of this deception is to be *unawakened.* The Enemy is too powerful at deception. So, we can be unawakened to two truths—the truth of Jesus and the truth of the Enemy. I was unawakened to the Enemy's real power.

I had been taught all my life what sin was, a very long list, but I never thought of it as being "unawakened."

In the words of Jesus:

> *"If I had not come and spoken to them, they would have no sin,*
> *but now they have no excuse for their sin."*

> — John 15:22

Now I get it!

Change your life just knowing that—

And, change your life by awakening to knowing this:

The Enemy's influence is real every day, every moment.

Fear = The Enemy = Headspace.

And, "Fear came into the headspace." Fear of what others think—fear of not pleasing others. Fear of not being good enough ruling our lives. Who defines good enough? "Fear is the enemy's sharpest tool." Guard your heart and your head. Pay attention to your thoughts—your headspace! I laughed at first sight of this word *headspace,* but then I understood just how important it was. Once we learn we have an opponent in our headspace, a very real external power, the battles become easier to win because we now know and understand how he operates—the separateness of the sides of the battle within our mind will then not easily steal away our divine relationship with God.

My new daily thoughts from deep within my soul:

> *Lord, help me to know what You want me to know.*

> *Let me see only you the clearest, hear you the loudest, and love you the most with all of my heart.*

> *May Your Will be done.*

The last week of April 2017, I would go to an event in Charleston, South Carolina. All of April, I felt filled with happiness and a lasting peace. During a walking tour with a small group of friends through the old town, we turned a corner, and suddenly, I was struck with extreme sadness. Tears spilled from my eyes. My friend Barb led me across the street, her arm around me, as I trembled with feelings I could not explain. One minute I had been laughing, the next, crying. "Where are we?" I asked her. "I feel like it has something to do with right here, right where we are." When we looked up, across the street our group stood as a tour guide related the history. An old slave market. A place where sadness would have been unbearable—humans, their families, now soul families, being separated from one another and sold to the highest bidder. I felt their pain. Their sadness. Their fear. This was my new reality.

One night, I was flying, the sky a shade of blue only ever seen in this dream. I told my husband as soon as I woke up, smiling as I remembered what I had experienced in my dreams. A few days later, friends were going skydiving and asked Buz and me if we wanted to go. My husband just looked at me. He knew. I had told him I had dreamed I was flying, so there was no question we were both going to skydive. I saw the blue. I saw a heart-shaped atoll underneath as I flew like a bird, free-falling through the sky. No wonder one of my favorite songs is "Freebird." My best friend Barb tells me she will play it at my funeral. She sent this beautiful excerpt:

> *"Free Bird .... I read this and immediately thought of you!*

I pray your trip is an amazing one!!

"Sometimes in life, you find a special friend. Someone who changes your life just by being part of it. Someone who makes you laugh until you can't stop. Someone who makes you believe that there really is good in the world. Someone who convinces you that there really is an unlocked door just waiting for you to open it. This is forever friendship. When you're down and the world seems dark and empty, your forever friend lifts you up in spirit and makes that dark and empty world suddenly seem bright and full. Your forever friend gets you through the hard times, the sad times and the confused times. If you turn and walk away, your forever friend follows. If you lose your way, your forever friend guides you and cheers you on. Your forever friend holds your hand and tells you that everything is going to be okay. And if you find such a friend, you feel happy and complete because you need not worry. You have a forever friend, and forever has no end."

—Unknown

We will celebrate that day, when my dot ends and my eternal life begins.

Jesus said so on the cross:

"Assuredly, I say to you, today you will be with Me in paradise."

— Luke 23:43

And that is where Gina is, and it does not matter where "is" is—whether right here in this dimension somehow still connected to this realm or a far off place—it just does not matter. It is a good place. A place of pure love. And it gives me peace to know my sister has a forever friend too. Her friend Jesus. And Gina is with Him in paradise.

Just by letting life happen, by quietly having a conversation with God every day from within the heart of our souls, God will know what we want Him to know. And we will know what God wants us to know. And as I would come to know next, there was always a Plan. And because of what happened next, I know God was with me every step of *The Miraculous Journey*. When God is with us, we will feel it all the way down to our toes.

LET ME SEE ONLY YOU THE CLEAREST, HEAR YOU THE
LOUDEST, AND LOVE YOU THE MOST, THEN I WILL
KNOW WHAT YOU WANT ME TO KNOW.

CHAPTER 23

She Talks to Angels

God had one more little piece to my puzzle. It was a long way to here. He gave me a cross to wear around my neck, so I could find my way, all the way, home to the only truth that mattered—His truth—His Son whom I met in the heart of my soul.

In June 2017, my husband and I took a Baltic cruise. We always plan to arrive in the port city a day or so early just in case we are unexpectedly delayed. Missing the boat's departure time and chasing the ship from port to port, just hoping to arrive before she sails again, is never a good way to start a vacation. Stockholm was our destination. We wanted a hotel close to the Vasa Museum, so I just picked one without doing any research. I liked the name Pop House, and it was within walking distance. Perfect.

When we checked in, I noticed inside the hotel a museum called ABBA. Still jet-lagged, I didn't make the connection until the next morning, but then it hit me: Abba was the group that sang "Dancing Queen," one of Gina's favorite songs. I escorted my husband to a quaint corner of the lobby, a crossword puzzle absorbing him while I toured the museum. The first exhibit reminded me of the songs Gina and I had danced to so many times. I felt a surge of emotional energy. A joy filled my heart, as though we were seeing it together. It crossed my mind that "Abba" is one of the most significant names used for God, "Abba, Father," referring to the intimate relationship we have with God, like a father has with his child. I smiled to think of the trusting relationship Gina and I had enjoyed with our dad. Our relationship with God was also like that for both of us. This museum was the perfect beginning to our vacation.

On the evening of June 28, 2017, the thirty-seventh anniversary of my sister's death, my husband and I arrived in Oslo after a week on the ship traveling throughout the Baltic countries. We had planned to spend a few days in Norway before leaving for a stopover in Iceland on our way home. We had one full free day to do as we wanted. This would be the day all of our plans fell through.

It is rare for me not to have every moment planned to perfection when I travel because there is always so much I want to see and do. However, when we arrived at the hotel in Oslo, we learned our plans had changed—we couldn't get a rental car that would allow us to guide our younger friends to the fjords as planned. A huge festival in Oslo meant no cars were available. We all agreed just to go our separate ways for the day and come back together after dinner later that night.

My husband and I decided to go with the flow. I had overheard a young woman in our hotel telling a friend about her recent trip to Drobak, a small coastal town along the Oslo fjord. Drobak—why not? We impulsively decided to take the ferry there. We scribbled down the ferry schedule and headed to the dock. Distractions around every corner drew our attention, but we stuck to the initial plan: Drobak. At the dock, the ticket machine would not cooperate with my credit card and produce our ferry tickets. My frustration escalated when I saw the ferry about to depart. We could have easily given up right then. Something inside told me, "Just get on that boat. You can pay them once on board. What is the worst that could happen? They'll kick us off at the next stop."

At the gangplank, I showed the ticket person my collection of paper slips, all the tickets I'd received from the non-cooperating machine. He let us board. It was a beautiful day for a ninety-minute ferry ride, which stopped in many enticing places. We thought about hopping off, each stop seemingly promising such adventure. But we stuck to Drobak. That was my destination. It felt right. As we exited the ferry in Drobak, I knew we had made the right decision. Lovely flowers adorned the homes, greeting us to a beautiful town. This place was perfect for photography, my renewed hobby.

For about two weeks before this, I had been having spontaneous thoughts that I wanted to buy a specific piece of jewelry: a simple cross necklace.

It would be a reminder of all I had experienced during the past months of rejuvenated faith. My husband would tell you that it's not unusual for me to want a new piece of jewelry. As an empty-nester, jewelry was often a reward to myself. I liked to collect jewelry from my travels, something that reflected the culture of each place I visited. I knew the Balkans were known for amber. As we visited the different port cities on the cruise, I'd looked at beautiful amber pieces here and there, in shops and with street artisans. And I'd picked up enough that I would be coming home with a complete set of amber—earrings, necklace, ring, and bracelet. That was certainly enough to satisfy, so I kept putting the desire for a cross out of my mind.

The night before this trip, I had the same thought—that I might want a white-gold or silver cross. I already had a yellow-gold cross, and I'd had a strong urge to find it and wear it on the trip. But I hadn't had time to look for it before leaving. One night, earlier on this trip, while on the ship, I had a flashing thought again to want a white-gold cross necklace. But, no, I already had a yellow-gold cross. But, yes, a white-gold or silver one would be nice. It's like I had that cartoon angel on one shoulder and a red-horned devil on the other. But this time the angels were whispering the loudest.

Strolling along the many streets of Drobak, we walked by a quaint artisan jeweler's shop. I suddenly felt a compelling desire to step back and go into the shop. I paused. *You have already purchased amber.* But the urge was real—it was now a familiar sense not to be ignored.

Listening to my heart, I stepped up to the door and walked in. Right away, I could see this was an individual designer, with only a few, beautifully created pieces on display. That can usually mean high-end and expensive, but I still walked up to the counter and asked the woman if she had any cross necklaces. The jeweler's wife reached under her counter and brought out a single, tiny small cross.

It came to me right away—the striking resemblance. This one-of-a-kind little cross was undeniably in the same shape as the symbol I'd drawn and the image in the water photo from the summer before. The black shadows on the tiny cross necklace reminded me of the muck place where I had dug, searching for my sister until I could dig no more. I stood there in that shop, tears of love expressing my joy.

No question about it, this was it. A clear message from God never to forget

IN FRONT OF THE JEWELRY STORE

the meaning of the cross. A simple cross necklace handcrafted by a jeweler, a divinely inspired design, waiting there an ocean away to become a gift from the spiritual realm. This was the truth that really mattered. The gift of the Cross, real love, a divine message. A gift not just for me.

Receiving the cross in June 2017 corrected my initial August 2016 perception of the image in the water. I listened to the simple urge from within, the urge to want *a cross*. The cross necklace brought clarity. The cross allowed me to see for myself the alignment—the true meaning of the Light image in the water—a cross with a soul at the foot of the cross—the message is the message of the Cross.

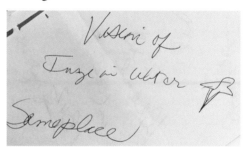

No more was I interpreting the image as two victims. That interpretation had been in my mind during those frenzied days in August, when I landed on interpreting it as a clue about where my sister's body was buried, even though for a brief flash of a moment I first interpreted it as the miracle of light that it was—angels lying on the water. But something that day in August at the muck place was taking me off the right path. My perception was influenced by thoughts shared with me by others—a six-year-old child, a compass, and even my own belief that there were multiple victims, something I still believe. Later, I finally came back to the realization that it was indeed a true miracle of light, zooming in on the unexplainable concentrated

balls of energy projecting the light into the outlined shapes that formed a very clear picture for all of us to see. But I still was not interpreting the shape as an image of a cross. Nor had I interpreted it as I do now: a soul at the foot of the cross. Gina's soul.

I can see clearly other moments when a thought would just come out of the blue, as though it came from a different place—sometimes from the heart of my own soul like the urge to walk into that jeweler's shop. And that day, the words of someone else, the criminal profiler in February, also flashed through my mind when I first saw the cross necklace. She had asked me months earlier, "Have you found the small trinket your sister left for you?"

I was still trying to understand all that had happened. But this message told me:

God will move heaven and earth to make His Will known.

Of course, I had to pause and contemplate all of the messages as I looked back at *The Miraculous Journey*. Messages a sister would certainly want a sister to have. And the very first message kept me focused on the water, and the water was where the miracles happened. She is breathing fine into the light of eternity, the gift received when the Word was up on the hill. Yes, Jesus. I do not pretend to understand these forces present in our physical world, but I do now see the reality of their existence every day. The powers behind what I experienced are undeniable. I hope curiosity ignited deep within you, just as it did in me throughout *the journey*. What I experienced was an intricately designed, predestined master plan—and its personal objective—to listen to my heart and to learn, and the ending result: love. It was not always easy to listen, or learn, but it was always easy to love my sister. I can embrace my sister's love, knowing she is right here with me, always and forever in my heart. The answers I had wanted were revealed during *the miraculous journey*, and it was orchestrated by an undeniable power we should never underestimate—the power of God.

Once I knew that finding Gina's physical body was not what mattered, would God still want me to know more truth? God is a righteous God. Was this little cross also a message guiding me back to the muck place—a resting place for my sister's physical body? Or was it so a sister could know where Gina's soul met Jesus? God's angels could have shown me the image in the water anywhere, but it was there at the muck place that the miracle happened. And it is there that we should consider its relevance to my sister. As Gina said to me, her last words as she headed out the door, "Listen to your heart, not your head." I listened to my heart for the answer. The image in the water is Gina at the foot of a cross. A soul ascended into heaven. God orchestrated this plan. I now can see the divine inspiration in our life that comes from a place of love. God knew my heart needed to be healed, and He knew the best way to my heart in the beginning was Gina. And now my heart was free of never-ending anger, hate, and unforgiveness, and there was room for love. God's love. To God be the glory. What a message!

I still wanted to know *exactly* who was communicating with me.

Why did I dream of "showing my art"? Who is the *my* in my messages? I questioned art every time I would wake and read the messages, but I never connected it to the graffiti until months later. I see now the graffiti on the bowling alley wall—the black headphones that I would see October 26, of course not really seeing the true message that day. And really, the artwork is in many places. The muck place was an amazing showing of artwork, a cross with a uniquely shaped image resembling a little girl in a dress at the foot of the cross, all designed to perfection. The tiny cross necklace was an exemplary piece of handcrafted art. The one doors at the museum a creative concept of colorful art. And the graffiti—no words to describe, yet the most important words. At one point during *the journey*, I had a thought from within: Listen Learn Love, the words written on the St. Albans bowling alley wall beside the black headphones. Now, taking my thoughts a step further, was it a more profound message?

So what came first—the proverbial question—the chicken or the egg? The thought in the mind of a graffiti artist becoming a personal message to me, a message God knew I would need in my own life's timeline, knowing I would

be standing right there years later. How could the messages on a wall, painted by someone at an unknown time from long past, become relevant in a future moment in time by matching a received message from the spiritual realm, and to emphasize the scope of this—a premonition? I would rationalize at the time that it must just be to get me to know I was at a place I was supposed to be, not where I was going to be. Really, does time even exist in that spiritual world?

When I first saw the black headphones on the wall in October, a vision message I had already had, I immediately wanted to search the room, to go down behind that bowling lane equipment, searching behind it for any clue to what had happened to my sister and why this message was given to me. My initial thoughts, influenced or not, interpreted the headphones as a sign that I was in a place relevant to my sister's murder. Later, much later, I *really* see *my* artwork—the words written beside it—*Listen Learn Love*—which seems to be the same path *the journey* had guided me on? The stepping stones to first listen so that I could learn, and in the end, knowing there is nothing in this world better than the unconditional love of Jesus I experienced.

And how do we reconcile that it was already known that I would be right there in Norway in that jeweler's shop on the anniversary weekend of my sister's death, God's intricately woven plan, a purpose in my life, playing out miraculously? I do not need to know the how, but I do know the why! This was a divine power at work. As I compiled the photos for this book, I noticed that even the Norwegian flag was showing me what I was to see and know. There could not have been a more perfect place. There is not a human anywhere in this realm smart enough to have designed *the journey* with its intricately masterminded plan. I certainly could not have made this amazing story unfold just as it did. It was hard enough just to write it all down so I could share the divinely inspired moving parts.

Later, I sent a note asking the jeweler what thoughts were in his mind as he made this one-of-a-kind cross. Marit, his wife, replied. "Of course I remember you and your happiness about the small silver cross. Walter made the cross shortly after we moved from Munich to Norway in 2012. We love thinking of the small cross having a 'good life' in America."

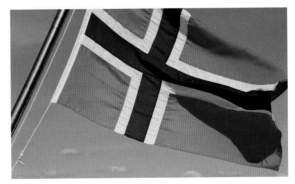

As I read her response, tears flowed again. He was German, and she was Norwegian. She got to return to her home after thirty years, and he got to live in her home, in awe of the grandeur of Norway, his new home. Marit said of his inspiration, "The first impressions he had in Norway were the huge stones, cliffs, and mountains, all made of strong granite. The cross was made, leaned in the strength of this stone."

What had been in the jeweler's mind was the strength of the *rock*. My March experience with Jesus was the same—a rock, strength. My thoughts pondered this verse:

"Trust in the Lord forever, for the Lord God is an everlasting rock."

— Isaiah 26:4, ESV

I now know a jeweler can be divinely inspired to design a cross in 2012, its purpose not yet known except to God, waiting there for someone— me—to spontaneously show up five years later and ask for it. The only one like it anywhere in the world, and I somehow ended up in this far off coastal town in Norway to receive a clear message of God's gift, one year after I had drawn the exact matching shape of the one-of-a-kind cross in a message. And now both matched an image in the water that I believe was created by the messengers of Light—God's angels. It is as if time does not exist when God's Will is at work. So if the cross story can happen as it did, then certainly someone painting on a wall could have had the in-fluenced thought in his head to draw black music headphones and write "Listen Learn Love." And, really, why not consider that all of our thoughts can be influenced—mine, Nola's, everyone's? It is not inconceivable that a creative thought can be inspired from that realm, even while painting a wall with graffiti, designing the day's Google search page, writing the lyrics of a song, or designing a simple cross necklace. A logical, closed-minded person would say, "There's no way that that Google page was designed for you to see. No way that song played just for you to hear. Not everything is a sign. You are just reading too much into it all." Am I? The digital journal of what I documented is an archive of proof. It is a trove of miracles. The miracles throughout 2016 were abundant, all leading to this very moment. The puzzle pieces were laid out on the table before I even began putting them together. Again, consider the many people put in my life's path— Nola, Elana, Andy, the Preacher, Peter Romano, Kim Jett, Katie Monroe, the grown-up ten year old...right down to the tipster—so many! Even the prior release of a book summarizing the 1980 composed story played a role. A prelude so I did not have to devote pages and pages retelling the composed story of 1980. How could there be that many coincidences! There never are. The power of it all is inconceivable within the limits of our own human understanding. What I do know is with God, all things are possible—anything and everything!

What an amazing way to live life in peace, just knowing God's got this.

Normally, every year at the end of June, the anniversary of Gina's death, I am overcome with sadness. Instead, this day, I was lovingly apprehended again, and led back to the right path by my winning spiritual army. *Who exactly is my spiritual army?* I thought of Gina with warm and loving memories, embracing life as fully as she would have wanted me to do. *The Miraculous Journey* had multiple purposes intricately interwoven. One of these purposes was for me—my own soul. My spirit's forgiveness of others, and my own peace so I could love unconditionally just as I am loved. Proof of God's love came just for me when I needed it most—a personal connection—a Divine relationship. There was always a divine plan and purpose. I just could not always see it while living it. What I had come through brought me to a solid self-worth that healed 1980, and healed 2014. God was always with me. Jesus was carrying me, the Holy Spirit was guiding me, and my angels were supporting me as were many others put in my path to help me see what I was to see. And, a question to ponder: *Is my own soul part of my spiritual army?*

The foundation was laid, so that when I received the gift of the cross, I was prepared for what was still to come. I could not keep *the journey* to myself. I knew I must share it. That was the plan.

I found so many truths, layered beneath the complexity of *the journey*. The messages continued as perplexing as before, but with a different intent. They were helping to answer questions that would arise in my mind about life. One day as I was struggling, trying to reconcile how destiny and free will can simultaneously exist with "the Plan," I had a dream message that seemed to tell me exactly what I needed to know!

> I saw myself falling from the sky, and below me I could see a vast thick, beautiful blanket of green. Like an animated green field of large wheat-it wasn't wheat but those were the only words I could think of to describe it. When my body entered

the green, it seemed it dropped through the green for a long time, like I was traveling for miles before landing on the ground upright. I was standing on dirt, and the green not so thick while I was in it, looking around from the ground. And life seemed to begin. I had to start finding my way, walking what did not look like a clear path to me...just walking through the green, turning right...turning left...crossing paths with people, changing paths because of these interactions with various people, and them changing their direction because they met me. And someone was up above, seeing every path taken clearly like a corn maze in the field that can be seen from above, yet we in the maze do not see it.

People cross our paths, both good and bad, influencing our life. And every now and then we just might cross paths with pure evil as did my sister. Evil is a very real force in our world. But the light will shine—it shines in the people whose lives are affected by the moments of grace and goodness that come from others during those moments of darkness.

The day my dad rode in the car with his daughter's killer could have easily been one of those moments when a choice changes a path. He could have been vengeful for his daughter's murder, but by the grace of God, he restrained himself that day. The power of faith that he gained from surviving his first cancer gave our dad the strength he needed to do as he did—to be a righteous man. We were always grateful that Daddy made the right decision in that moment when that decision could only have been made with God's love and strength in his heart. Had anger and vengeance won the spiritual battle, we would have lost not only Gina, but our dad also. And because of God's influence in his life, our dad remained in our life for many decades, sharing his wisdom with the generations to come.

We make choices every moment of every day, and those decisions guide us on a path in life. And this path becomes our life story. The path veers in all directions, and yes, I believe our spiritual army can see these paths and my own soul deep inside of me knows the destination—my life's purpose. We all cross paths every day, one with another, changing the zig-zag of our own lives. These moments happen every second we are in the dot of our life.

I create my own story when I decide how I will interpret everything that happens in my life—the thoughts in my own head. I have always understood that we become our thoughts. I learned early in life that whichever thoughts get fed are the ones that prevail. This thought process served me well in my life's path. The day I discovered I was pregnant in March 1981, I made one of those choices—to be a mother. My own thoughts could have easily changed that choice—*I am only twenty-one. I have so much I want to do before I have children. I am not even married!* Many thoughts could have influenced my decision and I could have made a different choice, a different path. This is free will. I could have chosen "reproductive justice," which seems to be the most recent buzz word for a woman's right to choose. I choose to think of that choice differently, not from a woman's view, but from the child's view, "soul justice." I knew that day a soul had been created and I was carrying Life inside of me. I do not believe I have the right to make a decision as to whether that Life lives or dies. And the result of that decision is now a caring man who will help the world. A brilliant son who is a Johns Hopkins PhD, a Mt. Sinai medical school graduate, and a Harvard resident physician. What will be God's purpose for his life? I am grateful every day that I chose that path. Life is life.

To simplify my life, I will just follow this advice:

> *"Trust in the Lord with all your heart, and do not lean on your own understanding.*
>
> *In all ways acknowledge Him, and He will make your paths straight."*

> — Proverbs 3:5-6, ESV

I will trust that this amazing spiritual army only wants what is best for my life.

I have a word for all of the women who were young, desperate, or alone when that one decision in their life was made—maybe because you felt you had no choice or maybe just because that is what others viewed as acceptable becoming your own belief. This word is for those who beat themselves up every day with shame, regret, and unforgiveness. The word is Forgive Yourself. Let God Heal You. Set Your Heart Free. Pay It Forward. Mentor other young women in the realities of the emotional challenges of the heavy burden that is carried as time passes. Know and believe that you can have authority over that which binds you.

The purpose of *The Miraculous Journey* is perplexingly complex—just like Life. This was a *journey* to many truths. My soul family and spiritual army whispered—no shouted—truth to me from within, through the hearts of our souls connected for eternity. This story was one of how a soul family's interwoven lives created a tapestry, as if time does not exist. It is about *Life*. Were these amazing unexplainable experiences simply to guide us to a more profound thought—to question the far reaches of our own mind, our own soul, our own heart?

How can we begin to explain the many, many amazing stories of *the journey*? My mind is still blown away by the complexity of it all. Parallel storylines that played out vividly in the minds of strangers. Similar storylines that intersected across time as though somebody somewhere just wanted truth known. Will these stories become straight lines like Dorothy Allison's straight line? A line that decades later crossed the butterfly spot—the first miracle in *the journey*. Only time will tell if their stories too will end in a straight line. Straight paths to truth—what truth?

"Call to Me, and I will answer you, and show you great and mighty things, which you do not know."

— Jeremiah 33:3

This is what 333 means to me now. That is exactly what I did and He did show me!

Promise kept again!

And, in my humble opinion, 1111 is a call to awaken to the truths by praising God in gratitude. There is only one book in the Bible with a chapter 111 and the first verse of this chapter says:

"Praise God."

— Psalms 111:1

The amazing day at the muck place when I captured that miraculous photo, I somehow knew it would be a great day. I got out of my truck and remembered I might need my phone to take pictures, so I reached back in and grabbed it. Just then the screen lit up—exactly 11:11; amused, I screenshot it. Somehow, deep down, when I saw 11:11, I just knew something miraculous was going to happen. Of course, right then I hoped as I did every day of *the journey* that I was going to find my truth about my sister's body. I found what she and my spiritual army wanted me to find!

I did not understand at first why I kept seeing the same numbers all of the time. I always had noticed 333 and 33. But new numbers began to surface while walking to the river butterfly spot. I would grab my phone, which I rarely did because it was too much trouble to take it out of the plastic bag I had it stored in. I noticed the time was exactly 11:33. After that happened the third day, my mind wanted a logical answer. I landed on searching for these numbers as if they were a clue like everything else—a clue on a map. Trying to justify why is what led me to the longitude/latitude theories. I surmised that if the Allison line could cross on a map as it did, then certainly a few numbers could be relevant! I did not understand then what I see now.

Now, when I see these synchronistic numbers, 11, 22, 33, 44, 222, 333, 444, 1111, I smile and my heart warms. I think of God.

So perplexing. Still perplexing.

Some believe these synchronistic numbers are the angels communicating with us in this realm. Some believe such synchronisms come from aliens. Some make jokes about it. Some say it is all just a coincidence or the person is just always looking, making it synchronistic. And the one that really gets my attention as an influenced thought is that some believe it is caused by themselves, reflecting their own power to manifest anything they want, a popular new thought theory. Many theories. I do not know how it happened, really how any of *The Miraculous Journey* happened, and I do not need to. I believe in God and His power. I believe in the Bible. What I do know now is that the angels were with me that day I grabbed my phone seeing 11:11, the same day the miraculous photo was captured when they lay on the water. I felt the angels with me. Kevin felt the goodness too. And, that day certainly was a day to Praise God. I know now, 1111—Praise God. This is not numerology. I believe it is communication to pay attention to what is relevant—God's words. There are many seeing these numbers. Why? Maybe as one becomes aware of the realities of a conscious spiritual realm, the synchronicities begin to occur. Maybe we are becoming closer to God for a reason yet to be seen. And as I have come to realize there would certainly be an external power that would want to redirect the interpretation to any theory that would lead people further away from God and His word instead of closer. Just a thought to ponder for those seeing those 1111s—I believe 1111 could be a call to Awaken to God. Simply *Praise God every time you see them* and watch what happens in your life! Once awakened, loving God is so effortless.

In the Old Testament, there are forty-four (44) prophecies throughout thousands of years about Jesus and his life. Can humans even begin to orchestrate these prophetic, connecting details? I see the Bible as an intricately woven masterpiece orchestrated by God as though time does not exist. And even though man was involved in the actual act of scribing in the beginning and throughout the ages, the words are divinely inspired. So, why not the numbers too?

The day I received the cross necklace, my husband and I had a lovely dinner in Drobak before catching the ferry back to Oslo. To end our beautiful day, I smiled when they brought our receipt—$1111.00 (Norwegian krones).

I was not surprised! Just amazed. When I see 1111, which now points me to Psalms 111:1, my heart smiles! Synchronicities need no explanation. Searching for the answer in the wrong place will just give you the wrong answer. The answer can be found in the place where answers can be found. A place not from a limited, human perspective. A place of omniscience.

This world is becoming quite interesting to me in its complexity. So to simplify life, I will choose this path:

> *"Praise the Lord! I will thank the Lord with all of*
> *my heart as I meet with His godly people."*
>
> — Psalms 111:1, NLT

Simple!

Jesus Christ is the main character in my life story—the Great I Am—the only way to eternal life. God's message sent to all is the message of the Cross. May we all have wisdom of peace just knowing of His gift of eternal life, and finding our way to Psalms 111:1—*Praise God, living every moment in a loving relationship* just as this message told me:

Acknowledgment is different than Relationship.

I believe a great question to answer is: Do we only *acknowledge* God, often only in a public, self-serving way? Or do we truly have a relationship with God—a personal loving relationship with the creator of all? We have a loving God, an amazing friend in Jesus who carries us when we need it most, and an army of angels sent to guide and protect us, so why do we ever need to waste our dot endlessly worrying about life? Let it go!

Now, when I open my eyes in the morning, the first image they land on is a piece of art I bought decades ago: a crucifix. As the years passed, the treasured crucifix was moved around the home. Before long, it landed in a place not often seen by me, where it was only dusted, acknowledged, and occasionally moved my heart, reminding me of a truth. We do the same to Jesus—he is often acknowledged; rote prayers are spoken, but they lose their meaning and connection to His powerful love. Religion can get the same way sometimes—recognized, stale, something missing,

sometimes even twisted. Most surprising is how we might be in awe when amazing moments happen in life, sometimes unexplainable miracles, but for some reason, the experience lands on the back shelves of our mind. I hope the story of the cross in *The Miraculous Journey* does not get put on the dusty shelf. Christmas and Easter are not just holidays that come around once a year to be "acknowledged." Christmas is an amazing everyday story of God fulfilling His promise. Seeing is Believing and many witnessed the life of Jesus shared in the Gospels as the shining light for our life. On the Hill is where I will find you...Underneath the Word is stronger. Easter is an everyday, every moment celebration—always remembering, never forgetting *Our Lord and Savior has Risen*.

Now my crucifix adorns the wall I see when I first open my eyes early in the morning. The light from the moon sometimes shines directly in from my window, lighting the center of my crucifix. Lighting up Jesus! Light in the darkness. A rectangle of light like the one door that He is. There have been many seemingly alluring doors throughout *the journey*, but there is only one door I need to know. This is my quiet moment of gratitude. Remember Mr. Odell who always welcomed two hungry little girls, graciously sharing his cereal? When I was a teenager, his daughter Donna became one of my best friends. One night, when I slept over, I saw her parents wake up in the very early hours to spend time together in prayer and reading their Bible. I recall as a teenager thinking that was the craziest thing I had ever seen. *Who wakes up at 3 a.m. to talk to God?* Now, I get it. I so understand what it means to truly be in a loving relationship. And that one intersection decades long ago in the path of my life, a crossing of paths, has become a relevant, impactful memory today. We do not need to have a relationship with an item on the wall! Or even a relationship with a little cross necklace. But we do sometimes need to be reminded just to have the relationship. I now spend time simply conversing with God. It is different. There is only one prayer I say aloud repeatedly: The Lord's Prayer—the one Jesus taught us in Matthew 6. All else comes from the heart of my soul. God always knows what I need. We can understand just how awe-inspiring the all-powerful, all-knowing, all-loving God is, and be comforted knowing He wants to have a relationship with us. God is the infinite eternal power of our existence.

How are we to know everything we are to know? We may never, but we can begin by getting back to the basics starting with ourselves—being kind, forgiving, just smiling, so we can *experience love*. Changing our daily lives helps us reach the higher levels of consciousness that naturally come when love, gratitude, kindness, and compassion all become a part of life. We can believe in the Spirit of Life.

We all are part of a story—the story of our life.

Each and every moment unfolding miraculously.

A part of God's plan.

A life full of miracles.

A purpose.

A life blessed by God.

The Miraculous Journey had multiple underlying purposes and messages for many. *The journey* began as a story about the spiritual realm told by a girl who questioned everything "ghosts." And yes, my journey began as a quest to know truth and uphold honor for my sister, a girl who so many believed was a "ghost." There were moments in *the journey* where I believed that the origin of my experience was my sister. And in many ways, it was—it was her life bearing fruit. *The Miraculous Journey* became a sisters' journey together. A story of a soul whose heart needed to be set free. A journey to truth, forgiveness, and unconditional love. A journey we walked together.

God has taken my sister's life story and used it to illuminate the only message that really matters...the message of the Cross.

This is a story about a cross. And a cross is symbolic of Jesus Christ. And someone somewhere wanted me to personally know that the soul at the bottom of the cross, my sister's soul, met Jesus. A message so important that God's angels lit up the water in the shape of a cross symbolic of Jesus

and His Eternal Love. And yes, a message I am sure my sister, my dad—my soul family would also have wanted me to have. A message to be shared with everyone. A message of utmost, urgent importance. We have one true story in this world about a *cross*, and it will be the most important story you will ever be told—to know what the cross means is to look into the window of your own soul—the straight path to love. *God is bringing us back to love.*

The power of Christ's love is in the message of the Cross.

After all, who besides God and His spiritual army would want us to have a reminder of the divine message of the Cross? And the ultimate purpose of *The Miraculous Journey* was the amazing image of light in the water—the Proof of God.

Allow me to recap why I personally believe what I experienced is Proof of God. While asleep, I wrote a message with a symbol drawn on July 26, 2016. I captured a photo of a light image that matched that symbol on August 12, 2016. But that would not have proven it because we all could say that the light image only resembled the symbol I had drawn and we could say it was angels sharing a different message or something unexplainable just as I did. But God was not finished. He knew more proof would be desired. So one year later, I receive a one-of-a-kind divinely inspired cross necklace designed in the same unique shape as the image drawn and the image perfectly formed on the water by light energy clearly not from this world. The message is the cross. Who would want us to remember the cross? Only God!

"For God so loved the world that he gave his one and only Son, that whoever believes in him shall not perish but have eternal life."

— John 3:16, NIV

The heart of the soul understands how the Holy Spirit can move through you, helping you to know what you need to know—what God wants us to know—wants us to remember. We can begin experiencing God's love by spreading the same message, a web of goodness and light, always remembering the truth of who Jesus really is and the message of the cross: Love.

I tried not to share my opinions too much and let you walk *the journey* just as I did, experiencing it step by step in the mindset of that moment. That was a challenge for a hard-headed girl! I already knew the end! Actually, it has not really ended. There is something else we must be sure we understand. Why would the Enemy not want us to know the truth about who Jesus really is? Clearly, so we do not know the most important message that matters—that our soul, one soul, can live an eternal life in Heaven. The master of deception's twisted truth of current times, dubbed as "New Thought," is that "Christ was just another teacher, another human who 'awakened' just like us. Just one of many ascended masters." NO! It is still the same old lie spreading faster than we could ever imagine into our Christian world through the New Age, New Thought movement. Believing that Jesus is just like us or that we are just like Jesus is a twisted mindset that leads us further away from God, away from who Jesus really is—The Son of God—*the real one who is going to help you.* The Enemy will use anything—facts, the end result, the direction, the misguided perceptions. They are all used against us for one objective—to win our soul away from eternity surrounded with pure love, in the presence of our Lord and Savior, Jesus, and of God, the Father.

Could this be one of the most important reasons Gina's story was used to share the message of Jesus and the cross? Has our world reached that tipping point just like once before when Jesus came to be with us for us? I believe God has faith in us—our love and simple actions one person at a time will create amazing results within the world we live. The divine mystery came to life for all of us, never to be forgotten.

I hope that those who can hear hear. I hope all who can see see. Hear and see a clear message that must be of utmost importance for the spiritual realm to have crossed the veil to share this simple, straightforward message—the message of the cross. Jesus is the Jesus of the scripture. The place where truth can be found. Plain and simple.

Just as the 44 prophecies are designed by an intelligence beyond human comprehension so, too, is the design of Jesus' life. From his birth to his crucifixion, his entire life was God's message for our everyday life. A message of love. A love that surpasses all. Simple and complex. God's plans are designed always with an objective in mind. We cannot always see it when we are living it, but looking back, we can see how the intricacies of His plan unfold miraculously in complex orchestration sometimes for a purpose still yet to be seen. No human could begin to design the intricacies of God's plan. The cross is complex in its many, many meanings, but to keep it simple, let's just think of Love. Love as I love you...a love beyond human comprehension.

Believe in your heart the only truth you ever need to know.

Now, please don't get all hung up over one word, one concept, one phrase. You will know I am talking to you if you start getting your nose out of joint just because I mention three *persons* or try to explain my beliefs, such as the Trinity, in the simplest way possible...and on, and on, and on. All of the chaos created for centuries about the most beautiful simple Message—The Cross—might just be hurling searching souls in a misguided direction toward the warm, and sometimes fuzzy, paths prevalent in today's world. And, just as I did a decade ago, *nit-picking* over every little word of someone else's interpretation of one Bible verse, taking my eye off the ball, to quote one of my dad's favorite cliches, the bigger, beautiful message of God's Love just might get ignored. My heart would say "Keep it simple! Keep your eye on the Prize! The Prize of Jesus! The Prize of Eternal Life!"

The message is simple: *Know Him* (John 8:19). Why should we?

Consider:

> *"...why do you stand gazing up into heaven?*
> *This same Jesus who was taken up from you into heaven,*
> *will so come in like manner as you saw Him go into heaven."*
>
> — Acts **1:11**, NKJV

Some people wonder who is Jesus Christ. Two verses explain it:

> *"Let us make man in our image, after our likeness."*
>
> — Genesis 1:26, KJV

And Jesus' words, *"...Because I live, you will live also."*

— John 14:19, NKJV

The three persons of the Trinity make up the Godhead....Each is separate yet of the same essence: The Father—The Son —The Holy Spirit—*all one together*—each with a separate role in relationship to us, always working together in perfect unity and harmony. One God, who created all, is in all, and over all. To simplify: Not 1 + 1 + 1 = 3, but 1 x 1 x 1 = 1!

"In the beginning was the Word, and the Word was with God, and the Word was God."

— John **1:1**. NKJV

There are those ones again! I hope everyone starts seeing ones like me!

And He gave us the way. The *one* and only way.

"Thomas said to Him.
'Lord, we do not know where You are going, and how
can we know the way?'
Jesus said to him.
'I am the way, the truth, and the life. No one comes to
the Father except through Me.
If you had known Me, you would have known my Father also;
and from now on you know Him and have seen Him.'"

— John 14:5-7, NKJV

Three parts all as one—the Father, the Son, and the Holy Spirit—coming together like a *candle flame lighting the dark.*

We live in a world created by an omnipotent God, a power beyond our human comprehension.

Our relationship with God, the Father, the Son, and the Holy Spirit, ever present here helping us to awaken to this truth—the very purpose of our existence is the relationship.

The Miraculous Journey was a personal journey that ultimately led to A Divine Message—a multi-purposed, multilayered journey. After all, it is God in control, perplexingly complicated, yet simple. There is such peace in just knowing there is a plan! That there is eternal life. Nothing is impossible when God's Will is to be known. Trust in your heart, not just your head, and experience the peace that passes all understanding. Life is just a dot on the circle of eternal life. And the dot, what we believe, determines where we spend the rest of eternity. Always remembering, and never forgetting, the one and only way.

Heaven is the perfect place to spend eternity. Gina knows.

The Miraculous Journey is a story of Light. His story.

Let the Light shine. Let the Spirit of Life spread. Let the Holy Spirit into your life and Let Life Happen.

I see the wisdom in Nola's words shared June 2016, but it took me until June 2017 to get it!

> Most of the time when your heart starts to heal, it is a little hard in the beginning because sometimes situations you have had in your heart for a long time come back to you. Just forgive and let it go.
>
> Instead of the anniversary of Gina's death reminding you of what happened to her in a sad way, encourage yourself and everybody to be happy and celebrate where she is now. She will be smiling and clapping at you all. Visualize Gina on that day smiling at you because she will. She wants that. She doesn't want to see anybody sad. I imagined her just now jumping happily like a little girl when she receives a surprise in her hands together and smiling at you all day.

I look back on this conversation and ask myself, "Really, Dlana, how could you have not gotten the message Nola shared?" It was so clear. The spiritual battle in my life was real, and I was right in the middle of it. The first line of Nola's message came true in January 2017—not a little hard, but a lot hard, and so true. By March 2017, my spiritual army had won! And the last line, how relevant these words became as I stood in Norway on the anniversary weekend of my sister's death receiving the most precious gift—the message of the cross, never to be forgotten. I imagine if souls do know what happens in this realm, then my dad was shaking his head in endearment, smiling as his last wish for me came true. I see my sister Gina jumping happily like a little girl when I received the surprise, our hands together—clapping and smiling with joy all day long, forever. I know I jumped for joy. The best day of my entire life.

A day made in heaven.

IN FRONT OF THE JEWELRY STORE

CROSS NECKLACE

MIRACLES OF A DAY MADE IN HEAVEN

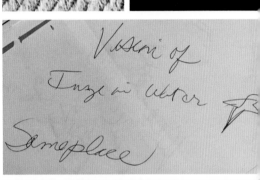

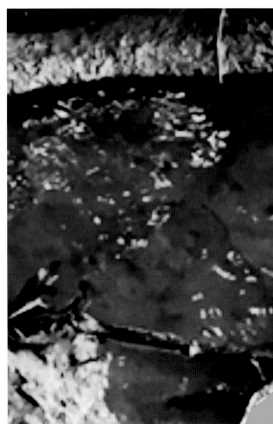

THE MESSAGE IS IN THE MIRACLES!!

God's Canvas
Author's Personal Photos
Love & Nature

THEN GOD SAW EVERYTHING THAT HE HAD MADE, AND
INDEED IT WAS VERY GOOD.

—GENESIS 1:31 NKJV

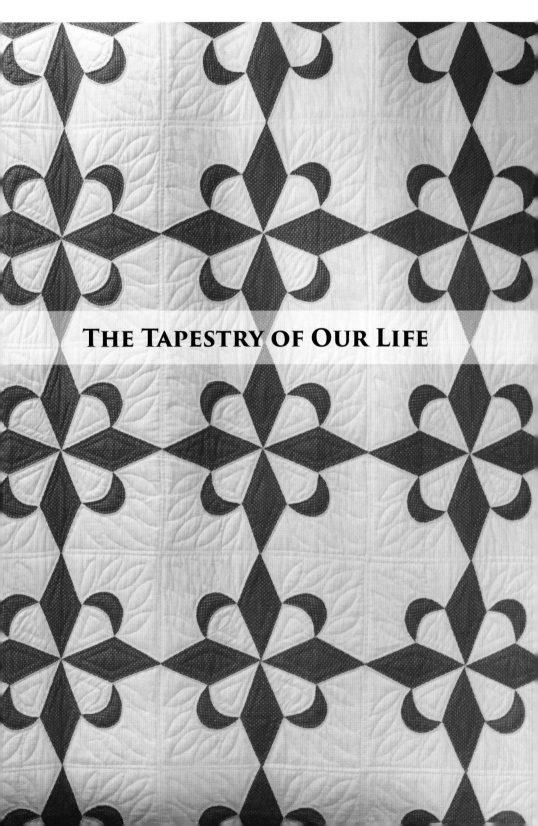

THE TAPESTRY OF OUR LIFE

DADDY AND HIS ROSES

G.P "Bunky" and JoAnne Bodmer

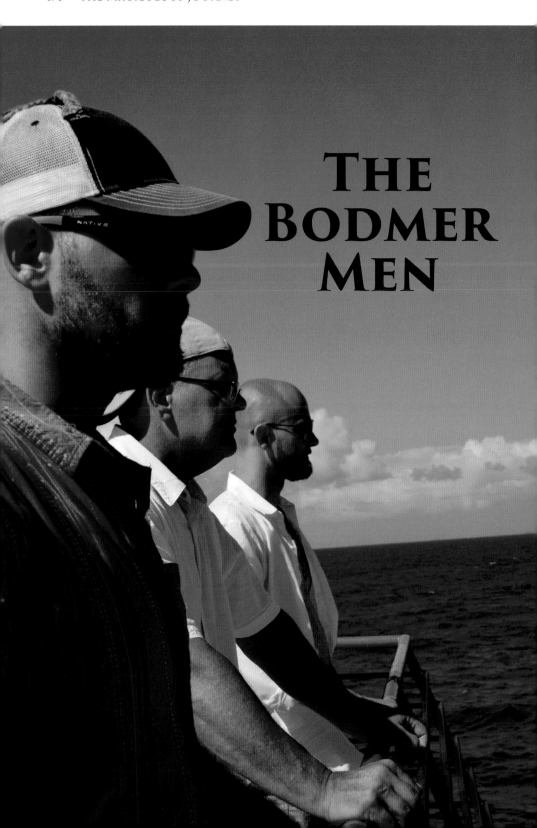

THE
BODMER
MEN

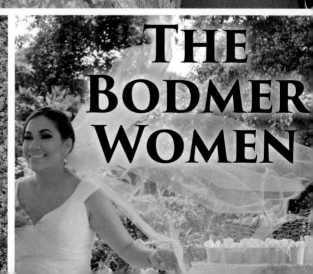

THE BODMER WOMEN

SPECIAL ACKNOWLEDGMENTS

DAN AND BEA

WILL AND ADRIENNE

Jack

Ruben

Ollie

Grand-dogs Samson and Pablo

Rocko, the NYC Cat

SPECIAL THANKS TO BUZZ
FOR SHARING THE JOURNEY WITH ME!

GINA RENEE HALL

MY LADY IN RED IS DANCING—HER LIGHT IS FOREVER SHINING BRIGHT

ABOUT THE AUTHOR
DLANA BODMER

Dlana likes to say her claim to fame is her two sons! She and her husband love traveling to new and exciting places with their family and spending time in nature hiking with their rescue dogs. She also loves her cats, Jack and Rocko. Her most favorite thing to do—snowboarding with her sons whooshing through the fresh powdery snow and a close second—eating!! Dlana loves to discover the hidden gems sharing delicious, savoring meals with her family.

Dlana has spent half of her life owning a business that provides a service to others. Her achievements have often led to requests from the business community to share and teach her methods of success. Now, Dlana serves an expanded audience by sharing an extraordinary journey that has no boundaries. Listen. Learn. Love.

Dlana has always lived life to its fullest! Despite a few bumps in the road, normalcy defined her everyday life—that is until age fifty-seven when

her world was turned upside down, inside out. Dlana's Miraculous Journey gives new meaning to Living Life to Its Fullest.

Dlana and her husband Buz reside in the small town of Lebanon, Virginia, nestled in the beautiful mountains of Appalachia America. For more information visit

THEMIRACULOUSJOURNEY.COM

About Dlana Hall Bodmer
Speaking Engagements

Dlana is focused on inspiring others. Through her genuine, down-to-earth, tell-it-like-it-is, forthright speaking style, she will have you laughing, crying, smiling, and ready to start on your own journey. Dlana can customize her presentations to focus on specific areas for varying target audiences. Her talks can be flexible for groups of all sizes, and her message is universal, whether in North America or abroad.

Dlana is committed to sharing The Miraculous Journey. Profiting on her sister's murder is not the objective—the light of Gina's life is and always will be. Dlana believes one of the purposes of her life is to share the compelling concepts interwoven throughout The Miraculous Journey.

Intriguing topics of interest can arise from Dlana's experiences. From Forgiveness to Forensics, Dlana is an open book when it comes to The Miraculous Journey and its multi-layered, multi-purposed messages. She is available to speak to an unlimited range of people —women or men, young or old —such as any group wanting to hear a motivational speaker, students, people in the criminal law field, cold case investigators, paranormal or supernatural enthusiasts, traditional church groups or atheists. No audience is too big or too small, too skeptical, too spiritual, or too religious, or can have too many questions because Dlana seeks to educate as well as entertain her listeners.

If nothing else, Dlana is approachable. She has spent a lifetime being a thought-provoking teacher of others. Providing simple explanations for complex concepts is her gift. Through open Q & A, engaged audience members can expand their own understanding of The Miraculous Journey—its complete purpose still yet to be discovered together. Dlana's experiences will be seriously contemplated, curiosity will be ignited, hearts will be opened, and the result will be a light shining like a beacon in our world—one person at a time.

For inquiries regarding events and public relations, please contact:

DHB LLC
Dlana Hall Bodmer
PO Box 3333
Lebanon, Va 24266
(276) 254-5343
or email Dlana: dlana@TheMiraculousJourney.com

REFLECTIONS

REFLECTIONS

Reflections

REFLECTIONS